Béla Bartók

Life and Work

Benjamin Suchoff

The Scarecrow Press, Inc.
Lanham, Maryland, and London
2001

SCARECROW PRESS, INC.

Published in the United States of America
by Scarecrow Press, Inc.
4720 Boston Way, Lanham, Maryland 20706
www.scarecrowpress.com

4 Pleydell Gardens, Folkestone
Kent CT20 2DN, England

British Library Cataloguing-in-Publication Information Available

Library of Congress Cataloging-in-Publication Data

Suchoff, Benjamin.
 Béla Bartók : life and work / Benjamin Suchoff.
  p. cm.
 Includes bibliographical references (p.) and index.
 ISBN 0-8108-4076-6 (alk. paper)
  1. Béla Bartók, 1881–1945. 2. Composers—Hungary—Biography. 3. Folk
 music—Hungary—History and criticism. 4. Béla Bartók, 1881–1945—Contributions
 in ethnomusicology. 5. Ethnomusicology—Hungary—History—Sources. I. Title.
 ML410.B26 S84 2001
 780'.92—dc21   2001049050
 [B]

♾™ The paper used in this publication meets the minimum requirements of
American National Standard for Information Sciences—Permanence of
Paper for Printed Library Materials, ANSI/NISO Z39.48-1992.
Manufactured in the United States of America.

For Eleanor

Contents

PART ONE

Bartók's Life

Preface

This book—the first comprehensive investigation of Béla Bartók as man, artist, and folklorist—is the outcome of more than forty-five years of my career in Bartók studies. I began in 1953, as assistant to the trustee of the New York Bartók estate, charged with the task of creating an archive "to aid in the study of Bartók's life, music, and folk-art works" (Victor Bator, *The Béla Bartók Archives*, 9). In 1958, when the greater part of Bartók's memorabilia had been identified and preserved, and other unpublished and published primary and secondary sources collected, my next assignment was preparation of the composer's folk music collections and essays for publication. Following the death of the trustee in 1967 and my subsequent appointment as successor-trustee of the Bartók estate, I continued the editorial and archival work until the termination of the estate in 1982. Thereafter my studies centered on theoretic-analytical examination of selected Bartók's compositions and arrangements, whose outcome appears in my book *Béla Bartók, Concerto for Orchestra: Understanding Bartók's World* (1995), and on the preparation of *Béla Bartók Studies in Ethnomusicology* (1997).

The next undertaking was the preparation of this book for music students, specialists, and performers, one that would fulfill József Ujfalussy's prediction that the time will eventually come "for a detailed, definitive, scientific study, reliable in all respects" (*Béla Bartók*, 1971, p. 5). Thus a two-part approach was adopted, in which the first, biographical portion includes the investigation of the background and development of Bartók's "New" Hungarian art music:

> the start for the creation of the "New" Hungarian art music was given, first, by a thorough knowledge of the devices of old and contemporary Western art music: for the technique of composition; and, second, by the newly-discovered rural music—material of incomparable beauty and perfection: for the spirit of our works to be created.
>
> Scores of aspects could be distinguished and quoted in regard to the influence exerted on us by this material: for instance, tonality, melody, rhythm, and even structural influence (*Béla Bartók Essays*, 363).

With regard to the music examples, the mentioned analytical approach is based on Bartók's principles of composition and incorporates constructs from the system of pitch relations developed by Elliott Antokoletz in his remarkable book *The Music of Béla Bartók: A Study of Tonality and Progression in Twenti-*

eth-Century Music (1984). The historiographic presentation emphasizes Bartók's long-lasting involvement with multinational musical folklore and traces his career and programs as an outstanding concert pianist. Recent findings from the investigation of expressionism in Bartók's compositions are supported in the narrative by the inclusion of the composer's relationship with Stefi Geyer and other women in his life, the impact on his compositions by the circumstances arising from Hungarian and international socioeconomic and political factors, and, in the Epilogue, by Zoltán Kodály's analysis of Bartók's personality.

Part Two examines Bartók's pioneering research in multinational musical folklore, with particular regard for the development of his musical language and its application to the compositions and arrangements comprising his "New" Hungarian art music. The concomitant objective: to provide the reader with an overview of Bartók's approach to systematic ethnomusicology, including the classification procedures he devised for the multiple thousands of vocal and instrumental melodies in his Arab, Bulgarian, Hungarian, Romanian, Ruthenian, Slovak, Turkish, and Yugoslav folk music collections.

The select bibliography illustrates the extent of my obligation to the many fellow researchers in Bartók studies, and I am also indebted to the staff of the Music Library at the University of California, Los Angeles. Above all, however, was my unique opportunity to compile and explore the inestimable resources of the New York Bartók Archive.

Finally, this book is dedicated to my wife, Eleanor, in recognition for her devotion to my welfare and work during the many years of my association with the Bartók estate.

Acknowledgments

To Boosey & Hawkes Music Publishers Ltd., acknowledgment is made for music examples from Béla Bartók's First Violin Concerto. Acknowledgment is made to Boosey & Hawkes Inc., New York, for music examples from the following Bartók works: Dance Suite for Piano, *Out of Doors* for Piano, First Piano Concerto, Sonata for Piano, Three Rondos on Folk Tunes for Piano, Rhapsody no. 1 for Violin and Piano, Twenty Hungarian Folk Songs for Voice and Piano, *Cantata Profana*, Forty-four Duos for Two Violins, Fifth String Quartet, Sixth String Quartet.

To Universal Edition A.G., Vienna, acknowledgment is made for music examples from the following Bartók works: Five Songs op. 15, Dance Suite for Piano, *Out of Doors* for Piano, First Piano Concerto, Sonata for Piano, Three Rondos on Folk Tunes for Piano, Rhapsody no. 1 for Violin and Piano, Twenty Hungarian Folk Songs for Voice and Piano, *Cantata Profana*, Forty-four Duos for Two Violins, Fifth String Quartet.

PART ONE

Bartók's Life

1

Early Musical Developments in Hungary[1]

Based on archaeological research begun in 1986 by Hungarian scholars in Xinjiang, a province in the northwest corner of China, recent findings suggest that the ancient Magyars stem from the Chinese Ugars, whose descendents still reside as a small community of 9,000 people about thirty miles east of Urumchi, the provincial capital. The evidence consists of archaeological objects excavated from 1,200 graves, such as similar weapons and identical burial methods and writing systems as those found in Hungarian cemeteries dating from the ninth and tenth centuries. Moreover, the investigators discovered seventy-three songs whose pentatonic structure is similar to the pentatonic melodies collected by Béla Bartók and Zoltán Kodály from Hungarian peasants in Transylvania and Bukovina during 1907–1916, and a pentatonic melody collected by Bence Szabolcsi from a Chinese informant in Shanghai in 1954 (Ex. 1.1).[2]

Ex. 1.1. (a) Chinese melody collected by Bence Szabolcsi in Shanghai, 1954, and (b) Hungarian-Csángó melody from the village of Hadikfalva (Bukovina), collected in 1914 by Zoltán Kodály.[3]

According to linguistic clues there was a prehistoric community of Finno-Ugrian tribes who lived along the banks of the Kama River—about midway between the upper half of the Volga River and the Ural Mountains. Eventually the community split into Finnish and Ugrian branches; about 500 B.C. the latter further divided into Ostyaks, Voguls, and ancestral Magyars and moved west-ward to the middle Volga region. Here they added horsebreeding to their main occupations of hunting and fishing. During the following centuries the ancestral Magyars separated from their Ugrian kinsmen and came under the dominating influence of the Bulgars, a race of Turki horsemen, who provided the Magyars with new techniques in martial arts and social and political organization. Thus, through conquest, clans were organized into tribes, each unit and subunit headed by a chieftain, and then into a tribal confederation or empire headed by an over-lord—the "king of kings."

Beginning about A.D. 830 the Bulgar-Magyar confederation was attacked by hostile tribes and moved farther west to take up residence on the banks of the Don River. Here they came under the political control of another Turki nation, the Khazars, but less than seventy years later rebelled against this suzerainty. The Khazars then enlisted the aid of the Petchenegs, another newly arrived Turki nation, and the Hungarians (Magyars, Bulgars, and the Avars, a former Khazar tribal unit) were driven ever westward, across the Dnieper River and into terri-tory held by eastern Slavic tribes. This area, "Great Moravia," also included the former Roman province of Pannonia (western Hungary); both territories were quickly conquered by the Hungarians who, in 896, established themselves as masters of the Middle Danube Basin.[4]

Árpád (d. 907) became the first overlord of the Hungarian tribal federation, which was really a loose organization of clans and tribes headed by about forty to fifty family chiefs. Unilateral rather than joint forays quickly established the tradition of rivalry for power between the successor Magyar kings and their ennobled subjects. When in 1000 A.D. Stephen I was crowned as the first Chris-tian king of Hungary, he consolidated his central authority by implementing a county system of the resident mixed society of basically Magyar and Slavic freemen, together with serfs and slaves acquired from conquered peoples, and established bishoprics and monasteries with crown lands. Later on Gregorian chant was taught in church schools, which led to widespread dissemination of Latin hymns in Hungary. Ex. 1.2 compares a Gregorian psalm melody and its related old-style Hungarian folk song.[5]

The resultant feudal society, castle centered and agriculturally based, lasted for two centuries. During that time a class of craftsmen and traders grew, at-tracting immigrants from western and central Europe. This influx of workers, along with the conquest of South Slav territories in 1198 and the expansion north and east into regions inhabited by Slovaks, Ruthenians, and Romanians, resulted in a greater Hungary containing a population of about two millions in the thirteenth century.

But in 1241 Mongol hordes invaded the country, devastating the eastern half of Hungary to the Danube River line, withdrawing only after they had inflicted very heavy losses in human life and property. The defeated king, Béla IV, had no alternative but to share his land and power with the Hungarian barons

a) Glo - ri - a Pat - ri et Fi - li - o et Spi - ri - tu - i San - cto,—

b) Szi - vár - vány ha - vas - sán fël - nyőtt roz - ma - ring- szál_____
(A rosemary bush that grows on snow-capped rainbow mountain)

Ex. 1.2. (a) First text-line of a Gregorian psalm melody, and (b) *BBSE*, 111, melody no. 83, mm. 1–2.

in order to reorganize the country's defenses. The old castle-centered way of life, however, was replaced by urban developments in the form of chartered towns free from feudal obligations. Thus, a class of burghers emerged, separated from the peasantry. In addition to this middle social stratum, another class was created—the lesser nobility—consisting of small landowners who had achieved minor nobility through military service as officers in the king's army.

In 1301 Andrew III, the last king of the Árpád Dynasty, died. The powerful clergy, whose properties and high offices were being expropriated by the barons, then succeeded in their attempt to place a non-Magyar ruler on the Hungarian throne: Charles I of Anjou was brought from Naples and crowned in 1308. By the end of the century, long after Charles had forcefully retrieved crown lands from the more powerful barons (c. 1321), slavery had ended and serfdom was gradually disappearing.

THE HABSBURG DYNASTY

In 1437 Albert of Habsburg—Holy Roman Emperor and King of Bohemia—became the first Habsburg to wear the Hungarian crown, but he died of the plague two years later. He was followed by Polish and Hungarian appointees until the restoration of the Habsburg Dynasty in the sixteenth century. These successions, however, required baronial support with its attendant cost in terms of special rights. On the other hand, political conditions were created, which enabled Hungary to resist the Turkish armies that invaded Transylvania in 1442 and the Serbian territory during the next decade.

The high cost of maintaining mercenary armies provided their officers with the opportunity to acquire lands in payment for their services, thus substantially increasing the class of feudal lords. Some of the peasants were able to purchase sizable acreage; others held smaller parcels, and a few were landless. But these gains were swept away in the war between the peasants and the nobles in 1514, an outcome of the aborted crusade against the Turks, in which the peasants were recruited by the clergy and given arms for the battle. The victorious nobles passed a law perpetually and universally binding peasants to the land and de-priving them of the right to own land. Dissensions had also risen between the nobles and the gentry, and, as always, between the nobles and their kings.

Finally, in 1526 the resurgent Turkish armies destroyed the weakened Hungarian forces at the battle of Mohács, overran the Great Central Plain (the Alföld), and occupied Budapest. The western (Transdanubia) and northwestern portion of the country were made part of the Habsburg Empire as the "Kingdom of Hungary." In the essentially depopulated area of Central Hungary, large numbers of Serbs took up residence as Turkish allies or as previous refugees from earlier Turkish invasions of the Balkans. Transylvania became a principality, tributary to the Sultan, consisting of Hungarians, Saxons, Széklers, and an ever-increasing population of Romanians. In 1557, the Transylvanian Diet proclaimed religious freedom, Protestantism became the dominant influence, and reformist clergy preached in the Hungarian language and called for a national collaboration to defend Christianity against the Turks.

Ex. 1.3. (a)"Ungarescha" in Jacob Paix' organ tablature book (1583), and (b) *BBSE*, 130, melody no. 139. The basic metric schema is 4+4+4+2 feet.

During the fifteenth and sixteenth centuries wandering singers of different European peoples made frequent visits to Hungary. In the meantime, Hungarian instrumental music was also being performed. West European musicians were recruited for the Transylvanian court, and Magyar bagpipers played dance tunes during their visits to European countries. In fact, ever since 1540 collections of dance tunes appeared abroad, including Hungarian melodies. This music, under the heading of titles such as "Ungarischer Tantz," "Passamezzo Ongaro," and "Ungaresca" (or "Ungarescha") were transcribed and printed in Germany and Italy. The "Ungaresca" was "a wild dance, partly of shepherd and partly of military character, accompanied probably by bagpipes." Example 1.3 illustrates a sixteenth-century "Ungarescha" and its rhythmic adaptation in a Transylvanian-Hungarian folk song.[6]

THE HUNGARIAN MINORITIES

After Mohács the barons took up residence in Vienna, adopted the language and customs of their Austrian royal hosts, and became more or less Germanized aristocrats to whom the Habsburgs entrusted the various high offices in the Hungarian army and governmental circles. In Transylvania, the first national musical style emerged: its most effective disseminator was the great Hungarian minstrel Sebestyén Tinódi (1505?–1556). Tinódi played a major role in establishing a people's music based on Hungarian poems conceived in song, which he published in a collection of pieces in Kolozsvár (now Cluj-Napoca, Romania) titled *Cronica* (1554). Ex. 1.4 shows the first half of an eleven-syllable Tinódi melody and its Transylvanian-Hungarian folk song variant with dotted rhythm.[7]

Ex. 1.4. (a) Sebestyén Tinódi, *Cronica* XIX, mm. 1–2, and (b) *BBSE,* 130, melody no. 138, mm. 1–4.

Toward the end of the century the great retreat of the Turks began, and in 1698 the absolutist Habsburg emperor, Leopold I (1657–1705), recovered the central and eastern Hungarian territories. His multifaceted plan: the re-colonization of depopulated or ungovernable Magyar districts with tractable foreign immigrants such as South Germans (Swabians) who flooded the western areas, reinforcing the German character of urban centers; a large group of Serbs was given national autonomy under the emperor, in the south of Hungary; Slovak colonists settled as far south as the Danube; new Slavonian, Székely (Hungarian-speaking people of Bulgar-Turki origin), and Romanian districts were also established along the southern tier; Ruthenians (a Ukrainian people) entered Hungary from the northeast, while Slovak expansion in the north enlarged the non-Magyar character of those areas; and the increase of more than a half-million Romanians in Transylvania effectively completed the encirclement of Hungary with a ring of national minorities. The Magyar barons, now thoroughly assimilated, sided with the Austrian emperors in attempting to Germanize the entire Hungarian nation.[8]

Western Hungary, under the Habsburg Monarchy, was pervaded by Germanic culture in castle and town. The ravaged, Turkish-occupied central Hungary was as previously mentioned, severely depopulated; in fact, the southern portion was essentially devoid of the Magyar element. The Principality of Transylvania, however, which now included Magyar refugees in addition to the resident

Székely people, became the preserve for traditional Hungarian musical life. Among these refugees were the heyducks *(hajdú)*—peasant mercenaries but originally herdsmen—who brought their recruiting dances into the territory. János Kájoni (1629 or 1630–1687), a Franciscan monk and church musician in Transylvania, collected Hungarian folk dance tunes, sacred and secular songs, and foreign instrumental and vocal pieces. One of his manuscripts, the *Kájoni Codex*, contains a popular art song whose Mixolydian melody appears as a nondiatonic (G-A-B♮-C-D-E♭-F♯-G) variant in a Hungarian folk song collected by Bartók in 1906 (Ex. 1.5).[9]

Ex. 1.5. (a) Popular art song from the *Kájoni Codex*, mm. 1–2, and (b) *HFS,* melody no. 304, mm. 1–4.

During the first decade of the eighteenth century a rebellion against the Habsburgs, was led by Prince Ferenc II Rákóczi of Transylvania—with a *"kuruc"* (kurutz) army consisting of landless lesser nobility and the Hungarian, Ukrainian, Slovak, and Romanian peasantry (who had been promised their freedom). Rákóczi's objective was the independence of Hungary, but lack of economic resources and the refusal of the aristocracy to participate in the rebellion forced a compromise solution in 1711 (the Treaty of Szatmár), which provided the Hungarian ruling class with—among other privileges—self-adminstration of counties, the right of the Hungarian diet to legislate, and unlimited seigneural powers over peasant labor.[10]

> Hungary's estates, comprising some 200 magnates, approximately 8,000 wealthy landowners, and about 135,000 families of the lesser nobility with 330,000 members, sought to preserve the old constitution, not for its own sake, but as a means of safeguarding the existing social order and aristocratic way of life from any major changes.[11]

In order to maintain control over the peasant class, prevent a possible attack from the Turks, and eliminate private armies, the Hungarian aristocracy demanded the presence of the imperial army. Under foreign, German-speaking officers, the army was formed by recruiting peasants and taxing the peasant class for the maintenance of the soldiery. And in the houses of the nobility, the ruling musical language of the century was "of German, Austrian, and Italian origin; no special attention was paid in these circles to the seemingly primitive Hungarian melodic treasure." On the other hand, the youth of the Hungarian

lesser nobility, who led a more or less common life with their serfs, were educated in Calvinist colleges and brought with them "a popular or popular-like
melodic treasure."[12]

The mentioned recruiting (*Werbung*, Hung. *verbunkos*) was begun by Hussar
officers in Hungarian rural villages toward the end of the eighteenth century, by
means of popular dance music performed on the bagpipe or by Gypsy bands.
The *verbunkos* melodies are strikingly similar to the tunes of the Hungarian
swineherd dance (*kanásztánc*, Ex. 1.6c), Romanian "Transylvanian" dance (*Ardeleana*, Ex. 1.6d), and Ukrainian round dance (*kolomyjka*, Ex. 1.6b). Furthermore, many instrumental *verbunkos* melodies were fitted with texts by poets
from the educated classes (Ex. 1.6a; cf. Ex. 1.3).[13]

Ex. 1.6. (a) Kerényi 182, popular art song from northeast Hungary, mm. 1–4; (b) Ruthenian folk song collected by Bartók in 1911, *BBSE* 232 (no. 63), mm. 1–4; (c) *BBSE* 233
(no. 64b), Hungarian folk song collected by Kodály in 1907, mm. 1–4; and (d) *RFM* i,
108 (no. 53), Romanian *Ardeleana* played on a peasant flute (*fluer*), collected by Bartók
in 1913, mm. 1–4.

The rise of the middle class during eighteenth-century Europe brought with
it a demand for the popularization of art and learning, such as plays oriented
toward the concerns and emotions of commoners. About the middle of the century, a form of comic opera arose, called *Singspiel* and adapted from English
ballad opera. This genre became the national form of German opera after 1750,
in which arias, choruses, folk-type songs, and other musical elements were connected by dialogue. And in Vienna, the German National *Singspiel* Theater was
opened in 1778 by Emperor Joseph II. Outside national opera but similar to
Singspiel folk-like songs, vocal music with keyboard accompaniment
(*Volkstümliche Lieder*) was composed in a simple style, usually strophic in form
and with architectonic (A B A) structure. These art songs, many of them with
amusing texts and memorable melodies, were published in numerous collections and disseminated to the point where they became actual folk songs sung
throughout Germany and beyond its borders.[14]

In 1812, in what is apparently the first Hungarian *Singspiel, Cserni Gyurka,* Gábor Mátray (1797-1875) merged Hungarian urban folk song, *verbunkos* music, and Viennese elements, all in an attempt to create a specifically Hungarian vocal style. The immense popularity of this new type of urban folk song quickly led to the production of thousands of Hungarian imitations, for the most part by amateur (so-called dilettante) members of the educated Hungarian classes. And the *verbunkos,* with its slow and fast forms, when removed from a military setting, grew into the national Hungarian musical idiom of the nineteenth century. Indeed, professional Hungarian musicians, such as the Gypsy band leader János Bihari (1764–1827), applied the instrumental *verbunkos* style to dance suites and other forms of chamber music (Ex. 1.7).[15]

I. Allegro vivace

II. Moderato

Ex. 1.7. Bihari, *Két Verbunkos* (Two *Verbunkos*), transcribed for keyboard (melody only): no. I. mm. 1–4; no. II., mm. 1–3.

THE KOSSUTH REBELLION

Beginning in 1850, the younger generation of Hungarian peasants adopted and transformed those popular art-song melodies which strongly resembled traditional rural folk song. This dynamic change in village musical life, referred to by Bartók and Kodály as the new style of Hungarian folk song, eventually affected the folk music of the national minorities.[16] Political changes, on the other hand, resulted in conflict between the Magyars and the various ethnic groups: the Language Decree of the Hungarian Diet of 1843–1844 made Magyar the official language in most areas of national life. At this time, because of financial hardship, radical ideas were growing among the lesser nobility. Its spokesman, Lajos (Louis) Kossuth, a young lawyer and writer, argued for major changes in the social structure, including complete independence from the Habsburg Monarchy and removal of the peasants' feudal status and obligations.[17]

Following the victory of the February 1848 revolution in Paris, on 13 March a popular uprising in Vienna forced the promise of constitutional rule for the peoples of the empire. Two days later a similar uprising broke out in Pest, and Kossuth, as governor of an independent Hungary, headed the preparations for military action. On 6 October the people of Vienna rose again, and on 2 December, Ferdinand V abdicated in favor of his nephew, Francis Joseph. When in May 1849 the Austrian army retreated to the frontier in disarray, the emperor appealed to Czar Nicholas I for military intervention. Finally, on 13 August 1849, the ill-fated Hungarian War of Independence ended, and Kossuth with other military and civilian leaders fled to Turkey.[18]

The *verbunkos* and the related *csárdás* (Hungarian national dance), in which slow (*lassú*) and fast (*friss*) sections alternate, received national emphasis and international attention during and following the Hungarian insurgency (Ex. 1.8).

Ex. 1.8. "Honvéd-dal és csárdás" (Soldier-song and [*csárdás*] dance) (1848–1849), for keyboard (melody only), mm. 6–11 and 1–6, respectively.[19]

The urban folk song genre—published in large numbers, with stereotyped piano accompaniments, in various collections—include many specimens written by such gifted musicians as Béni Egressy (1814–1851), Kálmán Simonffy (1832–1881), and Elemér Szentirmay (1836–1908). This material and the substantial number of songs composed by the dilettanti from the educated classes are known as *magyar nótuk* (national melodies; sing. *nóta*). These popular art songs were propagated by urban Gypsy bands at home and by such composers as Brahms, Liszt, and Sarasate abroad.

Ferenc Erkel (1810–1893), preeminent Hungarian opera composer, who "transplanted the idiom of Western opera into the Hungarian milieu," combined Italian opera techniques with *verbunkos* and *magyar nóta* forms (Ex. 1.9).[20] When the National Hungarian Royal Academy of Music was founded in Budapest in 1875 (renamed the Ferenc Liszt Academy of Music in 1925), with Liszt as president and principal of the piano performance faculty, Erkel was appointed as director of the institution. The faculty consisted of composers and pedagogues of German origin or German culture who had been exclusively educated by German Romanticism, including Robert Volkmann (1815–1883), followed by his successor, Hans (János) Koessler (in 1882), Ödön Mihalovich (1842–1929), and Jenő Hubay (1858–1937). Thus, the Academy of Music—the center of Hungarian musical education—together with the previously established Philharmonic Society (since 1853) and the Opera House (since 1884) were dominated by German musical tendencies.[21]

Andante
Minstrel (alto)

The world has four corners,
Our country has four enemies;
One external, one internal,
When one rests, another rises,
Alas! they are attacking on every hand.

Ex. 1.9. Erkel, *György Dózsa,* opera in five acts (1867). Adapted from the tragedy by Mór Jókai; libretto by Ede Szigligeti. Minstrel's aria, mm. 1–11.[22]

During the last third of the century, following the Compromise of 1867, the Habsburg Empire was reorganized to create the Dual Monarchy of Austria-Hungary. Although Hungary was granted its own bicameral parliament, separate domestic government, and autonomous financial administration, Francis-Joseph as *"k.u.k."* (Emperor and King) determined foreign policy and had unlimited control of the army whose language of command was exclusively German. Unfortunately, the unsolved problem of the national minorities was ignored—they were subject to the rule of the Hungarian nobility and its policy of forced Magyarization.[23]

Among the new legislative decrees were those uniting the sister cities of Buda, Óbuda, and Pest into Budapest (1872–1873), and the granting of full and equal civic rights to the Jews. In the absence of a Magyar middle class—the impoverished lesser nobility had turned to civil service as the only respectable form of employment—the Jews not only provided bankers, businessmen, lawyers, doctors, and intellectuals, but underwent linguistic assimilation and considered themselves to be integrated Hungarians. The growth of Budapest also brought an influx of Germans, Slovaks, and Croatians who likewise underwent Magyarization as the means for social as well as economic opportunities.[24]

In the 1890s, the stratification of Hungary's social structure was fairly well restricted, although it was possible for very rich Jews to acquire titles and even intermarry with aristocrats. At the top of the pyramid was the Habsburg court. Below this stratum were those Hungarian magnates who owned large estates, together with other wealthy aristocrats serving as diplomats, high-ranking officers in the army, or in top government positions. Following on the social scale was the "gentry," consisting for the most part of the lesser nobility, who exercised great power as county stewards, judges, and other important local officials. Next were the professionals: doctors, lawyers, professors, those who earned the academic degree of Ph.D., journalists, institutional directors, and even including bank clerks. All the above listed strata represented the Hungarian educated class, and some of its members possessed great refinement of taste, became patrons of the arts, and maintained distinguished salons for the performance of music. At the bottom were the ten million impoverished, landless peasants—farm workers, servants, and village Gypsies—comprising approximately 25 percent of the total population at the close of the century.[25]

2

Childhood and Youth: 1881–1899

Béla Bartók was born on 25 March 1881 in the Hungarian town of Nagyszent-miklós, now Sînnicolaul Mare, Romania. His baptismal certificate shows the name Béla Viktor János, after his father, godfather, and grandfather.[1] Bartók's grandfather, János Bartók (born 24 November 1816), moved to Nagyszentmiklós in 1863, serving as the county land steward and later the principal of the local agricultural school. His son Béla (born 19 November 1855), father of the composer, was appointed principal when János died in 1877. On 5 April 1880 Béla married Paula Voit (born 16 January 1857), a young Hungarian girl of German stock, who had come from Pozsony (or Pressburg, now Bratislava, Slovakia) to Nagyszentmiklós in 1876 for her first employment as a primary-school teacher. He arbitrarily added to the family name the prefixal title "Szuhafői" (of Szu-hafő, a village in Gömör County, now Gemerská, Slovakia) to emphasize that his family should be recognized as part of the Hungarian lesser nobility. However, recent investigations prove that the village cemetery contains only the family vault of István Bartók, a nobleman unrelated to the forebears of the composer.[2]

Why did "Szuhafői" Béla Bartók assume this pretentious title? Although professional status as an educator was also an indicator of gentry rank, such vocational pursuits did not carry the same perquisites and social prestige of the lesser nobility. The latter, who turned to civil administration following the loss of their estates, were admired and emulated for their conservative views, defense of historic Hungarian values, and admiration of Gypsy music. Thus the elder Béla Bartók identified his family with the lesser nobility, to the point where he adopted their manners and designed a personal coat of arms.[3] In his 1921 biography, the composer wrote that his father "played the piano, organized an amateur orchestra, learned the cello in order to play in his orchestra, and composed some dance music."[4] His father, moreover, was a highly motivated intellectual, founder and editor of the periodical *Gazdasági Tanügy* (Agricultural public instruction).

The original school, opened in 1799 as a private venture of the noble Nákó family, was granted a government subsidy beginning in 1863. During the elder Bartók's tenure, adverse circumstances threatened to terminate instruction. In 1886, however, he was reconfirmed as principal when the government assumed administrative control, designated the school building as the principal's residence, and began construction of a new, larger structure.[5] His drive to improve musical life by founding the Nagyszentmiklós Music League was thwarted by declining health, ethnic clashes, and local rivalries. The Serbs would not attend musical performances of the Swabians, and vice-versa; the Romanians were not a factor; and those who sided with the performances sponsored by the Nákó family denigrated the elder Bartók's orchestral concerts, and conversely.[6] Furthermore, Count Kálmán Nákó (1822–1902) was a formidable opponent, owner of a castle in Vienna as well as in Nagyszentmiklós, and whose musical taste apparently had been fashioned by his wife Berta (d. 1882). She was an accomplished pianist who had organized her own Gypsy orchestra and played with them in musical soirées at the Nagyszentmiklós castle and in a program of *csárdás* music for the benefit of indigent Serbians, at the Budapest National Theater. The elder Bartók's orchestra, on the other hand, consisted of Hungarian gentlemen, an educated Gypsy as the conductor, and the restaurant of the local Black Eagle Hotel as the venue. Their programs consisted for the most part of intermixed opera overtures, dance and vocal music, and Hungarian folk songs.[7]

Paula Bartók, a devoted mother and competent pianist, was struck by her son's interest in music at a very early age. Her memoirs of his childhood appear in a series of detailed letters to her grandson, Béla Jr., from 14 August 1921 to 5 November 1922. Although she gave birth to a strong, healthy baby, three months later he developed eczema on his face and body from an inoculation with a faulty smallpox vaccine. For a period of five years his facial appearance was affected to the point where he deliberately avoided people, because of the hurtful "poor little Bélushka" he invariably heard. He listened with much interest to the songs his nurse sang to him, and when he was eighteen months old, his attention intensified when his mother played a dance tune on the piano. The next day he pointed to the piano (he could not as yet speak) and nodded that she should play, shaking his head during her performance of different dance pieces until she reached the one she had played the previous day, whereupon he nodded his approval with a smile. Three days later, Mrs. Bartók decided to test his memory, to determine whether his recollection was only incidental, but he behaved the same way until she played the right piece. He was given a drum at the age of three, which he played with great delight:

> When I played the piano, he sat in his little chair, his drum on a footstool before him, and beat time precisely. When I changed from 3/4 to 4/4, he stopped beating for a moment and then went on in the correct time. . . . At the age of four he could play the folk songs he knew on the piano, with one finger. He knew forty songs, and if we said the first few words, he could immediately play the tune. Even at that time he had a good memory.[8]

During 1886 the child's eczema disappeared but was followed by other ailments that greatly troubled his parents. He often asked his mother for piano lessons, which she deferred because of his delicate condition. Eventually she started instruction on 25 March, his fifth birthday, limiting the lessons to fifteen or thirty minutes. Four weeks later, mother and son surprised the father with their performance of a little piece for four hands. There were a number of interruptions in the instruction, some of them due to the elder Béla Bartók's ailments.[9] In 1887, when the child's strength improved, he accompanied his parents to the Black Eagle restaurant where, on 26 March, he heard orchestral music for the first time.[10]

> I remember even today [21 August 1921] that their first piece was [Rossini's] *Semiramis* overture. The guests continued to eat and drink, but he immediately put down his knife and fork and listened intensely to the music. He was delighted but indignant: how could the others eat when they hear such nice music![11]

When the child was seven years old, his parents checked his musical hearing, noting with pleasure that he had absolute pitch, which they determined when the piano was played while he was in an adjacent room. He could immediately name every note, even simple chords. Up to this time Mrs. Bartók had provided him with primary school education, which he found easy and pleasurable. When she enrolled him in a Nagyszentmiklós primary school, she discovered that the teaching was poor and the requirements inadequate. Nevertheless, he quickly excelled in his studies, including the fourth primary grade which he completed when he was eight years old.

In 1888 disaster struck the Bartók family—now including a four-year-old daughter, Elza (Erzsébet Clementina Paula, born 11 May 1885)— when, after a protracted illness, the father died on 4 August at the age of thirty-one. Count Nákó rejected the widow's request for a small pension, and the bereaved family had to vacate the principal's residence in October and find temporary lodging elsewhere. She supported the family by giving piano lessons, resumed her son's music instruction with more regularity, and observed that he would not count beats, as he could keep time without it. Whenever he was praised by those who heard him play, the mother always told her child that such praise was only an expression of politeness.

> I did not want him to become conceited. It is true that if someone, no matter how intelligent, imagines that he knows this or that the best, his knowledge loses considerably by his becoming odious to others. I succeeded in making him modest, which might be prejudicial in life, but I have an aversion against conceited men and did not want my son to become such a person.[12]

Mrs. Bartók asked her older sister, Irma Voit (1849–1941), to join her and help with the household duties. During 1889, the family moved to Nagyszőllős (now Vinogradov, Ukraine), in northeastern Hungary, where the widow accepted a teaching position in a primary school. In her memoirs, she recalls that there was no musical life in this small town, and that her son grew up without any musical nourishment other than his piano lessons.

When he was nine years old and while I was sleeping in the next room after lunch, some tune struck his ear, one which he had neither played nor heard till then. He was unable to play it on the piano, because he did not want to disturb me. He told me about it after I was awake and then immediately played his composition. It was a waltz completely different from those he had heard till then.[13]

The music, notated by Mrs. Bartók and titled *Valczer Opus 1*, is basically a monothematic work, somewhat varied, consisting of six sections and a short interlude (Ex. 2.1).[14] Other compositions followed soon thereafter: Variation Piece, Mazurka, The Budapest Gymnastic Competition, Sonatina, and Wallachian [Romanian] Piece.

Ex. 2.1. Bartók, *Valczer Opus 1,* for Piano (1890), mm. 1–16.

That same year (1890) a visiting musician from the city of Sopron, Keresztély Altdörfer (organist and composer, 1825–1898), listened to Bartók's playing and compositions.

He [Altdörfer] was the first one to predict a great future for him, stating that Béla's talent was extraordinary and predicted great things for him in the music field. This made me very happy, and I tried to figure out how to have him take lessons from good teachers [even though] our financial circumstances were so modest.[15]

During 1891, Bartók's compositions were mostly polkas, some of them named for other children. He also wrote a second sonatina and began work on op. 20, a programmatic piece, *A Duna folyása* (The course of the Danube), eventually consisting of ten sections which were inspited by his school history and geography lessons (Ex 2.2).[16] Mrs. Bartók decided to take her son to Budapest for a second opinion of his talent, and she consulted Károly Aggházy (1855–1918) a former pupil of Liszt and professor of piano at the Academy of Music. Although Aggházy immediately accepted Bartók as a pupil and wanted him to enter the

conservatory without delay, Mrs. Bartók was unwilling to have her son live
with strangers or give up his academic studies.

Ex. 2.2. Themes from Bartók, *A Duna folyása* (The Course of the Danube) op. 20, for
Piano (1889–1891). The *Csárdás* section represents the river entering Budapest; the Allegro, in *kolomyjka* (round dance) rhythm, describes the river's departure from Hungary.

After they returned to Nagyszőllős, she had him tutored in Latin while he
finished the first grade in the upper elementary school. The next year she sent
him to her sister-in-law Emma Voit (d. 1916) in Nagyvárad, a larger town in
southeast Hungary (now Oradea, Romania), where the boy was entered in the
second grade of the Premonstratensian Gymnasium. He continued his piano lessons with Ferenc Kersch (1853–1910), an organist and choirmaster, whose main
interest was church music. Although Bartók learned many pieces, including
some that were too difficult, the instruction was somewhat superficial.

> His studies at school did not go well: the teachers were very peculiar, gave prefer-
> ence to the children of wealthy parents who had a private tutor at home, and were
> unfair to the other children. They wanted to fail him in algebra and geography
> (later on he always had the best marks in these subjects). He was very upset about
> this, and when he developed an eye disease, I made him quit school in order to
> prevent his having to repeat the same grade for a second year.[17]

In April (1892), Bartók returned to Nagyszőllős, and made his first public
appearance at a charity concert on 1 May. The program consisted of pieces by
Grünfeld, Raff, his own composition, *A Duna folyása*, and the first movement
of Beethoven's Sonata op. 53 (*Waldstein*).[18] The enthusiastic applause and the
laudatory press reviews impressed Mrs. Bartók's school supervisor to the extent
that he granted her request for a year's leave of absence to further her son's
musical education. The family moved to Pozsony, musically the foremost pro-

vincial Hungarian town, where Bartók made considerable progress in piano and composition with an excellent teacher, László Erkel (1844–1896).[19] Bartók attended the Hungarian-language Catholic Gymnasium, completing the second grade with distinction, and also had the opportunity "of hearing a few operas, more or less well performed, and orchestral concerts."[20]

Mrs. Bartók, unable to secure a teaching position in Pozsony, was reassigned to Beszterce (now Bistriţa, Romania) in September 1893. Here Bartók attended the third grade in the "szász" (Transylvanian Saxon) Gymnasium, where the instruction was exclusively in German. Although his rank was fifth out of forty-five pupils—notwithstanding an absence of many weeks due to bronchitis—his problems with German language instruction left him resistant and unhappy. Thus it seems likely that Bartók's resentment of Austrian and German domination of Hungarian education and culture in later life may have begun here. Another troublesome problem was the lack of a qualified piano teacher to further his musical education, for he was the best pianist in that small town. It was indeed fortuitous, however, that when a local forester and competent violinist, Sándor Schönherr, was unable to find an accompanist:

> someone told him that the twelve-year-old son of the new teacher plays the piano very well, but he hardly thought that a boy's knowledge would suffice as an accompanist. He nevertheless paid us a visit and was surprised to meet such a talent. They immediately started to play, and from then on there was a concert every week at our house. Among other Beethoven violin sonatas, they played the Kreutzer sonata (to me the most beautiful one, my favorite even today), thereafter Mendelssohn's violin concerto. This poor Schönherr committed suicide later on; we do not know why.[21]

The family returned to Pozsony in April 1894, following Mrs. Bartók's appointment to the faculty of the Pozsony Teachers' Training College. On the basis of his excellent scholastic record in Beszterce, Bartók was admitted to the Catholic Gymnasium as a scholarship student in the third grade. He had only six weeks to complete the requirements, notwithstanding the different program of instruction he had in Beszterce, and he reluctantly postponed music lessons as well as piano practice, in order to devote his waking hours exclusively to school studies. When the semester ended, he not only received a good report but a small cash award for having completed the third grade requirements in such a short time. At the beginning of the next school year, he resumed his piano lessons with Erkel and made very good progress, also doing well in his fourth grade studies. He was invited to play chamber music with several groups of amateur musicians, and thus became acquainted with a substantial number of works hitherto unknown to him. Free and discounted tickets to concerts and operas also broadened his musical horizon. The culmination of these experiences was his Sonata in G Minor for piano, the first piece in a new series of abstract works (Ex. 2.3).[22]

Ex. 2.3. Bartók, Sonata no. 1 in G Minor, op. 1 (1894), opening bars of the first two movements.

When Bartók entered the fifth grade in September 1895, his teacher of physics, mathematics, and geography was Dr. Frigyes von Dohnányi, father of the gifted composer, pianist, and conductor Ernő von Dohnányi (1877–1960). The elder Dohnányi, well known as a music-loving intellectual, frequently hosted musical gatherings at his home, where his son was the featured pianist. It was here that Bartók made the acquaintance of Ernő, who had earlier attended the Catholic Gymnasium and served as the organ accompanist at Sunday Mass. This position, assigned to the best student musician, was awarded to Bartók at the beginning of the school year. During the summer he composed his Sonata for Violin and Piano op. 5, his first composition in the genre. On 8 May 1896, he made his first public appearance at the Pozsony municipal theater—when the town celebrated the arrival of Hungary's millennium—where he provided the piano accompaniment to Antal Várady's melodrama *Rákóczy*.[23]

László Erkel died on 3 December. During the next two years Bartók continued his piano lessons with Anton Hyrtl (1840–1914), a music teacher who stressed the study of harmony.[24] On 3 November 1897—the "name-day" of Principal Károly Polikeit—the grammar school celebrated the event with a concert, in which the sixteen-year-old Bartók demonstrated his pianistic virtuosity by performing Liszt's Spanish Rhapsody. In July 1898, Bartók composed his Quartet for Piano, Violin, Viola, and Violoncello op. 20, from which two movements were performed on the principal's "name-day" celebration on 3 November. In addition, he played Liszt's piano transcription of Wagner's overture to *Tannhäuser* and arranged four pieces from Brahms's *Hungarian Dances* for the school orchestra. Other Bartók works performed were piano pieces, songs for voice and piano, and his first string quartet. He also began his career as a piano teacher and accompanied a violist on a fee basis, using his earnings to buy piano pieces and, for study purposes, such scores as Beethoven's Mass in D Major ("Missa Solemnis"). In his autobiography, Bartók states that:

> before I was eighteen I had acquired a fairly thorough knowledge of music from Bach to Brahms (though in Wagner's work I did not get further than *Tannhäuser*). All this time I was also busy composing and was under the influence of Brahms [Ex. 2.4] and Dohnányi (who was four years my senior). Especially Dohnányi's youthful Opus 1 [Piano Quintet in C Minor] influenced me deeply.
>
> When my education at the Gymnasium (high school) was concluded the question arose at which musical academy I should continue my studies. In Pozsony, at that time, the Vienna Conservatorium was considered the sole bastion of serious musical education.[25]

Ex. 2.4. Bartók, Three Piano Pieces op. 21 (June–July 1898), no. 1, Intermezzo in C Minor, mm. 1–4. Cf. Brahms, Intermezzo in A Minor, op. 76, no.7, mm. 18–22.

On 8 December, therefore, Mrs. Bartók took her son to Vienna for an audition with Hans Schmitt (1835–1907), renowned piano teacher who had written hundreds of etudes for the instrument as well as a book on the fundamentals of piano technique. Although Bartók was not an Austrian citizen, he was offered a Conservatory scholarship. However, following a consultation with his idol, Ernő Dohnányi, who had completed his studies at the Budapest Academy and recommended his teachers, István Thomán (1862–1940) for piano and János Koessler for composition, Bartók decided that he would follow in Dohnányi's footsteps and enroll in the Academy of Music.

While Bartók was pleased with his musical and secular education in Pozsony the past four years, the religious studies at the Catholic Grammar School were such that he abandoned his faith.

> Until the age of 14, like everyone else brought up to respect "authority," I was a devoted Catholic. . . . Between the ages of 15 and 16, in the divinity classes at school, we received exhaustive instruction in the history, ethics, rites and dogmas of the Church; as the divinity master was exceptionally zealous, we were taught even more, much more, than the prescribed syllabus. . . . The brilliant result of our divinity master's zeal was that since then I have ceased being a Catholic in principle. I left the issue of "God" and the "immortal soul" in abeyance—I could go neither forward nor back; I had to wait. At the age of 18, freed from the burden of

school work, I found time for reading more serious literature. A few years later I was greatly influenced by my studies in astronomy, a Danish writer, an acquaintance, and, above all, by my own meditations. By the time I had completed my 22nd year, I was a new man—an atheist.[26]

In January 1899, Bartók's piano audition with István Thomán at the Budapest Academy of Music was so well received that he was accepted as a student in the fall. In addition, Thomán provided him with a letter of introduction to János Koessler whose subsequent review of Bartók's piano quartet was equally enthusiastic (Ex. 2.5).[27]

Ex. 2.5. Bartók, Quartet for Piano, Violin, Viola, and Violoncello op. 20 (1898), opening bars of the last two movements.

The next month, Bartók fell seriously ill with pneumonia. His doctor prescribed complete rest, forbade piano playing, and subsequently limited school attendance to only a few hours daily. Fortunately, a schoolmate's regular visits enabled Bartók to keep up with missed lessons. During March he composed *Tiefblaue Vielchen*, a song for Soprano and Orchestra, perhaps intended to demonstrate the level of his scoring ability at the forthcoming Academy class in orchestration (Ex. 2.6).[28]

Ex. 2.6. Bartók, *Tiefblaue Vielchen* (Dark blue violet), for Soprano and Orchestra, mm. 1–4.

In June, Bartók earned his academic diploma following the successful completion of his eighth-grade examinations in mathematics, physics, religion, Hungarian history, Latin, Greek, and German language studies. During the summer months, Mrs. Bartók took her son to Eberhard, Carinthia, where his health was completely restored.[29]

3

Summary of Hungarian Musical Dialect: 1889–1905

When the Academy was opened in 1875, Liszt's nine piano students included Károly Aggházy and István Thomán.[1] After the death of Ferenc Erkel, Ödön Mihalovich was appointed director. Thus, when the Bartóks returned to Budapest at the beginning of September 1899, Mrs. Bartók found it:

> a disagreeable surprise that the Director (Mihalovich) did not want to enroll him without a test. I was fearful that he would not pass, as he had not practiced since February. I still remember, when we went up the stairs, that the Director was very grouchy. . . . [Bartók] played a Beethoven sonata and his own compositions. . . . The result was again excellent, I was very happy, and the Director kept holding my two hands and congratulating me about the talent of my son.[2]

Bartók was accepted as a student in the second grade, and Mrs. Bartók returned to Pozsony after she found a satisfactory boardinghouse for him. But her happiness was short-lived: at the beginning of October she received a registered letter from the landlady that her son was ill and she should immediately return to Budapest.

> that trip also remains unforgettable, for I imagined horrible things—in other words, it was terrible. He had bronchitis, which seemed dangerous on account of his previous ailment. I called a university professor [Dr. Ángyán] who said, after the examination, that it would be best that he give up the music profession and become a lawyer.

With tears rolling down his cheeks, Bartók protested that he would never be a lawyer, that such a life was not for him. Professor Thomán also interceded in his behalf, explaining to the doctor that, for Bartók, music was like water for fish, he would be unhappy in any other profession, and a musical career was a vital condition. Reconsidering his recommendation, Dr. Ángyán then advised Mrs. Bartók to take her son back to Pozsony and, after he had recovered, find a suitable place for him on the Buda side of the Danube, where the air would be better. When in December Bartók's health was restored, Aunt Irma accompanied him to the city and looked after him while he resumed his studies. But his room was uncomfortable and its location required too much travel time to the Academy. A nearer place was found for him in Pest, in the home of Emma Voit,

24

Mrs. Bartók's sister-in-law, who agreed to be responsible for his well-being. During the remainder of the 1899–1900 school year Bartók's health seemed to be improving, and he was given excellent reports by his teachers.[3]

The Academy Professors

In 1927, on the occasion of István Thomán's sixty-fifth birthday, Bartók wrote a most touching essay about his former teacher whose paternal concern and pedagogical activity went far beyond the classroom. Thomán, at his own expense, provided his pupils with musical scores and concert tickets, and, more important, invited his pupils to attend the frequent soirées he gave in honor of those great pianists—whom he knew and entertained personally—who visited Hungary. His pupils had the opportunity not only to observe at close hand the playing of these artists but also to demonstrate their own training, and in that way make an easier transition from the classroom to the concert platform. With regard to Thomán's pedagogy, Bartók recalls that:

> I must have been a real "savage" as a pianist when I first came to Thomán. My technique was good enough, but thoroughly crude. Thomán taught me the correct position of the hands and all the different "natural" and "summarizing" movements which the newer pedagogy has since made into a truly theoretical system and which, however, Liszt had applied instinctively and Thomán, a former pupil of Liszt, could acquire directly from his great master. Thus, the most initiated hands imparted to me the mastery of poetically coloring the piano tone.[4]

János Koessler, a born teacher, was a demanding taskmaster and a man of strict discipline, whose idol was his friend, Johannes Brahms (1833–1897). According to Otto Gombosi:

> Koessler's great knowledge of the classic masters, his deep love for romantic academicism, his artisan-like approach to "originality" and "ideas," his very limitations made him a good teacher. But he never understood the dilemma of a Hungarian composer of the unique makeup of a Bartók, because [Hungarian] national idiom was, to his mind, a matter of dialectal *couleur locale* applied to the one and only accepted and acceptable musical language, that of German academic Romanticism.[5]

The conflict between the aspiring Hungarian composer and his German preceptor began on 4 January 1900, when Bartók's sketches for a quintet were brought to class for evaluation. Koessler's verdict was "the whole thing is no good" and that Bartók should begin with a simpler piece in song-form. This harsh criticism evoked an antagonistic reaction which was expressed the next day, in Bartók's letter to his mother. He complained that Koessler spoke only in such generalities as the lack of adequate care in the choice of themes.

I don't really know what is not good . . . According to this, none of the themes is
of any value, but if they are not, I cannot see whether I shall be able to write
anything better in, say, a year's time. Why didn't he tell me last January that my
pieces are worthless? In my opinion, this quintet is in every respect better than the
quartet of last year.[6]

During the summer vacation, from June to mid-August, the Bartóks went to
St. Johann bei Herberstein (Styria) as a preventative measure to build up his
stamina. He composed a set of six love songs with texts by Goethe, Friedrich
Rückert (1788–1866), and Nikolaus Lenau (1802–1850), all of them with rather
bland accompaniments.[7] The fifth song contains an unrelated sketch of what
appears to be a fragmentary three-part fugue exposition, whose subject is based
on the D Hungarian-Gypsy scale: D-E-F-G♯-A-B♭-C♯ (Ex. 3.1).[8]

Ex. 3.1. Bartók's fragmentary sketch of a three-part fugue exposition (1900).

A piano was made available at the home of a local teacher, and Bartók began
the study of Liszt's B Minor Sonata. Soon thereafter, unfortunately, the owner
ended the arrangement: she had not supposed that he would play the instrument
with such force and was most anxious about maintaining its good condition.
Because Bartók was determined to keep up with his practicing, Mrs. Bartók
made plans for their return to Pozsony. On the afternoon of 17 August, while
she was packing their luggage he came down with a very high fever. A doctor
was consulted, whose diagnosis was a recurrence of pneumonia. In September,
after several weeks of rest and some improvement, although her son was still

very weak, they returned to Pozsony. Mrs. Bartók immediately contacted the family physician who examined the boy and informed her that Bartók's life could not be saved. Beside herself with worry and prepared for the worst, she called a specialist for a second opinion. To her great joy the doctor's prognosis was that Bartók would recover if he were taken to Meran (South Tyrol) for a lengthy convalescence. He should eat well, spend much time in the fresh air, and avoid the piano. In mid-November, after Mrs. Bartók made arrangements for an extended leave of absence from her teaching position, mother and son traveled to Meran. The success of the recommended regimen was such that in January Bartók was allowed to practice,[9] and by the end of March (1901) he was fully recovered and able to return to the Academy until the end of the school year. At a student performance he performed the first movement of Beethoven's Concerto no. 3 in C minor, accompanied by Thomán on the second piano, and was gratified that he had written an acceptable fugue for Koessler.

At this time in Hungary, Zoltán Kodály recalls that:

> The wave of independence following the [1896] Millennium celebrations was then reaching its climax. Public opinion demanded things Hungarian in every sphere of life: Hungarian words of command and Hungarian insignia in the army, and a Hungarian anthem instead of [the Austrian] *Gott erhalte*. . . . Bartók, too, wanted everything to be Hungarian, from language to dress. . . . Naturally in his music, too, he wanted to be Hungarian.[10]

During the next semester, with Thomán's encouragement, Bartók performed Liszt's Piano Sonata on 21 October, at the Academy's public concert celebrating the ninetieth anniversary of Liszt's birth. The glowing press review in the *Budapesti Napló* was reprinted in a Pozsony newspaper, Mrs. Bartók pasted the clipping in her scrapbook, and later quoted the review in a letter to her grandson.

> The first [performer] was Béla Bartók, who played Liszt's B Minor Sonata with a steely and fully developed technique. This young man has become more robust in the past two years. A year and a half ago he was so weak that the doctors sent him to Meran, that the winter cold shouldn't harm him. And now he thunders on the piano like a little Jupiter. The fact is that *today* there is nobody among the Academy piano students who could gallop with more success in the path of Dohnányi.[11]

Ten years later, Bartók's published recollection of this first encounter with Liszt's Piano Sonata was "at that time, although I tried, I could not like it. I felt the first half of the exposition was cold and empty, and I did not perceive the irony in the *fugato*."[12] With regard to composition, his output consisted of a short scherzo for orchestra (four minutes in duration) and a minuet for piano. This limited activity was probably due to the emphasis on piano performance: on 14 December he played Chopin and Liszt at his first professional engagement at the Budapest Lipótvárosi Kaszinó—a private concert and great social event, which was open to the press—and sent the fee of ten gold pieces to his mother as a Christmas present. Here, too, the general opinion of the press was that Bartók had a great future ahead of him as a pianist.[13]

At the beginning of 1902, Bartók realized that his creative work during the preceding two years not only lacked independence but was stylistically Brahmsian, even though he had enthusiastically studied Wagner's operas and Liszt's orchestral works in order to find "the new way so ardently desired." In fact, other than those knowledgeable classmates in Koessler's class, who were aware of his talent as a composer, his reputation at the Academy was only as "a first class" pianist. Thus he turned his attention to the study of Hungarian folk music, or—as he later put it—"to be more exact, what at that time was considered Hungarian folk music."[14] He therefore set four poems by Lajos Pósa (1850–1914) as his first attempt at writing "Hungarian" music (Ex. 3.2).[15]

Allegro

Ej-nye! Ej-nye! az a kis-lány ha-ra-gos

Ex. 3.2. Bartók, Négy dal (Four Songs), for Voice and Piano, no. 4, "Ejnye! Ejnye!" (Come! Come!), mm. 2–6. Note the Hungarian dotted- (that is, syncopated-) rhythm in the last two bars: ♪ ♩. | ♩ 𝄾 |.

On 12 February the Budapest Philharmonic Society gave its first performance of Strauss's tone poem *Also Sprach Zarathustra* (Thus spake Zarathustra; 1895–1886). Bartók recalls that:

> The work was received with real abhorrence in musical circles here, but it filled me with the greatest enthusiasm. At last there was a way of composing which seemed to hold the seeds of a new life. At once I threw myself into the study of all Strauss's scores and began to write music myself.[16]

Four days later he wrote to his mother about the "unbelievably wonderful" instrumentation in the Strauss work, how good it was to hear something entirely new, and that "Marvelous sections follow each other at every turn, the whole thing speaks of enormous genius and it is truly original. . . . In other words, I believe that Strauss is again somebody who has taken, that is, is taking the art of music one step further ahead."[17] A case in point is the fifth section in *Zarathustra,* "Von der Wissenschaft" (Of science), that—in view of the strictures Bartók met in Koessler's teaching about counterpoint—surely had great impact on the budding composer (Ex. 3.3).

The use of all twelve tones of the chromatic scale in the subject is only one of the several new approaches used by Strauss in fugal construction.[18] The so-called

Ex. 3.3. Strauss, *Also sprach Zarathustra,* op. 30 (1896), fifth section: (a) twelve-tone fugue subject, (b) end of the fugal exposition.

octatonic scale—apparently a Lisztian innovation—forms the passagework which serves as the transition to the third section, "Von den Freuden- und Leiden-schaften" (Of joys and passions) (Ex. 3.4).[19]

Ex. 3.4. Strauss, *Also sprach Zarathustra,* transitional octatonic passagework preceding the third section.

At an evening concert on 3 March, Bartók served as accompanist for Stefánia (Stefi) Geyer, a fourteen-year-old prodigy, who played the Émile Mathieu violin concerto.[20] On 24 March, the day before he reached his majority, Bartók informed his mother that he had begun teaching the piano to two students. One of them, an older, wealthy Jewish businessman, was "very musical but not a ·

good piano student." The other was Hortense ("Titi") Arányi, fifteen-year-old daughter of Police Superintendent Taksony Arányi, whose elder sister Adrienne (Adila) had recommended Bartók as teacher.[21] That evening Bartók made his first appearance as accompanist and soloist in the Royal Hall, where his performance of Schubert, Schumann, and Liszt pieces was acclaimed by the Budapest press. On 26 May the press reviewed Bartók's examination concert at the Academy and highly praised his performance of the Paganini-Liszt A-Minor Etude. Professor Thomán and Mrs. Emma Gruber, an accomplished composer and pianist, also attended the concert but were less satisfied with Bartók's playing of Chopin's *Barcarolle*, op. 60.[22]

When instruction ended in June, Bartók received the highest grade, *kitűnő* (excellent) in piano, chamber music, music history, music aesthetics, score reading, liturgy, and orchestration. In composition, however, Koessler's grade was a disappointing *jeles* (good).[23] Notwithstanding Koessler's cautionary evaluation, the rebellious Bartók returned to Pozsony for the summer recess and immersed himself in the study of Strauss's Nietzsche-based *Zarathustra* and autobiographical *Ein Heldenleben* op. 40 (A Hero's Life, 1898), particularly since Strauss's symphonic poems were then considered as the stylistic antithesis to the neoclassic symphonies of Brahms. Moreover, *Ein Heldenleben* had a special significance for the fervently nationalistic Bartók, inasmuch as the centennial of Lajos Kossuth's birth was celebrated in 1902, and the life and times of the exiled Hungarian revolutionary hero apparently struck Bartók as a promising subject for the creation of a specifically Hungarian symphonic poem. At all events, he prepared a reduction of the full orchestral score for piano solo and committed it to memory.

After his return to Budapest at the end of September, he was awarded the Liszt stipend of 200 florins for his achievements as pianist. In addition to his classroom schedule, he practiced 18 hours a week and devoted 12 hours to private piano teaching in order to earn extra funds for musical scores, tickets for Opera and Philharmonic performances, and other expenses.[24] He also began work on his Symphony in E♭, and in mid-October completed the sketch of the first three movements. On 12 November he wrote to his mother:

> Today I showed the slow movement to Koessler. He said: "An adagio must be about love; there is no trace of love in this movement. That is a serious fault. It is a general shortcoming of modern composition that it cannot produce adagios, this is why modern composers avoid writing them." What others cannot do he will not ask from me. If I cannot think of anything better I may leave the slow movement as it is, but it cannot be considered good [Ex. 3.5].[25]

On the other hand, Koessler was quite pleased with the third (Scherzo) movement. Indeed, when in June 1903 he learned that Bartók's intended to submit the work to the Philharmonic Society, his alternate suggestion was its first performance at the 1904 students' concert in the Budapest Opera House. (Ex. 3.6a).[26]

II.

Ex. 3.5. Bartók, Symphony in E♭, opening of the second movement [Adagio].

When Koessler saw Bartók's sketch, he undoubtedly recognized—and perhaps with more than a modicum of self-satisfaction—the thematic borrowings from the second movement of Beethoven's Ninth Symphony (Ex. 3.6c) and the third theme in Brahms Second Symphony (Ex. 3.6b).

But the ingenious, contrapuntal juxtaposition of two seemingly disparate themes resulted from Bartók's application of thematic metamorphosis he had recognized in his study of Strauss's scores, for example, the Nature motive in the opening bars in *Zarathustra* transformed into the "Hero's Deeds of War" motive in *Ein Heldenleben* (R.N. 43).

III. Scherzo

Ex. 3.6. (a) Bartók, Scherzo (third movement) from the Symphony in E♭ (1902–1903), mm. 1–12; (b) Brahms, Symphony no. 2 in D Major, first movement, mm. 82–87; and (c) Beethoven, Symphony no. 9 in D Minor, second movement, mm. 8–13.

On 12 November, Bartók informed his mother that he had been invited to Emma Gruber's salon, where he demonstrated his score-reading ability by transcribing Dohnányi's symphony at the keyboard, repeating several movements after supper. When he returned to his lodgings and replayed the score, he discovered that he had already memorized a substantial portion of the work. The letter continues with mention of a friendly invitation from the Arányi family, to attend an afternoon party for young musicians on the 23rd. He was especially interested to attend, because of the familial relation of the Arányi girls to the great Hungarian-born violinist, József Joachim, and—in step with Bartók's own nationalistic feelings—the refusal of the family to speak German.[27] He returned to the Gruber salon on the 15th, where he played his memorized transcription of *Ein Heldenleben*—an impressive feat that was received with much admiration— and was quite surprised when Mrs. Gruber asked him for lessons in counterpoint.[28] In addition to the weekly hour of instruction, he was frequently invited to her soirées, which provided him with the opportunity to perform as well as mingle with Academy faculty and outstanding students on a social basis. Mrs. Gruber (nee Emma Schlesinger; the family name was later changed to Sándor), an excellent musician and accomplished pianist, who later married Zoltán Kodály, made her salon "a meeting place for those with a more serious interest in music than that of the guests at most social gatherings."[29]

Also on the 15th, perhaps in expectation of the approaching Arányi party, Bartók sent a postcard to Adila, on which was neatly written a 22-bar canon he had composed, in retrograde inverse imitation for two violins. Although the notation consists of a single voice assigned to Violin I, two-part counterpoint results when the postcard is turned upside down and Violin II thus begins with the last bar (m. 22) and ends with first one (Ex. 3.7).[30]

Ex. 3.7. Bartók, *Duo,* for two violins. The lower staff represents the last four bars of the canon (mm. 19–20), turned upside down and juxtaposed with the upper staff to create a two-part counterpoint.

Bartók's 19 November letter to his mother states that he visited the Arányis to determine exactly what kind of party he would be attending, but perhaps he also wanted to find out Adila's reaction to his unique postcard. Whatever the reason, his letter reports that:

As I no longer teach them, the Arányi girls, Titi and Adila, behaved quite differently towards me, were very gay and dashed about the house upsetting everything. They promised an even rarer to-do on Sunday. I am really intrigued about this, so I'm going to it. In general they are different from other Jewish people I've met so far. (1) They live simply, and (2) they are anti-Semitic. This is something I don't understand, for so far as I know Joachim is also a Semite. However, it will all be the same in a hundred years.[31]

From then on Bartók was a regular visitor, for he had fallen in love with the lively Adila. She was fond of him but not in love with "a delicate lad" whom she often saw take nothing at meals but a glass of milk. From 1902 to 1905 he sent her more than sixty-five postcards, most of them mailed in Budapest. One postcard, dated 29 November, contains the first page of Bartók's composition for violin and piano (Ex.3.8), signed by the composer and headed "1902, nov. 23, emlékére" (in remembrance). Another one, with a picture of the new Szeged synagogue, is dated 11 April 1905.[32]

Ex. 3.8. Bartók, *Andante* for Violin and Piano (1902), mm. 1–2.

Word of Bartók's unique piano transcription of *Ein Heldenleben* reached the Academy faculty, and he was honored with the unusual invitation to play it at their annual meeting on 22 December. When faculty colleagues in Vienna were informed about the highly successful performance, he was asked to repeat the work at the Tonkünstlerverein on 20 January 1903. "It was an event which received widespread notice in the Viennese press. The performance was acclaimed in true Viennese style, though the critics did not miss the opportunity of denouncing Strauss's music."[33]

During January, Bartók composed the first piece (Study for the Left Hand; dedicated to István Thomán) of his Four Pieces for Piano;[34] on 8 February, no. 2 (Fantasy I; to Emma Gruber); on 13 October, no. 3 (Fantasy II; to Emsy and Irmy Jurkovics); and from June to September, no. 4 (Scherzo; to Ernő Dohnányi). This work clearly identifies Bartók as a virtuoso pianist, particularly with regard to the Study for the Left Hand—music whose composition apparently has an interesting background:

> During the years that Bartók lived in Pozsony as a secondary school student and already a recognized pianist, he took part in a soiree held by Géza Zichy (19 January 1898). Zichy had lost his right arm in a hunting accident and had trained himself into a virtuoso pianist with his left hand only. This is the most likely explanation of Bartók's interest in writing music for the left hand at this romantic period in his development as a composer and musician.[35]

Shortly after he finished the First Fantasy, Bartók lent the manuscript to Emma Gruber. She was delighted with the dedication as well as the music and practiced the piece until she was competent enough to play it at her salon. In Bartók's letter to his mother, dated 4 March 1903, he writes that Mrs. Gruber:

> played the whole thing for Dohnányi, who, during the whole time paced about restlessly and constantly mused over what this could be. Suddenly he exclaimed: "I've got it. This piece is either by Strauss or Bartók." So he finds it Straussian: he says it is very nice, but faddish. Mrs. Gruber always liked it. Mr. Thomán is very pleased with it now, he says it is rather Brahmsian. Dohnányi said later that it was modernized Tschaikovsky. Professor Herzfeld, for whom Mrs. Gruber played it on another occasion, heard it to be Lisztian. Somebody else felt it to be Wagnerish. But none of them are right. The truth is that there are oddities in it, for example, it starts like this, with this chord: [36] beautiful??

On 13 April, Bartók gave his first solo recital in his birthplace, Nagyszent-miklós—beginning with a Schumann sonata and ending with Liszt's Spanish Rhapsody—and gave the first performance of the Study for the Left Hand and the First Fantasy. The concert was the first formal one held in the town, organized by Othmár Jurkovics, Nagyszentmiklós district court judge, and the hall was filled. Four young girls, among them the two Jurkovics daughters who had been Bartók's childhood friends, brought a large, ribbon-bedecked laurel wreath to his lodgings. A romantic relationship with the elder girl, Irmy, began, leading to Bartók's dedication of the Second Fantasy to her and her sister Emsy.[37]

During May, Bartók completed the draft of the first and third movements of his Sonata for Violin and Piano (1903), and on the 25th, at the Academy public examination concert, he played Liszt's Spanish Rhapsody with such success that he was excused from the final examination in piano performance. He was also exempt from the composition test, because of the similar success of the third movement of his Sonata for Violin and Piano and the Study for the Left Hand, at a concert of the Academy composition class on 8 June. These concerts marked Bartók's last appearance as an Academy student, and he made plans for summer work on piano repertory under Dohnányi's tutelage, composition of the second movement of the Sonata for Violin and Piano, and completion of the piano score to his *Kossuth* Symphonic Poem, which he had begun on 2 April. A letter to his mother, dated 18 June, brought the news that:

> I said good-bye to Koessler yesterday, and he told me that he wants the Scherzo I was intending to send to the Philharmonic Society to be performed at an Academy of Music graduates' concert that will be held next year at the Opera. Well, as a matter of fact, I think he is right—I owe that much to the Academy. He listened to my *Kossuth* symphony and said that on the whole it is good. He would like me to orchestrate it during the vacation. In which case that too would be performed at the same concert.[38]

The Kossuth *Symphonic Poem*

During July, Bartók and his mother took up lodgings in the village of Passail (near Graz), where he worked on the orchestration of the *Kossuth* symphonic poem. The next month she returned to Pozsony while he visited with the Dohnányi family in Gmunden, a village in Upper Austria. Bartók worked on piano repertory under Ernő Dohnányi's tutelage, completed the orchestration of *Kossuth* and the Scherzo from the E♭ Symphony, and composed the middle movement of his Sonata for Violin and Piano as well as a new Scherzo (Four Piano Pieces, no. 4). He also prepared the following program notes for *Kossuth,* which are closely related to the type and sequence of sections in *Ein Heldenleben:*[39]

> The year 1848 is one of the most eventful in Hungarian history. It was then that the war for independence broke out: a life and death struggle whose aim was to escape forever from the domination of the Habsburg dynasty. The leader, the heart and soul of the revolution, was Lajos Kossuth. In 1849, as Austria saw that the war was going against her, she concluded an alliance with Russia. A crushing blow was inflicted upon the Hungarian Army, and the hope of an independent Hungarian state apparently was shattered forever.
> These events serve as the programmatic basis for this symphonic poem.
> The work consists of ten closely related sections, each with a superscription:
> I. *"Kossuth."* This section is intended to characterize Kossuth.
> II. *"Why are you so grieved, my dear husband?"* Kossuth's wife, his faithful companion, anxiously watches her husband's troubled, careworn face. Kossuth tries to set her mind at rest; but finally he can longer suppress his sorrow:
> III. *"Our country is in danger!"* —He is lost in melancholy contemplation of the glorious past:
> IV. *"Once we lived in better times. . . "*
> V. *"Then our fate changed for the worse . . ."* This theme characterizes the tyranny of the Habsburgs, their lawless use of force. With these words:

VI. *"Up and fight them!"* Kossuth is aroused from his musing; the call to arms has now gone out.

VII. *"Come, come! You splendid lads, you valiant Hungarian warriors!"* Kossuth's summons to the Hungarian nation, rallying them to his banner. Immediately there follows the theme of the Hungarian soldiers as they gradually assemble. Kossuth repeats his call to the assembled ranks, upon which they make a solemn oath to fight to the death. For a moment, very deep silence:

VIII. - - - - Then is heard the slow approach of the enemy, characterized by the motive of the Austrian hymn (*Gotterhalte*). The armies join in battle, assault after assault is made, then the battle subsides slightly. But suddenly the enemy launches its final attack, and their superior numbers overwhelm the Hungarians. The great catastrophe occurs: the remnants of the Hungarian army disperse and take refuge from the terrible vengeance of the victor.

IX. *"All is over!"* The country goes into deepest mourning. But even this is forbidden, and so:

X. *"All is silence, silence . . ."*

On 8 September, in a long, haranguing letter to his mother, Bartók complains that individual members of the Hungarian nation are indifferent to everything Hungarian, including the use of German instead of the mother tongue:

> This is how Hungarians act when they really ought to do all they can to foster the use of their mother tongue. Only thus can it become strong, at least within our own boundaries. . . . Everyone, on reaching maturity, has to set himself a goal and must direct all his work and actions toward this. For my part, all my life, in every sphere, always and in every way, I shall have one objective: the good of Hungary and the Hungarian nation. I think I have already given some proof of this intention in minor ways which have so far been possible to me.[40]

In addition to language and Hungarian-style clothing, the third "minor" way is reflected in *Kossuth* by Bartók's grotesque treatment of the Austrian anthem and use of typically Hungarian vocal and instrumental music. The first theme is based on *verbunkos* (recruiting music) rhythm and is related to the melodic contour and "heroic" rhythm of the first theme in *Ein Heldenleben* (Ex. 3.9).[41]

Ex. 3.9. (a) Bartók, *Kossuth* symphonic poem, section I, mm. 3–6, (b) Strauss, *Ein Heldenleben*, mm. 1–5.

The fourth-section theme is a close borrowing of a popular folk song (that is, a *magyar nóta*), composed by Ernő Lányi (1861–1923) and titled "Kossuth nóta" (Ex. 3.10).[42]

Ex. 3.10. (a) *Kossuth,* section IV, mm. 71–4, (b) Erno... Lányi, "Kossuth nóta," mm. 1–5.

In the eighth section, distortion of the Austrian anthem is achieved by chromatic compression of the melody (that is, changing diatonic scale degrees into chromatic ones) and simultaneously augmenting the individual note values (Ex. 3.11).

Ex. 3.11. (a) Austrian anthem (*Gotterhalte*), mm. 1–4, (b) *Kossuth,* section VIII, mm. 318–22.

The work ends with a funeral march, to portray the mourning that follows Hungary's defeat. The symbolic motif is a transformation of the second theme from Liszt's Hungarian Rhapsody no. 2 (Ex. 3.12).

Bartók's career as an international concert pianist began with his January recital at the Vienna Tonkünstlerverein, and his reputation as such was established when he performed the Beethoven "Emperor" concerto at the Vienna Concertverein on 4 November and "The very significant Dec. 14" recital in the Berlin Bechstein-Saal. In the latter concert, the great piano virtuosos, Leopold Godowsky (1870–1938) and Ferruccio Busoni (1866–1924), were impressed by the technical skill Bartók exhibited in his Study for the Left Hand. The program was for the most part the same one that he played in Nagyszentmiklós on 13 April, and one Berlin press report stated that "he stood out from his numerous colleagues who, year after year, seek to win public attention." [43]

Ex. 3.12. (a) Bartók, *Kossuth,* section IX, mm. 449–51, (b) Liszt, Hungarian Rhapsody no. 2, mm. 10–14.

Two works had their premiere performance at the Budapest Philharmonic Society concert on 13 January 1904. One was the violin concerto composed by Émile Jaques-Dalcroze (1865–1950) and performed by the eminent violinist, Henri Marteau (1874–1934), and the other was the *Kossuth* symphonic poem. The conductor, István Kerner, had a difficult time during the *Kossuth* rehearsals, because of the noisy interruptions by Austrian instrumentalists. The stormy scene was ended when he put down his baton and left the rehearsal room, returning only when the shocked players agreed to continue working on the music. According to the music critic of the *Budapesti Napló* (Budapest Journal), who was there at the time:

> When the orchestra reached the parodied "Emperor's Hymn," some members of the Philharmonic stopped playing, loudly protesting that they would neither play this part of the work, nor suffer anyone else to play it, as it was not permissible to play the Hymn thus distorted. . . . Under these circumstances, it is of interest to report that five members of the orchestra, all players of important instruments, were absent from the Philharmonic Concert today. They sent medical certificates, and their absence all but made the performance of the *Kossuth* Symphony impossible.[44]

Mrs. Bartók, aware of the rehearsal uproar, recalls how agitated she was before the concert, particularly when some gentleman sitting behind her said: "We'd better cross ourselves now, they're going to play the *Kossuth* symphony next. I wish it were over!"

> But when they had finished playing, there was a tremendous storm of applause, and that same gentleman applauded delightedly and went on cheering. I'll never forget the thunder of applause as Béla went on bowing, looking so happy (he was called back 8 or 10 times), and as for me, I wept for joy. . . . Then, the next day, all the splendid notices in the papers![45]

Bartók could hardly have hoped for more publicity than the work brought him in Hungary. The nationalist press overlooked the poor performance and concentrated on the behavior of the rebellious Austrian musicians, thus arousing the Hungarian chauvinists who despised the Hymn and all that it represented. In the 19 January issue of *Zenevilág* (The world of music), Pongrácz Kacsóh (1873–1923)—Academy classmate and devotee of the composer—points to Bartók's mastery of harmony, counterpoint, and orchestration, and acclaims him as Hungary's leading composer.

> With his first work this young man starts at the point, in depth of content and technical mastery which the most modern of the moderns, Richard Strauss, has reached at the height of a career of composition rich in artistic achievement. This man plays with that hundred-headed colossus which we call the modern symphony orchestra as if he had been writing nothing but symphonic poems throughout a long, long life.[46]

On the other hand, the Budapest music critics complained that too much emphasis was placed on Strauss's Germanic musical language or that *Kossuth* should have featured the national melodies (*magyar nóták*) that had served as an inspirational source for Liszt and Brahms. When the work was performed in England on 18 February by the Hallé Orchestra, Manchester, János (Hans) Richter (1843–1916) conducting, a lengthy review on the following day intermixes praise and censure.

> The mere fact that a young composer should attempt to follow in the footsteps of so tremendous a "Jack the Giant-killer" as Strauss would seem to betray the consciousness of great powers, and the degree of facility in handling great orchestral masses exhibited by Mr. Bartók would be remarkable in anyone, and is double surprising in so young an artist. . . .
>
> No justification of any kind can be found for such use as Mr. Bartók's of the Austrian Hymn. It cannot be pretended that the strains of the noble anthem have any fitness for musical purpose. They form a mere label, informing the listener that the reference is here to the Austrian host. Moreover, guying and degrading of the famous melody is altogether repulsive. . . . Apart from the function of the theme as a barefaced label, analogous to a piece of writing in the middle of a painted picture, "Yankee Doodle" would have served the purpose much better.[47]

The second movement of Bartók's Sonata for Violin and Piano was composed in September 1903, and the complete work was performed in Budapest by Jenő Hubay and Bartók on 25 January 1904. The first movement combines Hungarian *verbunkos* style and Lisztian construction. The variations in the second movement begin with "rhapsodic progression of *lassú-friss*" (slow-fast).[48] The third movement is in rondo form, features Hungarian-Gypsy scales, and owes much to Liszt's Piano Sonata in terms of Bartók's attempt to create a specifically Hungarian chromatic style.[49]

Bartók's manuscript of his Piano Quintet shows July 1904 as the completion date and October 1903 as the start.[50] Inasmuch as he was in Berlin that October,

it seems likely that he sketched the first movement and deferred further work
until after his involvement with the *Kossuth* premiere and other obligations were
ended in March 1904. Thus, after the music critics had chastised him for excluding popular national melodies from *Kossuth*, he may have felt it prudent to
include a *magyar nóta*—specifically a transformed version of the well-known
popular art song "Ég a kunyhó" (The hut is burning) as a theme in the quintet's
second movement (Ex. 3.13).

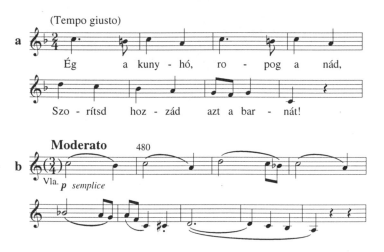

Ex. 3.13. (a) "Ég a kunyhó" *nóta*, (b) Bartók, Quintet for Piano and Strings (1903–
1904), second movement, mm. 479–87.

From the beginning of May to 8 November Bartók devoted himself to composition, piano practice, and the preparation of concert programs in the village
of Gerlice puszta, north Hungary (now Grlica, Slovakia). He rented a room in a
large boardinghouse which included a vacationing Hungarian family whose
nursemaid, Lidi Dósa, had been raised in a remote Transylvanian village. In
mid-August, he visited Bayreuth, attended six Wagner operas, and met János
Richter for whom he played sketches of his Scherzo for Piano and Orchestra.
During this creative "retreat" he completed the Piano Quintet and the Scherzo,
and composed the Rhapsody op. 1, for Piano and Orchestra. In his 1921 autobiography, Bartók recalls this time as the period when

> the magic of Strauss had evaporated. A really thorough study of Liszt's *œuvre*,
> especially some of his less well known works, like *Années de Pélerinage, Harmo-
> nies Poétiques et Religieuses,* the *Faust* Symphony, *Totentanz,* and others had
> after being stripped of their more external brilliance which I did not like, revealed
> to me the true essence of composing. For the future development of music his
> *œuvre* seemed to me of far greater importance than that of Strauss or even Wagner.[51]

The tonal language, rhythm schemata, and to a somewhat lesser extent the structure of the Rhapsody summarizes Hungarian musical dialect. The Lisztian flavor is apparent in the *Allegretto* part, where the rhythm schema of the third motif is a transformation of the second-theme schema in the Vivace of Liszt's Hungarian Rhapsody no. 13. The source of Liszt's theme, moreover, is a widely known popular art song, which was disseminated by Gypsy musicians and adapted by Hungarian and Slovak peasants (Ex. 3.14).[52]

Ex. 3.14. (a) Bartók, Rhapsody op. 1, for Piano and Orchestra, R.N. 14, (b) Liszt, Hungarian Rhapsody no. 13, mm. 126–8, (c) *HFS,* no. 73, mm. 1–3.

And the fourth motif of the *Allegretto* is a transformation of the first theme of the Vivace in Liszt's Hungarian Rhapsody no. 7 (Ex. 3.15).

Ex. 3.15. (a) Bartók, Rhapsody op. 1, mm. 626–29, (b) Liszt, Hungarian Rhapsody no. 7, Vivace, mm. 16–20.

Discovery of Indigenous Rural Folk Song

One day, while Bartók was working on his music, he overheard nanny Lidi Dósa—then eighteen years old—singing a somewhat familiar melody with an unusual text, "Piros alma leesett a sárba" (Ex. 3.16).[53]

The red apple fell into the dirt,
Who picks it up will not be unrewarded.

Ex. 3.16. "Piros alma leesett a sárba." (The red apple fell into the dirt).

At an interview in 1970, Dósa still remembered that Bartók "liked the tune . . . [and] he wanted to note it down. After he noted it down, he went to the piano and played it, then he asked me whether he played it correctly. Well, it was exactly as I sang it. . . . I had to sing continually, however, he only wanted to hear the ancient village tunes! He only liked those I had learned from my grand-mother."[54]

The impact of this impromptu "serenade" can be likened to Bartók's reaction when he heard Strauss's *Zarathustra,* that is, "roused as by a lightning stroke." Comparison of the source melodies in Ex. 3.17 with "Piros alma" (Ex. 3.16) provides the musical explanation.

Ex. 3.17. (a) Hungarian popular art-song melody (1883), mm. 1–6, (b) Slovak folk song, collected by Bartók in Gerlice puszta in 1906, mm. 1–6.[55]

The Hungarian art song shown in Ex. 3.17a "became popular among Hungarian, Slovak, and Moravian peasants; became, in fact, a peasant song. . . . Another probably derived from it is the popular Slovakian one . . . in which the Slovakian rhythm-contraction can be seen" (Ex. 3.17b, m. 5).[56] Bartók was obviously struck by "Piros alma" ending (Ex. 3.16, mm. 5–7) with the beginning bars of the art song (Ex. 3.17, mm.1-3). Another Dósa alteration was her use of the Dorian (B-C♯-D-E-F♯-G♯-A) and Aeolian (B-C♯-D-E-F♯-G-A) folk modes (Ex. 3.16, mm. 1–4 and 5–7, respectively) instead of the modern harmonic minor scale, B-C♯-D-E-F♯-G-A♯, in the art song (Ex. 3.17a). The third apparent difference was structural: Hungarian popular art songs invariably are quaternary (four-verse) stanzas; "Piros alma" is a ternary (three-verse) attenuated form.[57]

The immediate outcome of the fortuitous Dósa-Bartók encounter was his transcription and publication of "Piros alma" as Székely Folk Song for voice and piano accompaniment (Ex. 3.18).[58]

Ex. 3.18. Bartók, Székely Folk Song for Voice and Piano (1904), mm. 17–31.

The harmonic treatment is considerably different from the simple, functional chord progressions typical of nineteenth-century *magyar nóta* repertory. Although the piece is in B major, the lack of a key signature avoids the use of confusing accidentals in the accompaniment of the B-Dorian/Aeolian melody. Furthermore, the piano part is to a certain extent independent of the voice.

In view of the publication of this work, perhaps Bartók believed that popular art song thus "Székely metamorphosed" was indigenous Magyar folk song and therefore the more appropriate thematic basis for an innovative Hungarian style of composition. In order to substantiate his hypothesis, therefore, he decided to collect and analyze folk songs in Transylvanian Székely villages, and he applied for a grant-in-aid to study Székely folk music.

After his return to Pozsony, on 10 November Bartók gave a recital in which he played Liszt's Prelude (on an ostinato bass after J. S. Bach),[59] "Weinen, Klagen, Sorgen, Zagen" (Weeping, lamenting, sorrowing, quaking), repeating its performance in Vienna on 18 February 1905 (and on a number of occasions during the following decades). His penchant for this rather academic set of variations as a repertory piece can be explained in terms of tonal language: Liszt's use of the octatonic scale (Ex. 3.19).

Ex. 3.19. Octatonic configurations in Liszt, "Weinen, Klagen, Sorgen, Zagen," mm. 21, 24–25, 32 (as triads), and 69–70.

The premiere of Bartók's Piano Quintet, by the Prill-Jeral Quartet with the composer as pianist, was given on 21 November in Vienna's Ehrbar Hall. The favorable review, noting the positive audience reception, considered the work to be a serious one, replete with performance difficulties and reflecting the maturity of the composer.[60]

A humorous episode in Bartók's career was a fictitious review of the concert by the Grünfeld-Bürger String Quartet, on 4 December at the Royal Hall, in which Schubert's *Trout* Quintet was performed with Bartók as pianist. The Budapest critic reported that:

> On this occasion the composer, who is a gifted pianist, played the piano part in his own piano quintet. Here we had evidence of the warmth of his Hungarian heart as well as the wide knowledge he brought to the writing of the music. It is a work full

of interest, as evocative and imaginative as his other compositions. The audience loudly acclaimed him both as composer and performer. Bartók also played a piece by Schubert; his interpretation, in feeling and in technique, was of an outstanding order.

Bartók clipped the review and mailed it to a friend in Vienna, with the postscript: "What a gag that was! (The Grünfelds couldn't manage to learn my quintet)."[61] During the first quarter of 1905, Bartók took up lodgings in Vienna, occasionally traveling to Pozsony and Budapest for concert and other purposes, where he composed his Suite no. 1, op. 3, for Orchestra, a five-movement work whose instrumental forces are even larger than those used in *Kossuth*. A most interesting similarity is his transformation of the Austrian anthem in the first movement (Ex. 3.20). Here, however, the treatment is in *verbunkos* style: heroic, marchlike rhythms in the major mode, quite different from the distorted version in *Kossuth* (cf. Ex. 3.11).

Ex. 3.20. (a) Austrian anthem, mm. 1–8, (b) Bartók, Suite no. 1, op. 3, for Orchestra, first movement, mm. 1–9 (transposed to G for comparative purposes).

The first meeting between Bartók and Kodály, on 18 March, was arranged by Mrs. Gruber, for she was aware of the common interest both young men had in investigating indigenous Hungarian folk music. Kodály, two years Bartók's junior and also a composition student of János Koessler, recalls that:

> We went to the same school, we both studied at the Academy of Music but we never met, for Bartók always attended school on different days of the week than I. Bartók was a reserved and somewhat taciturn character, he scarcely made friends, even with his classmates. . . . Nor was I quick to make friends, and moreover I was always so busy that I had no time for society. . . . However, in 1905, a close contact developed between us.[62]

For Bartók—the locally acclaimed "Hungarian Tschaikovsky"—the meeting probably was a casual one; his focus was on the preparation for the fifth Rubinstein Competition as pianist and composer, to take place in Paris during August. And Kodály's agenda was research in Hungarian folk song, following an ongoing investigation of extant published collections as well as the melodies recorded on Béla Vikár's Edison phonograph cylinders.[63]

On 24 May Bartók was informed that his grant-in-aid had been approved, in the amount of a thousand kronen (Austrian crowns) for fieldwork in Székely territory. The next day he gave a charity concert for the benefit of the Budapest Music Education Society School, which included Liszt's B Minor Sonata. It was this performance that Bartók refers to in his statement that, "Some years later, I took up the work anew; its piano technique and the mastering of its difficulties interested me." And he precedes this remark with the comment that, "The few subdued introductory bars, the main thematic group of the exposition. . . . All these are among the great things in music." [64] Example 3.21 shows several innovative thematic constructions in the Liszt Sonata (Ex. 3.21).

Ex. 3.21. Liszt, B Minor Piano Sonata: (a) G-Phrygian mode, mm. 1–4, (b) nondiatonic G-Gypsy scale, mm. 5–7, (c) pentatonic scale sequence, mm. 105–10.

In addition, moreover, is the sequence of four octatonic-scale segments (mm. 8–11, 11–13, 13–15, 15–17), constructed from eleven of the twelve notes comprising the chromatic scale.

During June and July, Bartók stayed in Szilad puszta, near the small town of Vésztő (Békés County), with his sister Elza and her husband, Emil Oláh Tóth (then steward of the Wenckheim estate). While he was preparing for the forthcoming Rubinstein Competition, he commenced the first methodical collection of autochthonous Hungarian folk songs from the local peasant workers. [65] On 1 August he arrived in Paris, and two days later he auditioned as pianist for the Rubinstein jury. He was disappointed not only by his failure to win the first prize but by the lack of any other kind of recognition of his talent, for he believed that he was at least the equal of the winner, Wilhelm Backhaus (1884–1969). And on 8 August, Bartók's entries were rejected for the composition prize, a judgment that left him deeply disturbed at what he considered to be an unfair evaluation of his works. The judges voted to award certificates of merit instead of the monetary first and second prizes, and Bartók received second mention for his Rhapsody op. 1, for Orchestra and the Violin Sonata (1903). The latter work was substituted for the Piano Quintet, as there was not enough time to rehearse the Quintet with the string players. The next day Bartók wrote to his mother that there were only five competitors.

The other four composers' things were absolutely worthless. . . . I wouldn't say a word if a composer of any worth had beaten me for the prize. But the fact that those dunderheads declared my work unworthy of the prize shows how extraordinarily stupid they were. . . . There were 15 votes altogether to be cast by 12 judges: 5 Russian votes, 5 French, 3 German, one Hungarian and one Dutch. Of course it was the Russians and French who had the right to cast more than one vote. What kind of system this is I cannot tell. How can one vote on behalf of another person?!⁶⁶

A week later he wrote a long letter to Irmy Jurkovics, reporting on the negative results of the Rubinstein Competition and describing Paris museums, parks, and nightlife. He continues with the following comments delineating his future musical posture:

In reply to your letter, I must say that Bach, Beethoven, Schubert and Wagner have written such quantities of distinctive and characteristic music that all the music of France, Italy and the Slavs combined, is as nothing by comparison! Of all other composers, Liszt comes closest to the Big Four, but he seldom wrote Hungarian music. Even if, say, my [Kossuth] Funeral March could hold its own in one respect or another, no nation could possibly appear in the arena with a single 4-page piece, however magnificent it might be! In short: we are still far from being ready to start. Work and study, work and study, and again, work and study. Then we may achieve something. For we're in a surprisingly favorable position, compared with other nations, in regard to our folk music. From what I know of the folk music of other nations, ours is vastly superior to theirs as regards force of expression and variety. If a peasant with the ability to compose tunes like the one enclosed [the music examples have since been lost] had but emerged from his class during childhood and acquired an education, he would assuredly have created some outstanding works of great value. Unfortunately, it is rare for a Hungarian peasant to go in for a scholarly profession. . . . A real Hungarian music can originate only if there is a real Hungarian gentry.⁶⁷

Bartók was still in Paris during September, when his mother wrote that she was contemplating retirement from her teaching position. Her suggestion that she write to István Thomán about the possibility of a faculty appointment for her son was emphatically opposed in Bartók's response of 10 September. He explained that only the principal, Mihalovich, had sole jurisdiction, that professors cannot advise a principal in such matters, and that Mihalovich was already determined to get Bartók a teaching post whenever a new budget would provide the salary for an additional piano professor. Bartók's letter ends with a lengthy confession that he is a lonely man, notwithstanding such Budapest friends as Thomán and Mrs. Gruber.

There are times when I suddenly become aware that I am absolutely alone! And I prophesy, I have a foreknowledge, that this spiritual loneliness is to be my destiny. I look about me in search of the ideal companion, and yet I am fully aware that it is vain quest. Even if I should succeed in finding someone, I am sure that I would soon be disappointed.⁶⁸

Bartók was in Vienna during October, practicing Liszt's *Totentanz* for piano and orchestra and Bach's Chromatic Fantasia and Fugue for the Hallé concert in Manchester on 23 November and preparing the First Suite for its premiere by the Vienna Philharmonic Orchestra on the 29th. The reviews of the Manchester performance were outstanding, particularly in terms of Bartók's technical expertise: "He gets a big and virile tone out of the piano. . . . He was remarkably good in passages when the tone has at the same time to be sustained and gradually reduced in power; his pedaling was evidently very expert."[69]

Although the extant full score of the First Suite shows contiguous pagination throughout its five movements,[70] the second movement was not included in the performance. Notwithstanding this omission, the next month Bartók wrote a short autobiographical note for a Hungarian journalist, in which he states that: "A week ago my orchestral suite, in all its Hungarian-ness, caused a sensation *in Vienna*. . . . With patriotic greetings."[71] It is not known whether the Philharmonic conductor, Ferdinand Löwe, unilaterally decided on a four-movement rendition. But in 1915, when the Budapest Philharmonic performed only three movements of the Suite, Bartók's true feelings about such mistreatment of his work is tellingly conveyed in his letter to the orchestra's board of directors.

> As I did not want to cause a scene at the celebrations, I didn't protest when, on the occasion of your Gala concert in Vienna, you committed the barbarity of performing my 1st Suite in truncated form. . . . There is such a close thematic connection between the movements that certain bars of some of the movements cannot be understood unless one has already heard the preceding movements. . . . In these circumstances, I have to inform you that I should be greatly obliged if you never play any of my pieces again.[72]

During Bartók's stay in Vienna, he began writing his Suite no. 2, op. 4, for [small] Orchestra, completing the first three movements of what would eventually be a quaternary work. It may have been at this time that "he made a thorough study of [Kodály's] first collection, which appeared in the periodical *Ethnographia.*"[73] Kodály's essay, *Mátyusföldi gyűtés* (Mátjusföld collection) consists of thirteen folk songs that he had gathered in peasant villages in northern Hungary. Ex. 3.22 shows melody no. 9, apparently related to a *nóta* melody, which has the same alternation of folk modes that Bartók discovered in the song Lidi Dósa sang for him in 1904 (cf. Ex. 3.16).

Ex. 3.22. Kodály, "Mátyusföld collection," melody no. 9. The first melody section is in the G-Dorian mode (m. 1, E♮ sixth degree); the second section is G-Aeolian (m.7, E♭).

Bartók's "thorough study" of Kodály's collection, together with the few folk songs he had gathered from Lidi Dósa and from the peasant workers on the Wenckheim estate in Békes County, led him to the conviction that:

> what we had known as Hungarian folk songs till then were more or less trivial songs by popular composers and did not contain much that was valuable. I felt an urge to go deeper into this question and set out in 1905 to collect Hungarian peasant music unknown till then. It was my great good luck to find a helpmate for this work in Zoltán Kodály, who, owing to his deep insight and sound judgment in all spheres of music, could give me many a hint and much advice that proved of immense value.[74]

Thus, toward the end of 1905, Bartók apparently arrived at the conclusion that investigating Hungarian peasant music would yield the kind of melodic, rhythmic, and tonal idiosyncrasies needed to launch a new style of Hungarian composition. His First Suite is a remarkable confluence of stylistic elements typical of Hungarian national romanticism—*verbunkos* rhythm, *csárdás* dance, *magyar nóta* imitation, Gypsy ornamentation—and nineteenth-century art music—Liszt, Wagner, Richard Strauss. These elements, however, represent a summary of Hungarian music dialect until then—not a means for the future. Bartók then decided to join with Zoltán Kodály—fellow composer and adventuring folklorist with similar aspirations—in collecting hitherto unknown, rural Hungarian folk songs during the summer of 1906. Furthermore, they planned to compose appropriate piano accompaniments and self-publish the songs in a series of booklets for interested subscribers, with the expectation that the income earned would provide the financial means for future fieldwork.

4

Fusion of National Styles: 1906–1925

From 3 January to 16 February 1906 Bartók's concert appearances were for the most part shared events in which he participated as accompanist for instrumental and vocal artists and as soloist in his own compositions and works by J. S. Bach, Chopin, and Liszt. He met with Kodály in regard to their planned folk song publication, studied the latter's dissertation on stanza structure in the Hungarian folk songs that Kodály had assembled from personal and published collections, and began transcribing the field recordings previously made by Béla Vikár in rural Hungarian villages. But it was Kodály's findings that set Bartók on the right path for the future, scientific investigation of musical folklore: (a) except for children's songs and "regős ének" (Wassailing songs), the main corpus consists of quaternaries in which each of the four melody-lines corresponds to one text-line; (b) the basic types of tempo are strict dance-rhythm and parlando speech-rhythm; and (c) all melody lines follow the accentuation of the Hungarian language and thus begin with a downbeat.[1]

During the first two weeks in March, Bartók and Kodály drafted a circular, "Appeal to the Hungarian Public," which was sent to their acquaintances and other persons, announcing the forthcoming publication of two booklets, each containing ten folk songs (nos. 1–10 by Bartók, 11–20 by Kodály), for the price of three crowns.[2] From about 20 March to mid-May he was on tour as accompanist-soloist for the thirteen-year-old violin prodigy, Franz (Ferenc) von Vecsey, in Portugal and Spain. Among Bartók's sight-seeing experiences following the tour was a short excursion to Tangier, north Morocco, where he stumbled upon an Arab café and was struck by the unusual singing, to the point that he resolved to return some day, when he had the time and funds.[3] Thereafter he visited cities in Spain, France, and Italy before returning to Budapest on 29 May. Then, beginning the last week in June, he began the planned fieldwork in rural Hungarian areas.

> If we look at the map of his collecting tour in 1906, it is noticeable in how many different places he found his material. It would seem that his first intention was to gain a comprehensive picture of folk music in widely differing regions of the country. Naturally enough, he found that this would be impossible without the aid and support of his friends and acquaintances. . . . Most of the collection he made during the summer of 1906 originates from Békés County, in the neighborhood of Vésztő, Doboz, and Gyula.[4]

Some of the melodic, rhythmic, and formal characteristics in the peasant folk songs collected by Bartók that summer, which dramatically contrast the structural differences between such music and that of the *magyar nóta,* are illustrated in Ex. 4.1.

Ex. 4.1. (a) Two-section (mm. 1–6, 7–12) parlando melody, sung by Lidi Dósa in 1904, transcribed by Bartók as no. 7 in Twenty Hungarian Folk Songs for Voice and Piano (1906); (b) *HFS,* no. 49, a quaternary melody in dance tempo, in which the tonality of the first half is a nondiatonic folk mode, [G-A]-B-C-D-E♭ (mm. 1–4), and the second half is pentatonic, G-B♭-C-D-F (mm. 7–8 not shown); (c) *HFS,* no. 67, a quaternary melody in dance tempo, with three-bar phrases and change of time between duple and triple meter, mm. 1–6; (d) *HFS,* no 187, second half of a quaternary parlando melody in the Phrygian folk mode, G-A♭-B♭-C-D-E♭-F (mm. 5–8).

During August, Bartók returned to the village of Gerlice puszta in northern Hungary, which he had visited two years before, and collected 120 melodies, of which one-third were Hungarian tunes with Slovak text. Toward the end of the month, he wrote his mother that the village turned out to be a Slovak-Hungarian language border, and it was this circumstance which eventually led him to extend his research to linguistically Slovak territories. As one case in point, he found a Slovak folk song in the Dorian folk mode but with its "skeleton form" (that is, the principal tones of the melody) based on the symmetrical Hungarian pentatonic scale. In other cases, Hungarian words appeared in the Slovak texts or in the refrains, and a substantial number of melodies were direct borrowing of indigenous Hungarian tunes.[5]

Bartók's postcard to his mother, dated 10 September, states that he had been conferring with Kodály for three days about the proposed publication of Hungarian folk songs, and that "We are writing a preface in which we have some harsh things to say about Hungarian audiences."[6] In view of Bartók's statement and that the preface has been erroneously attributed to Kodály as sole author and Bartók as passive cosignatory, it is therefore given below in its entirety.

The purpose and method of publishing folk songs may be twofold. First, to concentrate on gathering all songs sprung from the people, considering completeness as the main aim, the individual values of the various songs being no object. Such a collection is something of a "comprehensive dictionary of folk-songs." The arrangement of its material should preferably imitate that of a dictionary, too. The best example of this kind so far is the Finnish folk song collection edited by Ilmari Krohn (Suomen Kansan sävelmiä. Four booklets up to 1906). The songs were published in one part, in a carefully written authentic notation, indicating all the variants. Nothing but a similar collection can serve as a basis for a scholarly study of folk songs.

The other purpose of publishing folk songs is to introduce them to the public at large and to encourage developing a taste for them. Naturally, for this purpose a "comprehensive dictionary" is not a suitable means, since it contains veritable gems and simple uninteresting pieces side by side.

A meticulous selection is needed, and the choice pieces should be presented in a musical arrangement in order to make them more palatable to the taste of the public. If brought in from the fields into the towns, folk songs have to be dressed up. However, attired in their new habit, they might seem shy and out of place. One must take care to cut their new clothes so as not to cramp their fresh country style. Whether arranged for choir or for the piano, the accompaniment should merely try to conjure up the image of fields and villages left behind. As for the authenticity of the melodies, the songs of the popular edition should not be second to those of the complete one.

Naturally, the first kind of publication presupposes that the work of collecting the material has been completed. In Hungary, where this work has scarcely begun, we cannot even think of it for some time to come. However, selecting the pick of the crop can be commenced from the very beginning. The present edition contains such selected songs, handpicked for the general public. By turning the entire income of this edition to the sole purpose of collecting folk songs, the first aim is also furthered.

A part of the 20 songs was taken from the recordings of Béla Vikár, an old enthusiastic collector of Hungarian folklore, acknowledgments are due to him for his kind permission to submit them; the other part of the collection was selected from the songs we have collected ourselves in our recent endeavors in this line. In consideration of the practice in this country, the melodies were also introduced into the accompaniment. In the subsequent booklets (their publication will depend on the results of the collecting tours), we shall not adhere to this practice at all times, since we wish to supply melodies to be sung and not to be played on the piano.

May these ancient manifestations of the spirit of our folk meet with half the amount of appreciation they deserve! It will take a long time before they can take their due place in our musical life, both in the homes and in public concert halls. The greater part of present-day Hungarian society is not Hungarian enough, nor naive enough and, on the other hand, not well-educated enough for these songs to find their way into the heart of these people. Hungarian folk songs in the concert halls! Sounds rather preposterous today. To be ranked with the masterpieces of song literature on a world scale and also with the folk songs of foreign nations! But, time will come when Hungarian music-making at home has become a common practice, and Hungarian families will not be content with the low music-hall songs imported from abroad, or with the imitation folk songs turned out in cheap series at home. Then we shall have Hungarian singers to sing our folk songs. By that time not only a mere handful of connoisseurs will know that there exists another kind of Hungarian folk song than the "Ritka búza" and "Ityóka-pityóka" type of sham popular songs.[7]

As the number of subscribers was less than they had anticipated, the two amateur entrepreneurs decided to publish one booklet of twenty songs (nos. 1–10 by Bartók, 11–20 by Kodály) titled *Magyar Népdalok* (Hungarian folk songs). They contracted for 1,500 copies at a cost of 750 crowns, a sum they could hardly afford, and the Budapest music publisher, Károly Rozsnyai, agreed to distribute the work. The sales were so disappointing that Kodály expressed his hurt feelings in a letter to Bartók, that "The fate of the booklet moves me deeply. I think a hearty, general and permanent 'to Hell with them' will do for the Hungarian public and then we had better not take any notice of them. After all, you can't feed asses on roast pheasant, it will disagree with them."[8] Unfortunately, at that time the Hungarian public was infatuated with *Die lustige Witwe* (The Merry Widow), the latest and most successful work by the Hungarian composer, Franz Lehár (1870–1948), which had its premiere in Vienna on 28 December 1905.

On 13 December the Academy of Music announced the retirement of István Thomán, because of severe illness, and that the Ministry of Culture had appointed Bartók as his successor. The next month, on 18 January 1907, Professor Bartók took over the advanced piano class whose objectives were to provide students with theoretical and practical instruction leading to a performer's career and award of a state diploma.[9] This appointment, unprecedented for such a young candidate and modest in terms of remuneration, provided him with the wherewithal to continue his fieldwork and the opportunity to augment his income by editing Hungarian editions of eighteenth- and nineteenth-century piano works. Indeed, he was particularly anxious to collect more folk songs from Slovak villagers in the northern Hungarian area he had visited in August, in view of the heterometric verse structure he found in Slovak folk song that is uncharacteristic of isometric Hungarian material. In the quaternary Slovak folk song shown in Ex. 4.2, the text of the second and third sections (mm. 9–11, 12–14) has a different structure (seven-syllable verses) from that in the first and fourth sections (eleven-syllable verses).[10]

Bartók continued his fieldwork in Hungarian and Slovak villages during March. On 15 May he attended the Academy concert by former students, which included his First Suite and a performance by the beautiful nineteen-year-old violinist Stefi Geyer, with whom Bartók fell hopelessly in love. He decided to use his grant-in-aid for the collection of folk music in Transylvania during the summer, and on 28 June he began his tour with a brief stopover in Jászberény (a

Pod lip - kou,   nad lip - kou,   ed - na ma - la   dve

E - šte je - dnu   ma - la daťʼ,   po - ša - la - sä   vi - mlú vač,

že - ňe - má,   že - ňe - dá,   že bi bu - lo   zla.

Ex. 4.2. Bartók, *SV.*ii, melody no. 531a.

small town near Budapest), joining Stefi and her brother as house guests of the the Geyers' uncle and aunt. Bartók, now twenty-six years old—bedecked with mustache, short beard, and pince-nez eyeglasses—collected Hungarian folk songs in the vicinity. Stefi's recollection is that "Bartók joined us under the pretext of collecting songs. It was obvious, however, that he was following me, because there isn't much to be collected in Jászberény and he hardly found anything."[11] At all events, when he prepared for departure to Transylvania on 1 July, she had agreed to correspond with him during his fieldwork.

The Discovery of Old-Style Hungarian Folk Song

It was probably in Csíkrákos (now Racul, Romania), a Székler village in the southeastern part of Transylvania, that Bartók first encountered ancient Magyar folk song. Its most striking feature is the pentatonic scale, notated as A-C-D-E-G-A and C-D-E-G-A-C in Bartók's "Csíkrákos, 14 Juli 1907" letter to Stefi. He also notated four melodies in skeleton form (that is, without ornamental notes), of which the first one appears below (Ex. 4.3).[12] Other features include "*tempo rubato, recitativo parlando*, and rich ornamentation."[13]

Parlando

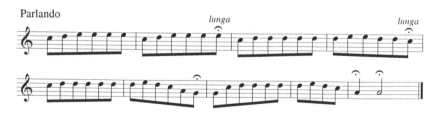

Ex. 4.3. Bartók, Transylvanian-Hungarian (Székler) folk song.

Inspired by his discovery of this ancient stratum of indigenous Hungarian folk song, he commemorated the finding by composing the fourth movement of his Second Suite, where the first theme is pentatonic and its rhythm is a *kanász-tánc* (swineherd's-dance) permutation. Furthermore, the accompaniment (B♭-F) emulates the drone and middle pipe of a Hungarian bagpipe. (Ex. 4.4).[14]

Ex. 4.4. Bartók, Suite no. 2 for Orchestra, op. 4, fourth movement, mm. 3–6.

Thus, when Bartók returned to the Budapest suburb of Rákospalota and completed the Second Suite on 1 September, its fourth movement represents the first adaptation of Hungarian peasant music peculiarities as source material for a new style of composition. On the other hand, however, his infatuation for Stefi Geyer prompted a return to German romanticism that persisted until she broke off their relationship toward the end of February 1908 and he vented his anguish by composing the First Elegy for Piano immediately thereafter.

The Stefi Geyer Episode

Bartók was so exhilarated by the receipt of Stefi's first letter,[15] that he responded with the mentioned Csíkrákos letter containing notated Székler folk songs (see Ex. 4.3). It is quite interesting that his next letter (27 July) also includes an excerpt from the Prelude to *Tristan und Isolde*. Following his 7 August postcard, containing another pentatonic melody collected in the village of Gyergyó-Kilyénfálva, on 16 August he sent a letter headed "dialog von Gyergyó-Kilyénfálva," which describes the difficulty he had in persuading a woman to sing. In the following excerpt, T = traveler (Bartók), W = Woman:

> T: I've heard from your neighbor that you know all kinds of ancient folk songs which you learned from the old folks when you were a girl.
>
> W: Me?! Old songs?! You shouldn't poke fun at me, Sir. Old songs! Ha, ha!
>
> T: Believe me, I'm not poking fun at you! I mean what I say! That's why I've made this long, long journey from Budapest, specially to look for these very old songs which no one remembers except here!

W: And what are you doing to do with those songs? Do you want to print them?

T: No indeed! What we want to do is to preserve the songs by writing them down. For if we don't write them down, then in years to come no one will know the songs that are being sung here now. You see, even now, the young people sing quite different songs; they don't care for the old ones and don't even learn them; and yet they are much prettier than the new ones, aren't they?! In 50 years no will have heard of them if we don't write them down now.

Bartók's fruitless cajoling continues, even though the woman insists on singing new songs or religious ones, until the exasperated traveler surrenders with: "And so on *da capo al fine* from morning till night, Monday to Sunday (day after day)! I can't bear it any longer. Impossible!"[16]

After he returned to Budapest, and overjoyed to receive Stefi's letter requesting that she be allowed to address him as a friend, his 20 August response includes a 12-bar melody with a repetitive Hungarian lyric whose translation reads, ":|: You're allowed to :| You may call me friend" (Ex. 4.5).[17]

Ex. 4.5. Melody composed by Bartók for Stefi Geyer, mm. 1–3, 10–12.

Bartók's letter also includes a second melody—his impression of Stefi (then nineteen years old)—and asks if it isn't the correct musical picture "of the approximately 14-year-old lively girl that I got to know in Jászberény?"(Ex. 4.6).[18]

Ex. 4.6. Bartók's musical impression of Stefi Geyer, which later became the first theme in the second movement of his Concerto no. 1 for Violin and Orchestra.

Stefi's answer becomes apparent in Bartók's letter of 6 September, in which he refers to her thoughts that "life is so beautiful! There's so much beauty in nature—the arts—science . . . ," tells her: "that is the most beautiful thing you have written to me so far," and continues with:

Suddenly, after those 4 or 5 delightful lines, you broach a weighty question such as we have never discussed as yet. But it had already occurred to me that there might come a day when we felt obliged to discuss this subject; and I am truly glad that at this time, in contrast to what has always happened so far, the initiative has not had to come from me. I was absolutely convinced—although we have never talked about it—that you were "godfearing." It wasn't difficult for me to put two and two together. This makes it all the more difficult for me to touch on this subject. I am almost afraid to begin.

Next follows a biographical narrative in which Bartók traces the course of his move away from Catholicism, from the age of fourteen till the completion of his twenty-second year, when "I was a new man—an atheist." The letter continues with lengthy discourses on philosophy, the "Holy Trinity of Christian mythology," mortality as opposed to immortality of the soul, and the purpose of life. He ends with: "Greetings from / AN UNBELIEVER / (who is more honest than a great many believers)."[19]

After Stefi received the aforementioned letter, she arranged a meeting with Bartók to disabuse him of any misconceptions he might have concerning her religious beliefs. Her obstinacy, even to the point where she would not accept any books from him, drove him to despair, to the point where he apparently brought up the subject of suicide. Her alarm was such, after his "impatient departure," that she immediately sent him a letter "not to do all kinds of foolish things." On 11 September, therefore, he responded that:

> By the time I had finished reading your letter, I was almost in tears—and that, as you can imagine, does not usually happen to me every day. Here is a case of human frailty! I anticipated that you might react like this, yet when you actually did so, I was upset. Why couldn't I read your letter with cold indifference? Why couldn't I put it down with a smile of contempt? Why should I be so affected by your reaction? . . .
>
> And yet I should add that it never occurred to me that you would write in precisely this way. I wouldn't have thought you capable of such dogmatism; that you believed in this or that just as you've been told to. Or maybe I am after all mistaken in thinking that you accept as true that clumsy fable about the Holy trinity? . . . Surely you can't be the slave of such notions! I must have got your letter all wrong, I am sure. If only you hadn't mentioned something about crossing oneself! . . . I would never attempt to talk you out of your faith, distressed as I am by your present state of mind.
>
> After reading your letter, I sat down to the piano—I have a sad misgiving that I shall never find any consolation in life save in music. And yet - - -

Ex. 4.7. Bartók's musical impression of the "ideal" Stefi Geyer, which was later revised as the first theme in the first movement of his Concerto no. 1 for Violin and Orchestra.[20]

Bartók took up his teaching duties at the Academy, beginning with what he found to be the onerous chore of student registration. On 8 October he wrote to Gyula Sebestyén (1864–1946), editor of *Ethnographia,* that he had transcribed twenty-eight ballads from his collection of Székler folk songs and was "at last" sending them for publication.[21] Later in the month he traveled to Nyitra County (now Nitrianska, Slovakia), where he resumed fieldwork in linguistically Slovak villages. In Darázs (Dražovce), on 27 October, he collected a folk song based on the Lydian folk mode, C-D-E-F♯-G-A-B, a pitch collection he previously found in a Slovak folk song he recorded in Gerlice puszta (now Grlica, Gemerská County).[22] This finding justified his conclusion that the Lydian mode is a scalar peculiarity of Slovak folk song. The next day he marked the event by notating the folk song on a picture postcard and mailing it to Stefi (Ex. 4.8).[23]

Ex. 4.8. Melody of a Slovak folk song, in the C-Lydian mode, as recorded by Bartók on 27 October 1907.

The following excerpts from Bartók's letters to Stefi, from 29 November to 8 February, provide a poignant memorandum of Bartók's anguish over Stefi's gradual withdrawal from their relationship.[24]

> On the evening of the 28th, I thought especially of you. The main theme of the last part of your concerto was born. Also some of the second movement was formed. Now the musical picture of the idealized St. G. is here, it is divinely ardent. Also the lively St. G. is here, it is funny, witty, amusing. Now one should write the picture of the indifferent, cool, silent St. G., but this would be ugly music.

> One day this week it became suddenly clear to me, as from higher inspiration, the indisputable necessity that your piece can only exist in two parts. Two opposite pictures, that is all. Now I only wonder that I did not see this truth before.

> This idealized picture has taken all my thoughts and feelings. I have never written such direct music before. I prefer it a hundred times, because it speaks about you and to you (only and solely). I really wrote it from my soul—I don't care if nobody likes it, only you should like it. The first movement is my confession to you.

> The full score of the violin concerto was finished on February 5th. I put it in my drawer. I do not know if I should destroy it or leave it there, so that it should be found after my death, or scatter the whole bundle of notated paper—my declaration of love, my best work—to the garbage dump. I cannot talk about it, show it to anybody, the sad outcome of my declaration does not concern the world.

Example 4.9 shows the "declaration of love" leitmotiv and its inversion as the opening bars. The undulating melodic contour brings to mind the fugue theme in Strauss's *Also sprach Zarathustra* (cf. Ex. 3.3a).

Andante sostenuto

Ex. 4.9. Bartók, Concerto no. 1, for Violin and Orchestra (op. posth.), first movement, mm. 1–4.

Stefi's response on 13 February brought the crushing decision to end their relationship, and she asked Bartók to present her with the manuscript of the Concerto as a parting gift. He decided to honor her request but had the presence of mind to delay the presentation until a copy of the score had been made. In the meantime, during a visit with Zoltán Kodály, Bartók noticed a poem lying on the piano and read it with growing interest. Kodály indicated that the author, Béla Balázs, had asked him to set the poem to music, but that he didn't find it a source of inspiration. Bartók then said, "Just good for me," and left with the poem.[25] Thereafter, Bartók inscribed the first page of the score with: "Dedication / For Stefi: / from times still happy. / Although it was only half happiness. . . ." And on the last two pages he added: "(It was also in vain, in vain that this poem came into my hands, for me there is no solace). / February 16." Following this comment are the stanzas from the Balázs poem, written on the left margin of the score, from which the following verses seem particularly appropriate to quote here as representing Bartók's state of mind:[26]

> My heart is bleeding, my soul is ailing,
> I roved amongst men,
>
> I loved with torment, with love of fire
> In vain, in vain!
>
> No stars are as far from each other
> As two human souls!
>
> Unquenchable desire burns me,
> As long as I live, as long as I live.

Later that month, the tormented suitor vented his unrequited passion in the Janus-like Elegy No. 1, op. 8b, for Piano, which looks back to the Liszt style of Romantic pianism as well as points ahead to a new tonal language. The Elegy also reflects Bartók's debt to Liszt as the source of thematic inspiration for programmatic purposes. Ex. 4.10 shows the motivic similarities between the first Elegy and Liszt's symphonic poem, *Les Préludes* (1854). It should be noted that motif 2 in the Elegy is constructed from the reordered degrees of the "declaration of love" leitmotiv as a transformation of motif 2 in the symphonic poem.

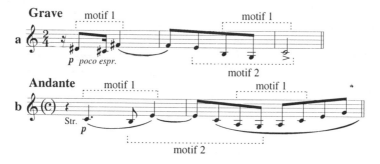

Ex. 4.10. (a) Bartók, Elegy no. 1, op. 8b, for Piano, mm. 1–3, and (b) Liszt, *Les Préludes*, mm. 3–4.

The programmatic content in the symphonic poem is based on Lamartine's poem "Les Preludes," which Liszt inscribed as the preface to his score. In view of the motivic relationships, perhaps the distraught Bartók found consolation in these lines which open Lamartine's poem:

> What is our life but a succession of preludes to that unknown song whose first solemn note is struck by Death? Love is the magical dawn of existence, but where is the life whose first enjoyment of such ecstasy is not disrupted by some tempest?[27]

The Elegy continues with changes in tempo, time signatures, and dynamics until the next transformation of the leitmotiv appears as a D♯-minor construction with a major seventh degree (D♮). The accompaniment, however, reveals that the pitch collection, together with that of the leitmotiv, forms the E Hungarian-Gypsy scale, E-F♯-G-A♯-B-C-D♯ (Ex. 4.11).

Ex. 4.11. Bartók, First Elegy, mm. 19–20.

Another example of Bartók's mindset is represented by the first movement of his String Quartet, op. 7, which opens with a transformation of the first theme in the second movement of the First Violin Concerto (Ex. 4.12; cf. Ex. 4.6).

Ex. 4.12. Bartók, String Quartet no. 1, op. 7, first movement, mm. 1–4.

According to Stefi Geyer, Bartók's last letter to her stated that: "I have begun a quartet; the first theme is the theme of the [violin concerto's] second movement—it is my funeral dirge."[28]

It was probably at the beginning of May that Bartók began composing his Fourteen Bagatelles op. 6, for Piano. This series of so-called experimental pieces was to a certain extent influenced by Debussy's music which Kodály brought from Paris the preceding July, analyzed its characteristic features, and shared his findings with Bartók.[29]

> From the beginning of this century the young Hungarian musicians, among whom I belonged, already oriented themselves in other domains toward the French culture. One can easily imagine the significance with which they beheld Debussy's appearance. The revelation of this art finally permitted them likewise to turn toward the French culture.[30]

> In 1907, at the instigation of Kodály, I became acquainted with Debussy's work, studied it thoroughly and was greatly surprised to find in his work "pentatonic phrases" similar in character to those contained in our peasant music.[31]

> In these [Bagatelles] a new piano style appears as a reaction to the exuberance of the romantic piano music of the nineteenth century; a style stripped of all unessential decorative elements, deliberately using only the most restricted technical means.[32]

As a case in point, the fourth Bagatelle is a transcription of an antique Hungarian melody (Ex. 4.13a) whose principal tones are based on the pentatonic scale, G-Bb-C-D-F, where the additional, nonaccented passing tones, Eb and A, convert the tonality to the Aeolian folk mode. The transcription (Ex. 4.13b) reflects the Debussy style of nonfunctional chord sequences as the means to harmonize the melody.[33]

Ex. 4.13. (a) *HFS,* melody no. 7a, mm. 1–4, and (b) Bartók, fourth Bagatelle, mm. 1–4.

Although Stefi had not intended to meet with Bartók again, their paths crossed on 3 May during a concert at the Budapest Fair in Városliget (Town Park). After Bartók played two Chopin pieces, she followed with a performance of the Vieuxtemps *Rondeau,* accompanied by Oszkár Dienzl.[34] Perhaps this apparently unwelcome association was the inspiration for creating the last two Bagatelles: no. 13 (Ex. 4.14a), with "(Elle est morte)" as the subtitle, and its Hungarian translation. "(meghalt)", placed above the leitmotiv in mm. 22–23; and "(Ma mie qui danse)" as the subtitle for no. 14 (Ex. 4.14b).[35]

Ex. 4.14. (a) Bartók, thirteenth Bagatelle, mm. 22–26, and (b) Bartók, fourteenth Bagatelle, mm. 9–14.

Furthermore, on 10 May Bartók wrote to the well-known violinist, Henri Marteau, inquiring whether he would like to have the Violin Concerto score and transcription for piano, that another artist shrank from its undertaking, and that his performance of the work would thereby save Bartók from an almost hopeless situation. Marteau's letter of 19 May stated that he could not play the concerto in 1908 and that Bartók should send him the music during the following year.[36]

In June, Bartók composed a set of pedagogical pieces under the title Eleven Piano Recital Pieces. The next month, after he had signed an agreement with his publisher, Károly Rozsnyai , he withdrew one of them and placed it as the Sixth Bagatelle. Inasmuch as his contract stipulated eleven pieces, he composed another one which begins with the leitmotiv, subtitled it "Dedication" as a musical memento of Stefi Geyer, and renamed the collection as Ten Easy Pieces for Piano (Ex. 14.15).

Ex. 4.15. Bartók, "Dedication" from Ten Easy Pieces for Piano (1908), mm. 1–8. The last four bars contain a transposed trichord, G-B-F♯, of the leitmotiv.

The First Encounter with Romanian Folk Song

Bartók returned to Transylvania for a brief walking tour during October, where he was "making merry" at the annual county fair in the village of Torockó (now Rimetea, Romania).[37] A fortuitous meeting with several young Romanian girls from the nearby village of Székelyhidas (now Podeni), resulted in the first collection of Romanian folk songs which he noted down by ear (he was traveling without his recording apparatus at the time). These unique specimens were completely different from his Hungarian and Slovak materials in terms of structure and modality. Three of the Romanian melodies were in the Phrygian folk mode, mainly characteristic of old people in Székely areas, with isometric (eight-syllable) text lines. The more important distinctions, however, were the melodic construction, consisting of three sections, and a refrain line with unintelligible syllables (Ex. 4.16).

Ex. 4.16. RFM.i., melody no. 353.

Bartók was especially struck by the apparently radical difference in repertory between young Romanian informants and their Hungarian peers: the latter
had discarded the Phrygian folk mode when the new style came into vogue
during the middle of the nineteenth century. He decided to extend his collecting
to the minority Romanian inhabitants of Transylvania, in order to determine
whether there were reciprocal influences with regard to their Hungarian neighbors. This change in direction proved to be of momentous impact not only on
his creative processes in terms of a new, unique musical language but also on
his investigative efforts in changing his ethnological emphasis from haphazard
collecting to scientific investigations which brought him international recognition as a foremost scholar in comparative musical folklore.

Another important event in Bartók's life occurred earlier in the fall, when
fifteen-year-old Márta Ziegler (1893–1967) entered the Academy of Music as a
student in his piano class. She and her sister, Herma, daughters of a Budapest
inspector-general of police, had been Bartók's private pupils in 1907, and he
found the family to be a congenial household where he was made welcome.
Notwithstanding the difference in age, teacher and student found in their relationship an attraction that transcended the latter's modest musical talent, as evi-
denced by the programmatic content of "Portrait of a girl," the first piece in
Bartók's Seven Sketches op. 9b, for Piano (1908–August 1910), which he dedicated to Márta in 1908 (Ex. 4.17).

Ex. 4.17. Bartók, first Sketch, showing the leitmotiv in mm. 52, 57–58, and 63 .

The expressive nature of the music is inherent in the cadential resolution of
the chordal leitmotiv (D-F♯-A-C♯) to a G♯-minor triad in mm. 52–53 and a G-
major one in the last two bars, as if to indicate that perhaps the composer has
tonally replaced Stefi Geyer with an "ideal Márta."

Bartók's Ten Easy Pieces and Seven Sketches also include transcriptions of folk tunes from his Hungarian and Slovak collections. As he later stated in a lecture-recital:

> Already at the very beginning of my career as a composer I had the idea of writing some easy works for piano students. This idea originated in my experience as a piano teacher; I had always the feeling that the available material, especially for beginners, has no real musical value, with the exception of very few works—for instance, Bach's easiest pieces and Schumann's *Jugendalbum*. I thought these works to be insufficient, and so, more than thirty years ago, I myself tried to write some easy piano pieces. At that time the best thing to do would be to use folk tunes. Folk melodies, in general, have great musical value; so, at least the thematical value would be secured. . . . I wrote [*For Children*] in order to acquaint the piano-studying children with the simple and non-romantic beauties of folk music. Excepting this purpose, there is no special plan in the work.[38]

After *For Children* for Piano had been printed in 1909, in two volumes based on Hungarian melodies, the publisher delivered copies to Bartók together with a letter regarding the future publication of another set based on Slovak melodies:

> I wish to emphasize that it would be better if the rules of classical harmony were even more strictly observed without any modernization than in the ones already published. I should not like to see a new trend in this undertaking but rather the beaten track on which you can continue from time to time.[39]

In addition to his own pedagogical piano works, Bartók prepared an annotated edition of Bach's Well-tempered Clavier published by Rozsnyai Károly in 1908. Beginning the next year, a substantial number of annotated editions of the standard piano repertory were published, such as sonatas (D. Scarlatti, Haydn, Mozart, and Beethoven), and other pieces (Couperin, Schubert, and Chopin). These editions were used in the Budapest Academy of Music and elsewhere in Hungary.

On 2 January 1909, Bartók had his first (and only) experience as a conductor, following Busoni's earlier request that he conduct the Scherzo movement of his Second Suite.

> Isn't it a wonderful experience to conduct an orchestra which responds exactly to what one wants! The effect on the audience was much the same as that of the waltz in Budapest. Two camps; hisses on one side, a storm of enthusiastic applause on the other, and I had 5 curtain calls. . . . The orchestra is splendid; everything sounded wonderful.[40]

During the first week in February, Bartók returned to northern Hungary for fieldwork in the same area he had previously visited. It is interesting to note that he sent a long letter from Darázs (Dražovce, Nitrianska), addressed to Márta and her sister Herma, which ends with five notated Slovak melodies, including one with its underlying text.[41] On 1 March—at long last!—the first complete performance in Hungary of Bartók's First Suite was given by the orchestra of the Budapest Academy of Music, conducted by Jenő Hubay. Thereafter, Bartók apparently organized the approximately 400 folk songs in his Slovak collection by village, in accordance with the procedure followed in the Slovak folk song series, *Slovenské Spevy,* and made plans to visit Transylvanian-Romanian peasant villages in Bihar County (now Bihor County, Romania) for an extended visit.[42]

Fieldwork in Romanian Villages of Transylvania

Bartók arrived in the village of Belényes (now Beiuș) on 19 July and was fortunate to enlist the help of Ion Bușiția (1875–1953), a music teacher at the local grammar school, as a traveling companion during the fieldwork. During the next three weeks he recorded vocal and instrumental pieces—especially bagpipe performances—and was "elated by the opportunity of coming in contact with pure, uncontaminated material," resulting from the scarcity of schools as well as transportation.

> For miles on end, in these parts, there are entire villages with illiterate inhabitants, communities which are not linked by any railways or roads; here most of the time the people can provide for their own daily wants, never leaving their native habitats except for such unavoidable travel as arises from service in the army or an occasional appearance in court. When one comes into such a region, one has the feeling of a return to the Middle Ages. Only then does one become convinced that in ancient times . . . music must undoubtedly have been a communal occupation.[43]

Eventually, after his Romanian collection had reached approximately 3,500 specimens, he concluded that: "Not withstanding the various foreign influences, the general picture is one of a material, differing, as a whole, from that of any other people. The difference is the result of the ensemble of various primary and secondary features which cannot be found elsewhere."[44] A primary feature is where the final tone of the melody is structurally the second degree of the scale (Ex. 4.18a, b). Secondary features include juxtaposed folk modes (Ex. 4.18a: F-Lydian, mm. 1–6, and G-Aeolian, mm. 7–9), and oriental (augmented second) scale fragments and G-Phrygian cadences (Ex. 4.18b: mm. 1–4 and 11–12, respectively). A primary feature of the texts is that their verses (that is, text lines) are not structured in stanzas, usually are in rhyming couplets, and frequently have refrain lines.[45]

Instrumental music is performed on the violin, peasant flute, bagpipe, and jew's-harp (mostly played by women and young girls). A primary feature of such music is the rhythm schemata which for the most part consist of various combinations of eighth- and sixteenth-notes in duple meter.[46]

Andante

a

Lento, rubato

b

Ex. 4.18. Bartók, *Chansons populaires* . . . , (a) melody no. 5, (b) melody no. 65.

After Bartók's return to Budapest in September, he composed the first of his Two Romanian Dances op. 8a, for Piano (Ex. 4.19b), inspired by a unique type of instrumental dance melodies he had encountered, whose indeterminate structure is based on motifs that are irregularly repeated throughout the piece and without any plan or coordination.[47] The source melody, a *Joc* (Dance) performed on a *Drâmbă* (jew's-harp), is made up of twin-bar motifs, such as the rhythm schema, 2/4 ♩♩♪♪ | ♪♪ ♪♪ ||, shown in Ex. 4.19a.[48]

(Vivace)

a

(Allegro vivace)

b

ppp

Ex. 4.19. (a) *RFM*.i, melody no. 648, mm. 31–34, and (b) Bartók, Two Romanian Dances op. 8a, no. 1 (1909), m. 3.

The revised version of Bartók's Rhapsody op. 1, for Piano and Orchestra, was given on 15 November by the Academy of Music orchestra, with the composer as soloist. The next day he married Márta Ziegler, and a week later the Budapest Philharmonic played the Second Suite. These works, together with the earlier performance of the First Suite, brought a storm of adverse reviews from the press, in which Bartók was belabored for "deliberate disharmony, use of bizarre modulations, and striving for originality at any cost."[49]

At the beginning of 1910, a Swiss pianist, Rudolph Ganz, was interested in performing pieces from the Fourteen Bagatelles and other Bartók works at a planned Budapest concert in 1911. He therefore wrote to the composer for help in obtaining copies of the music. Bartók responded that:

> Your kind lines (just received) have given me real pleasure, especially as I have
> had to endure an unbelievable number of attacks all provoked by these very piano
> pieces—here in Budapest as well as abroad. Besides these I have only 4 pieces,
> including a scherzo which Busoni in fact knows but hasn't yet played. Inciden-
> tally there is hardly anything new in those 4 pieces, and they should be looked on
> only as the promising work of a student, since I wrote them when I was 21.[50]

This acknowledgment of a shortfall in piano pieces suitable for public performance, together with invitations to appear as composer-pianist at the Festival Hongrois in Paris on 12 March and Budapest concerts of Bartók and Kodály
compositions in Budapest on the 17th and 19th, prompted Bartók's realization
that he had to address the deficiency forthwith.[51] The latter concert included ten
Bagatelles and the premiere of his First String Quartet played by the Waldbauer
Quartet, a group of exceptionally talented young musicians who became the
leading proponents and interpreters of Bartók's chamber works in Hungary and
abroad. Notwithstanding the excellent performances at each concert, the conservative audience and music critics reacted with intense dislike.

> Well known is the embarrassing scandal at the first Bartók-Kodály evening, which
> went so far as the throwing of rotten eggs by cliques from the upper class. It was
> at a time that the vulgar mock-poem appeared in a daily newspaper circulated
> throughout Hungary: "Kot-kot-kot-Kodály, little Zoltán, do not compose!" Simi-
> lar verses about Bartók were on everybody's lips, too.[52]

Bartók was no stranger to vehement abuse, nor did such reaction deter him
from his chosen path as composer. In fact, he considered himself to be "the
musician of Tomorrow," and, as he had earlier written to the Ziegler sisters,

> It is curious that in music until now only enthusiasm, love, grief, or at most, dis-
> tress figured as motivating causes—that is, the so-called exalted ideals. Whereas
> vengeance, the caricature, sarcasm are only living or are going to live their musi-
> cal lives in our time. For this reason, perhaps in contrast to the idealism mani-
> fested in the previous age, present-day musical art might be termed realistic, which
> without selection will sincerely and truly include every human emotion among
> those expressible.[53]

This Expressionist philosophy, born in the *Kossuth* symphonic poem and
sharpened in the "Stefi" Bagatelles (nos. 13 and 14), was tempered in his Two
Pictures for Orchestra, op. 10. The first Picture ("In Full Flower") reflects
Debussyian impressionism in terms of melodic construction, chords, and scalar
passagework based on nondiatonic, whole-tone scale degrees. The contrasting
second Picture ("Village Dance"), is a stylistic imitation of Transylvanian-Romanian instrumental dance music from Bihor County. A characteristic of the
Bihor musical dialect is the diatonic Lydian folk mode, a pitch collection whose

first four degrees also are whole tones (Ex. 4.20). Thus, the Western art-music structure of "In Full Flower" and the Eastern folk-music structure of "Village Dance"—seemingly disparate—are linked by the commonality of whole-tone pitch collections.

Allegro

Ex. 4.20. Bartók, Two Pictures for Orchestra, op. 10 (August 1910), no. 2, mm. 1–4.

Trailblazing a New Frontier in Ethnomusicology

Long after Bartók ended his fieldwork in the Romanian villages of Transylvania and was preparing the vast collection for publication, he stated that:

> I have to confess with regret that I did not heed all the requirements of folklore research in the first two years [1909–10]. At that time I attacked the problem purely as a musician, not minding extra-musical circumstances very much. The method of research changes according to the nature of the people whose folk music is in question; thus it took one or two years to familiarize myself with the new situation presented by Romanian folk music.[54]

As mentioned further above, Bartók had organized his transcribed Slovak folk songs according to village—the method followed in *Slovenské Spevy*—in order to achieve publication of the collection which, for the first time, points to the Lydian folk mode as a unique characteristic of certain specimens (see Ex. 4.8). On the other hand, however, a tetrachordal subset of the same mode is a unique characteristic of the musical dialect of Bihor County Romanian villages. Furthermore, he had already noted similarities as well as differences between the Hungarian-Slovak and Hungarian-Romanian melodies in his collection. Which musical characteristics are indigenous and which are borrowings from foreign sources? Bartók's deeply felt need to investigate these characteristics ultimately led to his outstanding contribution to comparative musical folklore: the determination of morphological elements by means of statistical treatment in the form of frequency of occurrence.

Between 1909 and 1910 Bartók struggled to find a way to sort the Bihor folk songs and, apparently at Kodály's suggestion, turned to the classification system devised by Ilmari Krohn (1867–1960) for Finnish folk songs, where the end tone as well as syllabic structure of each melody section constitute the major aspects of the sorting procedure.[55] He began to compile diacritic signs and special symbols to supplement the notation of text and melody, and he studied the volume of folk dance melodies published in 1908 by the Academia Română

(Romanian Academy) in Bucharest and the volume of sixty folk songs, including Christmas carols, printed in 1909 by a commercial publisher.[56] Perceiving these books as a window of opportunity for the publication of his own Romanian collection, on 29 April he wrote a letter of introduction to Dumitru G. Kiriac (1866–1928), a composer-member of the Academia Română, whose nationalist choral works Bartók had analyzed. He offered to send Kiriac some of the approximately 600 folk songs in the collection and asked if "it would be possible to collaborate with a Romanian philologist and have them printed."[57]

By way of background, in 1910 the "minority" Transylvanian Romanians—for the most part approximately a million illiterate peasants—comprised 55 percent of the region. While the makeup of the Transylvanian-Hungarian element (35 per cent) was the Székler people (about 550,000 peasants), the Romanians were governed under a policy of forced magyarization by a fraction of landowners and other members of the Hungarian educated classes.[58] It was the sociopolitical agenda of the Academia Română to underwrite scholarly publications which would promote understanding and appreciation of Romanian culture, particularly that in rural Transylvania. On 23 January 1911, following Kiriac's proposal to publish Bartók's Bihor collection, the Academia Română voted to add Bartók's transcriptions to their series of Romanian folklore studies and provide him with funds in connection with his recording activities.[59]

Transformation of Folk Music into Art Music

From 1906 to 1910 Bartók had not only collected a substantial amount of Hungarian, Slovak, and Romanian folk melodies but had arrived at a method for adapting them or their attributes as the means for creating compositions with different levels of inventiveness. The simplest level is "where the used folk melody is the more important part of the work. The added accompaniment and eventual preludes and postludes may only be considered as the mounting of a jewel." Obvious exemplars are the 1906 Hungarian Folk Songs (nos. 1–10 by Bartók), the Hungarian and Slovak pieces in *For Children,* nos. 3 (Slovak) and 6 (Hungarian) in Ten Easy Pieces, and no. 5 (Romanian) in Seven Sketches.

The second level is "where the importance of the used melodies and the added parts is almost equal," such as the Three Folk Songs from the Csík District (Hungarian), fourth Bagatelle (Hungarian, see Ex. 4.13), and the fifth Bagatelle (Slovak).

In the third level, "the added composition-treatment attains the importance of an original work, and the used folk melody (Ex. 4.21) is only to be regarded as a motto."

The penultimate level "is achieved by inventing and using themes which imitate certain features of [rural] music," for example, the first Romanian Dance (see Ex. 4.19), nos. 5 and 10 in Ten Easy Pieces, and "Village Dance" in Two Pictures (Romanian).

Ex. 4.21. Folk song melody (*RFM*.ii, no. 456b) used as a motto-theme in Two Romanian Dances op. 8a, no. 2.

The highest level is reached when "Even the most abstract works, as for instance my string quartets, where no such imitations appear, reveal a certain indescribable, unexplainable spirit—a certain *je ne sais pas quoi*—which will give to anyone who listens, and who knows the rural backgrounds, the feeling: 'This could not have been written by any but an Eastern European musician.'"[60] A case in point is the second Dirge, where the three rural backgrounds—Hungarian, Romanian, and Slovak—are represented by certain musical attributes whose remarkable integration reflects the fusion of national styles for creating an abstract composition (Ex. 4.22).

Ex. 4.22. (a) Bartók, Four Dirges op. 9a, for Piano (1909–1910), no. 2, mm. 48–55 and (b) 22–29; (c) Bartók, *Chansons populaires . . .*, melody no. 199, mm. 1–5 (cf. *RFM*.ii, melody no. 6281).

Ex. 4.22a shows the last repetition of the theme whose pitch collection is based on the old-Hungarian pentatonic scale (C♯-E-F♯-G♯-B) and dotted rhythm (♩♩ | ♩ ♩). The meter (3/4) and the syllabic structure (13 notes), however, are Slovak folk song characteristics. Ex. 4.22b shows the chromatic alteration of the theme to a hexachord of the octatonic scale (E-E♭-D♭-C-B♭-A), a nondiatonic pitch collection which occurs in Romanian mourning songs (cf. Ex. 4.22c: E♭♭-D♭-C♭-B♭-A♭-G-F). Moreover, whether subconsciously or by design, Bartók created the "Stefi" leitmotiv—F-A-C-E—in Ex. 4.22b, mm. 24–25.

Two happy events occurred during August: the birth of Bartók's first son, Béla, on the 22nd and the composition of Two Pictures for Orchestra op. 10.

After his return to teaching duties, Bartók made short visits to collect Romanian folk music in other Transylvanian counties and Hungarian folk music in the northern region of then Greater Hungary. During the latter fieldwork, county officials arranged for natural horn (*kanásztülök*) and bagpipe (*duda*) competitions as well as recording sessions for his collection of instrumental folk music.

> About ten horn-blowers and five bagpipers assembled, some doubling on both instruments. What a sight! They paraded before us in their hogherder's apparel: bright felt coat over the shoulders, the horn, the herder's whip. It is doubtful whether we will again meet five pipers playing together; indeed, it will be a long time before the market square of Ipolyság will resound to such piping.[61]

Earlier, in June, Bartók had written to the Turócszentmarárton Printing Company, printers of the *Slovenské Spevy* series, about the publication of his Slovak folk song collection. Their reply asked for the number of songs to be published and a statement of his terms. In his letter, dated 25 February 1911, he offered enough transcriptions of folk songs from Nyitra County to constitute a complete volume, arranged according to village. Instead of a royalty, he asked for copies of previously published issues and his own volume and included the transcriptions with the letter.[62] Meanwhile a letter from D.G. Kiriac arrived, dated 23 January, with the welcome news that the Romanian Academy had approved publication of the Bihor collection and would reimburse Bartók for the expenses incurred during his fieldwork. He set to work on preparation of fair copy of the text and music, which was completed in April 1912, and the book was published in Bucharest during November 1913.[63]

Duke Bluebeard's Castle, op. 11

From February to 20 September 1911, Bartók composed the score to his first stage work, a one-act opera set to a libretto by Béla Balázs. Balázs, a symbolist poet and disciple of Maurice Maeterlinck (1862–1949) had completed *Duke Bluebeard's Castle,* a "mystery-play," in the spring of 1910. The play, dedicated to Bartók and Kodály and published on 13 June, was motivated by Maeterlinck's tragedy, *Pelléas et Mélisande* (1892), the source of Debussy's opera (1902). Balázs created an opera libretto with eight-syllable text lines, in the style of ancient Székler folk ballads, intending it for Kodály, but the latter had no time to undertake the composition and recommended Bartók instead.[64]

The opera opens with a spoken prologue by The Minstrel, who asks the audience: "Where is the key to my riddle? Our eyelids' fringed curtain rises. . . . Is the stage within us or without? The castle, the tale, and the riddle are old. The play begins. Let us listen and wonder." As he recites the last two sentences, the orchestra plays a pentatonic theme that is similar to the first melody section of the second Dirge (Ex. 4.23; cf. Ex. 4.22a).

Andante

Ex. 4.23. Bartók, *Duke Bluebeard's Castle,* op. 11, mm. 1–16.

The opera consists of seven scenes, limited throughout to dialogue between Bluebeard and his latest wife, Judith. She has left her parents, her brother, and her betrothed as she follows her husband to his castle. When Judith enters the dark, cavernous hall, she notices seven black, locked doors. "Open them!" she demands, "Let the wind and the sunlight in!" But they represent the locked portals to Bluebeard's secrets, and when she asks for a key—"Give it to me, because I love you!" he tries to dissuade her from prying into his mysterious past. However, his love for her is such that he reluctantly grants her request. The following synopsis describes the action as Judith demands one key after another until she has opened all seven doors.

> *The Torture Chamber.* Deep moaning begins when Judith raps at the first door. She unlocks it and sees blood-encrusted scourges, fetters, racks, and thumbscrews.
>
> *The Armory.* Here she sees bloody lances, arrows, swords, and armor.
>
> *The Treasury.* The room is filled with golden ducats, pearls, rubies, fiery diamonds, and splendid raiments—all smeared with blood.
>
> *The Garden.* A magical garden with fragrant lilies, white roses, and red carnations, with blood seeping through beneath the flowers.
>
> *Bluebeard's Domain.* Meadows, forests, rivers, and mountains. Suddenly clouds red as blood gather. "Bluebeard, tell me where they come from?"
>
> *The Lake of Tears.* Judith sees a silent, motionless lake. "What water is this, Bluebeard?" "Tears, Judith, tears."
>
> *The Former Wives.* She demands the seventh key and opens the door. Three wives appear, adorned with crown, mantle, and jewels. Bluebeard explains that he found the first wife at morning, the second at midday, and the third at evening. The fourth—Judith, the most beautiful wife—he found at nightfall, and he places a diamond crown on her head, the mantle on her shoulders, and a pendant around her neck. She follows the other wives through the seventh door, and it closes after her. Bluebeard: "And there shall be darkness always . . . darkness . . . darkness."

Excepting Bluebeard's final recitative, the opera was completed on 20 September, in time for Bartók to enter the work in the Erkel Competition organized by the Budapest Lipótvárosi Kaszinó, but it was rebuffed as unperformable. Undaunted, during February 1912 he entered the opera in a competition sponsored by Rózsavölgyi, the Budapest music publisher. Here, too, he met with failure.

Bartók's piano piece, *Allegro barbaro*, composed sometime during 1911 and not given an opus number, is another work that "could not have been written by any but an Eastern European musician" (Ex. 4.24). On the one hand, the melody has a certain similarity to those heterometric Slovak folk songs which feature rhythm contraction (mm. 13–15). On the other hand, the major second and minor thirds of the melody are structural features of old-Hungarian pentatonic folk songs. Moreover, the blatting accentuation as well as the rhythm contraction resembles that of Hungarian natural-horn melodies.[65]

Ex. 4.24. Bartók, *Allegro Barbaro* for Piano (1911), R.H., mm. 5–18.

Bartók continued creating piano music with folklike themes in May, when he composed his programmatic second Burlesque titled "Slightly Tipsy" (Ex. 4.25b). it is based on a quaternary Hungarian 7-syllable folk song, designated "Bagpipes Polka" by the singer, which Bartók collected in 1910 (Ex. 4.25a).[66]

Ex. 4.25. (a) *HFS,* melody no. 180, and (b) no. 2 from Three Burlesques op. 8c, for Piano (1911), mm. 1–4. The first Burlesque was composed on 27 November 1908, the third Burlesque in 1910. The three pieces were published in 1912 by Rózsavölgyi, Budapest.

The New Hungarian Music Society

Bartók's letter to Frederick Delius (1862–1934), dated 27 March 1911, reports that:

> I've heard *Brigg Fair* was given a rather confused performance here. In this respect things here are quite impossible. Some of us at present are trying to get together a permanent first-class concert orchestra. With our present arrangement, we can never rely on having a worthy orchestral performance.
>
> If we do not succeed in our plans, I shall have to give up all hope for many years to come, of hearing my things performed (the compositions I plan writing), for I prefer no concert at all to a poor one from which it is impossible for either the audience or the composer to learn anything.[67]

In order to remedy this problematic circumstance, Bartók, together with Kodály and a number of other young musicians, founded the UMZE (Új Magyar Zenei Egyesület—New Hungarian Music Society).

> We could find neither a conductor who would understand our works nor an orchestra able to perform them. . . . The chief aim of the new organization would have been to form an orchestra able to perform old, new, and recent music in a proper way. But we strove in vain, we could not achieve our aim.[68]

In addition to orchestral performances, the UMZE planned to sponsor recitals and lectures, and to establish a magazine that would educate the public. This ambitious program required state funding, but the ministry of culture had no intention of underwriting the formation of an orchestra for the performance of avant-garde music. The UMZE thus was confined to fund raising by way of chamber music concerts, beginning with a recital by Bartók at Royal Hall on 27 November.[69] He played piano pieces by Couperin, Rameau, and Scarlatti, and accompanied a baritone soloist in folk song arrangements by himself and Kodály.

At the second concert, in the same venue on 11 December, he played works by Debussy and Ravel and accompanied a Viennese cabaret singer in songs by Mussorgsky, Reger, and Egon Wellesz (a composer and pupil of Arnold Schoenberg). During 1912, he did not play nor were his works performed in the third and fourth concerts. The fifth concert in the series was cancelled, and the UMZE disbanded because the Budapest concertgoing public was disinterested in attending performances of new music.[70]

Bartók's pessimistic letter to Géza Vilmos Zágon, dated 22 August 1913, provides the reasons why he was unable to join the latter in a new music venture.

> There is, however, an immense disadvantage in having me as a partner in the scheme, namely, that a year ago sentence of death was officially pronounced on me as a composer. Either those people are right, in which case I am an untalented

bungler; or I am right, and it's they who are the idiots. It therefore follows that since the official world of music has put me to death, you can no longer speak of my "prestige"– – –Therefore I have resigned myself to write for my writing-desk only. . . .

My public appearances are confined to *one sole field*: I will do anything to further my research in musical folklore! I have to be personally active in this field, for nothing can be achieved in any other way; while neither recognition nor public appearances are required for composing.[71]

Bartók commemorated his "sentence of death" in 1912 with the composition of the expressionist Four Pieces for Orchestra op. 12, whose lugubrious last movement is titled "Marcia funèbre" (Ex. 4.26).

Ex. 4.26. Bartók, Four Pieces for Orchestra op. 12, no. 4, mm. 1–5.

The other movements—"Preludio," "Scherzo," and "Intermezzo"—also reflect Bartók's gloomy mind-set and are replete with dissonance as well as marked by the absence of folk music influences. After he completed the sketch, he put it aside until the summer of 1921, when he prepared the full score for his new publisher, Universal Edition, Vienna.

Bartók's 1912 fieldwork included several Hungarian villages and many more Romanian localities in six Transylvanian counties. In January, in the northernmost Transylvanian county of Máramaros (now Maramureş), he discovered the unique "long-drawn" song (*hora lungă* or *cântec lung*), an improvisatory, non-ceremonial solo song, based on a single melody which is of an instrumental character.[72]

It may have been during the fall that Bartók was commissioned by Rózsavölgyi to create a method for teaching the piano "from the very beginning to the highest (virtuoso) degree." As he had no experience in teaching beginners, he asked a Budapest piano teacher, Sándor Reschofsky, to collaborate in the project. The resultant *Zongora Iskola* (Piano School) was published in May 1913.[73]

The Advent of the First World War

The attempt of the Balkan Slavs to distribute Turkey's European territories among themselves led to the outbreak of the First Balkan War on 18 October 1912. The Bulgarians advanced to the last line of defense before Constantinople, while the Serbs reached the Adriatic on 10 November, after overrunning northern Albania. Austria was unalterably opposed to such territorial access to the Adriatic and demanded Albanian independence. The ensuing international crisis was precipitated when Austria began to mobilize, as did Russia, following its warning to Bulgaria not to attempt the occupation of Constantinople. During May 1913 the Austrian threat of war against Serbia forced the latter to evacuate its positions, and on the 30th the Treaty of London ended the war.

Following a treaty of alliance between Serbia and Greece against Bulgaria on 1 June, the Second Balkan War broke out at the end of the month. Romania and Turkey entered the war against Bulgaria, which was rapidly defeated, and on 10 August the Treaty of Bucharest ended the hostilities. But the resultant Serbian expansion and the rising Romanian demand for union with Transylvania brought new concerns for Hungary in terms of maintaining its territorial possessions intact.

> While the vast majority of non-Hungarians remained steadfast and loyal to the dynasty and were also prepared to take up arms in defense of Hungary and the Monarchy, they were no longer prepared to accept national, political, economic, social, and cultural discrimination. In view of the spread of ambitious radical nationalism to Hungary's neighbors and Russia-backed neo-Slavism, the unsolved nationalities problem contained more explosive power for Hungary and the Monarchy than all the other political and social contradictions that beset the Habsburg patrimony.[74]

On 28 June 1914, Archduke Francis Ferdinand—the heir apparent to the throne of Austria—and his consort, Countess Sophie Chotek, were assassinated in the Bosnian capital of Sarajevo by a Serbian student. A month later Austria declared war on Serbia, followed by Russian mobilization against Austria. Then, during the first two weeks of August, declarations of war were made by Germany on Russia, France, and Belgium, and Britain on Germany and Austria. Among the outcomes of the First World War were the collapse of the Austro-Hungarian Monarchy and, at the 1920 Treaty of Trianon, the sundering of Greater Hungary.

Bartók continued his Slovak fieldwork for several days during the first week in January 1913. Thereafter, until mid-March, he concentrated on transcribing the Romanian material recorded during the preceding year and correcting proofs of his forthcoming Bihor publication. Then, from the 15th to the 27th of March, he returned to Máramaros County and collected more than 200 vocal and instrumental melodies, including additional variants of the *cântec lung* ("long-drawn" song). It may have been at this time that he decided to organize the recently collected material according to county perimeters—Temes-Torontál (Timiș-Torontal), Máramaros, and Hunyad (Hunedoara)—for publication by the Academia Română.[75] Another decision was to investigate the presumed Arabic sources of the *cântec lung*, and in April he wrote to Géza Vilmos Zágon in Paris for help in obtaining a French permit for travel in Algeria.

> This summer—in June and July, to be more exact—I want to go to Algeria; to be more precise, it is the region of the Biskra to which I want to go first, then to the "Grande Kabylie," to collect Arab and Berber music (with a phonograph, of course). I have applied to our Ministry of Culture, asking them to obtain for me an official letter of introduction from the French Ministry of the Interior to the Algerian authorities. But the Ministry of Culture informs me that the French will give no such thing to us (for political reasons!).[76]

Bartók's selection of the Biskra region was based on tour book information that the summer temperature there was cooler than elsewhere. Zágon succeeded in providing Bartók and his wife with the necessary letter of introduction, but after the travelers arrived at their Biskra destination in June they found great difficulties in collecting instrumental music: the first musicians they met played "coffeehouse music," and the only singers permitted to perform before foreign men were the Oueled-Nails (prostitutes). Nevertheless, a small number of pieces were recorded here as well as in other villages, before Bartók became ill and had to return to Budapest toward the end of the month.[77]

Prior to his departure for North Africa, the editor of *Slovenské Spevy* returned Bartók's manuscript of 134 Slovak folk songs that he had submitted in 1911, without an explanation for its rejection. Bartók was not only unaware that the publication had been discontinued in 1907, but that his precise notation of performance peculiarities and transcription of the texts in dialectal rather than literary form were rejected as representing peasant vulgarities which followed no rules.[78] Undaunted, from 21 to 25 November Bartók collected more folk songs in Slovak villages in Hont County, with the intention of making a complete survey of the folk music in that area, including the compilation of a monograph. Then, on 18 December, Bartók announced to a Romanian colleague that:

> The task of making a Complete Edition of Hungarian Folk Songs (containing approximately 5,000 songs) has been given to me and my colleague Zoltán Kodály (a first-rate musician), and in classifying them we have used Ilmari Krohn's system, with some slight modifications of our own. In order to be able to compare them with the songs of our neighbors, I have classified about 3,000 Slovakian songs by the same method.[79]

In order to fund this ambitious undertaking, Bartók and Kodály prepared a letter to the Kisfaludy Literary Society, titled "Draft of the New Universal Collection of Folk Songs," for support.[80]

It is indeed curious, if not enigmatic, that Bartók prepared a fair copy of a piano piece composed during his Academy years, titled the work *Danse orientale,* and sent it to the *Pressburger Zeitung,* where it was published as a facsimile on 25 December 1913 (Example 4.27).[81]

Ex. 4.27. Bartók, *Danse orientale* (first half of 1900?), mm. 1–4. The manuscript shows Bartók's signature under his remark, A "Pressburger Zeitung"-nak küldi (sent to the *Pressburger Zeitung*).

From 1914 to July 1917 Bartók maximized his fieldwork in Transylvania, notwithstanding the declaration of war by Romania against Austria-Hungary on 27 August 1916. His last visit added 128 melodies, bringing the total number of vocal and instrumental pieces in his Romanian collection to 3,404.[82] The collecting in the Slovak villages of northern Hungary ended in August 1918, bringing that total—for the most part vocal pieces—to 3,223 melodies.[83] Regarding the Hungarian fund, Bartók recorded specimens in Békés County from 1917 to 1918.

In the spring of 1914, a chauvinist Romanian reviewer of the dilettante kind attacked the recently published Bihor collection as—among other untenable conclusions—containing folk songs which "are not very melodious and would attest to the shortcomings of our national music . . . because Hungarian influence had dominated Romanian music in the region of Bihor." Bartók responded with a scholarly essay, "Observations on Romanian Folk Music," which was published in the July–August issue of *Convorbiri Literare* (Bucharest).[84] A second essay on Romanian folk music was the outcome of a lecture recital given by Bartók at the Academy of Sciences on March 18. The well-attended event, including the Budapest press, featured vocal and instrumental performances by Transylvanian-Romanian peasants from the village of Cserbel (now Cerbăl) in Hunedoara County.[85]

In the fall, Bartók was notified that his age-group would be called up for military service. Fortunately, he was rejected as "unfit for service (lack of stamina); they're quite right, too, with only 45 kg. to help me along I would find it a bit of an effort to do big march or quick advances (or retreats?), and with a great load on my back, too. I have even found time—and the ability—to do some composing: it seems that the Muses are not silent in modern war."[86]

During the preceding year, Bartók completed the transcription and study of his Maramureş collection and, in December, offered the work to the Academia Română as his next volume on Transylvanian-Romanian folk music.

Agreement to publish the Maramureş collection was promptly reached. If publication had not been interrupted by the "little event" of World War I, it would have been a smooth operation, and a second volume of Bartók's folk music ethnographies would have appeared without drawing on his personal resources. This work, however, did not come into print for almost a decade. World War I broke out before production was under way, and the Romanian Academy, sensing the dangers of political uncertainty, withdrew its offer. It promised instead that the publication project would be resumed after the war, in which Romania was not yet a participant.[87]

The mentioned agreement included engraving of the music examples by one of the leading firms in Europe, Röder of Leipzig, Germany. When the Academy failed to pay for the work already under way, Bartók felt obliged to complete the engraving and paid Röder's fee out of his own pocket. On 19 February 1915, he notified the Academy that the music examples would be ready in a few months.

> The rest of the work can be postponed till the end of the war. If, after the war, the Academy would renew its determination as to the publication of this collection, I would then place the corrected engravings at its disposal. If, on the other hand, you do not wish to have any further relations with me—(and this would be most regrettable, in fact, after your letter of September 1914 I consider this to be an impossibility)—then I will be the one who will carry the burden of the material responsibility.[88]

No response was forthcoming, and on 20 May Bartók wrote that "Communications have been too disrupted for me to venture into Rumanian regions; but I have been collecting among the Slovaks. . . . The amazing thing about it was that one could go on collecting exactly as in times of peace."[89] In place of fieldwork in Transylvania, he transcribed instrumental and vocal pieces from his Romanian collection for piano solo: Sonatina, Romanian Folk Dances, and Romanian Christmas Songs—all without opus numbers. The Sonatina is based on five Romanian peasant dances which are arranged in three movements {"Bagpipers," "Bear Dance," and "Finale"). There are six pieces in the Romanian Folk Dances, beginning with a "Joc cu Bătă" (Dance with Sticks; Ex. 4.28b) that captures the spirit of the original peasant performance, where the violin solo is accompanied by a second violin whose chords are easily bowed on its three strings by means of a flat bridge (Ex. 4.28a).[90]

The Romanian Christmas Songs publication consists of twenty melodies, divided into two series, from Bartók's collection of 454 Romanian carols (colinde) and Christmas songs (Cântec de stea), including a prefatory index of notated folk songs. There is also an appendix of revised melodies—four from the first series and seven from the second—for concert purposes. Thus Bartók's original, pedagogical purpose seems evident: to add a third volume of Romanian melodies to the previous publications of Hungarian and Slovak piano pieces for children. The unique rhythmic characteristics of these Romanian Christmas songs are additive rhythm (5/8, 4+3/8, 2+3+3/8) and change of time (2/4-3/4, 2/4-3/8, 6/8-7/8, etc.). In fact, when Bartók prepared the fair copy of the mentioned collection for publication in 1933, a number of melodies are notated in what he

Ex. 4.28. (a) *RFM*.i, melody no. 425, mm. 1–5, and (b) Bartók, Romanian Folk Dances (1915), no. 1, mm. 1–5.

designates as "Bulgarian" rhythm, where the quarter note is shortened to three sixteenths "whose rate of speed is about M.M. =300–420+." As a case in point, $10/16 = 3+2+2+3/16$.[90]

Intermittently between 1914 and 1918, Bartók also worked on Fifteen Hungarian Peasant Songs, a set of piano pieces for which he also provided an index of notated folk songs; from 1914–1916 on *The Wooden Prince* ballet; and from 1915–1917 on String Quartet no. 2. Although 1915 was a fruitful year, with regard to fieldwork, folk music studies, and especially the return to composition, Bartók was greatly disturbed by the unauthorized truncation of his First Suite at the Budapest Philharmonic Society concerts in Vienna, Budapest, and Dresden during November. In his letter to the board of directors, dated 10 December, he states that:

> It is generally accepted as improper and impermissible to omit movements from sonatas or symphonic compositions when these are played at a serious concert. This sort of thing can only be countenanced at "zoo" concerts or "young people's concerts" with anthology-type programs. My own composition, to which I now refer, is not only symphonic: there is such a close thematic connection between the movements that certain bars of some of the movements cannot be understood unless one has already heard the preceding movements.
>
> In these circumstances, I have to inform you that I should be greatly obliged if you would never play any of my pieces again. I feel all the more entitled to make this request since the deplorable state of Budapest's musical life has forced me to forgo all public appearances as a composer during the last 4 years and to withhold all my works written since then from public appearance.[91]

During the last week in December, Bartók returned to Zólyom County (now Zvolenská, Slovakia), the same region in northern Hungary he had visited in

April, July–August, and November, for fieldwork in Slovak villages. That summer his occasional host was József Gombossy, the regional chief of forestry,
whose precocious daughter Klára (b. 1901) was an epigone poetess of above-
average ability. She accompanied Bartók on his collecting tours, writing down
the dialectal peasant texts during the recording sessions. Klára and her older
friend, Wanda Gleiman (b. 1897), were piano pupils of the latter's widowed
mother, and both girls had an abiding interest in erotic poetry, particularly that
of Jutka Miklós (1886–1976)—at that time a fairly well known poetess who
was published in several Budapest magazines. According to recent investigations of Bartók's relationship with Klára, and soon thereafter with Wanda, he
was inspired to compose five songs for voice and piano in 1916. Text nos. 1–2
and 4–5 are plagiarisms created by Klára and sent to the naive composer as
original poetry, which he set to music in February. Wanda's similarly borrowed
poem became text no. 3 and was set by Bartók on 27 August (Ex. 4.29).[92]

Andante sostenuto

Kiss-es! My lips now   cry for kiss-es!   This is the   night of wild de - sire!

Ex. 4.29. Bartók, Five Songs op. 15, for Voice and Piano (1916), no. 3 ("Night of Desire"), mm. 2–6.

Although the fair copy of the five songs had been prepared in 1918, Bartók
later submitted only the first three songs to Universal Edition for publication.
According to his correspondence with the publisher that year, for "various reasons" he withdrew nos. 4 and 5. Apparently it was at this time that Wanda informed him of the spuriousness of Klara's texts. Then, in his letter dated 14
January 1923, Bartók informed the Universal Edition that he had no objection
to printing the three songs if the publisher considered their appearance to be
particularly important. But he emphasized that the author of the texts, who wished
to remain anonymous, was unknown to the public, and that he neither had nor
could obtain permission to publish them. In view of possible future copyright
problems, Universal Edition decided to shelve the work.[93]

From February to April, Bartók composed a second group of songs—Five
Songs op. 16, for Voice and Piano—to texts of Endre Ady (1877–1919), the
renowned founder of modern Hungarian poetry. Here, too, the erotic motif pre-
vails, ending with the plaintive fifth song, "I cannot come to you" (Ex. 4.30).
With regard to musical content, opp. 15 and 16 represent a new approach in
Bartók's treatment of accompanied vocal material. The piano no longer func-
tions in a supportive role but engages the voice in a dialogue between equal
protagonists. An extension of this concept can be seen in the first and second
sonatas for violin and piano that he composed in 1921 and 1922, respectively.

Ex. 4.30. Bartók, Five Songs op. 16, for Voice and Piano (1916), no. 5, mm. 51–56.

Another innovation occurs in the Suite op. 14, for Piano. This work, also created in February, reflect's Bartók's treatment of the piano essentially as a percussion instrument, rather than its previous, romantic notion purely as a stringed instrument. In a New York radio broadcast on 2 July 1944, Bartók was asked if he considered the Suite to be representative of his abstract piano compositions and, if so, what qualities make it abstract. Bartók's response:

> If by abstract music you mean absolute music without program, then yes. The Suite op. 14 has no folk tunes. It is based entirely on original themes of my own invention. When this work was composed, I had in mind the refining of piano technique, the changing of piano technique into a more transparent style—a style more of bone and muscle opposed to the heavy chordal style of the late romantic period, that is, unessential ornaments like broken chords and other figures are omitted, and it is more simple style.[94]

But the work reflects the atmosphere of folk music in the first movement, with its Romanian *Ardeleana* rhythm schema: ♩ ♫♫♪ | ♫♪ ♫♪ | ♩ ♫♫♪ | ♩ ♩ ‖, and in the third movement, where the melody is "tinctured with oriental (for instance, Arabic) influences."[95]

Moreover, in a January 1945 summary, Bartók states that he deliberately used only the most restricted technical means that he consistently followed, beginning in 1908, "in almost all of my successive piano works, with more or less modifications, as for instance in the Suite op 14 (accentuating in some of its movements the percussive character of the piano)."[96] Perhaps the mentioned change in piano technique prompted Bartók to discard the Suite's original second movement of the five he had composed (Ex. 4.31a).[97] In any event, there are apparent stylistic similarities between that movement and the piano accompaniment of op. 16, no. 1 (Ex. 4.31b).

Bartók composed another piano piece in 1916, based on two Slovak folk songs he collected in Zvolenská County on 25 April and a third one on the 30th (Ex. 4.32). He gave its first performance on 9 March 1927, during a Budapest Radio broadcast, which he referred to as "Három szlovák népdal" (Three Slovak folk songs). That same year he composed two more piano pieces, similarly based on Slovak folk songs, and, during their Budapest Radio performance on 28 October, he referred to them as "Két kis rapszódia népdalokra" (Two little folk-song rhapsodies). Apparently it was not until 1930, the year of publication, that Bartók referred to the pieces as rondos.[98]

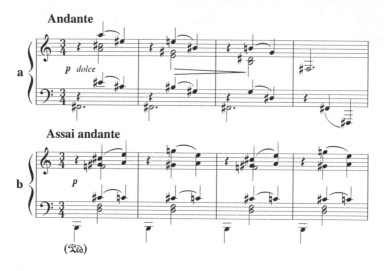

Ex. 4.31. (a) Bartók, Suite op. 14, for Piano (1916), discarded second movement, mm. 1–4, and (b) Bartók, Five Songs op. 16, for Voice and Piano (1916), no. 1, mm. 1–4.

Ex. 4.32. *SV*.ii source melodies used in Bartók's Three Rondos on Folk Tunes for Piano (1930), no. 1.

The Wooden Prince, op. 13

It was in May 1916 that Bartók resumed work on the score to *The Wooden Prince*, which he had begun two years before, following successful negotiations with the Budapest Opera House to compose the music for an hour-long ballet to the libretto by Béla Balázs. In fact, on 1 June he received a grant of 400 krönen as an incentive to complete the work.[99] The Bálazs libretto had been published in the Christmas issue of *Nyugat* in 1913, but it was only after the premiere of the work in 1917 that he wrote about the symbolism underlying his creation.

> The wooden puppet symbolizes the creative work of the artist, who puts all of himself into his work until he has made something complete, shining, and perfect. The artist himself, however, is left robbed and poor. I was thinking of that very common and profound tragedy when the creation becomes the rival of the creator, and of the pain and glory of the situation in which a woman prefers the poem to the poet, the picture to the painter.[100]

And, too, perhaps the preference of the composition to the composer! Bartók's empathy with the symbolic content apparently provided him with the inspiration to begin working on the ballet soon after the Bálazs libretto appeared in print. The music, beginning with a prelude, consists of seven dances which are linked together by interludes. There are six characters: the prince, the princess, the fairy, the wooden prince, the forest, and the streamlet. The following narrative follows the sequence of events as described in the piano score.[101]

PRELUDE. When the curtain rises, the stage shows a grotesque and primitive picture. On the left are a tiny castle on a hill, a streamlet encircling the hill, and a path leading from the castle to a tree bridge and from there into a forest. A second path runs across the stage to another hill on the right. On it stands a second, tiny castle. The fairy stands on the left, at the foot of the hill, and the princess is seated in the woods.

FIRST DANCE. *Dance of the princess in the forest.* The door of the second castle opens and the prince emerges. The fairy drives the princess back into her castle, but not before the prince sees her.

INTERLUDE. The princess is seen in her room, seated at her spinning-wheel. The prince falls in love, decides to go to her, and runs toward the forest. The fairy then enchants the forest.

SECOND DANCE. *Dance of the trees.* The forest springs to life, and the prince is terrified at the sight.

INTERLUDE. The prince walks towards the forest, a fight ensues, he succeeds in passing through, and he continues on towards the tree bridge. The fairy then enchants the streamlet.

THIRD DANCE. *Dance of the waves.* The prince repeatedly tries to cross the bridge but the waves lift it out of reach.

INTERLUDE. Baffled, the prince walks back through the forest. An idea comes to mind: he places his cloak on his staff and lifts it high, in order to draw the attention of the princess towards him. Although she notices the staff and cloak, she is not distracted and continues at her work. A second idea occurs to the prince: he fastens his crown to the staff and lifts it high. The princess looks but fails to react to the sight. A new plan occurs to the prince: with a pair of scissors he shears his golden locks, fastens them to the staff, and lifts the ensemble high. When the princess sees the staff with the golden locks, she has an overwhelming desire to take possession of it, and comes tripping down from her castle to the pretty toy. The prince steps from behind the staff and stretches his arms wide to embrace her. While the princess evades his advances, the fairy enchants the bedecked staff, and it begins to move in the guise of a wooden prince. The prince tries to prevent the princess from reaching the puppet, but she finally manages to do so.

FOURTH DANCE. *Dance of the princess with the wooden prince.* The princess and the puppet dance until they exit the stage, leaving the prince behind in greatest despair.

INTERLUDE. The prince lies down and falls asleep. The fairy steps out of the forest, goes to the prince and gently comforts him. At her command all objects around her are enlivened and, rendering homage to the prince, dance before him. She takes curly golden hair from the calyx of a large flower and puts it on the prince's head. Then she adorns him with a crown taken from another flower. From a third flower she takes a cloak of flowers which she drapes on his shoulders. Taking his hand, she leads him to the hill: "Here you will be King over everything!" Suddenly, the princess appears with the puppet, its wig, cloak and crown are in a disorderly state.

FIFTH DANCE. The princess, trying to make the puppet dance, pulls and pushes him about. His dancing becomes poorer and poorer. Finally, she begins to despise him, angrily pushes him away, and he falls to the ground. And now she catches sight of the prince in his radiant splendor.

SIXTH DANCE. With her most fascinating smiles the princess tries to persuade the prince to dance with her.

INTERLUDE. Touching his heart, the prince makes a disavowing gesture and turns away from the princess.

SEVENTH DANCE. The princess tries to entice the prince, but the forest comes to life and prevents her from approaching him. Her attempts to force the obstacles aside are fruitless.

POSTLUDE. Finally, she discards her crown and cloak, shears her hair, and buries her face in her hands. At the sight of the princess in such pain, the prince tries to consoles her. She is ashamed of her bareness, but he persists and takes her in his arms. A long kiss. The enchanted objects around them resume their original shape and places. The curtain slowly falls.

Bartók's letter to his mother, dated 21 March 1917, describes his good fortune in working with Egisto Tango (1876–1951) an outstanding, conscientious Italian conductor. The latter devoted several weeks studying the score, then informed the Opera House director that thirty rehearsals would be needed.

Just think of it—30 rehearsals! So far Tango has proved magnificent. His refusing to conduct the work, unless he's given the opportunity to study it in detail first, is the finest thing a conductor can do. You can imagine anyone else, less gifted and with less preparation, would have done it on 5 or 6 rehearsals—and how! God protect us from that! Tango has also said that he is very pleased to have the opportunity to conduct a Hungarian work for once, but went on to say that he would not have conducted anyone else's work, only mine. . . . Therefore: praised be Tango, for ever and ever, *Amen.*[102]

On the other hand, the score presented an insuperable problem for the Swedish choreographer, who was unable to cope with Bartók's music. Balázs's bitter recollection of the premiere states that:

> May 12 [1917] was the first night of the ballet. It was a success the like of which was never recalled at the Opera. They called me back at least thirty times. They raved for more than half an hour. The next day the papers gave Bartók full recognition, but for me mostly abuse. . . .
>   In the days before the opening night, it was rumored that the libretto would be successful, but not the music. This distressed me very much, and it would have been bitterly humiliating. That it happened the other way around might have pleased me if they had at least acknowledged one thing, or had been aware of it: the fearful work I did for Bartók, and that I did it for him alone. That I broke the symphonic music down for the stage, since it is devoid of all stage timing and spacing (I, who am not a musician, and not a director!), that I drilled music which musicians do not understand into houseporters' daughters, that I got across that every moment corresponded to a phase of the music (with ballerinas who were not even accustomed to doing this to the music of Delibes).[103]

Acclamation of the ballet by the audience and the Budapest press brought a change in the public's perception of Bartók's stature as composer, to the extent that on 7 June the Opera House proposed a double bill—*Duke Bluebeard's Castle* and *The Wooden Prince*—for their 1918 repertoire, with Egisto Tango as the conductor. On the 17th Bartók notified the Opera that he would review the score and submit it on 15 July. It is interesting that he set out to collect folk music—with Tango as his traveling companion!—in three Transylvanian counties, during the last three weeks in July.[104] From time to time in the ensuing months, until the premiere of *Duke Bluebeard's Castle* in May 1918, he revised the work throughout, for the most part making relatively superficial changes. Substantial revisions were made in the First Door and Third Door scenes, and, more important, he finally achieved success in his long-postponed attempt "to find a more satisfactory way to bring the work to a close, musically and dramatically."[105]

In his autobiography, Bartók speaks of the "promising beginnings" of 1917, which were followed by "the complete political and economic breakdown of 1918. The sad and troubled times that followed for about a year and a half were not conducive to serious work."[106] After Emperor Francis Joseph died on 21 November 1916, he was succeeded by Charles I (King Charles IV of Hungary). In 1917, during March, revolution broke out in Petrograd, followed by Hungarian workers' demonstrations in May, and thereafter by the Bolshevik October

Revolution. In January 1918, the Vienna munitions workers' strike spilled over
into Hungary, and the mutiny of Hungarian army units in May was followed by
a general strike in June. The Republic of Austria was proclaimed on 12 November, the Republic of Hungary proclamation on the 16th. Although the national
minorities had previously supported the Dual Monarchy, beginning in November their councils took over the civil administration of Transylvania, northern
Hungary, and the territories along the southern tier of the country.[107] New borders were drawn in the territories surrounding dismembered Hungary, which
effectively prevented Bartók from traveling in those areas.

The difficult political and economic times as well as the termination of
Bartók's Romanian and Slovak fieldwork were somewhat tempered by the public acceptance of his compositions in Hungary, the creation of new works, and a
contract with the Vienna publisher, Universal Edition. In 1917, Bartók completed two folk song arrangements: Eight Hungarian Folk Songs, for Voice and
Piano (begun in 1907) and Fifteen Hungarian Peasant Songs, for Piano (begun
in 1914). He composed the Second String Quartet op. 17, from 1915 to October
1917, and, from 1917 to 1918, arranged a group of four Slovak folk songs for
unaccompanied male voices and another group for mixed voices with piano
accompaniment. During 1918, he composed Three Studies op. 18, for Piano,
and began work on his third stage work, *The Miraculous Mandarin* op. 19.

In his third lecture at Harvard University during February 1943, Bartók discussed the peculiar Arab chromatic style that he heard during his fieldwork in
North Africa. He remarked that "As I have known such Arab melodies since
1913, it is quite imaginable that they may have influence my works (following
that year) with their chromaticism. . . . My first "chromatic" melody I invented
in 1923; I used it as the first theme of my Dance Suite. This music has some
resemblance to the Arab melody you just heard."[108] In the Second String Quartet, however, the first theme in the second movement (Ex. 4.33a) resembles the
narrow-range, chromatic style of Arab folk melodies as well as their ornamental
tones and repetition of short motives (Ex. 4.33b).

Ex. 4.33. (a) Bartók, String Quartet no. 2, op. 17 (1917), second movement, mm. 19–24,
and (b) Bartók, "Arab Folk Music from the Biskra District," melody no. 38, mm. 1–4.[109]

Beginning in March or April, Bartók worked on the Three Studies op. 18.
This thorny work marks a new change in direction with regard to piano technique and musical language, along the lines of the innovative Bagatelles, such

as nos. 8–11.[110] According to Bartók's letter to Universal Edition, dated 11 April 1918, he was working on "concert etudes of greater extent and very difficult." On the 18th he indicated "6 or 7 etudes assembled under one opus number." Then, on 11 July 1919, he wrote that three etudes were ready, but he did not mail them until April 1920, the year of their publication.[111] As the music clearly shows, Bartók extended his musical language almost to the threshold of so-called atonality, by means of what he would eventually describe as "a new chromaticism."[112] This phenomenon, together with the virtuosic pianism involved, is perhaps as difficult for the listener as for the performer. On 21 April 1919, during the Budapest Academy of Music concert devoted to his music, Bartók not only gave the Studies its premiere but repeated it immediately thereafter as the closing work.[113]

In response to an invitation to play certain works at proposed concerts in Zagreb and Bremen in 1926, Bartók responded that:

> What we must be careful to avoid is any attempt to put on such works as my two Sonatas for violin or the piano Etudes and Improvisations in places where the level of appreciation is as low as it is in Hungarian country towns. Such works would merely arouse antagonism in an audience which has not been trained to listen.[114]

During similar negotiations in January 1934, his letter of the 20th states that: "I am a bit surprised by what you write regarding the program: we agreed at the time, that it was to be a *Hungarian-Slovak* evening." His counterproposal was six groups of pieces drawn from his vocal, choral, and piano arrangements.

> By the way: I cannot play the 3 Etudes (!). I haven't played them—ever or anywhere since 1918 [*sic*]; and the piano Sonata would give the audience a fright, so there would be no sense in putting it on the program. But to you (and anyone else who might be interested) I would gladly play it in private (before or after the concert).[115]

The Miraculous Mandarin, op. 19

In mid-August, Bartók enjoyed a fortnight holiday "in lordly splendor" at a baronial estate, where he "spent most of the time in the laundry, of course; I collected lots of songs from the washerwomen. . . . As soon as I got home, I set to work . . . to set Menyhért Lengyel's libretto to music."[116] The author (1880–1974), an acclaimed Hungarian playwright, had published his dramatic work, *The Miraculous Mandarin. Pantomime grotesque,* in the January 1917 issue of *Nyugat.* He signed a letter of agreement with Bartók on 21 June 1918, in which the composer was given the exclusive right to set the pantomime to music.[117] In a letter to his wife, dated 5 September, Bartók outlines his plan for the opening of the work: "It will be hellish music if I succeed. The prelude before the curtain goes up is going to be very short and will sound like the horrible pandemonium, din, racket, and hooting: I lead the honorable audience from the crowded streets of a metropolis into the Apaches' den."[118] The following narrative is an abridged version of the original libretto.

INTRODUCTION. A squalid upper-story room, used as a cache for goods stolen by three thugs. Outside, representing the life and hubbub of a huge city, are vibrating lights and a mixture of confusing cries and noises.

MIMI AND THE THREE THUGS. They have no money. The First Thug pushes Mimi to the window, tells her to show herself and get someone to come up to the room. The thugs hide behind the furniture and wait.

THE OLD GALLANT. He is a quaint, dapper old man, wearing a shabby top-hat; coat shiny with wear and ironing; withered flower in buttonhole; and a cheap, gaudy tie. He enters the room, smiling with the assurance of a gallant, puts his hat on the table, and tries to put his arms around Mimi. She steps back and asks: "What about the money?" He ignores the question and pinches her arm and cheek while she attempts to evade his amorous moves. The thugs spring forward, toss him from hand to hand, and finally throw him and his hat down the stairs. The First Thug pushes her to the window, and again the three men hide themselves. Mimi sways her hips, leans from the window, and smiles as she waves her hand.

THE YOUNG STUDENT. He rushes up the stairs and through the door, wearing short pants and big shoes. He has rosy cheeks and blond hair, and stands helplessly— not knowing what to do with himself. Mimi beckons him to step nearer, puts her arms around him and quickly explores his pockets. She only finds a handkerchief: "Have you got no money at all?" When he shakes his head sadly, she takes pity on him, puts his hands around her waist, and they start waltzing slowly. Their movements become more inhibited, they stop and look at each other, laugh and then kiss. The thugs jump out from their hiding-places, pull the couple apart, and throw the boy out the door. The First Thug draws his knife and threatens Mimi: "Get back to the window!"

THE MANDARIN. He is Chinese, with a broad yellow face, wearing a silk skullcap from under which a long, black pigtail falls on his back. He is richly dressed in a silken coat, velvet trousers, and fine boots. Around his neck is a gold chain, and he has many diamonds on his fingers. He stares at Mimi with unblinking, serious eyes. She is afraid of him and edges backwards, but the thugs keep pushing her forwards. She motions to the Mandarin to sit down and begins to dance provocatively, locking the door and then dancing faster and faster. Seeing his oddly stiff and unmoving posture, and dizzy from her dancing, she laughs and drops heavily on his lap.

The Mandarin is transformed by her actions, his chest heaves, he twitches and shudders in mounting excitement. The frightened girl stops laughing, jumps to her feet, and backs away. The Mandarin rises, moves towards her then pursues her as she flits between table and chairs. He becomes nimble and alarmingly grotesque as he whirls about, until he finally catches the girl and sinks with her to the floor. Suddenly the thugs attack the Mandarin, holding him down as they free Mimi and search his pockets. While the gold coins roll out on the floor, they remove the gold chain from his neck and the diamond rings from his fingers. The thugs decide to suffocate the Mandarin, and smother him with pillows and blankets. They signal to each other that he is dead. But the Mandarin's head emerges from the bedding, his eyes fixed on the girl. The Third Thug produces a long knife, motions to the others to hold onto the Mandarin, and stabs him in the belly. The Mandarin staggers, recovers, and leaps at the girl, but the thugs seize him. One of them pulls out a pistol and shoots the Mandarin in the head. When the smoke clears, he has a hole in his forehead, totters, but again recovers and resumes his chase of the girl with grotesque movements.

The Mandarin is seized for the third time. "He doesn't die! How can we kill him?" One of the thugs points to the chandelier. They lift up the Mandarin on a chair, wrap the pigtail around his neck, and tie its end to the chandelier. Then the chair is kicked out from under his feet. He is hanged. The light goes out. Darkness. Silence.

Suddenly a strange light appears in midair: the Mandarin's rotund belly begins to glow as the mysterious light reveals the Mandarin's body. His glaring eyes, like a pair of flashlights, are fixed on the girl, with animalistic craving. The terrified thugs creep under the bed, but Mimi, unafraid, remains standing in the middle of the room and smiles at the Mandarin. She signals to a thug to cut the Mandarin down but the terrified cutthroat refuses to leave his cover. She reaches under the bed, drags him out, and places the knife in his hand. She forces him to mount the table and sever the pigtail.

The Mandarin drops to the floor, rises, and runs to Mimi. She takes him in her arms and holds him in a long embrace. He clings to her, his body trembles, and blood slowly flows from the wounds in his belly and forehead. His body gradually slackens. A smile appears on his contorted face, for his desire has been fulfilled. The exultant girl lowers the body to the floor—to the sounds of a strange, discordant, exotic music. The Mandarin is dead.[119]

Beginning in October, Bartók contracted influenza and was bedridden until the end of the month. On the 31st, in Budapest, the Hungarian October Revolution broke out with demonstrations by soldiers and civilians. The November dissolution of the Austro-Hungarian Monarchy disrupted the economy, and by mid-December the massive numbers of the resultant unemployed were increased by the return of more than a million demobilized soldiers and refugees from the occupied territories.[120] Early in 1919, when Mihailovich retired as director of the Academy of Music, Dohnányi was appointed his successor. Kodály accepted the post of deputy director. Bartók heard that he would be the next director of the Opera, but he was much relieved when a transfer to the National Museum was offered, where he would take up duties as head of a new, independent department of musical folklore. Although the transfer never materialized, he did serve as a member of the music directorate at the Academy.[121] During May, Bartók completed the sketch of the *Miraculous Mandarin*, then postponed work on preparation of the orchestral score until 1924. The ensuing events until the end of February 1920 are summarized in Bartók's first report to the New York *Musical Courier,* which was published in the March issue of the magazine.[122]

Hungary is in the throes of reaction. The reestablishment of the monarchy is almost a certainty, and the dictatorship of the military is crushing the intellectual life of the country, just as the dictatorship of the proletariat crushed its economic existence before. There has never been a darker period in the history of the country. Red Terror and White terror alternately follow following upon four years of war and starvation have left Hungary a mere shadow of its former self. Whether under these conditions Hungarian national culture, which has fought for its existence for generations under the old monarchy, can develop or even live is a question. . . .

The outbreak of the war naturally brought certain interruptions in its train. . . . [Egisto Tango] was planning a performance of Stravinsky's *Sacre du Printemps* when the October revolution broke out in 1918; all connections with other countries were interrupted for a very long time, and it thus became impossible to procure the necessary music.

The Socialists, who then came into power, were very progressively inclined toward all matters pertaining to art, and this soon found its expression in the musical life of the city. . . . Then came the month of March, 1919, and with it the Communist dictatorship. In principle, this regime favored the progressive home talent even more than its predecessor. . . .

Unfortunately, the Socialist rule as such was a disappointment, and that of the Communists even more so. . . . Serious and fruitful work was an impossibility, and a feeling of relief was general when the dictatorship collapsed on July 29, 1919.

But—out of the frying pan into the fire! In the period of conservative reaction that followed, Dohnányi and Kodály were dismissed from the positions as heads of the High School; all their reforms were annulled, the best instructors swept aside, and all this under the false and thin pretext of routing out Bolshevism.

Beginning in September, Bartók requested and was granted a six-month leave of absence from his teaching duties, which was extended in December to a full year. His preoccupation was the transcription and classification of thousands of folk songs in his Hungarian collection, assisted by his wife and even his son. According to Bartók's letter to his mother, dated 28 November 1919, "The little one now helps me with the arrangement of the folk songs; he can indicate the cadences in each line of the melody with numbers as well as the number of syllables in each line of the text, and the compass of the melody! And he does it quite well, though mechanically, of course."[123] An underlying reason for the requested leave was the unsettling, politically oriented turmoil at the Academy of Music. That circumstance as well as other factors led Bartók to consider the possibility of seeking employment outside Hungary.

But I have been making what enquiries I can in 3 different countries about the chances of making a living. For in this country, though one can make a living, for the next 10 years at least it will not be possible to do any work, i.e. the kind of work I am interested in (studying folk music). In other words, if I have a chance to do this kind of work abroad, I see no point in staying here; and if it's impossible to make a living from this kind of work abroad, either, it would still be better to teach music, in Vienna say, than in Budapest; for there at least they have good musical institutions (orchestras, operas, etc.), whereas everything is being ruined here because our best musicians, our only ones—Tango, Dohnányi, etc.—are being hounded from their posts.[124]

There were some brighter occasions following the critical acclaim of Dohnányi conducting the Budapest Philharmonic performance of Two Portraits op. 5 on 3 November and the Rhapsody op. 1 for Piano and Orchestra, with Bartók as pianist, on 29 December. Between those events, Hubay was appointed director of the Academy and, in February 1920, a Budapest newspaper announced that he would also serve as president of a new Council of Music and Bartók would be included as a member. But the latter immediately served written notice to the paper on the 20th—which was not published—that "I have received no official approach on this matter; nor would I wish to be a member of any musical council from which the greatest musicians are excluded.[125]

Concurrent with his Hungarian folk song research during the autumn of 1919, Bartók discovered that to a certain extent his Slovak collection could be similarly classified This material includes seventy-three melodies collected by Antal A. Baník (b. 1900), a Slovak folklorist who had been providing Bartók with published Moravian folk music collections and corresponding with him up to 1918.[126] It appears that Baník discussed Bartók's Slovak folk music research—including the determination of reciprocal relationships among the Czech, Moravian, and Slovak folk songs—with Miloš Ruppeldt (1881–1943), a professor at the Bratislava (formerly Pressburg, later Pozsony) Academy of Music and Performing Arts, who served as a representative of the *Matica Slovenská* (Slovak Literary Society). Some time later, Ruppeldt asked Bartók to bring the Slovak collection and sample field recordings to Bratislava for evaluation with regard to prospective publication by the Society. Thus, in mid-July 1920, Bartók applied for a passport from the Czechoslovak Consulate, which was not issued until 20 August, and two days later Bartók sent a letter to Ruppeldt, to the effect that it was quite unlikely that the required export license would be granted for a phonograph and sample recordings.

> From the beginning of September, I will no longer be free; after a yearlong vacation I must again start my activity as a professor. But my wife has the intention to travel to Pressburg [that is, Bratislava] in September, in the event she receives the Czech visa. At this opportunity she would bring the first part (about 1/7th of the entirety) of my Slovak collection in a fair copy, so that it could be seen what it is all about. She would then also negotiate orally what must be done further—because in view of my critical situation, I cannot say anything in writing. So I ask you to make it possible that my wife receives the Czech visa without difficulties.[127]

Bartók's letter also mentions that a likely reason an export license would be withheld stems from the attack against him by official circles in May, which was circulated by the newspapers, for his "strictly scientific" essay on the rural music dialect of the Transylvanian Romanians in Hunyad (Hunedoara) County. This essay was originally published in *Ethnographia* (Budapest) in February 1914. After the German translation appeared in *Zeitschrift für Musikwissenschaft*, in March 1920, the polemics began with an article, "Béla Bartók in the service of Walachian 'Culture,'" published in the *Nemzeti Ujsag,* in which Bartók was denounced as unpatriotic. On 23 May the newspaper published a follow-up by the same author, who accused Bartók of subversive activities by publishing an essay in a foreign journal as "an effective way to gain popularity in the eyes of the Walachians.[128]

When Bartók refused to respond to such calumny, the hue and cry was taken up by Hubay's statement as Academy director, which was published on the 25th in the *Szózat*. His pronouncement reflects a transparent obeisance to the repressive, counterrevolutionary regime of Miklós Horthy (1868–1957), the recently elected Regent of Hungary.

> At the present time, when we must fight for the maintenance of our integrity to the last drop of our blood, I cannot regard it is other than culpable for us to be in any way concerned with the culture of our minorities.
>
> Bartók always showed a particular sympathy for Walachian tunes, a considerable number of which he mistakenly incorporated in his collections of Hungarian folk songs. . . . In Bucharest, people will now spread it about that Transylvania is an exclusively Walachian musical region. . . . These questions must not today be judged from a scholarly point of view, but only from that of the national interest of Hungary, which at the present time is, in any event, more important than details of scholarship to which in general no great significance can be ascribed.[129]

The next day, in the same newspaper, the indignant Bartók replied with a passionate, yet scholarly rebuttal of Hubay's assertions as well as the previous unwarranted attacks, ending his defense with the following queries:

> Who is unpatriotic? Someone who spares neither trouble nor pains for more than a decade to acquaint himself with Hungarian folk music, or rather someone who greets this work with indifference and, moreover, with hostility and trumped-up charges? My last question: Is not that man a "malicious propagandist" who out of ignorance, malevolence or misrepresentation dares to forge the charge of unpatriotic conduct against an article which serves the cause of the Hungarian nation?[130]

Bartók's only composition in 1920 is the Improvisations op. 20, arrangements of eight Hungarian folk songs for piano, in which "I reached, I believe, the extreme limit in adding most daring accompaniments to simple folk tunes."[131] The inspiration for this dissonant work, apparently begun in the summer, may have been Bartók's mind-set arising from the mentioned polemics. On the other hand, perhaps it was his analysis of Stravinsky's *Pribaoutki* (1914), published in the April 1920 issue of *Melos* (Berlin), that prompted the creativeness. In

Bartók's essay, "The Influence of Folk Music on the Art Music of Today," he illustrates how the influence of completely tonal folk music is made compatible with the "atonal trend" in contemporary composition. Ex. 4.34a shows the Russian folk-song motive in Stravinsky's *Pribaoutki* no. 4, "in D minor, with the underlying *ostinato* accompaniment."[132]   Ex. 4.34b shows the beginning of a Hungarian folk song[133] and its accompaniment in Bartók's Improvisation no. 8.

Ex. 4.34. (a) Stravinsky, *Pribaoutki* for Voice and Instruments (1917), no. 4 ("Le Vieux et le lièvre"), mm. 1–2, and (b) Bartók, Improvisations op. 20, for Piano (1920), no. 8, mm. 5–7.

Stravinsky's folk song arrangement shows a melodic phrase in the D-Aeolian mode, D-E-F-G-A-B♭-C. The ostinato accompaniment, however, is based on the fifth ("dominant") degree, A, and includes two "foreign" degrees, C♯ and G♯ (Ex. 4.34a). The resultant pitch collection of modal and nondiatonic degrees forms discrete octatonic sets built on D as the first ("tonic") degree and A as the fifth ("dominant") degree: D-E-F-G-G♯/A-B♭-C-C♯. In the accompaniment, however, the tonal emphasis provided by the emphatic rendition of the dominant implies a reordered formation of the mentioned sets, where A replaces D as the tonic: A-B♭-C-C♯/D-E-F-G-G♯. This interaction of modal and octatonic pitch collections results in atonality, inasmuch as a single principal tone (that is, "tonic") is not firmly established. According to Bartók, "The compositions maintains—despite all that atonality—a domineering A which gives a solid basis to the whole."[134]

Improvisation no. 8 is based on Bartók's innovative polymodal chromaticism, with B as the principal tone.[135] The first three bars of the melody and its accompaniment consist of ten degrees, B-C-D♭ (C♯)-D-E♭ (D♯)-E-F♯-G♯ (A♭)-A-B♭ (A♯). When these degrees are grouped according to the modes to which they belong, a B-Phrygian/Major polymode is formed, B-C-D-E-F♯-A/B-D♭-E♭-E-F♯-G♯-B♭. Note the melodic emphasis of "tonic" B and "dominant" F♯.

In October and November, two articles were published by music critics in England that attracted widespread interest in Bartók's works. The first one, by Leigh Henry in *Musical Opinion,* states that "Bartók has given us a new interpretation of a tradition, and at the same time opened up to us a new realm of musical possibilities. These achievements place him among the significant and

important of contemporary composers."[136] In the second article, by Cecil Gray
in the inaugural issue of *Sackbut,* reference is made to Bartók's First String
Quartet as "probably the finest achievement in quartet writing since Beethoven,"
and to *Two Pictures* and the Second String Quartet as works that "take rank with
the finest achievements of the century."[137]

On the occasion of Bartók's fortieth birthday on 25 March 1921, *Musikblätter
des Anbruch* published a special issue devoted to Bartók, the first journal to
accord him such recognition; Kodály contributed a biographical study of Bartók to *La Revue Musicale*; and Aladár Tóth—an outstanding Hungarian music
critic—praised Bartók in an article published by *Nyugat.* In a letter dated 8
May, Bartók reviews his economic situation and other personal matters since
1919, beginning with the "living expenses for the three of us are twice my year's
salary. So I have to devote all my spare time to money-making." He cites such
activities as "piano concerts, writing articles for foreign periodicals, and writing books about the folk music of Hungary and other countries," and he continues with:

> It is obvious that, in these circumstances, I have no time for composing, even if I
> were in the right mood for it. But my mood is far from right—and no wonder. The
> fact is, I am homeless: it is impossible to get any kind of a flat, and even if I could
> find one, I wouldn't be able to afford it. And I am hopelessly cut off from the one
> thing that is necessary to me as fresh air is to other people—the possibility of
> going in with my studies of folk music in the countryside. There's no time or
> money for it! It now seems that nowhere in the world is there any real interest in
> this work. I've made every attempt to find some opening, and I would have gone
> *anywhere* I was invited if there had been the opportunity for going on with this
> work.
>
> Yet at this moment my compositions are arousing interest abroad. In Novem-
> ber I was the subject of a 12-page (approx.) article in a London music periodical
> in which the writer placed me in the ranks of the world's greatest composers, not
> merely the greatest living composers but of all time. . . . all this, however, is but a
> moral victory. And anyhow, even if they were to make me the High Pope of Mu-
> sic, it would be no help to me so long as I remain cut off from peasant music.[138]

The adoption of the Treaty of Trianon in 1920, which transferred immense
territories and their inhabitants to the newly created boundaries of Czechoslovakia, Romania, and Yugoslavia, was a grievous loss which affected the Hungarian nation in different ways. A case in point is the attendance at and positive
reception of young audiences and the press to the performance of new music.
Reflecting this change was Bartók's "Debussy-Stravinsky Evening" concert at
the Music Academy, on 23 April, which also included two pieces from
Schoenberg's op. 11 for piano. A partial compensation for Bartók's lost opportunity to continue his Slovak and Romanian fieldwork was the publication of
his research, beginning with a joint venture with Kodály which was completed
on 15 March: *Erdélyi Magyarság: népdalok* (Transylvanian Hungarians: Folk

songs).[139] He was elated when on the 29th he signed a contract with *Matica Slovenská* for the publication of his Slovak folk music collection.[140] During October, he finished his seminal work, *A magyar népdal* (The Hungarian Folk Song), in which the material is classified in three stylistic categories: Old, New, and Mixed.[141]

Bartók's introduction to the music of Karol Szymanowski (1882–1937) occurred during Jelly d'Arányi's holiday in Budapest. Now an internationally recognized violinist, she met with Bartók in October, with the express purpose of their playing together, including Szymanowski's *Trois Mythes* op. 30, for Violin and Piano (1915). Bartók was not only impressed with Jelly's performance but even more so with her radiant personality, to the point where he fell in love—again hopelessly. As Jelly later wrote in her diary, following the composition of Bartók's First Violin Sonata, "It is good and great that I should have inspired that gorgeous sonata—but apparently a woman can't inspire the soul of a man without doing great harm. It is sad, too sad, that I should make this great man suffer."[142]

At the same time he was working with the violinist Zoltán Székely in preparation for a concert to be given at the Budapest Vigadó. On 6 October, he wrote to his publisher for the score of *Mythes,* and on 12 November the Székely-Bartók duo gave the work its first Budapest performance.[143] Meanwhile, inspired by Szymanowski's composition as well as the anticipated relationship with Jelly, Bartók began work on the First Violin Sonata and completed the first two movements on 9 November. In her letter to Bartók's mother, dated 19 October, Márta Bartók writes that:

> Béla took me my surprise with the news—that he composes! Again at long last. I hardly contained myself this morning when, as a birthday present, he showed me the violin sonata on which he's working. . . . Well, could anyone get a more beautiful present than this? I am so happy. How afraid I was that all the deprivations of recent years would finally enfeeble Béla's ability to work—and how grateful I am to Jelly Arányi, whose wonderful playing on the violin has drawn out of Béla this (as he tells it) long dormant plan.[144]

Bartók completed the First Violin Sonata on 12 December, in which a more or less independent function of the piano—following Szymanowski's innovation—replaces the traditional, supportive accompaniment.[145] The next year Bartók returned to Transylvania for a series of concerts in February, followed in March by his first tour of England. Jelly performed the Violin Sonata to mixed reviews; one critic, however, was remarkably perceptive:

> The sonata is not a fusion of both instruments, but is a sort of duologue: impassioned on the part of the violin; restrained, logical and rhythmical on the part of the piano . . . Puzzling as this sonata was at first hearing, it was sufficiently arresting in its quality of feeling to make one think that, after all, Béla Bartók may be something of a genius.[146]

Following his London stay, on 3 April Bartók and Jelly were in Paris at the Hotel Majestic, where they began preparations for their concert on the 8th. At that time Jelly was in her late twenties, unmarried, and totally committed to her brilliant career. Since Bartók was apparently unable to comprehend that her appreciation of his gifts as composer and pianist, and that her enthusiasm and delight in their music making did not carry over to the personal relationship he was obviously seeking, she decided to limit their association to rehearsals. Thus she was able to avoid a possibly awkward situation that might have affected their performance. As her letter to her father, dated 22 April, reports:

> Last Saturday I had about the most exciting musical event in my life. Bartók and I played his sonata at a concert, and all the greatest living composers came to hear it; that was in the afternoon, and in the evening they all came to a soireé to hear it once more—Ravel, Stravinsky, Szymanowsky and many other less important ones. . . . Bartók is going tomorrow—we are glad, as he is a little difficult to be with—, I must say he was a very great success both here and in London.[147]

Following Bartók's departure from Paris for a scheduled Frankfurt concert on 24 April, the program consisted of his piano works, the First Violin Sonata— with Adolf Lehner as violinist— and the First String Quartet played by the Lehner Quartet. Bartók stayed on for the performance of *The Wooden Prince* and *Duke Bluebeard's Castle* at the Frankfurt Opera House on 13 May. At an earlier time during this year he wrote his autobiography and an essay, which for the first time disclose specific features in the development of his new musical language.

> A new chapter in the history of Hungarian music was begun at the beginning of this century, together with a revival of the literary impulse. Some young musicians, born about 1880, turned their attention to the hitherto unknown music of the Hungarian peasants and set out themselves to collect on a large scale and in a more or less scientific way the blooms of this music. Among others, these men are Zoltán Kodály, László Lajtha, Antal Molnár, and the present writer. The collecting was later extended also to the music of other nations coexisting on Hungarian soil, primarily that of the Slovaks and Romanians. . . . This musical material, and especially that which belongs to the Hungarian race, constitutes the only Hungarian musical tradition which could serve as a base for a serious effort whose intention was the creation of a Hungarian musical language and which had a direct and decisive influence on the works of the above folkloristic composers.[148]
> The outcome of these studies [of the musical material] was of decisive influence upon my work, because it freed me from the tyranny of the major and minor scales. The greater part of the collected treasure, and the more valuable part, was in old ecclesiastical or old Greek modes, or based on more primitive (pentatonic) scales, and the melodies were full of most free and varied phrases and changes of tempi, played both *rubato* and *giusto*. It became clear to me that the old modes, which had been forgotten in our music, had lost none of their vigor. Their new employment made new rhythmic combinations possible. This new way of using

the diatonic scale brought freedom from the rigid use of the major and minor keys, every tone of which came to be considered of equal value and could be used freely and independently.[149]

The outcome of Bartók's Parisian misadventure with Jelly d'Arányi was her decision to avoid further communication or appearances with him. Notwithstanding this tacit rejection, he composed the Second Violin Sonata (July–November) for her but had to give its premiere with Imre Waldbauer on 7 February 1923 in Berlin. When a tour of England was made possible through the auspices of the newly formed International Society for Contemporary Music, which included a request for Jelly to perform the two sonatas with Bartók on 7 May in London, he added her initials as dedicatee of the Second Violin Sonata—at the end of the fair copy.[150]

While the sonatas share a number of stylistic features whose predominant commonality is the use of Romanian source material, the obvious difference is the number and form of movements: three (sonata, ternary [ABA], rondo) in no. 1 and two (rondos) in no. 2.[151] The less obvious dissimilarity is the abstract nature of the former as opposed to the programmatic content of the latter. Specifically, the two movements of the Second Violin Sonata replicate the performance of a composite piece by Romanian peasant instrumentalists, beginning with a slow, mournful "When the shepherd lost his sheep" (Ex. 4.35a) and followed by a fast dance tune designated "When the shepherd found his lost sheep." (Ex. 4.35b) The slow piece—intended to express sorrow over one of the most tragic events in shepherd life—was based on a Transylvanian improvisatory genre that Bartók discovered in 1913.[152]

In addition to composition during the second half of 1992, Bartók prepared the fair copy of the 763 melodies comprising the first volume of his Slovak folk

Ex. 4.35. (a) *RFM*.i, melody no. 747 ("When the shepherd lost his sheep"), mm. 1–6, and (b) *RFM*.i, melody no. 293bis ("When the shepherd found his lost sheep"), mm. 1–8. The melodies were played on a *trişca* (a recorder-like peasant flute).

music collection. On 8 October he wrote to *Matica Slovenská* that the remaining two volumes hopefully would be ready for delivery by the end of January.[153]

Bartók's letter to Universal Edition, dated 23 April 1923, refers to his composing dances for small orchestra, commissioned by the municipal council of Budapest for the jubilee festival-concert in November. Dohnányi and Kodály were the other composers selected to provide the music in celebration of the fiftieth anniversary of the unification of Buda, Pest, and Obuda to form the Hungarian capital. The sketch, designated "táncszvit" (Dance Suite), was completed on 6 July.[154] Other good news was the long-awaited publication of Bartók's 1913 collection of Romanian folk music from the Transylvanian county of Maramureş by Drei Masken Verlag (Munich).[155] On the other hand, unfortunately, the postponement and subsequent abandonment of the book by the Academia Română forced Bartók to underwrite the engraving costs of the music examples then under way. The promised volumes of Slovak folk melodies were not ready, and Professor Vilmoš Figusch, representing *Matica Slovenská,* met with Bartók to determine the status of the project.[156] The intervening circumstances were such, however, that it was not until October that Bartók could hand over only the first two volumes ready for press.[157]

The aftermath of Bartók's unsuccessful pursuit of Jelly d'Arányi, coupled with his recent attraction toward Ditta Pásztory (1903–1982)—a gifted student in his Academy piano class—was the mutually agreed divorce from Márta. His mother's depression and anxiety, stemming from her close relationship with her daughter-in-law, brought a letter from her son, dated 13 August, in which he explains that:

> I believe that it will be well thus, it will be better than it has been up to now. Only to Márta it will be far worse; this is the only thing that saddens me. So that I truly should not have asked this sacrifice of her; this I did not know how to do, although the human *raison* should be the commandment. But she persuaded me to this change, and I could not say no, after all, I was not the only one to be considered. Little Béla accepted the situation readily enough—he understood the "specialness" of the matter. Consequently I hope that you too will become reconciled to it.[158]

The orchestral score of the Dance Suite, dated 19 August, consists of five dances, each followed by a *ritornell* (an Interlude of Hungarian character). The dances also show the influence of Arab, Romanian, and Ruthenian folk music, thus creating a unique fusion of national styles that reflects the results of Bartók's folk music research to date. In the first dance, for instance, the opening theme of the first dance combines narrow range, chromatic Arab melodic style with Ruthenian *kolomyjka* dance rhythm (Ex. 4.36). This is followed by melodic strands whose rhythm schemata can be attributed to the influence of Hungarian and some Slovak folk songs, ♩♫ | ♫ ♩ and ♫♫ | ♪♩ ♪ | ♪ ♩., as well as the Romanian bagpipe motif, ♩♫ ♫♩. It is interesting that none of the other dances show the influence of the most characteristic Slovak folk music products.

Ex. 4.36. (a) Bartók, Dance Suite (1923), first movement, mm. 1–5, and (b) *BBSE,* melody no. 16, Arab *Qṣeida*-song, mm. 9–12.

Bartók and Ditta Pásztory were married on 28 August 1923. From 30 November to 12 December he was in England for concerts with Jelly and Adila (m., Fachiri) d'Arányi, recitals of his own works, and the Rhapsody op. 1, for Piano and Orchestra. Unfortunately, the performance of both violin sonatas was received negatively by the London press, and his percussive piano touch offended those critics who were adherents of the Tobias Matthay (1858–1945) approach to piano technique.[159] While Bartók was staying in the same London home as Henry Cowell (1897–1965), he heard Cowell playing piano music in which his innovative tone-cluster technique was featured. Bartók was struck by these peculiar sounds and asked permission to use tone-clusters in his own music.[160] According to Cowell's recollection, in his letter dated 23 April 1946:

> (of course I wrote him that they are public property, and I was delighted). I did have a great many discussions with Bartók on how he developed,—slowly a bit at a time—many unusual chords and rhythms, not by direct imitation of the folk music of Hungary, but by developing into sophisticated musical means strong suggestions from this folk music. He mentioned many times what he called "rhythmical punctuation" by means of sudden, biting discords injected into rather simple melodic and harmonic fabric—he had these classified, so far as his own use was concerned, into more or less biting sounds, taking the place of periods, commas and semicolons in written language.[161]

During 1924, Bartók's seminal study, *A magyar népdal* (The Hungarian Folk Song) was published in Budapest, and the articles he wrote on Eastern European folk music and various Hungarian subjects were printed in *A Dictionary of Modern Music and Musicians* (London). Other than the performance of the Second Violin Sonata at the Academy of Music on 5 February, his concerts were piano recitals in which the programs were divided between his folk music arrangements and works from the standard repertory. Bartók's second son, Péter, was born on 31 July. Thereafter the happy father celebrated the event by composing Village Scenes for Voice and Piano, an arrangement of seven Slovak folk songs from his collection, which he completed in December and dedicated to his wife. The work is a tableau of rural life in five movements: I. Haymaking, II. At the Bride's, III. Wedding, IV. Lullaby, and V. Lad's Dance.

The increasing international interest in Bartók's works carried over in 1925 to requests for his personal appearance as pianist. The pressing need to augment his Academy income forced him to accept such engagements, whose preparation in terms of time and energy were disincentives with respect to composition. Furthermore, he had an equally compelling need to work on his folk music collections, particularly a new project for a volume of Romanian carols and Christmas songs, that had interested the Romanian Ministry of Culture.

> When I was in Bucharest, in the autumn, it turned out that, actually, the most they can do at the moment is to purchase the material; there's no money for printing it, and it's quite uncertain when they will be able to give it to the printers. The head of the Music Department of a British publishing house, the Oxford University Press, was here recently; he would like to publish this collection in London. He is going to talk to the Bucharest people about it. This solution would be very much to my liking, and I think the people in Bucharest would like it too. For the Oxford Univ. Press is a firm known throughout the world; and everyone takes notice of its publications.[162]

The most significant tour was in Italy—Milan, Rome, Naples, and Palermo—during the last two weeks in March, and in Trieste on 7 December. In addition to selections from his own works for piano, Bartók's programs included D. Scarlatti and Beethoven sonatas, and pieces by Chopin, Debussy, Kodály, and Liszt. At this time or perhaps in July, when Bartók took his family on holiday in the Lake Como region, he purchased editions of Baroque keyboard music published by Ricordi, Bratti, and Breitkopf & Härtel.[163] He subsequently transcribed selected pieces of cembalo and organ music by G. Frescobaldi (1583–1643), M. Rossi (1600–c. 1660), A. della Ciaia (1671–1755), B. Marcello (1686–1739), and D. Zipoli (1688–1726). These transcriptions not only provided him with additional works for future concerts in Italy and elsewhere concert material but—of substantially greater importance—gave him a fresh insight on the contrapuntal techniques practiced by Bach's Italian predecessors and contemporaries.[164]

The Dance Suite had its first performance in the United States on 3 April, by the Cincinnati Symphony (conducted by Fritz Reiner); in Czechoslovakia on 19 May, by the Prague Philharmonic (Václav Talich); and in Holland on 15 October, by the Amsterdam Concertgebouw. Bartók was the soloist in performances of his Rhapsody, op. 1 on 9 September, by the Budapest Philharmonic (Dohnányi) and in the 15 October Amsterdam program, immediately following the performance of the Dance Suite. The contrast in style between the two works—representing a difference of more than fifteen years in their composition—was particularly noted by Bartók in an interview on 22 November: "I must compose a piano concerto. This is sadly lacking. This will be my next work."[165]

Finally, he was also determined to offset the folk music arrangements in his piano recitals by composing original, abstract works to replace the older pieces previously selected from the Bagatelles, Elegies, and Burlesques.

5

Synthesis of East and West: 1926–1945

Bartók's last stage of development was the synthesis of Eastern folk-music materials with Western art-music techniques of composition, beginning in the summer of 1926 with an intense burst of creative energy. His output was the Piano Sonata (June), *Out-of Doors* for Piano (June–August), Nine Little Piano Pieces (31 October), the First Piano Concerto (August–November), and two piano pieces that eventually were incorporated in the *Mikrokosmos*. In certain respects, the 1924–1925 period of Bartók's dormancy preceding the composition of those innovative works is strikingly similar to the 1905–1926 "stagnation" period antedating his remarkable 1907–1908 output: original piano pieces (opp. 6–9b), First Violin Concerto, First String Quartet, and Two Portraits. The basic dissimilarity between the two periods was in regard to the source of inspiration or motivation that led to the mentioned works. The earlier period was followed by the ill-fated love affair between Bartók and Stefi Geyer; the later one, by his deeply felt need to compose stylistically up-to-date piano works, including a concerto, to meet the growing, international clamor for his personal appearance as composer-pianist. In fact, his 1926 concert season began in Budapest on 14 January, with a recital of piano pieces he had previously performed during the preceding two years; followed by the Rhapsody op. 1 with the Berlin Philharmonic (conducted by Bruno Walter) on the 18th and in Baden-Baden on the 21st. During his return to Italy in March (Bergamo, Cremona, and Firenze), he repeated the programs given in other Italian venues during the preceding year.

A second source of motivation was the concert of Stravinsky works given by the Budapest Philharmonic on 15 March with the composer as soloist in his Concerto for Piano and Wind Instruments (1924). Bartók, who attended the concert, was aware of the highly successful Stravinsky tours in Europe and the United States, in which Stravinsky also played his Second Piano Sonata (1924) and conducted his orchestral works.[1] Bartók recognized the Bachian influence in the Concerto, and his later recollection is that:

> This is Stravinsky's neoclassical period of which the *Pulcinella* music is only a preparatory study. It really starts with his Octet for Wind Instruments, followed by his Concerto for Piano, piano pieces, and many other works too numerous to mention here. Just at the beginning of this period, when I once met Stravinsky in Paris, he told me that he thinks he has the right to incorporate into his music any material he believes to be fit or appropriate for his purposes. . . . With this convic-

tion, Stravinsky turned to the music of a bygone time, to the so-called classical music of the seventeenth and eighteenth centuries, for a new starting point.[2]

Stravinsky's stylistic changeover attracted so much attention that it gave rise to a "back to Bach" label. Bartók avoided such stereotyping by turning to the music of Bach's Italian predecessors and contemporaries, such as Girolamo Frescobaldi (1583–1643) and Azzolino Bernardino della Ciaia (1671–1755). Thus, the first movement of Bartók's First Piano Concerto begins with the transformed fugue subject of the *Canzone* (second movement) of della Ciaia's G Major Sonata (Example 5.1).

Ex. 5.1. (a) Azzolino della Ciaia, G Major Sonata, second movement, mm.1–5, and (b) Bartók, Concerto no. 1 for Piano and Orchestra, first movement, mm. 38–44.

In a 1927 interview, Bartók states that he uses more counterpoint in his newer works than he did in the older ones and offers the following explanation:

In that way, again, I keep clear of nineteenth-century formulas, which were generally homophonic. I study Mozart. Did he not marvelously combine the contrapuntal and homophonic ideas in certain of his slow movements, and especially in the "Jupiter" Symphony? I have studied the pre-classic contrapuntists, both the organ and the clavicembalo writers, and I intend to do some reading of the old vocal contrapuntists.[3]

Several years later, when a musicologist asked Bartók why he had made so little use of counterpoint, the composer's letter offers further clarification about the subject:

> In my youth my ideal of beauty was not so much the style of Bach or Mozart but Beethoven. Recently it has changed somewhat; of late I have been much occupied with pre-Bachian music, and I believe that traces of this can be observed in the Piano Concerto and Nine Little Piano Pieces.[4]

While Bartók was in Paris during March 1939, the remarks he made at an interview were subsequently published in a biographical study as "Bartók's own testimony." These remarks, quoted below, have provided a significant clue toward understanding the makeup of his unique world of composition.

> Kodály and I wanted to make a synthesis of East and West. Because of our race, and because of the geographical position of our country, which is at once the extreme point of the East and the defensive bastion of the West, we felt this was a task we were well fitted to undertake. But it was your Debussy, whose music had just begun to reach us, who showed us the path we must follow. And that, in itself, was a curious phenomenon when one recalls that, at that time, so many French musicians were still held in thrall by the prestige of Wagner.
>
> Debussy's great service to music was to reawaken among all musicians an awareness of harmony and its possibilities. In that, he was just as important as Beethoven, who revealed to us the meaning of progressive form, and as Bach, who showed us the transcendent significance of counterpoint.
>
> Now, what I am always asking myself is this: is it possible to make a synthesis of these three great masters, a living synthesis that will be valid for our own time?[5]

Bartók, of course, was well aware that he had achieved the "living synthesis" in his 1926 compositions. The "East," described in the preceding chapter, embodies the morphological elements that are most characteristic of Eastern European and Arab folk music: melodic, rhythmic, and scalar structures. The synthesis is brought about when selected folk music structures are transformed and integrated with the structural techniques of Western European art music. For example, in the third movement of Bartók's Sonata for Piano, the rhythm schema of the first theme (Ex. 5.2a) is an attenuated transformation of Hungarian *kanász-tánc* (hog-herder's dance) rhythm (Ex. 5.2b). The Sonata shows an 11-note (6+5) structure; the dance has 13 notes (7+6) and itself is a transformation of the Ruthenian *kolomyjka* (round dance) 14-note (8+6) schema.

Ex. 5.2. (a) Bartók, Sonata for Piano (1926), third movement, mm. 1–8, and (b) rhythm schema of the Hungarian hog-herder's dance.

Bartók completed the preparation of two fair copies of his book on the Romanian *colinde* (Winter-solstice songs) and presented one of them to the Romanian embassy, for transfer to Bucharest. The other copy was mailed on 1 May to Oxford University Press for editorial purposes, notwithstanding the London publisher's failure to contact Bartók concerning the publication status of his book on the Hungarian folk song.[6] During the next months he set to work on preparing the fair copy of the remaining part of his Slovak folk song collection, with the intention of delivering it to *Matica Slovenská* in September or soon thereafter.[7]

With regard to the other works composed during the summer, the *Out of Doors* for Piano is a suite of five pieces whose chromaticism reflects Bartók's new tonal language. The impressionist fourth piece, *Musique Nocturnes,* brings to mind stylistic features in Debussy's *Préludes* for Piano. It is noteworthy that *Musique Nocturnes* also marks the first appearance of the "Night's music" genre—the sound of frogs, crickets, and nocturnal noises—that Bartók invented to commemorate his field trips and holidays in Békés County and other rural areas of Hungary and Transylvania.

Nine Little Piano Pieces may be considered an extension of Ten Easy Pieces (1908) with regard to difficulty or as pedagogical material. The essential difference between the two compilations is textural: chromatic counterpoint is the guiding principle of the former, beginning with *Four Dialogues* in the style of Bach's Two-Part Inventions.

It was at this time that Bartók established a more or less routine lifestyle that would enable him to cope with the pressing demands on his time and energy. His elder son recalls that:

> Giving recitals and piano lessons (he consistently refused to give lessons in composition), tired him chiefly because he always and everywhere insisted on giving his best. Five to six hours of practising daily, or playing with his pupils, took up much of the time he could have devoted to pursuits dearer to his heart, particularly his work on folk music. He was only too delighted, therefore, when, in 1934, he was invited to join the Hungarian Academy of Sciences. . . .
>
> He had no recreations in the conventional sense of the word. He never visited the cinemas, cafés, or other places of amusement, and would seldom go to concerts. His principal pastime was—work. During the school year he would leave the house rarely—with the exception of visits to the family or to give his lessons

at the Academy of Music. He read the newspapers avidly and would buy one every day, sometimes more than one. He was interested in everything in it, editorials, economic news, politics, and the arts.[8]

On 27 November, the premiere performance of *The Miraculous Mandarin* was staged in Cologne, under the direction of Jenő Szenkár (1891-1977), the Hungarian-born chief conductor of the Cologne Opera. He recalls that:

> At the end of the performance we were confronted with a chorus of whistling and booing! Bartók was present—even during all the rehearsals he generally sat in the auditorium. The uproar was so deafening and threatening that the safety curtain had to be lowered! . . . Then, on the following day came—the reviews! What was published . . . can barely be repeated![9]

Later that day Konrad Adenauer, the lord mayor, informed Szenkár that the "dirty piece" must be dropped immediately from the season's program. When the latter considered offering his resignation, Bartók begged him to reconsider: "He was convinced that his time would certainly come!"[10]

Bartók's final concerts of the year were given at the Academy of Music on 8 December, which included the premiere of the Sonata for Piano and six of Nine Little Piano Pieces, and on Budapest Radio on 30 December (Liszt, Beethoven, Chopin, and Debussy works). The next year he featured his transcriptions of Italian keyboard music at early January recitals in Genoa and Velence, and on the 26th, in Kecskemét, his program was for the most part devoted to Scarlatti, Mozart, Beethoven, Chopin, and Debussy. On 1 July Bartók was the soloist in the first performance of the First Piano Concerto, Wilhelm Furtwängler conducting, at the Frankfurt Opera House. And on 26 July he played the Sonata for Piano in Baden-Baden, where the International Society for Contemporary Music (ISCM) held its concert, and he had the opportunity of hearing Alban Berg's *Lyric Suite* for string quartet. This happenstance apparently motivated Bartók to resume writing in this genre after a ten-year hiatus.[11] Thus, beginning in September, he composed the Third String Quartet in an unusual "Prima parte" and "Seconda parte" binary form.

While Bartók was working on his Slovak folk music collection, it seems likely that this activity prompted him to complete the Three Rondos on [Slovak] Folk Tunes begun in 1916. Reading from a copy of the manuscript, he played the first performance at the Academy of Music on 29 November, where the program title is listed as "Három kis rapszódia népdalok fölött" (Three little rhapsodies on folk songs). The second and third rondos include folk songs which feature the characteristic Slovak Lydian mode (Ex. 5.3).[12]

Concurrent with his return to teaching in October, Bartók continued concertizing in Hungary, including the First Piano Concerto, and in Germany, where he also played the Rhapsody op. 1, for Piano and Orchestra. In December, he departed Cherbourg for New York to begin an extended tour of the United States sponsored by the Pro-Musica Society.

Ex. 5.3. Source melodies from *SV.*i in Bartók, Three Rondos on Folk Tunes. No. 5 (*Meno mosso* in Rondo III) shows the first half of the melody as a G-Lydian hexachord and the second half as a G-major pentachord. No. 318b (*Allegro non troppo* in Rondo II) has G-Mixolydian (mm. 1–8) and Lydian (mm. 9–14) pentachords.

Following his arrival in New York on 18 December, Bartók and the New York Philharmonic, Willem Mengelberg conducting, began rehearsing the First Piano Concerto as the inaugural work for his American debut. Unfortunately, because of inadequate rehearsal time, the concerto was replaced by the Rhapsody op. 1, to the disappointment of the audience and music critics who had been expecting "new music atonality." The same work was performed by Bartók with the Philadelphia Orchestra, Fritz Reiner conducting, on 30 December. Among the reports in music periodicals and New York newspapers that publicized Bartók's forthcoming tour was his interview—including demonstrations at the piano—with an American journalist, which was held at the Academy of Music prior to the composer's departure from Budapest.

> It is true that I thought that at one time my development would eventually bring me to the exclusive use of the twelve-tone system, but now I am of another belief, because: First, I have never written a work that is genuinely atonal, or of the twelve-tone system. . . . Second, I now believe that I should hold to tonality, in spite of earlier tendencies to the contrary [the two violin sonatas]. My new works [the 1926 Piano Sonata and Concerto for Piano and Orchestra] evidence a more decided tonality as compared to my works of four or five years ago. . . .
> I do not care to subscribe to any of the accepted contemporary musical tendencies, for instance those which may be considered as objectively impersonal, or consisting of a solely polyphonic or homophonic nature. My ideal is a measured balance of those elements. I cannot conceive of music that expresses absolutely nothing.

I consider it as inadvisable to devote myself rigidly to a certain definite tendency in music, so that one becomes dominated by set rules. This attitude of mine
is dictated in part by a natural reaction against any outcropping of "romanticism,"
which too is an exaggerated form of a definite tendency.[13]

The tour also included a lecture-recital in which Bartók discussed the modal
characteristics of Hungarian, Romanian, and Slovak folk songs, and demon-
strated the ways in which the folk modes influenced his harmonic processes.[14]
His itinerary, beginning in January 1928, included the following venues: Los
Angeles, San Francisco, Seattle, Portland (Oregon), Denver, Kansas City, St.
Paul, Chicago, Detroit, Cleveland, Cincinnati, Boston, and New York. And he
was most gratified that he had the opportunity to appear as soloist in the First
Piano Concerto, Fritz Reiner conducting the Cincinnati Symphony Orchestra at
Carnegie Hall, New York, on 13 February and at Emory Auditorium, Cincin-
nati.[15]

Following his return to Budapest, on 16 March Bartók played a mixed group
of piano pieces at the Academy of Music. Two days later he was the soloist in
the First Piano Concerto with the Budapest Philharmonic, Ernő Dohnányi conducting, on 23–24 March, with the Cologne Philharmonic, and on 19–20 April
with the Kroll-Opera Symphony in Berlin. He concluded the concert season
with a Budapest Radio broadcast on 2 May.

In the meantime, Bartók completed the final section of his Slovak material
and on 16 May wrote to *Matica Slovenská* that he was ready to hand over the
fair copy for engraving the music. He also asked permission to prepare an additional appendix which would not only list approximately 8,000 tunes in the
previously published Slovak, Moravian, and Czech folk-music collections but
indicate their variant relationships among the melodies comprising the three
volumes of the projected publication.[16]

Three major works were composed during the summer: Rhapsody nos. 1 and
2 for Violin and Piano, and the Fourth String Quartet. The First Rhapsody is
essentially a transcription of folk music in a binary form, which Bartók also
arranged for violoncello and with orchestra. The Prima parte ("lassú" [slow]) is
based on two folk tunes, a Romanian instrumental melody and a Hungarian folk
song. The Seconda parte ("friss" [fast]) is based on Transylvanian-Romanian
source melodies played on the violin for Sunday dance recreations.[17] The first
movement begins with a *De ciuit* ("Calling to the dance") in the G-Lydian folk
mode. The third dance in the second movement is a *Pre loc* ("In place") dance
of the *Ardeleana* ("Transylvanian") type, in D major, whose rhythm is that of
the Ruthenian *kolomyjka* (Ex. 5.4).

The unusual construction of the Fourth String Quartet is in palindromic or
so-called bridge or arch form, that is, five movements whose "character corresponds to classical sonata form." III., the slow movement, is the "kernel," II. is
a scherzo and IV. its variant movement, and I. is in sonata form and IV. has the
same thematic material but lacks the traditional development section.[18]

232. De ciuit   215. Pre loc

same thematic material but lacks the traditional development section.[18]

Ex. 5.4. *RFM*.i. source melodies in Bartók, Rhapsody no. 1 for Violin and Piano (1928).
The Second Rhapsody also is in binary form, but has three Romanian instrumental melodies in the Prima parte, and one Ruthenian and six Romanian tunes in the Seconda parte.[19]

On 2 October *Az Est*, a Budapest newspaper, reported that Bartók's Third String Quartet had been awarded First Prize of $6,000 in the Philadelphia Music Fund Society's competition. He found this difficult to believe until a check arrived from Philadelphia, informing him that he shared the prize with the Italian composer Alfredo Casella (1883–1947). In his 29 October response to a congratulatory cable from Fritz Reiner, he writes that:

> There's no need for me to stress that the money 'came in handy'; we are able to breathe more freely now, to say nothing of the publicity we've had. You can hardly imagine the sensation this caused in Budapest. Six thousand dollars! I told everybody, from the very outset, that it couldn't be as much as that—but all to no effect; it is by now common knowledge that I have won 6,000. . . .
>
> PS. Meanwhile I have written another string quartet, a much longer one this time; there are 5 movements (would thereby any chance be another competition somewhere?!!).[20]

More than two years had elapsed since Bartók's inquiry to Oxford University Press about the publication status of the English edition of his Romanian *colinde* book. Finally, on 17 November he informed the publisher that the Academia Română in Bucharest would be glad to publish the collection:

> Before making any agreement with them, I must have your decision, If you can not publish it, let me know it. . . . But if you decide to publish it, we must make an agreement (contract) containing the date before which the work must appear.
>
> If it can not [be] published by you, you may give back the manuscript next March (4th and 5th) when I shall be in London. (Bucarest [*sic*] has an other copy of the manuscript.)[21]

Bartók's tour of Russia began with a recital in Kharkov on 9 January 1929, and was followed by appearances in Odessa, Leningrad, and Moscow. Before the end of the month he was in Switzerland, playing a concert at the Basel Conservatory on the 29th, the Zurich Town Hall on the 31st, and the Winterthur Staathaussaal on 1 February. It is indeed interesting as well as fortuitous that Stefi Geyer appeared with him in the performance of the Second Violin Sonata and the Romanian Folk Dances, for their meeting forged a new, professional

Bartók arrived in London on 3 March and met with Hubert J. Foss, head of the music division of Oxford University Press, concerning the projected Hungarian and Romanian folk-music publications. That evening he appeared as soloist and accompanist (for Zoltán Székely) in a program of his works at the Arts Theatre Club. The first hour was broadcast over BBC, thereafter he played the "too difficult for a radio audience"—Piano Sonata. One of the attendees recalls that:

> [Bartók] later played the Piano Sonata in which, playing from memory, he came to a complete halt twice, his memory having failed. Each time he sat perfectly still for a moment, then started off again, apparently quite calmly (though I doubt he was as calm as he looked) at some point previous to that at which the disaster had occurred.[23]

The French section of the Pro Musica Society presented the "Festival Béla Bartók" at the Paris Conservatoire on 13 March, with the composer as pianist and accompanist, the Roth Quartet, József Szigeti, and a vocalist in selections from op. 16 and Hungarian folk-song arrangements. The next month, on the 12th, the Santa Cecilia Academy of Rome sponsored a.Bartók-Szigeti concert. After the performance, writing on a picture postcard from the Café Greco, Bartók informs his wife that: "Poor Szigeti was quite shocked because the audience was rather noisy during my violin sonata. He has never experienced such a thing before, but I'm pretty hardened in this respect."[24]

In May, Emil Haraszti (1885–1958)—a Budapest music critic with a long-held aversion to Bartók's music— initiated a newspaper debate concerning Hungarian peasant music, Gypsy music, and popular art song. He wrote that Gypsy music is the "dearest music of the Magyars . . . what a sterile undertaking it is [by Bartók and Kodály] which blacklists the Gypsy in order to impose on the Hungarians an official art of one particular trend [Hungarian peasant music]."[25] Bartók's tacit response was the composition of Twenty Hungarian Folk Songs— his last arrangement of Hungarian folk songs for voice and piano—which was published in 1932 in four volumes: I. Mourning songs, II. Dance songs, III. Diverse songs, and IV. Young people's songs. The last song in the work is a simple example of Bartókian polymodality, that is, the melody is in the D-Mixolydian folk mode, D-E-F♯-G-A-B-C♮ and the accompaniment is in D-Lydian, D-E-F♯-G♯-A-B-C♯ (Ex. 5.5).

In June, *Matica Slovenská* remitted the last royalty payment, and their representative, Miloš Ruppeldt, informed Bartók that the publisher would like to eliminate the songs of Hungarian origin. Bartók's response, dated 20 June, emphatically states that he is unable to leave out any part of the delivered material, as the recommended truncation would be an unscholarly procedure. And he refers Ruppeldt to the publisher's contract, in which there is a related clause concerning the author's rights: "—In a word, I must adhere strictly to this clause of the contract."[26]

Più allegro

Ex. 5.5. Bartók, Twenty Hungarian Folk Songs for Voice and Piano (1929), no. 20, mm. 29–34.

During May 1930, Bartók continued his transcription of Hungarian folk songs, arranging five of them for unaccompanied mixed chorus. Then, on 8 September, he completed the composition of his choral masterpiece, the *Cantata Profana,* for double mixed chorus, tenor and baritone solo, and orchestra. Bartók's original music is set to a *Colindă* folk text of pagan origin and is unrelated to the Romanian source melody (Ex. 5.6).[27]

Andante

4a. Cel un - cheş bă - trâ - nă   Cel-un - cheş bă - trâ - nă El - că - şi-o ďa - vu - tă

Ex. 5.6. *RFM*.iv., melody no. 12bb with text no. 4a.

Bartók's adaptation of the Romanian folk text maintains its basic six-syllable versification as well as in his English translation below. Another borrowing is the rhythm schema: 3/8 ♩ ♪ | ♪♩ | ♫ ♪ |, which is transformed in the Cantata as a "flattened" Hungarian dotted-rhythm pattern: 9/8 ♩ ♪ ♪♩ ♩ ♪ |. The text in the third movement provides a synopsis of the work:

Once upon a time there
Was an aged man, he
Had nine handsome boys.
Never has he taught them
Any handicraft, he
Taught them only how to
Hunt in forests dark.
There they roamed, hunted
All the year around, and
Changed into stags in
Forests dark and wild.
Never will their antlers

Enter gates and doors, but
Only woods and shrubs;
Never will their bodies
Wear a shirt and coat but
Only foliage;
Nevermore their feet will
Walk on houses' floors but
Only on the sward;
Nevermore their mouth will
Drink from cups and jugs but
From the clearest springs.

In 1933, Bartók published his observations on Romanian folk music, stating that—from the point of view of the musical aspects—the Christmas songs (*Colinde*) are the most important category of traditional rituals.

> We must not think of the *Colinde*, however, in terms of the religious Christmas carols of the West. First of all, the most important part of these texts—perhaps one-third of them—have no connection with Christmas. Instead of the Bethlehem legend we hear about a wonderful battle between the victorious hero and the—until then—unvanquished lion (or stag), we are told the story of the nine sons who—after hunting for so many years in the old forest—have changed into stags, or we listen to a marvellous tale about the sun who has asked in marriage the hand of his sister, the moon, and so on. Thus here are texts truly preserved from ancient, pagan times! One of the festivals of pagan peoples was that observed at the time of the winter solstice. Afterwards, by chance or design, the celebration of Christmas was established at the same time. It is not surprising that in the subconscious mind of the Christianized pagan peoples the two holidays have become as one. What is really miraculous is the fact that after so many hundreds of years the pagan texts have been able to survive undisturbed.[28]

At the time the composition of the *Cantata Profana* was undertaken, the calamitous, worldwide depression that had begun with the New York stock market crash in October 1929 impacted severely on the Hungarian economy. Nearly a third of the country's industrial workers lost their jobs and were without unemployment insurance. Even the educated classes were afflicted: university graduates were unable to find work, there were few job opportunities for engineers and teachers, and state employees suffered substantial cuts in salary. But of much greater significance was agrarian Hungary's reduction in foreign trade, which had been based on a large volume of agricultural exports and now was reduced to a minimum. Thousands of landed peasants farming small acreage were ruined, and over one million agricultural laborers and farmhands were impoverished, many of them to the point of near starvation. Their plight as well as the encroachment of fascism in Hungarian politics may have been the motivating factors that led to the creation of Bartók's highly expressionist choral work.

It is therefore thought-provoking that the orchestral introduction to Bartók's secular Cantata (Ex. 5.7) includes a quotation from the opening bars of Bach's *St. Matthew Passion* (Ex. 5.8), notwithstanding Bartók's professed atheism.[29] Apparently there is a symbolic significance on dramatic and musical levels: "the Bach thematic quotation, which elicits the crucifix and mankind's freedom from sin, may have been intended by Bartók to symbolize the magical transformation and ultimate freedom of the sons."[30]

The mentioned completion date includes the first draft—choral parts with Romanian text and condensed orchestral score—and the full score with Hungarian, Romanian, and German text. Later on, Bartók also worked on drafts of an English translation.[31]

Ex. 5.7. Bartók, *Cantata Profana,* mm. 10–13.

Ex. 5.8. Bach, *St. Matthew Passion,* mm. 1–2.

Preparation of the Cantata fair copy, however, was delayed for several years. In 1932, responding to a query from his friend Sándor Albrecht (1885–1958), Bartók indicates that:

> The choral and solo parts are very difficult but not the orchestral parts. However, it is not going to be published (or performed) for the time being, because I am planning to add to it 3 [*sic*] more pieces of similar length in such a way that, while they will be linked together by some connecting idea, it would be possible to perform each of three separately. It will be 1 year or 2 at least before I can see whether there is any likelihood of my achieving this.[32]

The "connecting idea" apparently was embedded in an allegorical poem that Bartók left unfinished, as expressed in the following lines:

> Three different worlds contended with each other
> Three different worlds, three different countries.
> The name of the one was the country of the sunrise,
> The name of the second was the country of the sunset,
> The name of the third was the country of the south.
> Then up spake the country, the first kind of country,
> The first kind of country, the country of the sunrise,
> "Finer than both of you, better than both of you,
> I am the loved one of the bright sun himself,
> The bright sun visits me before you,

Visits me before you, so dearly he loves me."
Then up spake the second, that fine and lovely country.
Fine and lovely country, country of the sunset.
"Finer than both of you, better than both of you,
I am the loved one of the bright sun himself,
The bright sun himself stays with me the longest,
Stays with me the longest, so dearly he loves me."
Then up spake the third, that fine and lovely country.
"Finer than both of you, better than both of you,
I am the loved one of the bright sun himself,
The bright sun himself smiles on me more warmly,
Smiles on me more warmly, so dearly he loves me."
Thus they contend, the fine and lovely countries,
The countries of the sunrise, the sunset and the south.[33]

During a September (1932) discussion with Universal Edition, when the publisher asked Bartók to hand over the Cantata for printing, the composer expressed his wish that the Cantata "only in *Hungary* should not be performed for the time being, because the text is created from Romanian folklore." Then, in his letter of 12 October, he states that:

Now times are uncertain to such an extent that one, so to speak, lives from one day to the next and actually does not know whether in the morning a world revolution, world war, or, in other respects, something wonderful has erupted, so I have decided not to wait for the conclusion of the remaining three parts of the Cantata but to give over to you the already completed part in question, according to your wish.[34]

Returning to other happenings in 1930, on 27 October Bartók received a request from the Romanian folklorist Octavian Beu for information about the composer and his works, which would be incorporated in a lecture on Bucharest Radio. After Bartók provided him with a detailed list of compositions, books, and studies in Romanian musical folklore, on 3 December Beu sent him a copy of the lecture for evaluation, in which he describes Bartók as a *compositorul român* (Romanian composer). At this time Bartók already had been described in Slovak reviews as a Slovak composer, because his concerts featured a number of his Slovak arrangements. In order to disabuse Beu of his similarly misguided notion, Bartók's letter of 10 January 1931 emphatically states his views that:

I consider myself a Hungarian composer. The fact that the melodies in some of my original compositions were inspired by or based on Romanian folk-songs is no justification for classing me as a *compositorul român*; such a label would have no more truth than the word "Hungarian" applied to Brahms, or Schubert, and is as inappropriate as if one were to speak of Debussy as a Spanish composer, because their works were inspired by themes of Hungarian or Spanish origin. In my opinion it would be better for you and other scholars to give up these labels and confine yourself to remarking that "here or there, in this or that composition, there are themes of Romanian inspiration". If your view were correct, I could just as easily be called a "Slovak composer"; and then I should be a composer of three nationalities! As I am being so frank, I should like to give you some idea of what I think about all this.

My creative work, just because it arises from 3 sources (Hungarian, Romanian, Slovakian), might be regarded as the embodiment of the very concept of integration so much emphasized in Hungary today. Of course I do not write this for you to make public; you will yourself beware of doing so, for such ideas are not for the Romanian press. I only mention it as a possible point of view which I encountered about 10 years ago, when I was attacked in the most violent manner by our chauvinists as a musical Scotus Viator. My own idea, however—of which I have been fully conscious since I found myself a composer—is the brotherhood of peoples, brotherhood in spite of all wars and conflicts.

I try—to the best of my ability—to serve this idea in my music; therefore I don't reject any influence, be it Slovakian, Romanian, Arabic or from any other source. The source must only be clean, fresh and healthy! Owing to my—let us say geographical—position it is the Hungarian source that is nearest to me, and therefore the Hungarian influence is the strongest. Whether my style—notwithstanding its various sources—has a Hungarian character or not (and that is the point)—is for other to judge, not for me. For my own part, I certainly feel that it has. For character and milieu must somehow harmonize with each other.[35]

From 19 January to 7 February Bartók made his first concert tour of Spain and Portugal. After his return to Budapest, he was summoned to the French embassy and awarded the Chevalier of the Legion of Honor in recognition of his impending fiftieth birthday. This was followed by a notice that he would be honored as one of the recipients of the Corvin Wreath, to be presented by Regent Horthy. Bartók, deeply offended by Hungarian cultural policies, deliberately absented himself from the gala festivities—the much-publicized attempt to stage *The Miraculous Mandarin* at the Opera House had been foiled by a number of factors, above all the efforts of the authorities to change the meaning and staging of the pantomime.[36] The only recognition of Bartók's anniversary was in the form of a newspaper tribute on 29 March:

> In Hungary today one showy celebration succeeds another. In such a country, who would want to honor Bartók in the same way? This spiritual giant is a solitary hermit among us. We must respect his seclusion and remain silent. And if we are permitted to say a few words we must not squander them in some anniversary greeting but rather try to interpret the significance of the silence which surrounds the fifty-year-old Bartók.
>
> That silence seems to tell us that it is not for us to honor an artist who achieved an honorable position without any assistance from us; that it is not for us to hasten with gifts to an artist whom we made no haste to accept the gifts he had to offer; that it is not for us to disturb the privacy of an artist whom we ourselves would have none of. We have no right to feel proud of an artist who was born among us but whom we did not accept as one of ourselves.

The time is not yet ripe for a Bartók celebration in Hungary. First we must work for this genius, then we can honor him. The bronze for his statue in the public square can be molded only by the fire of our devotion and understanding. If during his remarkable career as an artist we have allowed him to reach the age of fifty without fostering such feelings in our hearts, then let us set to work and in the next ten years repair all our omission. Until then every celebration is an act of hypocrisy. That is the significance of this silence.[37]

It was during 1931 that Bartók wrote a number of important essays on musical folklore, which were published in Hungary, Romania, Czechoslovakia, Austria, Germany, and the United States.[38] He also had the satisfaction of—at long last!—receiving copies of the English edition of *A magyar népdal* from Oxford University Press. In order to supplement his income, he made two orchestral transcriptions of previously published folk-music arrangements for piano. These were brought out by his Budapest publisher Rózsavölgyi, as Hungarian Sketches and Transylvanian Dances.

When in May Arturo Toscanini refused to conduct the Italian fascist anthem in Bologna and had been attacked and beaten in the street, Bartók, in behalf of the UMZE (New Hungarian Music Society) drafted a circular letter to all divisions of the ISCM, in which he urges them to support "the creation of a worldwide organization for the institutional protection of the freedom of art."[39] In July, following his 1930 election to the Committee of Intellectual Cooperation of the League of Nations, Bartók attended the first session in Geneva, as the sole appointee for music. He made two motions he believed would enable musicians to precisely interpret a composer's intention: (a) to publish a list of all authentic editions available to the public, in order to offset the plethora of annotated editions currently in vogue, and (b) to publish a list of facsimile editions currently available as well as provide financial assistance to museums for photocopying manuscripts of outstanding musical works.[40]

> We discussed many lofty motions there . . . but what I would like to say to those people is this: as long as one is unable to put the world in order economically and in other ways; so long as, for instance, currency restrictions make it difficult for even works of culture to pass the various frontiers, grandiose garrulity about "intellectual cooperation" is completely useless. Even if I said it, it would of course be in vain.[41]

In December 1930, while Bartók was in Freiburg for the performance of his First Piano Concerto, he met with Erich Doflein (1900–77), a German violin pedagogue, who had earlier asked the composer to transcribe pieces from *For Children* for violin duo, to serve as exercises in Doflein's forthcoming *Violin School*. Bartók said he would prefer to compose original pieces, and in May 1931 sent sixteen duos for advanced players. In response to Doflein's request that easier pieces were needed, including those for beginners, Bartók composed several batches during the next months, including pieces for beginning players,

Ex. 5.9. (a) *YFM*.i.(p. 459), "Zaplet" (Interweaving) dance melody, mm. 1–5, and (b) Bartók, Forty-four Duos for Two Violins (1931), mm. 1–5.

until forty-four duos had been received by Doflein in September.[42] With the exception of two original pieces, the duos consist of arrangements of vocal and instrumental melodies in Bartók's collections of Arab, Hungarian, Romanian, Ruthenian, Serbian, and Slovak folk music. The only Serbian piece (Ex. 5.9b) was arranged from the source melody (Ex. 5.9a) that Bartók collected in March 1912, from a village *tambura* player in the Banat region (now Romanian territory).[43]

Bartók had a frustrating experience following the Geneva conference. He had previously accepted a position to teach at the Mondsee Austro-American Conservatory of Music, from 10 July to 26 August:

> It is a very queer setup here at the Mondsee Conservatory. Only 2 pupils registered, instead of the minimum of 8. From sheer necessity, [the assistant school organizer] Mrs. Carter "enrolled" a few days later for the piano faculty!!); so did [the school organizer] Mrs. Peeples (for composition, but after a few lessons she switched over to the piano!); I was left wondering when Mr. Kienzl would "enrol" for "atonal composition" or some such thing. As for me, I am giving 8 lessons to these 4 pupils, of course; how they will settle the financial side of the problem between themselves is none of my business. . . . The whole thing doesn't make sense! Which, by the way, I suspected before I came.[44]

Bartók's return to Hungary at the end of August was coincidental with the resignation of the prime minister, Count István Bethlen (1874–1947), on the 24th. Growing dissatisfaction under the impact of the economic crisis led to Bethlen's ouster and was followed by austerity measures that failed to improve the financial situation. Bartók himself had no concert engagements until the relatively few appearances during the first half of 1931. On the other hand, he was able to devote his time and energy to the Second Piano Concerto—which he had begun in October 1930—and complete the work during September and October. The first two movements have an unusual instrumentation, where the first movement is for the most part limited to the piano and woodwinds, and the second movement—a ternary Adagio-Presto-Adagio form—is restricted to the piano and strings in the slower tempi.

> I wrote my First Concerto for Piano and Orchestra in 1926. I consider it a success-ful work although its writing is a bit difficult—one might say very difficult!—as much for orchestra as for audience. That is why some years later (1930–1931), while writing my Second Concerto, I wanted to produce a piece which would contrast with the first: a work which would be less bristling with difficulties for the orchestra and whose thematic material would be more pleasing. This intention explains the rather light and popular character of most of the themes of my latest concerto: a lightness that sometimes almost reminds me of one of my youthful works, the First Suite for Orchestra, op. 3 (1905).[45]

The second unfortunate incident in Bartók's dealings with the *Matica Slov-enská* (hereafter: *Matica*) began on 30 March 1930, when their editor indicated that preparation for publication had started and requested the name and specific location of the Slovak villages where the melodies had been collected. Bartók's enthusiastic response the next month included hand-drawn maps and a request for a specimen proof page before printing the book. But he was unaware that the publisher intended to transform the dialectal peasant texts into their proper liter-ary form, in accordance with their previous folk-song publications, and that the respective village priests and school teachers would be consulted and editorial emendations entered directly in Bartók's manuscript.[46]

It was not until a year later that he felt constrained to repeat his request for a specimen proof of the music and ask when it would be forthcoming. His request was met in June, and on the 19th, Bartók returned it with his corrections and asked for a second proof as well as first proofs of additional pages.[47] These were enclosed with several typescript pages of the texts, which had been prepared by the editor as a proposal for publishing the texts in a separate volume. On 8 August, Bartók responded that:

> I am pleased to hear your plan to publish the texts separately from their melodies. In that way, the texts also could be grouped according to their content; the separa-tion is justified scientifically only by such a presentation. . . . but every text must be provided with the number to which it belongs. . . . The texts marked with the exact numbers of melodies should be sent to me, I will group them according to their content and send them back (ballads, soldiers' songs, humorous, etc. and unclassifiable songs).[48]

It was not until 6 January 1932 that Bartók's concert career resumed with a performance on Budapest Radio of his Baroque transcriptions and Beethoven's Sonata op. 109. He was in Paris on 21 February as soloist in the First Piano

Concerto, with the Paris Symphony Orchestra conducted by Nicholas Slonimsky, and in Glasgow on the 29th for an all-Bartók program of his piano, vocal, and violin pieces. And on 4 March he played the Rhapsody op. 1 as part of an all-Bartók radio broadcast with the BBC Orchestra, Henry Wood conducting. On the 11th he set out for Cairo as a participant in the Congress for Arab Music, where he joined the section on recordings.

> The function of this section not only consisted of advising the Institute for Orien-
> tal Music on the making of phonograph or gramophone recordings and establish-
> ing a phonogram shop, but also to audition Arab musicians. In the latter case we
> were to select from the performed music the material seemingly best suited for the
> planned, on the spot gramophone recordings. (The musicians were brought from
> different Arabic territories by the Egyptian Government.) Since we dealt with the
> kinds of Arabic music still living, rather than with abstract or theoretical questions
> concerning it, a consequence of our activity was a much closer contact with Ara-
> bic life than had our colleagues in other sections.[49]

In May, Bartók moved his family to a house on Csalán út (Nettle street; now preserved as the national Bartók shrine), thus requiring a change in schools for his eight-year-old son Péter. Bartók had been dissatisfied with the instruction previously given in the mandatory singing classes; he therefore arranged with the school authorities to have Péter excused from such classes; the father would personally attend to his son's music education. Bartók apparently was motivated for this pedagogical undertaking by his work on the violin duos as well as the 1913 *Zongora Iskola* (Piano School) publication. In October, when Universal Edition asked him to write some very easy piano pieces, he replied that:

> It coincides very well with my own plans that you are just now asking for some
> very easy piano pieces from me: during this past summer I wrote several—about
> 35—beginning with the easiest (like the pieces that Rózsavölgyi published in the
> "First Term") and progressing in difficulty. But because I have a many-sided project
> in mind, it will be a long time before I can complete it.[50]

The project, designated by Bartók as *Mikrokosmos* (Little world) for Piano, was completed in 1939. The "many sides" can be construed as (a) pieces for beginners, advanced students, and concert artists, (b) piano technique and musicianship, (c) music theory, (d) folk music arrangements, and (e) Bartók's principles of composition.[51]

Turning next to the publication status of Bartók's Romanian *colinde* book, another two years had elapsed since he discussed matters with Oxford University Press in London. At that time (1928) the publisher stated that the English translation of the texts had begun the year before. Bartók was troubled by the delay and lack of communication, and he decided to address the problem by suggesting a collaboration with the Academia Română or another Bucharest publisher for the parallel production of English and Romanian editions. On 2

July 1930, therefore, he again contacted his Romanian colleague, Constantin Brăiloiu (1893–1958) for assistance with cooperative production problems as well as correction of orthographic and other errors in "the texts I am setting to the music."[52] On 16 February 1931, the fifth year of his unsatisfactory dealings with Oxford, he demanded the immediate return of his manuscript: "When—after a certain time (in five, ten or twenty years)—you will be ready to publish it, you may get it from me once more, but—for the moment—I must have it at my disposal." Instead of the manuscript, Bartók received a penciled draft of half the translated texts, which was followed by Oxford's letter in May, approving collaboration with a Romanian publisher and asking for another copy of part of the manuscript—including the music examples—which had been lost by the publisher's staff. Somewhat encouraged yet concerned by the careless handling of his work, Bartók's response of 31 May outlines the steps that could be taken for production of the music examples and the Romanian texts from the Bucharest copy of the manuscript.[53] He was not aware that the partial draft of the English texts had been prepared in 1927 by a Mr. Rothchild, who died before the work was completed, and that for some reason the publisher deferred the appointment of another translator.[54]

Because of economic conditions, Brăiloiu was unable to find a Bucharest publisher for the Romanian edition, and Bartók decided to investigate the possibilities for self-publication, including the production of a holographic fair copy of the music examples. On 11 January 1932, Bartók wrote to Universal Edition about the costs involved and the feasibility of heliographic printing of music notation.[55] In addition to the *colinde* melodies, Bartók decided to undertake the production of fair copy of his vast Romanian folk music collection, including revision of the Bihor County melodies published by the Academia Română in 1913.

The indefatigable Bartók next pursued the *Matica,* his delinquent Slovak publisher, because there had been no communication since the preceding August. On 15 June, therefore, a week prior to the contractual deadline for publication of his Slovak folk-music collection, his letter to Sándor Albrecht describes his future course of action:

> I ask your help in a somewhat unusual matter. It concerns the following:
> Many years ago I sold the manuscript of my Slovakian collection to Matica Slovenská. They are obliged to publish it by June 22 this year, otherwise I have the right to buy back the manuscript from them, that is, they are obliged to return the manuscript to me if I return to them the original price, almost 10,000 č.k [Czech crowns: about $400].
> I need someone whom I could authorize to execute this transaction and I would ask you for this task. The procedure would be like this:
> The Sl.M. sends you (or its representative living in Pozsony) the manuscript; you make sure that it is complete (I would send you detailed information concerning this later) and you inform me about it. Then I would write to one of my friends to send you the money. If you get the money, the transaction could take place.—If

you could undertake this task, I should know when you are not in Pozsony, lest the manuscript would arrive there at that time.

Of course, I have to be prepared for the SL.M. raising difficulties or simply ignoring completely my demand. In that case, I would need a lawyer. Could you recommend somone?[56]

On 22 June, Bartók sent a registered letter to the *Matica*, in which the detailed instructions given to Albrecht are repeated. Having had no response, he sent another letter with the same instructions on 22 July, with a postscript stating that: "Should I not receive an answer to this letter by 22 August, I will be forced to take the necessary legal steps to obtain what is due me."[57] The *Matica*, meanwhile, perhaps because they were opposed to editor Ján Valašťan-Dolinský's suggestion for a fourth volume of texts, replaced him with Ivan Ballo, Slovak music critic, as the third in the series of editors.[58] Unfortunately, Ballo unnecessarily wasted much time in preparing new instructions for the printer, notwithstanding that Bartók had already furnished a detailed list as an addendum to the manuscript, and he requested a fee of 40,000 Czech crowns, approximately four times the amount Bartók received as full payment for creating the entire work. The *Matica* refused to pay such a large sum for Ballo's editorial work, demanded the immediate return of the manuscript, and, for whatever reason, decided not to inform Bartók of these events.[59]

Bartók's threat of a lawsuit prompted *Matica*'s reply, on 4 August, that the first part of the work was in press, the other parts would also go to the printer, and—because of the serious illness of one of their colleagues—they apologized for not responding sooner. Bartók therefore granted a temporary postponement of his demand, providing that he received proofs before the end of the month.

Unfortunately, Bartók was stricken with influenza for five weeks, with further complications from bronchitis. It was not until October that he was able to press on with his negotiations, albeit reluctantly, with what he now referred to as "the ugly *Matica* case," which was further confused by complaining letters from Ballo about the publisher's failure to pay his fee. Later in the fall, when Bartók tried to intercede in Ballo's behalf, the *Matica* advised Bartók that editorial fees were not negotiable. He therefore offered to edit the complete manuscript himself if the publisher would provide a Slovak linguist, familiar with various peasant dialects, to edit the texts, as well as a qualified musician to correct the unsatisfactory German translations of the Introduction and Notes to the Melodies. While the *Matica* agreed to this new proposal, they failed to inform Bartók that litigation had commenced against Ballo for recovery of the manuscript.[60]

Even though Bartók had been bedridden during his illness, he was nevertheless able to complete the classification of his Romanian material and begin the study of the available published collections of Serbo-Croatian folk music. His peace of mind was further disturbed by the political events during this period, as the continued deterioration of the Hungarian economy and the ensuing increase in social tensions led to Horthy's appointment of Gyula Gömbös, the minister of defense, as prime minister on 1 October. Gömbös, a notorious demagogue and anti-Semite, attempted to introduce a total fascist dictatorship by means of internal espionage, censorship of correspondence, and wiretapping.[61]

In November, Bartók arranged six Transylvanian-Hungarian folk songs for male chorus (*Székely dalok*), of which three pieces were published in 1933 by the Swiss Workers Choral Society. He was awarded the Romanian "Meritul Cultural" Order of the Knight's Cross on 3 December, and on the 13th, fully recovered from his illness, he played Bach, Mendelssohn, and Schubert works on Budapest Radio. He appeared as soloist in his Second Piano Concerto in Frankfurt on 23 January 1933, Hans Rosbaud conducting the Frankfurt Radio Symphony Orchestra, an event which marked his last appearance as a concert artist in Germany. Bartók's only Budapest performance that year was a recital of piano pieces (Kodály, Brahms, and Beethoven) on Budapest Radio. His refusal to perform his own works in Budapest was emphasized when Louis Kentner appeared as the soloist in Bartók's Second Piano Concerto at the Vigadó Hall (Otto Klemperer conducting the Budapest Concert Orchestra) on 2 June, and the same orchestra, with Bartók at the piano, repeated the work at the Vienna Musikvereinsaal on the 7th.[62] His other performances of the work were in Strasbourg on 9 August, and in London (Adrian Boult conducting) on 8 November. On 2 November, in Glasgow, he gave a recital of his own works, his transcriptions of Baroque keyboard music, a Beethoven sonata, and Kodály pieces. And in December, a similar program was presented in the Transylvanian towns of Oradea (formerly Nagyvárad) and Cluj-Napoca (Kolozsvár).

Another, equally important part of Bartók's public life in the 1930s was such scholarly activities as ethnomusicological and musicological lectures and essays on folk music, his compositions, and works of other composers. His papers were read at international meetings of scholarly societies and on radio stations, and subsequently published in a number of languages.[63] In connection with the mentioned Swiss publication of three pieces from his choral work *Székely dalok*, Bartók prepared essays on Hungarian and Romanian folk music for the *Schweizerische Sängerzeitung*.[64] Among Bartók's outstanding achievements in comparative musicology is his treatise *Népzenénk és a szomszéd népek népzenéje* (Hungarian folk music and the folk music of neighboring peoples), which he quoted on Budapest Radio on 21 November and again on 15 January 1934.[65]

An interesting sidelight of Bartók's piano recitals was his approach to programming his compositions according to venue. He preferred to feature his folk-music transcriptions in Hungarian provincial towns such as Békéscsaba, where the local impresario had requested original pieces for the 15 February Bartók Festival concert. Bartók responded that, "I am a bit surprised by what you write regarding the program: we agreed at the time, that it was to be a *Hungarian-Slovak* evening." Bartok's objection was based on the fact that Békéscsaba was mainly Slovakian and that his program emphasized that the concert was for that national minority.[66]

When Bartók decided to undertake the preparation of his Romanian folk music collection for publication, beginning in 1932, he discovered that:

> my transcriptions of the records were not sufficiently exact. This meant the revision of all the old notations and even the making of new transcriptions of some of the recorded melodies. In addition, the systematic grouping of the whole material had to be done and, finally, master sheets of the complete musical part had to be prepared.
>
> Had I attended to these three stages of the work in succession, as they should have been done, I could not have completed the work till today. But, since 1933, I saw that there was no time to lose, that it was uncertain as to how long this work could be pursued if at all in Europe. Therefore, the three types of work had to be started at the same time parallel to each other.[67]

Fortuitously, in 1934 the Hungarian Academy of Sciences was authorized to publish the Hungarian folk melodies collected by Bartók, Kodály, and other folklorists. Bartók was granted a leave of absence from his teaching duties and transferred to the Academy's folk-music section as head of the newly-organized publication subcommittee. Beginning in September, Bartók usually worked every other day on transcription of phonograph recordings or editing the notations prepared by his assistants.[68] The new, flexible schedule provided the freedom for completing the studies of his Romanian collection, particularly the research related to his earlier hypothesis that certain melodies contain elements borrowed from Bulgarian or Yugoslav folk-music sources.[69] He eventually found that a small percentage of Romanian dance tunes are in so-called Bulgarian rhythm, that is, asymmetrical patterns such as 7/16, which are derived from symmetrical 2/4 time (Ex. 5.10).[70]

Ex. 5.10. Bartók, *RFM*.i, (a) variant melody no. 243dd in 2/4, mm. 5–8, and (b) no. 243ee in 7/16, mm. 5–8.

Bartók was indeed surprised when on 5 June a telegram arrived from the Library of Congress, Washington, D.C., with a proposal for a string quartet, which he accepted by return wire.[71] Two months later he began composing the Fifth String Quartet and completed its five movements on 6 September.[72] The third movement, a ternary Scherzo and Trio, is cast in Bulgarian rhythm, beginning with the first theme in 4+2+3 time (Ex. 5.11).[73]

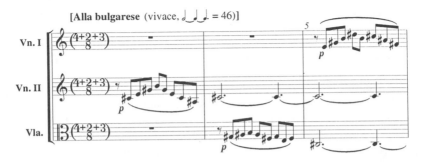

Ex. 5.11. Bartók, String Quartet no. 5 (1934), third movement, mm. 3–5.

The arching melodic contours consist of disjunct intervals, and the sectional repetitions are isorhythmic structures, that is, each one consists of 4+2+3 eighths. In 1910, the second year of his field trips in Transylvania, Bartók collected a Romanian instrumental melody whose quick tempo and additive schema prompted him to later revise it in 4+2+3/16 Bulgarian rhythm (Ex. 5.12).

Ex. 5.12. Bartók, *RFM*.i, no. 272, mm. 1–4.

Similarity in contour and additive rhythm mark the folk tune as a possible structural source for the Scherzo theme. While the contour of the Romanian melody also describes an arch, its intervals are conjunct, and the quaternary sectional arrangement (not shown) is isorhythmic for the first half of the melody but heterorhythmic (that is, rearrangement or substitution of values) in the last two sections.

The brief correspondence between Bartók and Oxford University Press toward the end of the year, in which Bartók stated that the unsatisfactory English translations of the Romanian *colinde* texts had to be redone, led the unwilling publisher to cancel the contract and return the manuscript. In January, Bartók decided that he would underwrite the publishing costs of the musical part of the book and thereafter deposit typescript copies of the Romanian texts in several European university libraries for interested readers.

Ultimately, Bartók had the fifty pages of the introduction, the title page, and the other nonmusical parts printed in Hungary, while the printing of the music and the binding was done in Vienna. He personally carried the Hungarian printer's contribution to the Austrian printer. His own German translation of the nonmusical sections was double-checked by Mrs. Müller-Widmann, his trusted friend in Basel, Switzerland. He conducted a long correspondence about the quality of paper to be used, its price, etc. He personally sponsored a private subscription campaign, had twenty copies sent to friends, and had prospectuses printed in Vienna.[74]

For many years Zoltán Kodály had been encouraging Bartók to write choral music, to the point where the latter took up the study of Palestrina's works.[75] Perhaps Kodály's successful results in composing choral pieces for school children and arranging for their performance in public concerts was the stimulus Bartók needed to turn to similar choral writing. During 1935, he composed Twenty-seven Choruses, for two- or three-part children's or women's unaccompanied chorus, based on Hungarian folk poetry. After the premiere of his children's choruses on 7 May 1937, Bartók reported that:

> It was a great experience for me when—at the rehearsal—I heard for the first time my little choruses coming from the lips of these children. I shall never forget this impression of the freshness and gaiety of the little ones' voice. There is something in the natural way these children from the suburban schools produce their voices, that reminds one of the unspoiled sound of peasant singing.[76]

It is also interesting to note Bartók's response to a request by the editor of *Magyar kórus* (Budapest), shortly before his emigration to the United States in October 1940: "I do not think that I can write a preface and annotations; for one thing, I haven't time, and apart from that, I wouldn't know what to write about or what to explain."[77] While a number of the children's choruses are fairly accessible with regard to technical difficulty and tessitura, all of them are stamped with Bartók's unique tonal language in which the folk modes, their transposition, and their chromatic alteration are predominant—hence the editor's felt need for the composer's input. As a case in point, the first verse of *Huszárnóta* (Hussar song) is in G major and the second verse in the G-Lydian folk mode (Ex. 5.13).

Ex. 5.13. Bartók, Twenty-Seven Choruses (1935), *Huszárnóta*, mm. 1–6.

Bartók followed the Twenty-seven Choruses with the composition of *From Olden Times* (1935), three choruses for unaccompanied men's voices, based on the transformation of texts from old folk songs and art songs. The first piece opens with "None more miserable than the peasant," in the dirge-like E-Phrygian folk mode (Ex. 5.14, mm. 3–5). The same verse is repeated in the second melody-section (mm. 6–8), in D-Dorian. The next verse, "For his poverty is bigger than the sea!," is emphatically rendered in the third section by the contrasting C-Lydian folk mode (mm. 8–12).[78]

(Parlando)

Ex. 5.14. Bartók, *From Olden Times* (1935), three choruses for unaccompanied men's voices, no. 1, mm. 3–12.

On 1 December, László Rásonyi, a Hungarian-born philologist and professor at the newly founded University of Ankara, wrote a letter to Bartók, in which he inquired whether Bartók would be interested in undertaking a visit to Ankara for lecture purposes. The local Halkevi, aware of Bartók's stature as artist and scholar and wishing to avoid one-sided German orientation, wanted Bartók to address three questions: "(1) The connection between Hungarian and Turkish music (the ancient pentatonic music); (2) The development of Hungarian music and its current state (how its modern music is in connection with folk music); and (3) How could a national Turkish music develop?"[79] Bartók's affirmative, lengthy response, dated 18 December, included the suggestion for a field trip to collect village music in the Ankara vicinity as well as a request for published Turkish folk music collections and a visit to the Istanbul music folklore center: "because I shall only be able to give useful hints after having been informed what was done till now and what was neglected."[80]

Ten days later the conservative Kisfaludy Literary Society announced its 1935 sestennial awards in the Budapest papers, and Bartók was infuriated when he read that he had been awarded the music prize (a Greguss Medal) for his Suite no. 1, op. 3, for Large Orchestra (1905). His rejective letter underscores the erroneous reason for the award, namely, that the first performance of the work was given in its entirety in 1929.

> But even if the above-mentioned statement were true—which it is not—the award itself cannot be justified. I am, it is true, very fond of that particular work of mine—it was in fact an outstanding achievement for a young man of 24. Nevertheless, in the period between 1919 and 1934, numerous works of greater merit and maturity were performed in Hungary, for instance [Kodály's] *The Spinning Room* or the *Dances of Galanta*. . . .

And lastly I take the liberty of declaring that I do not wish to accept the Greguss Medal, neither now, nor in the future, nor during my lifetime, nor after my death.[81]

On 3 February 1936, The Budapest Academy of Science awarded Bartók a chair as a working member, in recognition of his scholarly achievements in musical folklore since 1906. In his inaugural address, "Liszt Problems," Bartók considered the following four questions:

1. The response of the general public to Liszt's compositions. Audiences preferred the less significant ones, such as the rhapsodies, because they were unduly influenced by superficial elements and lacked the capacity to see what was really essential in Liszt's important works.

2. The impact of Liszt's works on the further development of music as an art. Much of Liszt's invention indicated possible developments which he himself failed to exploit, and which were only fully utilized by his successors. In this respect, his œuvre was more important than Wagner's.

3. The erroneous statement in Liszt's famous book on Gypsy music, that what the Gypsies in Hungary play, as well as Hungarian peasant music itself, is of Gypsy origin. Liszt is not wholly to blame for his conviction: nobody then had any idea that the study of problems in the domain of folklore research required hard work, scientific methods, and the collection of facts from the widest possible firsthand experience in some of the thousands of Hungarian villages.

4. The justification for regarding Liszt as a Hungarian. Here it was Liszt's own attitude which was decisive. Although he did not know the Hungarian language, he was born on then Hungarian territory and on countless occasions called himself Hungarian. Everyone, Hungarian or not, should know of this and let the matter rest at that.[82]

In April, Bartók received an official invitation from the Ankara Halkevi to visit in May and lecture on the methods for the study of folk music in general and the principal elements of his methodology in particular. In view of his forthcoming concert performances and a suggested five-point program for Ankara—three lectures, a performance with orchestra, collecting Turkish folk music, and discussions on future tasks—he asked for a postponement until October.[83] Fortuitously, he had prepared a lecture, "Why and how do we collect folk music?", for Budapest Radio the preceding December, which was published in Budapest and Ankara in 1936.[84]

Bartók purchased a recently published Turkish primer for the second grade, which he annotated in Hungarian and French with Rásonyi's help. The latter, who was visiting Hungary during the summer, also assisted Bartók with the translation of a volume of Turkish folk texts that had been published by the Hungarian Academy of Sciences in 1889. He found many difficulties in his study of the Turkish language, particularly "the twisted sentences, contracting into one sentence what is expressed in other languages by ten. Fortunately, this rarely occurs in the texts of the folk songs."[85]

On 23 June, Paul Sacher, founder and conductor of the Basel Chamber Orchestra, offered Bartók a commission "to write for the Basel chamber orchestra a piece for strings alone or with some other orchestral instruments." Bartók's response on the 27th indicated that he was thinking of a work for strings and percussion instruments—piano, celesta, harp, xylophone, and percussion—and he hoped that this would not cause any difficulties.[86] The score of Music for Strings, Percussion, and Celesta, completed on 7 September, is a masterpiece of musical structure. The first movement is a strict fugue based on a four-section chromatic subject. The second movement, in sonata form, illustrates the diatonic expansion of the subject "to such a degree that its relation to the original, non-extended form will be scarcely recognizable."[87] The third movement, in rondo form, is an orchestral realization of the "Night's music" that made its first appearance in *Musique Nocturnes* from Bartók's *Out-of-Doors* for Piano. And the fourth movement, a rondo-like suite of folk dances, again quotes the fugue subject in diatonic expansion, but here its relationship is readily apparent.

Bartók's visit to Turkey began with his arrival in Istanbul on 2 November. His week-long stay gave him the opportunity to listen to the sixty-five records, produced by commercial companies, of mostly peasant performers who had been brought to Istanbul. He found that, among other deficiencies, the performers were itinerant musicians who could not be authentic sources of village music, and neither the texts nor the melodies had been transcribed. The next week he was in Ankara for his concert and three lectures, but illness prevented him from undertaking the planned field trip until his recovery ten days before his scheduled return to Budapest.[88]

> His companions were the composer A. Adnan Saygun, whose task was the collecting of data from the performers as well as the jotting down of the texts, and two composition teachers from the Ankara Conservatory of Music, who were to witness how musical folklore is collected on the spot.
>
> Having been warned by his Turkish escorts that it would be necessary to fraternize with the peasants for weeks before they finally would be induced to sing, Bartók set out with mixed feelings.[89]

In the event peasants were met who were intimidated by Bartók's presence, Saygun would explain that Bartók was only a descendant of Turks who had settled in Hungary, and that his accent had become more or less different. Then Bartók would repeat a contrived sentence in Turkish, whose English translation is: "In the cotton field are much barley and many apples, camels, tents, axes, boots, and young goats." The Turkish sentence was constructed with words that would be almost the same in Hungarian:[90]

> Hung.: *Pamuk tarlón sok árpa, alma, teve, sátor, balta, csizma, kicsi kecske van.*
> Turkish: *Pamuk tarlasinda çok arpa alma, deve, çadir, balta, çizme, küçük var.*

Nevertheless, Bartók was considerably handicapped by his inability to talk to the peasants directly or get them to sing together. The greatest shortcoming was his failure to record songs performed by women: Moslem women did not sing in public.[91]

While Bartók was in Ankara, the *Cantata Profana* received its first performance in Budapest on 9 November—six years after it had been completed. The second performance was given a month later at the Vigadó Hall, at an all-Bartók evening sponsored by the Budapest Education Committee. Finally, after an absence of many years, the composer agreed to participate in the program, as pianist in the Rhapsody op. 1. One critic concluded that: "It is now clear that Bartók's work arouses so much interest that there is no difficulty in filling every seat in the Vigadó."[92]

On 17 January 1937 Bartók's provocative lecture, "Mechanical Music," was given at the Budapest Academy of Music. He defined the term "as a music in whose creation not only the human body but also some kind of machine is involved."[93] He explored various types of music machines, such as the player piano, gramophone records, radio broadcasts, and films (motion pictures), and compared their output with live music if at some future "the reproduced music will necessarily be exactly the same as the live music which has been recorded."

> But even in that case there will be an irreplaceable superiority, for which there is no substitute, of the live music over the stored, canned music. This substitute is the variability of live music. That which lives changes from moment to moment; music recorded by machines hardens into something stationary. It is a well-known fact that our notation records on music paper, more or less inadequately, the idea of the composer; hence the existence of contrivances with which one can record precisely every intention and idea of the composer is indeed of great importance. On the other hand, the composer himself, when he is the performer of his own composition, does not always perform his work in exactly the same way. Why? Because he lives; because perpetual variability is a trait of every living creature's character. Therefore, even if one succeeded in perfectly preserving with a perfect process a composer's works according to his own idea at a given moment, it would not be advisable to listen to these compositions perpetually like that. Because it would cover the composition with boredom. Because it is conceivable that the composer himself would have performed his compositions better or less well at some other time—but in any case, otherwise.[94]

A concert of Bartók works, performed by the composer and Zoltán Székely, was given on 9 February at the Cowdray Hall in London. The feature of the evening was the premiere performance of twenty-seven pieces from the *Mikrokosmos* for Piano (published in 1940).[95] The London press responded with such colorful tidbits as: "Percussive steps to an Hungarian Parnassus"; "the piano pieces are science, as interesting no doubt to write (and, for those who can, to solve) as chronograms and palindromes, and as devoid of musical vitamins"; and "If for children, then these pieces must be for an iron age."[96]

During the preceding August, Székely wrote a letter to Bartók with the proposal that he compose a concerto for him. Two months later, Bartók responded that it "is certainly feasible. You do know, however, that I can only work on such things during the summer, thus you couldn't expect the manuscript before the end of September 1937. . . . We might meet at the end of January and finalize the matter."[97] Prior to the meeting, however, Bartók was in Basel on the 21st, for the premiere of Music for Strings, Percussion, and Celesta: "The performance was a triumph for the musicians and the composer; the last movement had to be repeated. . . . The quite unusual success of this first performance motivated my friends and myself to ask Béla Bartók for a chamber music work for the Basel section of the I.S.C.M.[98]

In the weeks following, Bartók's concerts included Hilversum (2), Paris, Brussels, and London (2); Zoltán Székely participated in several programs; and Bartók also gave a lecture on folk music at the Amsterdam Conservatory of Music.[99] During this time, Bartók and Székely took up the matter of the latter's previous request for a concerto, in which the composer pressed for a work in variation form. Székely, however, insisted on the traditional violin concerto, whereupon Bartók yielded and requested Székely to draft the letter of agreement. On 17 March, Bartók's letter to him states: "You also didn't do anything concerning the Violin Concerto!!" This memorandum apparently led to negotiations beginning in April, including Universal Edition, that continued to mid-September.[100]

In mid-May, Bartók completed the major part of his transcriptions of his Turkish folk music collection and initiated steps to obtain a joint Turkish-Hungarian publication.[101] On the 29th, he wrote to Paul Sacher about the proposed Basel commission, stating that:

> In principle I would agree to the matter, but first, the deadline seems to me to be a bit too close, second, I cannot commit myself completely, i.e. I could accept only with reservations; the performance would depend on how much time I have available for work this summer. That means a sure acceptance on my part could only be expected at the beginning of September. What kind of chamber music could it be? How about, for instance, a quartet for 2 pianos and 2 percussion groups"? Or a piano trio? Is a piece for voice and piano considered chamber music or not?[102]

Bartók's July vacation was spent in Carinthia, where he began work on the Basel commission and the comparative study of the Turkish material received from A. Adnan Saygun. On the 7th, he mailed his critique of the shortfalls in the Turk's transcription technique, including suggestions for improvement, and pointed to problems in the submitted French translations.[103] Székely visited him toward the end of the next month and was delighted when: "he showed me the first two pages of the violin part of the Violin Concerto beautifully written out, but the piano reduction was nothing yet, just a few notes. I played and he accompanied me at the piano from his sketch, so that much was ready at that time. The conception was fixed as it would be, as it came out later, and that seems a very remarkable thing, since the work was only finished a year later."[104]

On 2 September, Bartók informed Sacher that the "complete work—my choice is the quartet for 2 pianos and 2 percussion groups—is almost finished. which means you can count on it."[105] And on the 14th, subsequent to the request of the Secretary General of the Hungarian Academy of Sciences, Bartók submitted a report on the status of the work being done on the comprehensive collection of Hungarian folk songs:

> We have been engaged in preparing these for the press since September, 1934. During this time I have revised the transcriptions of all the phonograph cylinders, 1,026 in number. Meanwhile, Kodály has selected all relevant material from what is already in print. We have copied and partially systematized the song material—necessary for purposes of comparison—of the neighboring peoples of Hungary (Bulgarians, Serbo-Croatians, Slovaks, Poles, Ukrainians).

The report concludes with an estimate of another three years to have all the material—approximately 12,000 songs—ready for the printers. Further, Bartók calls attention to the separate task of comparison with the German material "which can only be accomplished in the folk song archives in Berlin."[106] On the 23rd, his letter to Hungarian Radio forbade the transmission of his piano recitals over the German and Italian broadcasting systems. This brought a personal attack by the Hungarian press, to the point where, on 10 October, he felt obliged to make the following statement for publication:

> The reason for my decision is simply that I have never performed either for the Italian Radio or for that of the Third Reich, and indeed, I have never been directly invited to do so by either of those two countries. In the circumstances, I do not consider it right that they should be allowed to transmit performances I gave for the Budapest Radio, just like that, as a free gift.[107]

For the past several years the main objective of Hungarian foreign policy was the revision of the Versailles Peace Treaty. The government's aspirations were strengthened when Britain's policy of appeasement, implemented by Neville Chamberlain after he became prime minister in May 1937, attempted to secure peace with Germany and Italy, at the expense of considerable concessions. Concluding that the Western Powers would not oppose cooperation with Germany, a pro-German policy was initiated, which not only led to a Nazi-type Arrow-Cross movement and the so-called first anti-Jewish law but, in November, to participation in Hitler's scheme of aggression aimed at the dismemberment of Czechoslovakia.[108]

Earlier in the year, when the members of the New Hungarian String Quartet decided to reorganize, Zoltán Székely was invited to take over the leadership as first violinist (Sándor Végh moved to second violin, and Dénes Koromzay and Vilmos Palotai remained as violist and cellist, respectively). He agreed to the proposal on the condition that the other musicians also take up residence in Holland. Koromzay recalls that:

We were all unmarried and free, and moving to Holland wasn't too bad an idea . . . The political winds were not exactly blowing our way in Hungary. In fact, the quartet was very badly located if we wanted to play concerts, because Germany was completely out of the question with a total Nazi regime, and Naziism was spreading in Hungary too. . . . . Later Bartók certainly *had* to leave Hungary. We didn't have to leave. Bartók was one of the most direct and outspoken men in the world, and he made such strong anti-Nazi statements that he would have been the first to be picked up by the Gestapo when they came, or even by the Hungarian Nazis when they eventually came into power.[109]

Bartók's 1938 concert tour began on 16 January, when he and his wife were the pianists in the Basel I.S.C.M. premiere of the Sonata for Two Pianos and Percussion. During the next two weeks, he gave performances in Holland, London, Brussels, and Luxembourg, and while he was en route to Budapest on the 31st, he wrote to Sándor Albrecht that:

> I didn't even have time to do anything in that Sl.Mat. [*Matica Slovenská*] affair.— It has occurred to meanwhile that I could, perhaps, have my entire Slovak collection copied in Budapest from the rough draft, and that would hardly cost more than buying back the whole manuscript. But first I would have to take a good look at that rough draft at home and see if it wasn't a bit too rough! If I decide this will be the solution, then you would have collected the [repurchase monies] all for nothing; and then we would have to think about ways and means of getting them to me. One way is a trouble, the other way is a trouble—and I have hundreds of other troubles as well; if I had not turned grey years ago, I would certainly do so now. . . . I'll have a look at that rough draft as soon as I get home . . . and then I'll write to you again.[110]

Bartók's worst fears were realized when, on 13 March, the annexation of Austria by Germany was quickly followed by positioning of German troops on the western borders of Hungary and Bohemia. In Vienna, the owners and editors of Universal Edition lost control of their publishing house, and the A.K.M. (performing rights organization) was likewise Nazified. These seizures signaled an end to Bartók's royalty income as well as future publication opportunities in occupied Europe.[111]

In 1933, Boosey & Hawkes (London) became agents for Universal Edition. This association gave the Publisher, Ralph Hawkes, direct contact with Bartók's music as well as the events concerning the latter's refusal to allow his music to be broadcast in Germany. Hawkes recalls that:

> As soon as the *Anschluss* with Austria was proclaimed, I realized that both Bartók and Kodály were, so to speak, marooned in Budapest. Their works were published largely by Universal Edition, and as this house was obviously going to be "put in order" by Hitler's propaganda minister, these great composers, Aryan though they were, in view of their liberal and free attitude, would be in difficulty. A few days after the sensational news of the occupation of Vienna, I phoned Kodály in

Budapest and said that I would immediately fly there to talk with him and Bartók. I arrived the next evening and met them both. There certainly was no reticence on Bartók's part in agreeing to publish all his future works with us. . . . We talked about future plans and other forthcoming works far into the night. Thus, the foundation of Bartók's association was laid.[112]

One of the plans related to the safe shipment of his compositions. On 13 April, therefore, his letter to Mrs. Müller-Widmann contains a request to "give shelter to my manuscripts" which he and possibly someone else (Stefi Geyer) would bring to her at some future time. But the main thrust of the letter concerns his thoughts about emigration, in view of "the imminent danger that Hungary will surrender to this regime of thieves and murderers."

> The only question is—when and how? And how can I go on living in such a country or—which means the same thing—working, I simply cannot conceive. As a matter of fact, I would feel it my duty to emigrate, so long as that were possible. . . .—And then I have my mother here: shall I abandon her altogether in her last years?—No, I cannot do that! So much for Hungary, where, unfortunately, nearly all of our "educated" Christians are adherents of the Nazi regime; I feel quite ashamed of coming from this class.[113]

During the next two months, Bartók shipped more than twenty manuscripts, each one placed in a numbered envelope,[114] which eventually were received by Boosey & Hawkes and later transhipped to New York after Bartók's arrival there in October 1940. On 20 June, the Bartóks were in London, performing the Sonata for Two Pianos and Percussion at the I.S.C.M. concert. Earlier that afternoon, Bartók played pieces from *Mikrokosmos* at "one of the intimate little Concerts we give in our [Boosey & Hawkes] Organ Studio in London."[115] According to the critic of the *Musical Times*:

> A group of piano pieces from Bartók's "Mikrokosmos" made the impression of terrific energy that everything connected with him does. He "impacted" into the room (there is no other way to describe the mental effect of his entrance, though his actions were quiet) and proceeded to play all sorts of little sketches, each one as if cut by a lapidary's tools, instead of written by a pen. Then he vanished again, leaving a wake of applause.[116]

Other than a short holiday in Braunwald during the first half of July, Bartók was in Budapest for the remainder of the summer. In his letter to Bartók on the 24th, Sándor Albrecht wrote that he had discussed the *Matica Slovenská* contract with Dr. Ivan Marcovič, a noted Czechoslovak attorney and political figure, who offered to write to the publisher on Bartók's behalf and without fee. Albrecht then inquires: "Now I ask you to please write to me again exactly what you want: the return of the manuscript or the publication of the songs. I assume that you will want the first one, because you will probably not want to take care of the publication after waiting ten or more years!"[117] Bartók's response indicates his doubt that the publisher would consider new offers brought through indirect channels, such as return of the manuscript to Bartók, without financial obligation, if they fail to engrave about a hundred melodies per month:

> Missing the term of publication happened several times; the only trouble is that I don't have enough money to buy back the manuscript, since I lost (and I will lose) money in consequence of the Austrian incidents. In any case, I will notify the *Matica* that they lost the right of publication and are obliged to give the manuscript back to me when I shall want it.[118]

On 11 August, József Szigeti's letter to Bartók brought the news that Benny Goodman—the renowned jazz clarinetist—was willing to commission "a clarinet-violin duet with piano accompaniment for him," for a fee of three hundred dollars. Szigeti suggested that: "If possible, it would be fine if the composition were to consist of two independent parts (which could perhaps also be played separately, (like the First Rhapsody for Violin), and we hope, of course, that it will also include a brilliant clarinet and violin cadenza![119]

By mid-September Bartók wrote to Székely that:

> I was diligent: the score for the first and second movements is ready, the third movement in sketches (with the exception of the coda that was planned to be short also, by the way) is also ready, five pages of it are already orchestrated. I think the third movement turned out very well, actually a free variation of the first (thus I got the best of you, I wrote *variations after all*).[120]

In the meantime, the terms of the Benny Goodman commission had been settled on the 5th, and Bartók completed the sketches ten days later. During the last two weeks, the German-Czech crisis—resulting from Hitler's demand for cession of the Sudetenland—brought Czechoslovakia's full mobilization. This action was followed by supportive discussions among Britain, France, and Russia. In order to avoid an international crisis, Mussolini persuaded Hitler to convene a conference at Munich on the 29th, at which Czechoslovakia and Russia were unrepresented.

The settlements effectively dismembered Czechoslovakia, for the conferees agreed to the Sudetenland takeover, the autonomy of Ruthenia (renamed Carpatho-Ukraine) and Slovakia, and Hungary's claim to those areas in Slovakia and Ruthenia occupied by Hungarians. In the latter case, however, it was decided that Hungary should negotiate with Slovakia, but settlement could not be reached and serious clashes erupted on the border. The Hungarian leaders therefore renewed their pro-German policy, and on 2 November the Axis Powers decided, in the so-called First Vienna Award, to give the largely Hungarian-inhabited southern strip of Slovakia to Hungary.[121]

On 9 October, Bartók's letter to Mrs. Müller-Widmann expresses his dismay about the news of her illness and sanatorium confinement and summarizes the impact of the Munich conference—"You can't imagine to what extent this has strengthened [Hitler's] following in this country"—and continues with:

> As for me, I have been working hard this summer. I have finished the Violin Concerto and two pieces (commissioned) for Szigeti and the American jazz clarinetist Benny Goodman (3 pieces, to be exact, 16 minutes altogether). . . . I am leading an even more retired life here, if that is possible; I do not feel like meeting people, everyone is suspected of Nazism. I work nearly 10 hours a day, exclusively on folk music material; but I would have to work 20 hours to make real progress. A distressing situation—I would so very much like to finish this work before we are involved in the next world catastrophe that's hanging in the air. And, at this rate, it will take a few more years![122]

During November, Bartók and his wife were on tour, performing the Sonata for Two Pianos and Percussion in Amsterdam and Brussels, and Bartók played piano recitals in Antwerp, Brussels, and Paris. And on 31 December, he completed the Second Violin Concerto. Toward the end of January, Bartók's letter to the *Matica Slovenská* Board of Directors unambiguously terminates his unrealized Slovak folk music publication.

> For about a year I had intended to declare to you what follows:
> 1. The stipulations of our recent Agreement of about 6 or 7 years ago—in which I granted you a certain *respiro* [respite]—have been repeatedly violated by your further unjustified delaying and silence. In consequence a) you have definitely forfeited your right of publication of the folk music material I have given respectively sold to you, b) you are obliged to return to me the manuscript I handed you for the purpose of publication, when I claim it, under the modalities laid down in our Contract. . . . 3. Unless an answer to this letter is received by me not later than 28th February 1939, I shall consider your silence as your agreement with its contents.

The second paragraph of the letter demands a reply to Bartók's previous inquiries as to the whereabouts and condition of the phonograph records—from which Bartók made his transcriptions—that had been delivered with the manuscript, since there was circumstantial evidence that they had been mishandled to the point of unsuitability.[123] A month later, the *Matica* responded that they had no further interest in publishing the work or in any copyright claim to it, and that they would return the manuscript on the condition that Bartók reimburse them for the royalty previously paid to him. In addition to denial of the mishandling charge, they defended their abrogation of the contract on the basis of the opinion of their experts: that the work gives a one-sided picture of the actual character of the true Slovak music, presents difficulties in the reconstruction of the texts, and raises insolvable problems with regard to restoring the uniformly transposed melodies back to their original tonality.[124]

Meanwhile, Bartók and his wife were on tour in Switzerland and Paris, playing the Sonata for Two Pianos and Percussion, and the former as soloist in the Second Piano Concerto. Unfortunately, the Bartóks were unable to attend

Székely's performance in the Amsterdam premiere of the Second Violin Concerto on 23 March, since they were preparing for a concert of two-piano works by Mozart and Stravinsky the next day.[125] The Dutch press was unstinting in praise of Bartók's masterpiece: "'The Concerto is a great work' . . . 'The new Concerto is a great victory.' . . . 'Bartók has reached new heights and has managed to solve all problems, has fused all aspects together to form a new work.' . . . 'The new Concerto is a work that one can love. Bartók is a giant, and in this work he uses everything he has arrived at in the past and everything is in perfect balance.'"[126]

Following the success of the Violin Concerto, Bartók agreed to Székely's proposal that he compose a work especially for the New Hungarian String Quartet.[127] Apparently Bartók felt that he could undertake the commission in addition to the one suggested by Paul Sacher in November and confirmed in March, namely, a string piece for the Basel Chamber Orchestra. Then, in response to Sacher's request for the title of the new piece and offer of an honorarium of a thousand francs, Bartók's letter of 1 June states that:

> As I had told you in March, I can only start working in August, so that I can definitely inform you by the end of August, when the work has progressed enough. As you can see, the order of work is the same every year. Besides, my idea is a kind of concerto grosso alternating with concertino; but I would like to know whether you have the right people for the solo-string quartet in your orchestra. I would like the idea of an alternating solo and tutti.[128]

On 1 August, Bartók was the houseguest of the Sachers at their chalet in Saanen, where he composed the Divertimento for String Orchestra. On the 18th, he wrote to his elder son that he felt like a musician of olden times, the invited guest of a patron of the arts, and that he lived alone—"in an ethnographic object: a genuine peasant cottage"—whose furnishings were the last word in comfort, including a piano that had been brought from Berne for his use:

> Luckily the work went well, and I finished it in 15 days (a piece about 25 minutes), I just finished it yesterday. Now I have another commission to fulfill, this time a string quartet for Z. Székely (i.e. for the "New Hungarian Quartet"). Since 1934 virtually everything I have done has been commissioned.[129]

On or about 18 August, Bartók began writing the Sixth String Quartet but left it unfinished when he returned to Budapest the next month. He had drafted the first three movements and part of the fourth movement when a radio broadcast on the 24th announced the signing of the nonaggression treaty between Germany and Russia. The manuscript shows a sketch of the forty-five bars which open the last movement, and then six transitional bars which are followed by two themes in folk-dance style. The first theme is based on Romanian bagpipe motifs (Ex. 5.15) and the second one, an original melody in Bulgarian rhythm, alternates 8/4 and 9/4 time.[130]

Ex. 5.15. Bartók, String Quartet no. 6 (1939), fourth movement, discarded folk dance theme in Romanian bagpipe style.

Immediately following the mentioned radio announcement Bartók notified Ralph Hawkes and his concert manager, Walter Schulthess, that he was compelled to leave Saanen for Budapest at once. On 1 September, German forces invaded Poland, Britain and France declared war on Germany on the 3rd, and two weeks later Russia invaded Poland. Bartók's attention during these weeks was concentrated on the myriad details connected with the imminent publication of three works (Second Violin Concerto, Divertimento, and *Mikrokosmos*) in a race against time before communications between Hungary and Britain were broken off.[131] Although he was further occupied with preparing for a number of concerts, on 2 November he was able to complete the 153 pieces and 33 exercises comprising the *Mikrokosmos*.[132] Later that month he returned to the unfinished Sixth String Quartet and, among other modifications, revised the fourth movement (the fair copy of the work is dated Saanen-Budapest, 1939, VIII–XI). But the "tempo giusto" of the Romanian village dance, conceived in Switzerland, was now replaced by the "parlando-rubato" mourning song for the murder of Europe.[133]

November also brought the news that arrangements had been proposed by the Library of Congress for a Bartók-Szigeti concert in April, at the Elizabeth Sprague-Coolidge Festival in Washington. Of more immediate concern was the precarious economic situation, which apparently motivated the Bartóks to play two-piano concerts in Italy during the first two weeks in December. On the 16th, Bartók's mother died; unfortunately, his illness prevented his attending her funeral.[134] He was overwhelmed with grief, and in his letter to Mrs. Müller-Widmann on 2 April 1940, he mentions that it was most difficult to endure the self-reproaches for "all the many things I could have done to differently to make my mother's life easier and to comfort her in her last years. It's too late now, nothing can be repaired or set right again—nothing, never."[135]

In addition to the 13 April concert in Washington, others were scheduled for Bartók, as pianist and lecturer, by the New York office of Boosey & Hawkes. Another appearance was arranged by Dorothy Parrish (Bartók's private piano student in Budapest from 1935 to 1937) at Juniata College in Huntington, Pennsylvania. In his 18 January response to her request for piano lessons during the visit, Bartók gladly agreed—"perhaps $10 for lesson would not be too high for you?"—and he continued with:

> As for the works to study, you may choose whatever you like from all the works by Beethoven (except the last sonata, and the "Hammerklavier"), by Mozart, Bach, Schubert, Chopin, Schumann, Debussy, and—Bartók! You will get this letter probably in the beginning of Febr. and will have more than 2 months to prepare works. (I forgot to mention Liszt: all works, excepted the most "hackneyed",—is this the right expression?[136]

During January, he played Beethoven's First Piano Concerto at the Music Academy, and at the same venue an evening of two-piano music with his wife, including the premiere performance of four transcribed pieces from *Mikrokosmos*. But most of his time was occupied with correcting a substantial number of proofs and related material from that work and the Divertimento for String Orchestra, tasks which were not completed until the end of February. He described this period as being drowned in work:

> which I got through in a mechanical sort of way, some of it in connection with my trip to America; finally I fell ill (*not* as a consequence of the work, it was simply 'flu), and the trip had to be postponed. So it will be tomorrow when I leave Europe. The boat is due in New York on Apr. 11 . . . But this boat was my last chance. I had to try it.[137]

The Festival concert consisted of violin and piano sonatas by Beethoven (*Kreutzer*), Bartók (no. 2), and Debussy, and Bartók's First Violin Rhapsody. In his review, "The Return of Béla Bartók and the Gulf between Those Who Admire Him and Those Who Are Left in Doubt," Oscar Thompson asks the question: "Why, when [Bartók] is internationally famous, is his music so seldom played, as compared to that of many other composers?" He provides the reader with two reasons, noting that "Bartók has written relatively little music for symphony orchestra, the medium by which most of his more popular contemporaries have reached a wider public," and that his piano and violin concertos are not played, because "pianists or violinists are chiefly concerned with whether the music they play is grateful for the soloist."[138]

Bartók's solo recital at Juniata College on the 15th was followed by violin and piano concerts in Pittsburgh, Chicago, and New York. In one of the reviews of his Chicago performance, he is hailed as "one of the great living pianists."[139] On 22 April he was at Harvard University for a lecture on "Some Problems of Folk Music Research in East Europe," in which he stated that:

Eight or ten years ago, if we wanted to examine the Serbo-Croatian material, we found ourselves up against a few obstacles. The available material consisted of about 4,000 tunes, for the most part in pre-war transcriptions made by ear, without the aid of an Edison phonograph or gramophone. Subtleties of execution and grace-notes can scarcely be studied at all, since they are lacking in these rather amateurish transcriptions; but at least types and classes can be established.[140]

Among the attendees was Albert B. Lord, a Junior Fellow at Harvard, whose letter to Bartók, dated 23 April, states that the late professor Milman Parry had deposited a large collection of Yugoslav folk music recordings at Harvard; a description of the collection, assembled from 1933 to 1935, would be mailed to Bartók; and that Bartók should meet with George Herzog and Samuel Bayard, the two other scholars interested in the musicological aspects of the collection, in New York.[141]

Following concert appearances on the 23rd (Curtis Institute of Music, Philadelphia) and 24th (Museum of Modern Art, New York), Bartók recorded the *Mikrokosmos* and other works at the New York studio of CBS Records.[142] Earlier in the month, Columbia University voted to confer the degree of Doctor of Music, *honoris causa,* for Bartók's "distinguished service to the art of music," at the forthcoming commencement on 4 June.[143] Because Bartók was quite concerned about rescheduling his 18 May departure from New York, the university agreed to hold the award in reserve until his return to the United States.[144]

On the evening of 1 May, Bartók's concert appearances ended at the university's McMillan Theater, with a gala performance of his works, which included the First String Quartet (a New York Philharmonic quartet), a group of Hungarian folk songs for voice and piano, the First Violin Rhapsody (with Szigeti), and piano pieces. This concert was the springboard that provided the opportunity for Bartók's discussions of a future position at the university with Columbia professors Herzog, Douglas Moore, and Paul Henry Lang. Moore, newly appointed as chairman of the music department, offered to investigate the possibilities of obtaining a grant from the university's recently established Alice M. Ditson Fund—set up for "the aid and encouragement of American musicians"; Herzog and Lang were to look into the possibilities of Bartók's transcribing the heroic songs from the Parry Collection at Harvard (working, however, under Columbia's auspices), which had not been previously examined and whose transcription was needed as illustrative material for Albert B. Lord's planned book on the textual aspects of those songs.[145] Also at this time, the Boosey & Hawkes concert management was arranging for another, more extensive tour of the United States by Bartók in the 1940–1941 season. Thus, on 17 May, he wrote to Dorothy Parrish, in English, that:

After so many troublesom [*sic*] days, tomorrow I will try my voyage to Hungary, full of misgivings – – – There are plans (excepting concertising) to make it possible to me (and to my wife too, of course) to stay here longer, perhaps for several years. I am not authorized to give details, but I hope these plans can be turned into reality. So, if there will be still a possibility to come over next fall, I will stay here for a longer periode [sic].[146]

It is interesting that, on 15 May, a trust agreement was signed by Bartók as Grantor and Boosey & Hawkes Inc. and Dr. George Herzog as Trustees, for the sale of the manuscripts of *Mikrokosmos, Contrasts,* Divertimento, Violin Concerto [no. 2], and Sixth String Quartet, "First, to pay for the publication of the Grantor's collection of Romanian and Slovakian folk music until the entire cost for the production and publication of the said collection shall have been paid in full." Work on the Romanian material had been initiated by Bartók in April, when he paid a commercial printer to produce the instrumental melodies and part of the vocal melodies in 500 sets of unfolded sheets sets, from the master sheets Bartók brought from Budapest.[147]

On 20 May, Douglas Moore requested Columbia to establish a research scholarship for Bartók, beginning in the fall, to "advise and assist" in the growth of its already outstanding collection of records of primitive and folk music, and "as a concrete objective, it is proposed to invite Mr. Bartók to examine an important collection of 4,000 records of Jugo-Slav music collected by Harvard University, of which Professor Herzog of the Department of Anthropology has been requested to make a musical analysis. It is hoped that this material will throw new light on Homeric problems."[148]

Among the tasks awaiting Bartók in the weeks following his return to Budapest was the correction of Twenty-seven Choruses proofs and their compilation in booklet format. He then informed the publisher (*Magyar kórus*) that:

> I do not think that I can write a preface and annotations; for one thing, I haven't time, and apart from that, I wouldn't know what to write about or what to explain.
> Owing to recent developments, I find it impossible to write more choruses or indeed anything at all—and this is probably how it will be for the rest of the year. What the future will bring—only Wotan (and his earthly deputy) knows. At the end of Sept. I have to go to America once again (if it's possible). My wife will be going with me, and we shall be staying for a longer period.[149]

Concurrently, Bartók and his assistant (Jenő Deutsch, a former pupil) completed the master-sheet autography of the Romanian vocal melodies "in an unfavorable haste and anxiety." Bartók then prepared an inventory of specially selected folk-music collections and stowed them in a large trunk for shipment to New York.[150] The month of August was wholly taken up by "troubles and upset . . . unthinkable hindrances and difficulties" Bartók met in his attempts to expedite the departure from Hungary. The first obstacle was the newly required permission of the war minister to leave Hungary before passports could be issued. Then followed the circuitous events of obtaining the necessary visas, particularly the delay cause by "the ridiculous and senseless . . . accursed and silly" demand of the American consulate for a moral certificate:

The Portugese visa is immediately obtainable if I have already the American visa and the boat-ticket! Spanish immediately if I have already American and Port. visa; French visa in 2–3 weeks, if I have the other 3 visas; Swiss visa in 3–4 weeks if I have the other 4 visas; Italian visa in 4 weeks if I have the American visa . . . These preparations are to make one crazy: I am half-dead and half-mad by all these troubles and worries. And I repeat again: it would be disastrous for me not to be able to undertake this journey.[151]

On 6 September, Bartók wrote to Mrs. Müller-Widmann, with copies to Stefi Geyer Schulthess and Paul Sacher, that the American visa would be granted the next day and the transit visas in four weeks, and he asks for immediate assistance and a temporary loan in obtaining tickets from Geneva to Lisbon. His suggested itinerary is via Milan to Geneva, then autobus to Barcelona and railway to Lisbon, but that it would be preferable to travel directly to Lisbon from Geneva if an autobus is available.[152] The final arrangements, mostly by autobus, were quite different! On 12 October, Bartók and his wife traveled from Budapest to Geneva, via Yugoslavia and Italy, where they were met by Stefi Geyer; from Geneva to Nîmes on the 15th; the next day continuing on to Barcelona; thereafter, by railway via Madrid, arriving in Lisbon on the 19th; and embarking for New York (via Bermuda) on the 20th.[153] Unfortunately, the vehicle broke down en route to Barcelona, and the Spanish Customs examination was very severe. Part of the Bartóks' luggage had to be left behind, including the trunk with folk-music materials, for later transport to Lisbon. But after they arrived in Lisbon, Bartók was quite distressed when he was told that it would be sent to New York as soon as possible.[154]

Bartók's first will, signed in Budapest on 4 October, restates the provisions of the New York trust agreement and maintains all the dispositions made therein concerning the sale of the manuscripts and the utilization of the income (Section II.). The penultimate section (VIII.) directs that:

My funeral should be as simple as possible, without clergy. If after my death it should be desired to name a street after me or locate a memorial tablet which bears any relation to me in a public place, then it is my wish that as long as the former *Oktogon Tér* [then called *Mussolini tér*] and former *Körönd* [*Hitler tér*] are named after those men whose name they bear at present, and moreover, as long as there is any square or street in Hungary named after these two men, no square, street or public building should be named after me in this country, and no memorial tablet connected with me should be placed in any public place.[155]

On 8 October, Bartók and his wife appeared in their farewell concert, at the Budapest Academy of Music, with the Capital Orchestra conducted by János Ferencsik. Bach and Mozart concertos were the featured works, including her first solo appearance, ending with his playing of pieces from *Mikrokosmos*. "And now we are here, with sorrowful hearts, bidding farewell . . . who knows for how long, perhaps forever! It is hard, very hard to say farewell."[156]

The Exile in America

Immediately after Bartók's arrival in New York on 30 October, he was again beset with "troubles and worries" that:

> began with our baggage (6 heavy trunks) which are still in Lisbon. We arrived in N.Y. only with the clothes which we have been wearing. Evening dresses etc., all our linen, all our music being in our baggage, we had to buy all the articles necessary for our appearances. . . . In addition there were some other disappointments, too; so our time was until now [26 November] not very agreeable.[157]

The Boosey & Hawkes Artists Bureau had arranged a coast-to-coast series of thirty-two concerts—some with lectures on piano playing or folk music—for the 1940–1941 season, beginning with the Sonata for Two Pianos and Percussion on 3 November in Town Hall (New York) and ending with a concert of music for two-pianos at the Baltimore Museum of Art Auditorium on 16 April 1941. The mentioned "disappointments" include the temporarily delayed Columbia appointment until the required funds were on hand, and the failed attempts by the Artists Bureau to obtain an engagement during the next summer. Following a conference with Bartók in November, the bureau contacted the University of Michigan, Western Reserve University, and the Oberlin Conservatory, offering his availability during July and August as teacher of piano classes and lecturer on piano teaching and modern music. The Michigan administrator responded that "in case the engagement would come through [Bartók] would be appointed to the rank of guest professor, which would carry the highest available honorarium."[158]

Bartók was under the impression that his Columbia University appointment involved permanence (as such a position would have done at a European university). In the Hungarian farewell notices his post was described as a professorial one, and he surely understood it as such. He was not informed that it was to be a temporary research fellowship of a kind usually given to doctoral candidates, nor that it was financed by a special fund that made no allowance for renewal or permanent appointment. He already had a worldwide reputation as a composer, and his assumptions were based on his awareness of his stature; the Columbia appointment, unknown to him but regarded at the university as a matter of common knowledge, was in conflict with those assumptions.[159] Furthermore, on 25 November, Bartók was "doctorated":

> It was some ceremony. Before it could take place, I had to be measured in yards, feet, and inches, so that they would know the size of my head, width of my shoulders, etc., and send in the details. At the University, we all had to put on our academic gowns and hoods and march in solemnly two by two to the sound of discreet organ music. We had been given exact instructions. When my name was called, I had to stand up, when the president addressed me, I had to take off my gown, and when he came to the end of his speech, I had to proceed toward him, so

that he could hand me my diploma, while the pink velvet sash of the Order of Music was placed on my back; and then I could go back and sit down. And that is exactly what happened.[160]

On 3 December, Bartók was in Ohio for two concerts at the Oberlin Conservatory of Music. His morning lecture-recital, titled "Contemporary Music in Piano Teaching," consisted for the most part of pieces from *For Children* and *Mikrokosmos*. In his introductory remarks, he stated that:

> Already at the very beginning of my career as a composer I had the idea of writing some easy work for piano students. This idea originated in my experience as a piano teacher; I had always the feeling that the available material, especially for beginners, has no real musical value, with the exception of very few works—for instance, Bach's easiest pieces and Schumann's *Jugendalbum*. I thought these work to be insufficient, and so, more than thirty years ago, I myself tried to write some easy piano pieces. At that time the best things to do would be to use folk tunes. Folk melodies, in general, have great musical value; so, at least the thematical value would be secured.[161]

The next concerts were on the 5th and 7th, playing the Second Piano Concerto with the Cleveland Orchestra, conducted by Artur Rodzinski. When he returned to New York, a furnished apartment in Forest Hills (Borough of Queens) had been rented by his wife. The subway was close by, the surroundings more congenial, and the janitor spoke Hungarian. They were "beginning to become Americanized, e.g. with regard to food. . . . My head is bursting with new words of every kind: the names of subway stations and streets; subway maps, scores of possibilities for changing from one to the other—all absolutely necessary for living here, but otherwise futile."[162]

Other Bartók performances of the Second Piano Concerto took place in Pittsburgh, on 24 and 26 January 1941, with Fritz Reiner as the conductor. On the 23rd, the Bartóks played Bach's Concerto in C Major for Two Pianos, accompanied by the Saidenberg Little Symphony in New York's Town Hall. Columbia University informed Bartók of his appointment as Visiting Associate in Music at a monthly salary of $300, expiring on 30 June unless renewed. Confirmed concert engagements and expected music royalties for that period were estimated to yield an additional $400 per month. Thereafter, however, the financial picture was uncertain if not bleak, especially with regard to the temporary Columbia appointment.

The Bartóks were in Boston on the 4th, joining with Szigeti and Benny Goodman in a concert of works by Mozart, Debussy, and Bartók. The same day—three months after the Lisbon departure!—the six trunks arrived in New York. During the next four weeks, Bartók was on a cross-country concert tour, beginning with Monticello College (Illinois) on the 14th, Denver's Broadway Theater on the 18th (with Szigeti), Brigham Young University on the 20th (with his wife), Mills College (California) on the 28th, the University of Washington

(Seattle) on 3–4 March, and the University of Kansas City on the 10th. Thereafter, following his return to New York, he began work on the Milman Parry Collection at Harvard, which had been brought to Columbia for study:

> The [2,500] records had been collected on an expedition in 1934 for the purpose of tracing sources of the Homeric legends, but the music had not previously been examined.
> Bartók was enthusiastic about the project and delighted with the material and the working conditions. It was understood that he was to work when and as he pleased and that no teaching or social duties demands were to be made upon him. A further grant was obtained from the Ditson fund to underwrite the expense of publication of the work.[163]

Bartók's last two concerts of the season, including two-piano works with his wife, were given on 29 March at the Detroit Institute of Art and, on 16 April, at the Baltimore Museum of Art. At about that time, he also prepared an illustrated lecture about "the methods and ideas of the contemporary Hungarian composers" for Douglas Moore's class in twentieth-century Tendencies in Music. Bartók emphasized that he never used peasant tunes in his original works, only in his transcriptions, which:

> are discernible either by their titles or by some added subtitle or footnote indicating the origin of the themes. . . . If there is no indication of origin, then there have been no folk melodies used at all. These are my original works. . . . You may want to ask in what way does the influence of folk music appear in such original works. First, it appears more or less in the general spirit of the style. To describe this spirit in words is, of course, sometimes rather difficult; to discern it is largely a matter of intuitive feeling, based on some kind of experience with folk music material. Secondly, in many cases themes or turns of phrases are deliberate or subconscious imitations of folk melodies or phrases.[164]

In connection with the impending renewal of Bartók's contract in May, the Boosey & Hawkes Concert Bureau apparently decided to draw on his new association with Columbia University and publicize his availability as a lecturer as well as pianist at universities and colleges during the coming 1941–1942 semesters. The following list, prepared by Bartók, was printed and mailed as a flyer to selected institutions:

Lectures on Piano Music:

1. *Contemporary Music in Elementary Piano Teaching.* This lecture is accompanied by many examples at the piano, giving only easy pieces.

2. *Béla Bartók's Piano Compositions Written with a Pedagogical Purpose.* Lecture-recital with many examples on the piano, easy and difficult pieces.

3. *Contemporary Music in Piano Teaching.* A cycle of three lectures, each about one hour, with many examples on the piano, easy and more difficult pieces.

Lecture on Hungarian Art Music:

4. *The Relation Between Contemporary Hungarian Art Music and Folk Music.* With many different music examples.

Lectures on Folk Music Research:

5. *Some Problems of Folk Music Research in East Europe.* With examples played on gramophone records. Some examples (scales and melodies only) are played on the piano. Slides are used in illustrating this lecture.

6. *The same lecture can be divided and extended into three lectures:*
   a. Hungarian Folk Music
   b. North-Slav and Romanian Folk Music
   c. South-Slav (Serbo-Croatian and Bulgarian) Folk Music
Each lecture will have a duration of about one hour and is illustrated with gramophone records, slides, and a few examples on the piano.

Bartók's satisfaction with the ambiance at Columbia University is described in a letter to Zoltán Kodály, in which he notes that: "I almost feel as if I were continuing my work at the Hungarian Academy of Science, only in slightly altered conditions, even the setting resembles its nobility. When I cross the campus in the evening, I feel as if I were passing the historic square of a European city."[165] By 18 April, his familiarity with the Parry Collection had reached the point where he decided to summarize its contents in a report to Douglas Moore and, a year later, in an essay for publication in the *New York Times*: "These poems seem to be the last remnants of a folk usage at least several thousand years old, expressed in words and music, leading back perhaps to antiquity, to the times of the Homeric poems. Nowhere else can be found a similar usage, not even in other countries of the Balkans."[166] Of greater significance, however, is Bartók's finding that transcription of the nonepic materials in the collection would provide an inclusive picture of Yugoslav folk music; a task that would require another year of research but, as Moore had suggested, could result in a book on Serbo-Croatian folk songs.

While Bartók was in Seattle for his concerts at the University of Washington, the head of the music department, Professor C.P. Wood, inquired whether Bartók would be interested in an appointment as visiting lecturer on the Walker-Ames Foundation, for a period of up to nine months, at a proposed salary of $300 per month. The position was somewhat similar to the one at Columbia: no fixed requirements of class teaching or public lectures and the opportunity for laying the groundwork for continuation in research on regional primitive (Indian) music. When Bartók expressed interest in receiving a formal proposal, Wood's letter, dated 22 May, summarizes their discussion, adding that: "If you are at all interested in the idea, I should like to have you give me in reply some outline of what you think might be accomplished during your appointment."[167]

When Bartók replied on 9 June, his appointment at Columbia University had not only been extended to 30 June 1942 but also included a subsidy for publication of Bartók's Yugoslav folk music research by the Columbia University Press. He therefore indicated his interest in Wood's proposal, stating that he could not accept another appointment until the present one expired. While he found the conditions suitable, he asked for a reconsideration of the allocated grant with regard to travel and living expenses. His letter concludes with a threefold plan of working: (1) To transcribe all the recorded Indian material held by the University, (2) To give weekly lectures to students interested in the method for such transcription, eventually extending the lectures to the related subjects of the collection and scientific study of folk music, and (3) Seminars and conferences with students interested in transcribing folk-music records.[168]

The delay in Bartók's response can be partially attributed to the distractions during his change of residence from Forest Hills to Riverdale (Borough of the Bronx), since the relocation was made from a small furnished apartment to a much larger unfurnished one.[169] But the more important circumstance was the complicated procedures Bartók had to undertake—certificates, affidavits, photographs, etc.—in order to obtain a nonquota immigrant visa. Without this visa, his son Péter would not be allowed to enter the United States, and a necessary step after obtaining it was to reenter from Canada. His pessimistic outlook on the future is given in his 29 June letter to his elder son in Budapest:

> It is not true, of course, that I have been invited to take up an appointment as a "professor". . . . The reason for inviting me here (apart from the fact that it would help me personally) was so that I could accomplish certain research work, that is, to study and transcribe this incomparable material on Yugoslav folk music. . . . I will have finished working on this material—or so I expect—by next summer. Afterwards, possibly at some other university, I could go on to transcribe some Indian material (there is plenty of material which has not been worked on), but I don't feel very much inclined to do that: it is a field of study very remote from the folklore areas I have dealt with so far, and to start on it now would mean frittering away my energies.[170]

Two transcriptions were the outcome of his work with the Parry Collection heroic songs that were recorded in Novi Pazar during 1934. The first transcription, "No. 4. The Captivity of Đulić Ibrahim," consists of diverse text lines selected from the 1,811 lines comprising the epic, and it includes the *gusle* introduction and accompaniment (Ex. 5.16). The second transcription, "No. 27. The Battle of Temišvar," was not engraved for publication.[171]

GUSLE   ♩ = 146
(1)
Record No. 1237b

Ex. 5.16. Bartók's transcription of "No. 4. The Captivity of Đulić Ibrahim," *gusle* introduction, mm. 1–2.

In June, the Concert Bureau had been able to book only eleven appearances for the Bartóks during the 1941–1942 concert season. With the exception of the Second Piano Concerto in Chicago and a recital in a Los Angeles theater, the performances were the usual piano recitals and lectures at colleges and universities. Ralph Hawkes recalls that:

> During 1940 and 1941, I spent a good deal of time in the United States and travelled extensively, with the promotion of the contemporary music section of the Boosey & Hawkes Catalogue as my main interest. To promote Bartók was no easy matter and many were the times I met with blank refusals either to perform his works or to give him and his wife engagements to play. Apathy and even aversion to this sort of music was to be found everywhere. Some organizations and conductors who were outspoken in their refusals were noticeably prominent in performing his works after his death, when general recognition made it impossible to ignore them any longer.[172]

In addition to the minuscule distributions for the very few performances of his works in the United States, Bartók's royalty income was reduced as the result of European wartime currency regulations. It was difficult for the London office of Boosey & Hawkes to obtain royalties from Europe, and the New York office was unable to provide Bartók with advances without permission of the Bank of England. He was cut off from his Hungarian pension, and the modest Columbia University emolument would terminate on 20 June 1942. His pessimism was such that he seriously contemplated a return to Hungary:

> Our prospect of breaking into the concert world is not very bright: either our agent is bad, or the circumstances are not favorable (and will become even less so in the near future, as a result of wartime atmosphere). In these circumstances, we should then have to return to Hungary, no matter how the situation develops there. By that time things won't be much better even here. No one need feel gratified by our return—from any higher point of view—for it will not be much use to anyone. All it would mean is that, if things are bad everywhere, one prefers to be at home.[173]

In the meantime, Bartók continued his negotiations with the University of Washington during the summer, which resulted in a mutual agreement to postpone consideration of his appointment until such time as Columbia University decided to renew or discontinue his work on the Parry Collection. On 7 July, Mrs. Bartók left for Riverton, Vermont, to spend the summer as the houseguest of Agatha Fassett; Bartók joined them shortly after 21 July, when Boosey & Hawkes delivered the complete sets of mastersheets and the unformatted individual melodies from his Romanian collection. During his stay in Vermont, Bartók assembled the remaining 363 mastersheets by using transparent adhesive tape to link the newly proofread melodies into leaves. After his return to New York in September, he had them printed in the event "something should happen to that unique copy."[174]

The second transcontinental tour was preceded by Bartók's lecture on East European folk music and recital of his piano pieces at Wells College, New York, on 18 October. The next month he was the soloist in two performances of the Second Piano Concerto, with the Chicago Symphony Orchestra conducted by Frederick Stock. The same lecture and a somewhat similar program of his piano pieces was presented on the 26th at Stanford University, California. He arrived in Portland, Oregon, on the 28th and made an excursion the next day to Seattle, where he conferred with Professor Wood about such technicalities as availability of gramophones and copying machines, what Indian folk music material was on hand, and if and how the Indian texts were already transcribed.[175] Bartók returned to Portland and, on 1–2 December, repeated his lecture-recital program at Reed College and, on the 3rd, at the University of Oregon. He was in Los Angeles on the 5th, where he played a piano concert at the Wilshire Ebell Theater—a venue with 1,500 seats—where the disappointed sponsors were hard pressed to sell or give away 200 tickets. While Bartók was on tour, George Herzog met with Douglas Moore concerning the status and scope of Bartók's work on the Parry Collection. Although Moore was willing to support Bartók's transcription of the Serbo-Croatian epics as music examples for Harvard's planned publication of the material, he also wanted to realize his own plan for a Columbia book by Bartók based on transcription of the folk songs. Thus, on 21 November, Herzog wrote to Albert B. Lord that:

> We think that it would be best to take sections of the material which are outside the epic material and work them up as essays which could be published here . . . as a small book. One could either take a generous selection of lyrical songs, or, as another possibility, discuss briefly lyrical songs, having another essay on the instrumental pieces, again another on the ballads, and build up a little unit from these three subjects.[176]

The concert season continued on 6 January 1942, at Chicago's Orchestra Hall, when Béla and Ditta Bartók played music for two pianos, including Colin McPhee's transcription of Balinese Ceremonial Music, four pieces from *Mikrokosmos,* and Bartók's recent transcription of the Suite no. 2, op. 4, for Orchestra (1905–1907). The next evening they performed at Northwestern University. After Bartók returned to New York, he asked Douglas Moore for an extension of his engagement, which was granted until the end of the year, and the other good news were the safe arrival of Péter Bartók in Lisbon—following a long and tedious journey from Hungary—and a special permit for him to enter the United States. The third two-piano concert was held at Amherst College, and the fourth one—including a reception in honor of Bartók—was sponsored by the United States section of the ISCM at the MacDowell Club, New York, on 24 April. The concert was the last appearance for 1942, since the Boosey & Hawkes Concert Bureau was unable to secure other bookings. Moreover, the management reported that only one engagement had been secured for himself and his wife in

1943: the first U.S. performance of the Concerto for Two Pianos and Percussion—a 1940 transcription which Bartók had made, albeit reluctantly, at the behest of his publisher—with the Philharmonic-Symphony Society of New York, conducted by Fritz Reiner. Bartók was extremely upset by this unfortunate turn of events, as he indicates in his letter of 2 March 1942:

> Our situation is getting daily worse and worse. All I can say is that never in my life since I earn my livelihood (that is from my 20th year) have I been in such a dreadful situation as I will be probably very soon. To say dreadful is probably exaggerated, but not too much. Mrs. Bartók bears this very valiantly: the worse the happenings, the more energetic, confident and optimistic she is. She tries to do some work, teaching for instance. But how to get pupils or a job! . . . I am rather pessimistic, I lost all confidence in people, in countries, in everything.[177]

Several days after he posted this letter, he received a negative response from the president of the University of Washington, in which Bartók's proposed appointment for the fall of 1943 or the full academic year of 1943–1944 could not be confirmed because of the hazards of war: "we have no present way of knowing what our income will be on our invested funds. . . . [by the spring of 1943] we should be able to know whether our finances will be sufficient to justify carrying through the proposed appointment."[178] On 20 April, however, the Bartóks received the joyful news that their son had arrived from Lisbon:—"I met him quite unexpectedly at our subway station 231st street; it was like a scene in those old stories. . . . It is quite amazing how he could find his way after so many difficulties." At the beginning of the month, however, Bartók's health took a sudden, adverse turn: "I have every day temperature elevation (of about 100°) in the evening, quite regularly and relentlessly! The doctors cann't [sic] find out the cause, and as a consequence, cann't [sic] even try a treatment. Is that not rather strange? Fortunately, I can do my work."[179]

Bartók's essay "Race Purity in Music" was published in the March–April issue of *Modern Music,* in which he addresses the question: "Is racial impurity favorable to folk (peasant) music or not?" It seems evident that he selected the topic as a reaction to Nazi dogma, which mandates that "purity of race should be preserved, even by means of prohibitive laws":

> It is obvious that if there remains any hope for the survival of folk music in the near or distant future (a rather doubtful outcome considering the rapid intrusion of higher civilization into the more remote parts of the world), an artificial erection of Chinese walls to separate peoples from each other bodes no good for its development. A complete separation from foreign influences means stagnation: well assimilated foreign impulses offer possibilities of enrichment.
> There are significant parallels in the life of languages and the development of the higher arts. English is impure in comparison with other Teutonic languages; about forty per cent of its vocabulary is of non-Anglo-Saxon origin. Nevertheless it has developed incomparable strength of expression and individuality of spirit.

As for the development of Europe's higher art music, every musician knows what far-reaching and fortunate consequences have resulted from the transplantation of the fifteenth-century musical style of the Netherlands to Italy, and, later, from the spread of various influences of Italy to the northern countries.[180]

It was probably in December 1941 that Bartók had completed his essay on the Parry Collection of epic poems and sent a copy to Douglas Moore. Thereafter, on 20 January, Moore discussed the essay with a member of the Ditson Committee and thereby succeeded in obtaining an additional grant to underwrite a Bartók book on Yugoslav folk music. During February, Bartók met with Herzog, Lang, and the editor of Columbia University Press to discuss the details, including the appointment of Albert B. Lord as coauthor. The next month Bartók was gratified to learn that his appointment at Columbia would be extended until the end of the year and that Harvard had shipped a number of new records to Herzog, all of them containing lyric songs. On 1 June, Bartók was able to write that he was working on two projects: "Rumanian Folkmusic of Transylvania and Banat (in preparation): about 2400 melodies, introduction, etc., Serbo-Croatian Folkmusic (in preparation, going to be published soon by Columbia University Press): 80 melodies, very detailed introduction (containing examination of some general aspects of the problems connected with research work in folk music)."[181]

Although the classification procedures of the two materials had much in common, so that Bartók could prepare their introductory studies more or less parallel to each other, his progress was slowed by the need to compare the Banat and Yugoslav melodies, in order to determine whether there were any reciprocal influences.[182] He therefore remained at home during July, and his wife spent the summer with Agatha Fassett in Vermont. In August, however, he decided to accept Victor Bator's invitation to visit as a houseguest at the latter's summer home in Nonquitt, Massachusetts. On the 18th, he received an invitation from Harvard University as a visiting lecturer on the Horatio Appleton Lamb Fund, from February through April 1943, for an honorarium of $2,000.

At this time, the United States was feverishly gearing up its war effort against Japan, since the latter's drive for conquest of the Pacific theater was at its height. Millions of citizens had left their homes to join the armed forces or government agencies and little attention, time, and money was left for the arts. On 31 December, Bartók's letter reports that:

> At Columbia, I am "dismissed" from Jan. 1 on; they seem to have no more money left for me. This is annoying because little more than half the work (connected with the Parry collection) could be achieved during these 2 years; and I hate incompletness [sic]. If it ever can be continued, Heaven only knows. But from Febr. on, I am invited to Harvard University to give there a certain number of conferences and lectures during the 1st semester. This gives us a respite until the next fall (no possibilities with concertizing or lecturing; we have a "unique" engagement in Jan. with the New York Philh. Society, but this is a "family" busi-

ness, the engagement was made through my friend Fritz Reiner who is guest conductor in some of these concerts).

So we are living from half-year to half-year. I still don't know what to decide about Seattle. What you write in your letter in this connection, is not very encouraging.

I was very busy during the whole year with my book. One, you know, is on Serbo-Croatian folkmusic, this I have finished in October; it ought to be published by the Columbia Press, as an Appendix to my work done there. The other is on my Rumanian folkmusic material: 2500 melodies published in two volumes, of course, with introductions and all. There is hope that it will be published.—All this was a rather tiresome work (and my struggling with the English language) but very interesting indeed. . . .

So, with my books and articles I am gradually advancing to the position of an English writer (I don't mean it seriously, of course!); I never had an idea that this will be the end of my career! Otherwise, my career as a composer is as much as finished: the quasi boycott of my works by the leading orchestras continues, no performances either of old work[s] or of new ones. It is a shame—not for me of course.[183]

As mentioned above, the Bartóks played the American premiere of the Concerto for Two Pianos and Percussion on 21 January 1943, at Carnegie Hall. During the concert, Bartók briefly extemporized on his own, bewildering his wife and the conductor, until he returned to the score. He later explained that: "the tympanist is the one who started everything. He played a wrong note, suddenly giving me an idea I had to try out, and follow through all the way, right then. I could not help it—there was nothing else for me to do."[184]

Bartók decided to commute to Harvard University for his lecture series, although he had been offered dormitory lodgings there. His jottings show his intention to give the following lectures:

1. Revolution, evolution [in music]
2. Modes, polymodality (polytonality, atonality, twelve-tone music)
3. Chromaticism (very rare in folk music)
4. Rhythm, percussion effect
5. Form (every piece creates its own form)
6. Scoring (new effects on instruments), piano, violin as percussive instruments (Cowell)
7. Trend toward simplicity
8. Educational works
9. General spirit (connected with folk music)[185]

The incomplete draft of the fourth lecture presents an account of the three prevailing kinds of rhythm formations in Eastern European rural music, ending with a projected description of the patterns "which we call 'Bulgarian' rhythm-formations."[186] It seems likely that he may have been considering an extended adaptation of the remarks on Bulgarian folk music from his 1940 Harvard lecture on "Some Problems of Folk Music Research in East Europe."[187]

Bartók's sudden breakdown followed the third lecture, and the university insisted on a two-week hospital stay, including a complete physical examination, at their expense. Finally, after an X-ray reading was interpreted as tuberculosis, Bartók was discharged, resigned his lectureship, and returned home to convalesce. While he was bedridden, he began work on preparing his Turkish folk-music collection for publication, including correction of the English text translations that had been made in Budapest.[188] But his "condition was getting worse every day. His fever was constantly high, his weight down to 90 pounds, and he was not even able to turn in bed. His doctor's opinion was that if no change occurred he could not last more than a week. . . . Mrs. Bartók, completely fatigued by day and night nursing, was in no condition to take charge of the situation."[189] In desperation, she called Ernő Balogh for help. He immediately contacted ASCAP's board of directors for assistance, and the society responded by sending "the best doctors, specialists, and nurses to Bartók, who had been moved immediately to one of New York's finest hospitals. Later, Bartók was sent to the country, to the south in the winter, to the northern mountains in the summer. His family was sent with him when his condition required it."[190]

During the five weeks Bartók was a patient at Mount Sinai Hospital, Victor Bator and József Szigeti created a "Béla Bartók Research Fund" from contributions made by interested musicians and other supporters and, by special arrangement with Columbia University, donated the money needed to provide Bartók with an extension of his appointment until the end of the year.[191] In response to Szigeti's appeal, Serge Koussevitzky—conductor of the Boston Symphony Orchestra—responded with: "I trust to find another way to help Bartók morally as well as financially."[192] Shortly after, the conductor visited the composer at the hospital, proposed a Koussevitzky Foundation commission of a thousand dollars for an orchestral work, and, notwithstanding Bartók's protests, gave him a check for half the fee. Mrs. Bartók recalls that:

> They agreed upon purely orchestral work; it was Béla's idea to combine chorus and orchestra. I am so glad that plans, musical ambitions, compositions are stirring in Béla's mind—a new hope discovered in this way quite by chance, as if it were incidentally. One thing is sure: Béla's "under no circumstances will I ever write any new work—" has gone. It's more than three years now—. And to whom do we owe most thanks for this? You know, of course: to Szigeti.[193]

Although the doctors informed Bartók that he was suffering from polycithemia (abnormal increase in red blood cells), he was not told that the medical diagnosis was leukemia (an incurable cancerous disorder, marked by an abnormal increase in white blood cells). But his fever abated, he regained some lost weight, and felt well enough to return home. He opened negotiations with the New York Public Library as a potential publisher of a two-volume edition of his Romanian instrumental and vocal melodies, and he indicated that the printed music was available in the form of 500 sets of unfolded sheets. Following their receipt of a complete set of gathered and folded sheets, the library turned to G. Schirmer, the well-known New York music publisher and printer, for a production estimate, including Bartók's introduction and notes to the melodies. When the printer indicated that they were unable to use the furnished printed pages and quoted a price of approximately $2,000 per volume, the total cost was substantially higher than expected, and on 26 June the library withdrew.[194]

Earlier in June, the University of Washington renewed its offer of an appointment, but on the 30th, Bartók had to decline: "The doctors cannot find the cause of my illness; therefore, no cure and no treatment is possible, and the prospects of the future are rather gloomy. For the time being I can not even think of accepting a job anywhere!"[195] Another letter, on the 28th, iterates his frustration with the medical diagnoses based on X-rays:

> *It does not account for the high temperatures!* So we have the same story again, doctors don't know the real cause of my illness—and, consequently, can't treat and cure it! They are groping about as in a darkness, try desperately to invent the most extraordinary hypotheses. But all that is of no avail.[196]

At the end of the month, thanks to ASCAP's generous support, a small cottage was available in Saranac Lake, New York, for his convalescence. He took with him the various drafts of the Turkish material, for he decided to prepare fair copy of the extra-musical portion (introduction, texts and translations, etc.) and offer that much smaller work to the New York Public Library, in place of the rejected Romanian proposal.[197] On 31 July, in response to an inquiry from Ralph Hawkes, Bartók indicates that there is no perceptible change in his health and continues with a detailed description of the various medical opinions:

> Now about the doctors. End of March they made the statement, it is tuberculosis of the lungs, and were extremely glad to have found out this, at last. Later, however, they it appeared, for several reasons, that the disease can not be tuberculosis; so they shifted to other hypotheses. . . . They turned to "monilia", and finally to "Beck's sarcoid". These two are very interesting (not for me!) ailments. The only trouble is that neither of them can be proved! So they are groping about in the darkness and are entirely at the end of their wits.—This is the rather disconcerting picture of the situation. Of course, no treatment is possible, if they don't know what the trouble is.[198]

During August, Bartók's high fever abated to the point where he felt well enough to undertake the Koussevitzky commission. On 15 August, Bartók began composing the Concerto for Orchestra on the blank staves of his Turkish field sketchbook. It is most interesting, if not significant, that Bartók's draft begins with the *Elegia* (third movement) and its introductory variant of the "darkness" theme from his opera *Duke Bluebeard's Castle* (cf. Ex. 4.23), and ends with the first movement whose *Introduzione* opens with different variants of the theme (Ex. 5.17).[199]

Ex. 5.17. Bartók, Concerto for Orchestra (1943), "darkness" theme" variants in the first movement, mm. 1–6 and 12–16, and third movement, mm. 1–5.

In connection with the forthcoming renewal of his contract with Boosey & Hawkes, Bartók asked his publisher to print the two volumes of Romanian folk music. On 10 September, however, the company assured him that they would undertake the publication but that it "must be postponed until the war is over."[200] He therefore turned to the New York Public Library with a new proposal, stating that:

> nothing can be done with the Rumanian material for the time being. Fortunately, however, I have another work, to offer for publishing, about half the size of the Rumanian one. It is the "Turkish Folk Music from Asia Minor."
> This work contains the first collection of Turkish folk music ever made by systematic research work, and ever published. The Introduction contains a description of how to determine the approximate age limit of rural folksong material, in certain specific cases. Such problems have never yet been described and published. Therefore, this feature of the book has an international significance. Besides this, many other highly interesting questions are treated in the Introduction.[201]

On 8 October, Bartók completed the fair copy of the Concerto for Orchestra. He returned to New York on the 12th, where he and his wife moved into the Woodrow Hotel. Several days later, he was able to hear the Second Violin Concerto for the first time, played by Tossy Spivakovsky and the New York Philharmonic-Symphony, Artur Rodzinski conducting, at Carnegie Hall. On the 15th, the New York Public Library wrote that they were not optimistic about publishing the book on Turkish folk music and had decided to postpone consideration of his recent proposal.

During November, Yehudi Menuhin had scheduled a performance of the Second Violin Concerto in Minneapolis, Minnesota (Dmitri Mitropoulos conducting) and the First Violin Sonata in Carnegie Hall (accompanied by Adolph Baller). Since the playing of the Sonata would be Menuhin's first performance of the work, he wanted Bartók's critical opinion before the concert and sent him a request for an audition. When Bartók agreed to the critique, the audition was held at the apartment of Menuhin's friend.

There were no civilities. Baller went to the piano, I found a low table, put my violin case on it, unpacked, tuned. We started to play. At the end of the first movement Bartók got up—the first slackening of his rigid concentration—and said, "I did not think music could be played like that until long after a composer was dead."

Knowing that I had just performed his great Concerto, Bartók probed to see how well I had grasped it, asking particularly my opinion of a passage in the first movement. "It's rather chromatic," I offered. "Yes, it's chromatic," he said, but then, nudging me toward the point he was making: "You see that it comes very often?"—which it does, some thirty-two times, never exactly the same. "Well, I wanted to show Schönberg that one can use all twelve tones and still remain tonal."[202]

The outcome of this meeting was Bartók's acceptance of a $500 commission to write a solo violin work for Menuhin. Another commission in the same amount was offered by the American Ballet Theater for a piano reduction of the Concerto for Orchestra score. The company was interested in a staging a dance performance of the Concerto, and Bartók agreed to prepare an arrangement for use by a rehearsal pianist. And on 29 November, in response to a letter from the University of Washington, he indicated that the earliest time he could come to Seattle would be January 1945, adding that he would write again in April whether his situation up to that time had developed favorably as expected.[203]

On 14 December, Bartók deposited the mastersheet draft of the first two volumes of *Rumanian Folk Music* "at the Columbia University Music Library— there they are available to those few persons (very few indeed) who may be interested in them."[204] Two days later he was en route to North Carolina, since ASCAP had decided to underwrite his stay at the Albermarle Inn, Asheville, during the winter months. Shortly after his arrival, he set down his gloomy thoughts concerning the European war.

> There is no end in sight—and the destroying of Europe (people and works of art) continues without respite and mercy. Personally, I do not know how long I can endure the insecurity of this Gypsy life. (But for 1944, at least, my living expenses are secured, no worry about that.) And the destiny of poor Hungary, with the Russian danger in the background—the prospects of the future are rather dark.[205]

In his letter to Szigeti, dated 30 January, Bartók states that: "Here I have started on a very interesting (and, as usual, lengthy) work, the kind I have never done before. Properly speaking, it is not a musical work: I am classifying and writing out fair copies of Wallachian [i.e., Romanian] folksong texts." He also mentions a recent letter from Eugene Ormandy, in which the conductor, after hearing the Second Violin Concerto on the radio, "thinks that such a viol. con certo had not been written since Beeth., Mendels. and Brahms. Sic Ormándy!"[206] By 1 February, the fair copy of the Concerto for Orchestra piano reduction had been prepared, and on 14 March, the first draft of Menuhin's commission—the

Sonata for Solo Violin—was drafted. In a humorous letter to his wife, dated 21 April, he describes how "a concert of birds is heard from dawn till evening, but at night, however, the crickets take over the empire."[207]

Bartók returned to New York on the 28th, and wrote an essay, "Hungarian Music," for the 4 June issue of the *American Hungarian Observer* (New York). Although most of the essay is a rehash of previous writings on the subject, his remarks about the stylistic differences between his works and those of Zoltán Kodály are indeed instructive.

> Although we have a common outlook upon rural music and its part in the development of higher art music, there is a very marked difference in our works. Each of us has developed his own individual style, despite the common sources which were used. And this is very fortunate indeed, because it shows that rural folk music as a source provides various possibilities for the creation of higher art music and that the use of it as a basis does not necessarily render the results uniform.
>
> It would be going too far to give here a detailed description of the differences between Kodály's works and mine. I will mention only one essential difference— a difference in procedure which may account (at least partly) for the differences in style. Kodály studied, and uses as source, Hungarian rural music exclusively, whereas I extended my interest and love also to the folk music of the neighboring Eastern European peoples and ventured even into Arabic and Turkish territories for research work. In my works, therefore, appear impressions derived from the most varied sources, melted—I hope—into a unity. These various sources, however, have a common denominator, that is, the characteristics common to rural folk music in its purest sense.[208]

On 1 July, Bartók deposited his Turkish folk-music study at the Columbia Library, and on the 5th, left the city with his wife for another summer at Saranac Lake, under the continuing auspices of ASCAP, where he resumed work on classification of the Romanian folk texts. Two weeks later, however, Columbia University Press sent the copyedited manuscript and its typescript revision of Bartók's preface and introduction to Yugoslav Folk Music (the working title).

> The Columbia Press have been disturbing me in my work. For a month, I have been chewing over colons and semi-colons, new paragraphs, and I have drafted hundreds of new counter-proposals. The battle will take place in October. In case you can't guess what its all about, I'll whisper it: they have sent me the revised and typed copy of the preface to the Serbo-Croatian volume. All the trouble they must have taken and the number of corrections is really astounding. Only they've often gone too far. The whole thing is very interesting and, above all, most instructive, but sometimes tiresome and annoying just because of this over-fussiness.[209]

Bartók returned to New York on 5 October, this time to an apartment on 57th Street, and not only continued the folk music research that he had pursued throughout the summer but, during November, turned his attention to a critical review of the Serbo-Croatian texts and translations that Albert B. Lord had been preparing as the second part of the volume. On the 26th, he attended Yehudi Menuhin's premiere performance of the Solo Violin Sonata at Carnegie Hall. The New York music critics turned out en masse, and their reviews were for the most part quite favorable. The Olin Downes "Menuhin Thrills Capacity Crowd" article ends on this humorous note:

> One listener was heard to remark ironically after the performance that unfortunately Mr. Menuhin had played a wrong note in the middle of the second movement. She had the critics there. Not one of them could have taken oath in distinguishing between the alleged wrong note and the alleged right one![210]

Several days later, the Bartóks traveled to Boston to attend the rehearsals and premiere performance of the Concerto for Orchestra. Bartók later reported that "Koussevitzky is very enthusiastic about the piece, and says it is 'the best orchestra piece of the last 25 years' (including the works of his idol Shostakovich!)."[211] Moreover, one of the reviews describes the music as "akin aesthetically to Bach. . . . The Concerto, by the way, is fearfully difficult. Yes, if a composition of transcendent musical art may be defined as one which, in its own way, is a summation of all that has gone before, then the Orchestra Concerto is a work of art—and a great one."[212] When a former Bartók student sent him the program of her recent concert devoted to works by Bach, Beethoven, Brahms, and Bartók, he wrote that:

> I received your "Four B" program this morning. Was this a deliberate act of yours? This reminds me of a criticism appearing Jan. 1944 in the San Francisco Chronicle and saying: "the sonata (1st violin sonata, played there by Menuhin) emphasizes again what has often (?!?) been suggested in these columns—that Bartók is the fourth in the procession of the great B'^{s} of music." This is, by the way, an amplification of the "jeu de lettres" invented by Bülow—if I remember well—at the occasion of the first performance of Brahm's [sic] 1st symphony.[213]

The Concerto for Orchestra was given its New York performance by the Boston Symphony on 10 January 1945, with the composer again in attendance. The audience and the press found the work enjoyable and engrossing, and Koussevitzky "repeatedly led Mr. Bartók from the wings, and finally left him alone on the stage with the applauding audience."[214] Later that month, he accepted a commission to compose a viola concerto for William Primrose. During February and March, he worked on the mastersheet draft of the third volume of *Rumanian Folk Music* (completed on the 30th) and corresponded with Albert B. Lord concerning the Serbo Croatian texts and translations. He was also uncertain whether his health would allow him to take on commissions for a concerto for two pianos and a piece for orchestra. And in April, he was surprised to learn that he was one of four exiles who had been elected by the people of Budapest as members of the new Hungarian parliament.[215]

In addition to the mentioned commissions, Bartók was considering a seventh string quartet—to satisfy his publisher's repeated request—and a piano concerto for his wife. Since he was unable to practice or concertize, he thought that "if she could play it in 3 or 4 places then it would bring in as much money as one of the commissioned pieces I refused."[216] A rejected commission, proposed by the well-known Hollywood musician Nathaniel Shilkret, was an orchestral prelude for his forthcoming record album titled *Genesis*. Shilkret had commissioned celebrated composers (Stravinsky, Schoenberg, Milhaud, and others) to write movements for the album, but there were problems with regard to certain rights he demanded, which were contrary to Bartók's contract with Boosey & Hawkes. During the negotiations, Bartók wrote to an intermediary that:

> We have been receiving some extremely depressing news from Hungary: appalling devastations, terrible misery, chaos threatening (a great number of Hungarian newspapers are finding their way—presumably through the Russian Embassy— to a Hungarian Communist newspaper here, which reproduces them in facsimile; also a few people have received news through private channels). As I see it, for the time being one cannot even think of returning to Hungary. Nor is there any means of doing so—neither transport nor (Russian) permit. But even if there were means, in my opinion it would better to await developments. Heaven know how many years it will be before Hungary can pull itself together in some measure (if at all). And yet, I too, would like to return, for good – – – – –[217]

During June, the Columbia University Press had many problems with producing the special symbols Bartók used in the introduction and the notes to the melodies. In addition, there were unresolved questions about the collaborative work during the ongoing preparation of Part Two (texts, translations, and text-melody conformity). As Bartók had earlier written, "The gestation of the elephant is nothing in comparison with the time needed to give birth to this book— provided that it will not miscarry in the meanwhile."[218]

On 30 June, Bartók and his wife returned to Saranac Lake for the summer, and, on 2 July, he was in Montréal for his successful immigration to the United States the next day. This was followed by his acceptance of a lectureship at Harvard University, during the spring of 1946.[219] He completed the first draft of the Third Piano Concerto and, in August, worked on the mastersheet draft of the score as well as the first draft of the Viola Concerto. When he continued to have elevated temperature toward the end of the month, they decided to return to New York on the 30th. On 8 September, he wrote to William Primrose that:

> I am very glad to be able to tell you that your Viola Concerto is ready in draft, so that only the score has to be written, which means a purely mechanical work, so to speak. If nothing happens I can be through in 5 or 6 weeks, i.e., I can send you a copy of the orchestral score in the second half of Oct., and a few weeks afterwards a copy (or if you wish more copies) of the piano score.
> Many interesting problems arose in composing the work. The orchestra will be

rather transparent, more transparent than in the Violin Concerto. Also the sombre, more masculine character of your instrument executed some influence on the general character of the work.[220]

During mid-September his conditioned worsened, and when his temperature suddenly dropped on the 21st, his doctor had him admitted to the West Side Hospital. On September 25, the day before he died, Mrs. Bartók spent the night in his room. In the morning, after Péter arrived, Bartók began to breathe with difficulty.

Then Béla, smiling, looked in the direction of the armchair where I had spent the night—however, he did not say a single word. Péter held his right hand, I the left; his breathing, after a short while, became weaker, stopped completely, and he passed away quietly with a delicate smile on his face.[221]

PART TWO

Folk Music Research

6

Hungarian Folk Music

After Bartók and Kodály set out in 1906 to collect hitherto unknown Hungarian rural folk songs, it soon became apparent that significant structural differences occurred among the melodies, to the point where specific types could be established. Furthermore, a substantial number of variants were found, which required a means for determination of prototypes.

> Previously, even when collecting, the main importance was generally attributed to the text. The melody was noted down only as a secondary aspect, and the material was gathered eclectically and out of a regard for musical beauty and attractiveness, or perhaps just a few melodies were chosen out of many of similar character; in short, the viewpoints of scientific examination were neglected. And these viewpoints require the collection of all available material in order to obtain as many variants as possible. The old publications are selective, consider the text as the main aspect, and so forth.[1]

Fortunately, a method for the lexical ordering of a large corpus of Finnish folk songs had been developed by Ilmari Krohn (1867–1960) for the second volume of *Suomen Kansan Sävelmiä* (Melodies of the Finnish people).[2] His procedure, based on stanzas of four lines, is the determination of the melodic cadence of each line, beginning with that of the fourth line. The groups thus established are subdivided according to the cadence of the second line; further subdivision is made according to the cadence of the first and, finally, the third lines.[3] Bartók and Kodály decided to adopt Krohn's method, with "slight modifications" for lexically grouping the melodies of the Hungarian people, particularly by the use of caesuras (end tones) instead of such melodic cadences as dominant–tonic (V–I) and subdominant–tonic (IV–I). The following list represents a brief summary of salient features:

a. All melodies are transposed so that the last melody-section (a section is that part which overlies a text line) ends on G.

b. The caesuras of the other melody sections are designated by appropriate numerals, to indicate pitch.

c. The melodies are then grouped according to the number of sections in the tune: four-, three-, then two-section melodies.

d. The main caesura (the end tone of the second section) of each melody is determined. Its height—beginning with the lowest pitch—determines the basic sorting. Thereafter, classification is in accordance with the caesura of the first section and, finally, the third section.

e. The next differentiation is in rhythmic terms, from lowest to highest syllabic number of the underlying textlines, in which isometric melodies (having the same syllabic structure in each melody section) precede heterometric melodies (having one or more sections with a different syllabic structure).

f. The final classification is based on ambitus: tunes with narrow range precede those with wider range.[4]

In 1913, Bartók and Kodály drafted a plan for a "monumental Hungarian 'Corpus Musicae Popularis' edition," classified according to the modified Krohn-System and supplemented with the following indices "showing the collection from all sides."[5]

1. Alphabetical index of first textlines.

2. Topical index of the texts.

3. Toponymical list of communities and their songs, as determined by serial number.

4. Optional thematic catalogue to facilitate finding the songs.

5. Index of collectors or sources.

6. List of texts which underlie several melodies and of melodies sung to different texts.

7. A complete bibliography for each song.

8. Optional index classifying the material according to genre and subject matter, for those readers who want to use the collection exclusive of musical considerations.

It was not until 1923 that Bartók and Kodály succeeded in publishing a joint edition of 150 Transylvanian Hungarian folk songs, the first publication of Hungarian material grouped on a lexicographic basis.[6] Bartók transcribed most of the melodies, and Kodály was responsible for the editorial control, including the preface, classification procedure, and index tables. Before this event, however, Bartók had developed an alternative, "grammatical" methodology which was published the next year in his consequential study, *The Hungarian Folk Song*. His systematic approach begins with the basic treatment described in (a), (b), and (c) above. The next step is division of the melodies into the three style-categories of Hungarian folk songs: Class *A*. Old Style, Class *B*. New Style, and Class *C*. Mixed Style. Each of the three classes thus obtained is then ordered according to rhythm: Subclasses I. *Parlando* (or *Parlando-rubato*) and II. *Tempo giusto*. Next follows the grouping of each subclass into syllabic structures as described in (e). Thereafter, subgroups are formed with regard to caesuras (d), and the last stage is melodic ambitus (f). In the event still further classification is needed, the individual melodies are analyzed for sectional content structure (A B C D, A A B B, A A B A, etc.).[7]

Bartók's approach was readily adaptable for the classification of the peasant melodies of Hungary's pre–First World War minorities since the Mixed Style category comprises those Hungarian folk songs which show Slovak and other foreign influences. Kodály, on the other hand, emphasized the lexicographic principle of grouping all melodies according to melodic design, thus enabling the reader to locate each tune quickly and easily, and, moreover, bringing together all variant melodies as far as possible. In addition, his interest was centered on indigenous Hungarian products, including folk songs influenced by Gregorian chant, folk hymns, and popular art-songs.[8] There are no differences, however, between the grammatical and lexicographic methods with regard to the symbolic representation of caesuras. After each quaternary melody has been transposed to g^1 as the *tonus finalis*, the end tones of the first three melody-sections are indicated by the related roman or arabic figures (Ex. 6.1).

Notes

Figures   I   II   III   IV   V   VI VII   1   2   3   4   5   6   7   8   9   10   11

Ex. 6.1. Bartók, *HFS,* 7. Accidentals are added as needed (♯VII, ♭3, etc.).

A. The Old Style of Hungarian Peasant Music

Among the oldest-known songs in this class are nonceremonial quaternaries, consisting of *parlando* isometric melodies with eight-syllable textlines (Ex. 6.2), and those with twelve- and six-syllables. Comparatively recent are *tempo giusto* melodies with eight-, seven-, and eleven-syllables. The symmetrical Hungarian pentatonic scale, G-B♭-C-D-F, is a characteristic feature of all Class A melodies.[9]

8, vii–5   M.F. 1610b), Csikverebes (Csik), Kovács Balázs, 61é., 1912 (Lajtha).

−Ki - csi ma - dár   jaj be fenn szálloz, __   Mi az o - ka   a - lább   nem jársz?

−A - lább száll - nék, de nem me - rek,____   Mer én_ sen - kit_   sem üs - mé - rek.

Ex. 6.2. *BBSE,* 220, melody no. 44a.

Above the melody are the symbols indicating syllabic structure and range, followed by the number of the recording and the performer's data (place, name, collector). The main caesura (♭♭), representing the end tone of the second line) is enclosed in a box. The secondary caesuras (5 and 1, representing *d* and *g*, respectively) are bracketed and placed as indicated.

Other characteristic features of Class *A* melodies are the main caesura ♭3 (*b*♭*b*)—which in a few instances eventually became 1 (*g*¹) or 5 (*d*²)—and stanzas with nonarchitectonic structure (A B C D, A B B C, and A⁵ B⁵ A B).

> These old-style tunes are to be considered as purely Hungarian creations; so far as we know, nothing similar in style and character is to be found in any other country. The *parlando-rubato* eight-syllable tunes exercised a strong influence upon the peasant music of the Rumanian districts adjoining the regions of the Székely [people]. . . . Out of the rhythm of the seven-, eight-, and eleven-syllable tunes in adjustable *tempo giusto* rhythm was evolved the rhythm of most of the tunes representing the new Hungarian musical style (Class *B*).¹⁰

B. The New Style of Hungarian Peasant Music

The new style probably began to develop during the second half of the nineteenth century.¹¹ It is characterized by four architectonic (that is, rounded) structures: A A B A, A A⁵ B A, A A⁵ A⁵ A, and A B B A, The A B B A content-structure is a uniquely Hungarian form, usually with 5 (*d*) as the main caesura, the rhythm is for the most part *tempo giusto*, and there are hardly any ornamental tones (Ex. 6.3).

Ked - ves lá - nya vol - tam az a - nyám - nak,   Még - is o - da - a - dott egy o - láh - nak;

An - nak a - dott, a - kit nem   sze - ret - tem,   Gyász lesz vé - le az é - gesz é - le - tem.

Ex. 6.3. *HFS,* 244, melody no. 93a. Collected by Bartók in 1906.

Synopsis. The most common scales are the Dorian, the Aeolian, and the modern major; the Mixolydian is fairly frequent, the Phrygian and the modern minor less frequent.

The number of syllables to a line varies from six to twenty-five; but lines of twelve syllables or more may be considered as extensions of ten- or eleven-syllable lines.

The new style, undoubtedly, is a Hungarian creation. It exercised a considerable influence upon the more recent Slovak and Ruthenian peasant music, but hardly any on the Rumanian.¹²

C. Other Tunes in Hungarian Peasant Music

This class of mixed styles probably came into being under indirect Western European (possibly German) influences, probably through Czech-Moravian-Slovak channels. Many of the same melodies are found in both Hungarian and Slovak peasant music, and there are three- and two-line stanzas in addition to the prevailing quaternaries. Also included here are the melodies of the ancient ceremonial songs (wedding songs, harvesting songs, match-making songs, and so forth).[13] There are seven subclasses, further divided into groups (Table 6.1).[14]

TABLE 6.1
Strophic Structure in Class C Melodies

I. Isometric strophes: *Parlando* or invariable *Tempo giusto.*
    1. 5-syllable lines (no. 152)
    2. 6-syllable lines (153–78)
    3. 7-syllable lines (179–85)
    4. 8-syllable lines (186–205)
    5. 9-syllable lines (206)
    6. 10-syllable lines (207–11)
    7. 11-syllable lines (212)
    8. 12-syllable lines (213-4)
    9. 13-syllable lines (215)
   10. 14-syllable lines (216)
II. Isometric strophes: adjustable *Tempo giusto*
    1. 6-syllable lines (217)
    2. 7-syllable lines (218–21)
    3. 8-syllable lines (222–25b.)
    4. 10-syllable lines (226–7)
    5. 11-syllable lines (228–34b.)
III. Heterometric strophes: invariable *Tempo giusto*
    2.–5. Double-line melody sections (235–45)
    6.–11. Two lines of different syllabic length (246–61)
   16. Miscellaneous constructions (262–68)
IV. Heterometric strophes: adjustable *Tempo giusto*
    1., 3., 5. Double-line melody sections (269–74
    6.–11. Two lines of different syllabic length (275–94)
   16. Miscellaneous constructions (295a.–300)
V. Melodies in *Kolomyjka* rhythm (301–55)
VI. Two-section melodies (306–7)
VII. Three-section melodies (308–20)

Example 6.4 is a Class C folk song whose melody is that of the *kalamajkó* dance "which, curiously, bears no relation to the *kolomyjka* tunes of the Ruthenians. It was borrowed from the Czech fund, the Slovakian being the intermediary. Perhaps its origin should be sought even farther west. . . . That the tune is of Western origin is quite obvious."[15]

Ka - la - maj - kó an - nak ne - ve, Ug - rán - do - zik, mint a fe - ne,

Hány - ja - ve - ti lá - ba - it, Nem saj - nál - ja i - na - it.

Ex. 6.4. *HFS,* 285, melody no. 250.

As Bartók recalls in his autobiography, his investigation of Hungarian peasant music began in 1905 and was based entirely on musical grounds, since what
he had known as Hungarian folk songs until then were folklike "trivial songs by
popular composers and did not contain much that was valuable."[16] Beginning in
1906, however, he turned to scientific research as the means of determining
autochthonous Hungarian products, based on his discovery of old-style pentatonic melodies in remote villages of Hungarian Transylvania, Western European influenced new-style tunes among the younger peasants of Hungary proper,
and Slovak rhythm schemata in certain Hungarian mixed-style folk songs.

> The outcome of these studies was of decisive influence upon my work, because it
> freed me from the tyrannical rule of the major and minor keys. The greater part of
> the collected treasure, and the more valuable part, was in old ecclesiastical or
> Greek modes, or based on more primitive (pentatonic) scales, and the melodies
> were full of most free and varied rhythmic phrases and changes of tempi, played
> both *rubato* and *giusto.*[17]

The influence of Hungarian folk music on Bartók's Concerto for Orchestra
is apparent in the first movement, where the first theme of the *Introduzione* is
based on alternating major seconds and perfect fourths in the symmetrical pentatonic scale, F#-A-B-C#-E. This type of scalar structure and the frequent use of
major seconds and perfect fourths are characteristic of old-style Hungarian folk
song (see Ex. 5.17).[18] Moreover, the so-called dotted rhythm is "especially characteristic for certain types of Hungarian rural music. Our dotted rhythm is a
combination of the following three rhythmic patterns: ♪♩. , ♩. ♪, and ♩ ♩. Among
these, the first one, with an accentuated short value and a nonaccentuated long
value, is the most important. It is this rhythmic pattern which gives that well-
known rugged rhythm to many Hungarian pieces."[19]

7

Slovak Folk Music

During July 1906, while Bartók was in Békés County to undertake the collection of Hungarian peasant music, among the hundreds of recorded songs were isometric melodies with a pentatonic base (*HFS*, Class *A*, no. 66) or architectonic A B B A content-structure (Class *B*, no. 122), or heterometric syllabic structure (Class *C*, no. 268). Apparently it was the surprisingly large number of mixed-style melodies that prompted him to return to the northern Hungarian village of Gerlice Puszta during August. It was there, in 1904, that he recorded his first Hungarian folk song (Class *C*, no. 313).[1] The second visit added 120 melodies, of which one-third were Hungarian tunes with Slovak text. It was this fieldwork that led Bartók to extend his research to linguistically Slovak territories, and he continued collecting Slovak folk music until 1918, when the political events following the First World War interrupted his travels. His Slovak material consists of 1,620 melodies and approximately 1,200 variants, and he studied and classified more than 8,000 related melodies that had appeared in Slovak folk music publications.[2]

Bartók began with the lexical classification method as a preliminary study, in order to assemble variant melodies "in close sequence according to the conformity of the melodic line (whose character is somewhat determined by the final notes of the melody lines).[3] Then he followed the grammatical method as shown in Table 7.1.

TABLE 7.1
Classification of Slovak Folk Melodies

Class *A*. Four-line melodies
    Subclass I. With so-called nondotted rhythm
        Group a) Isometric melodies (nos. 1–421c)[4]
            Subgroup 1. 5-syllable lines
                Type β) Isorhythmic structure
                Type γ) Heterorhythmic structure
            2. 6-syllable lines
                α) *Parlando-rubato*
                β) Isorhythmic
                γ) Heterorhythmic
            3. 7-syllable lines
                β) Isorhythmic

γ) Heterorhythmic
4. 8-syllable lines
   α) *Parlando-rubato*
   β) Isorhythmic
   γ) Heterorhythmic
5.–11. 9–15-syllable lines
   β) Isorhythmic
   γ) Heterorhythmic
 b) Heterometric melodies (422–1047b)[5]
   Divided into 30 subgroups, according to stanza structure[6]
 II. With so-called dotted rhythm[7]
   Patterns such as ♩. ♪♩♩, ♩ ♩ ♪♩., ♪♩. ♪♩., and so forth
 III. With A A⁵ A⁵ A, A A⁵ B A, A B B A architectonic structures,
   further with A A B A architectonic structure and dotted rhythm[8]
Class *B*. Three-line melodies[9]
 I. With nondotted rhythm
 II. With dotted rhythm
Class *C*. Two-line melodies
 I. With nondotted rhythm
 II. With dotted rhythm
Class *D*. Melodies with indeterminate structure[10]
 I. Children's songs and play songs
 II. Other melodies with unclear or incomplete structure
Class *E*. Instrumental music[11]

Old Style Melodies

Bartók's fieldwork in northern Hungary unearthed certain specimens, all of them improvisation-like variants of a single melody—collected in Zólyom County (now Zvolenská, Slovakia) in 1915—that represent very old, autochthonous Slovak folk songs, and he designated them *valaská* (Shepherd's songs) or *detvanská* (from the village of Detva).[12] Other original Slovak melodies are certain lullabies, haymaking-, harvesting-, wedding-, and Midsummer Night songs.[13]

Mixed Style Melodies

The most extensive part of the material contains uncommonly varied types of isometric as well as heterometric stanzas, and the most striking feature is the frequency of occurrence of the Lydian mode, G-A-B-C♯-D-E-F♯, which is completely missing in the Hungarian material. Most of the melodies are in near relation to Moravian melodies, and other tunes apparently originate from Czech and German sources—especially the so-called *tercelő* (accompaniment in thirds) melodies—which arrived in Slovakia through Moravian intermediation.[14]

The rhythm of these melodies is mostly *tempo giusto*, 2/4, and the notes are nearly always quarters and eighths; frequently as ♫ ♩ or ♪♩ ♪. A character-

istic syllabic structure, designated by Bartók as Slovak rhythm-contraction, is:
2/4 ♩ ♩ | ♫ ♩ | ♩ 𝄾 | ♩ ♩ | ♫ ♩ | ♩ 𝄾 | ♬♬ ♩ ♩ | ♬♬ ♩ ♩ | ♩ ♩ | ♫ ♩ | ♩ 𝄾 |.
Symbolized as *a a a a* (six-syllable heterorhythmic Type γ), this isometric quaternary illustrates rhythm-contraction of the third line into two bars, where each
of the other lines consists of three bars.[15]

New Style Melodies

The Hungarian influence in the Slovak melodies with so-called dotted rhythm
is (a) direct adoptions from the Hungarian Class *B* material, for the most part
A A⁵ A⁵ A, A A⁵ B A, A B B A, and A A B A content-structure, and (b) original
Slovak peasant melodies with Hungarian dotted-rhythms or with their last lines
characteristic of the more recent Hungarian folk songs: 2/4 ♩ ♫ | ♫ ♩ | ♩ 𝄾 ‖
and 4/4 ♬♬ ♫ ♩ | ♪ ♩. ♪ 𝄾 ‖.[16]

In the fourth movement (*Intermezzo Interrotto*) of Bartók's Concerto for
Orchestra, the first theme is in Slovak folk-song style, particularly with regard
to emphatic rendition of A♯, the characteristic fourth degree of the E-Lydian
mode. And in the first movement of Bartók's First Piano Concerto, the Introduction (R.N. 1–2) is obviously Slovak Mixed Style (♫ ♩ and ♪ ♩ ♪) in rhythmic structure (see Ex. 8.2).

8

Romanian Folk Music

Bartók's fieldwork among the Transylvanian-Romanian minority peasants of former Greater Hungary began in Toroczkó (now Torockó, Romania) in November 1908 and continued until 1917.[1] He collected and transcribed more than 3,600 instrumental and vocal melodies, of which 3,404 were published during his lifetime (1913, 1914, 1923, 1935) and posthumously (1967, 1975). He continued working on the material intermittently, following the end of the First World War, and his research ended the year of his death, when he completed the classification of the song texts in New York on 30 March 1945.[2]

Bartók's first publication, the 1913 edition of 371 melodies from Bihor (formerly Bihar) County, was completed in May 1912 and published by the Academia Română in Bucharest. The material represents the simplest type of classification: instrumental melodies are grouped as violin, peasant flute, and bagpipe pieces; quaternary melodies with eight-syllable lines are sorted according to the modified Krohn-System; and there are eight unclassified melodies (nos. 363–71) originating from popular (urban or Hungarian) folk songs. During the 1930s, Bartók revised most of the melodies for publication in *RFM*. i–ii.[3]

His next project, ordering the 229 vocal and 156 instrumental melodies material collected in Torontal (Torontál) County, was apparently completed prior to his fieldwork in Maramureş (Máramaros) County during March 1913. When he returned to Budapest, however, he decided to postpone further work on the Torontal collection and arrange the Maramureş material, which he completed in November 1913. He then sent the fair copy to the Academia Română for publication, but production was temporarily postponed and subsequently canceled when the First World War broke out (see pp. 79–80 above).

In 1914, Bartók published his treatise on the music dialect of Hunedoara (Hunyad) County folk songs. Bartók's unique study and the eight unclassified melodies were revised in the 1930s and published in *RFM*.ii.[4] The book-length study of Romanian folk music from Maramureş finally appeared in a German edition in 1923, and it was reprinted in an English edition in 1975, as *RFM*.v.[5] The fourth monograph was the collection of Romanian *colinde* (Winter-solstice songs), assembled from various Transylvanian counties and completed in April 1926. It was Bartók's intention to introduce a new dimension in systematic ethnomusicology by classifying the texts as well as the melodies, and he concluded a contract with the London publisher, Oxford University Press, to publish the work in English, including translation of the Romanian texts. It was not until 1931, however, that Bartók finally realized the hopelessness of his efforts to achieve satisfactory text translations and cancelled the contract (see pp.120–21, 125–26 above):

> The second publication by the same publisher was to include my collection of Rumanian Colindas (Winter-solstice songs). Their extremely interesting texts were supposed to appear in original as well as English. After several years of delay, the translation to English prose was completed, one part in archaic English, the rest (by someone else) in most unsuitable Kitchen-English. The publisher did not want to change this, though. Result: I published the book at my own expense; however, only the musical part, because of lack of sufficient funds. The texts are still in manuscript, even today.[6]

Each of the five volumes comprising the posthumous edition of Bartók's *Rumanian Folk Music* has a different synoptic grouping of the melodies (and of the texts where applicable): "Apparently every body of material of distinctive character requires a distinct system of classification, constructed especially for the purpose."[7] The following exposé, therefore, provides the classification system in tabular format, findings, and other data for each volume.

RFM VOLUME ONE: INSTRUMENTAL MELODIES

TABLE 8.1
Classification of Romanian Instrumental Folk Melodies

Class *A*. Dance melodies (nos. 1–542bis)
    Subclass I. Short-section 2/4 melodies
        Group 1. Two-section melodies
            Subgroup 1. 5-syllable lines
        2. Three-section melodies with the main caesura at the end
        of the first section
        3. Three-section melodies with the main caesura at the end
        of the second section
        4. Four-section melodies
    II. Long-section 2/4 melodies
        Group 1–4. Same as in Subclass I.
        Group 5. Five-section melodies
    III. Four-section melodies differing from Subclass I and II
        Group a). In 2/4, one bar per section
        Group b). In 2/4, three bars per section
        Group c). In 2/4 time, eight bars per section
        Group d). Heterometric melodies: sections have unequal
        number of bars
Class *B*. Dance pieces without any determined structure

Original form. Irregular repetition of one or more motifs
(543–681)
"Skeleton" form (Appendix I). The extracted motifs are
grouped systematically into four groups: 1. Two 2/4 bars,
2. "Shifted rhythm" motifs, 3. Four 2/4 bars, and
4. Miscellaneous types
Class C. Instrumental melodies normally sung with text (682–758)[8]
Subclass I. *Parlando* melodies with determined structure
Group 1. Two-section melodies
Group 2. Three-section melodies with the main caesura at
the end of the first section
Group 3. Three-section melodies with the main caesura at
the end of the second section
Group 4. Four-section melodies.
Subclass II. *Tempo giusto* melodies with determined structure
(730–737)[9]
Subclass III. Melodies of mourning songs[10]
Subclass IV. *Parlando* melodies with no determined structure
Group 1. Various melodies
Group 2. *"Cântec lung"* melodies[11]
Class D. Instrumental melodies connected with wedding ceremonies
(759–763)
Class E. Alphorn melodies and their imitations on other instruments
(764–809)

Instruments

1. The VIOLIN is identical with the European violin, including the tuning. The instrument's literary name is *vioara,* a designation, however, never used by the peasants of the explored territory. Instead, it is called *higheghe* (from the Hungarian *hegedű*). When a "band" of two violinists plays, the second violin has a flat bridge and three strings tuned to *g, d*[1] and *a.* This arrangement allows the three strings to be bowed together by a loosely strung bow, in order to play an accompaniment of trichords. Another type of accompaniment is played on a two-stringed guitar, which is tuned to the perfect fifth, *d–a.*

2. The PEASANT FLUTE is a recorder-like instrument made from wood, about 12–15 in. in length, with six fingerholes and a whistle-like mouthpiece. The LONG PEASANT-FLUTE, about 25–30 in., and generally is provided with five fingerholes. The DOUBLE PEASANT-FLUTE consists of two flutelike pipes of equal length wrought from a single piece of wood. One of the pipes has six fingerholes, the other has none. There two kinds of LONG PEASANT-FLUTE WITHOUT FINGER HOLES, with or without a whistle-like mouthpiece.

3. The BAGPIPE exists in two types in the explored territory. (1) The Balkan type has only two pipes, the chanter and the drone. (2) The Eastern Central-European type has three pipes: the chanter, the middle pipe (made of the same piece of wood), and the drone.

4. The ALPHORN is made of a fir trunk about 7–8 ft. long, with a diameter of about 4–5 in. at its broader length Since it has no fingerholes, only harmonics can be produced. This rather bulky and heavy instrument is used by shepherds (mostly women and girls in certain areas).

5. The JEW'S-HARP is a favorite instrument of the women folk, which seems to be restricted to women's or children's leisure-time activities.

6. PERCUSSION INSTRUMENTS were rarely used in the explored territory. Bartók found only a kind of side drum with one drumhead, which was played with a single drumstick. The designation of certain dances, on the other hand, seems to indicate that an instrument with two drumheads is used in many other villages, especially in Bihor County.

Dance Genres and Their Choreography

Bartók lists eighty different genres, including counties and metronomic tempi. A second list provides the usual order of dances at the "ever-recurring" Sunday dances in certain village dance recreation. There are detailed descriptions of almost half of the listed genres, including some illustrative line drawings to indicate dance steps.

> The pieces called *Când păcurarul a găsit oile* ("When the shepherd found his lost sheep"; no. 79), though never accompanied by dance, evidently belong to the class of dance music, since they *are* dances. For expressing joy, dance music, of course, is more appropriate than any other kind of music. Besides, these pieces, when performed, may be regarded as dances with an imaginary solo dancer, the shepherd. There well may be the latent supposition that the outburst of exultant joy leads to dance-like gambols.[12]

Musical Characteristics

The greater part of the material can be reduced to a skeleton pattern of ♫♫ in each bar, eight bars in the short sections of Subclass *A. I.* 4 and sixteen bars in the long sections of Subclass *A. II.* 4. This supposedly original rhythmic pattern is transformed in instrumental pieces: ♫ is substituted for ♪ to form combinations of ♫♫♪, ♫♫, and ♫♫. Each of the latter two combinations may be further transformed into an eighth-note triplet.[13]

Bartók collected sixty-nine melodies in fast tempo, whose nonsymmetrical combinations of ♪ and ♪. "gives them a very peculiar and exciting 'limping' character which distinguishes them from any other rhythmic formations."[14] They are designated as "Bulgarian" rhythms, because of their frequency in Bulgarian folk music as well as discovery by Bulgarian musicologists. Among the varied combinations in melody no. 130a are: 3+4/16 ♪. ♫♫, ♪. ♫, ♪. ♫♫, and

♪. ♫♫.[15] The "heroic" melody type (e.g., no. 232) has combinations of ♪. and ♪ instead of even ♪ values, which give a march-like character to the pieces. Sometimes ♫♫ groups are substituted for ♫ pairs .

"Shifted" rhythm can be found in some pieces of Subclass *A*. II (e.g., no. 18) and motifs of Class *B*. Ex. 8.1, a bagpipe motif, shows how this rhythmic peculiarity occurs when the shifting of an unaccentuated phrase transforms its repetition to an accentuated formation. The basic thirteen- or fourteen-syllable schema of this bagpipe motif is similar to that of the Hungarian *kanásztánc* (Swineherd-dance), Romanian *Ardeleana* (Transylvanian [dance]), or Ukrainian (Ruthenian) *kolomyjka* (Round dance): 2/4 ♫♫♩| ♫♩ | ♫♫♩ |♩ ♩ ‖ or ♫♫♩| ♫♫♩ | ♫♫♩|♩ ♩‖. Apparently the Ukrainian schema was the source for the *kanásztánc,* which led to the Recruiting-dance type (*Verbunkos*) and, eventually, to the Romanian *Ardeleana.*

Ex. 8.1. *RFM.*i, Appendix One, motif 228. The brackets delineate the phrase and its shifted repetition. Motif 228 occurs in Class *B* melody nos. 559, 564, 571, 575, 579, and 589.

The Class *B* melodies with motif-structure "seem to be a primitive state of folk music preceding the era of determined-structure formations." Appendix I comprises 323 motifs (excluding variants), "mostly using five or six diatonic degrees. It is amazing indeed what a variety can be achieved with such scanty means."[16]

The mentioned programmatic genre—"When the shepherd found his lost sheep"—is the conceptual source for the third movement of Bartók's Sonata no. 1 for Violin and Piano (1921) and the second movement of no. 2 (1922).[17] Romanian "shifted" rhythm is featured in the first movement of Bartók's First Piano Concerto (Ex. 8.2).

Ex. 8.2. Bartók, Concerto no. 1 for Piano and Orchestra (1926), first movement, mm. 13–18.

The first movement of Bartók's Second Piano Concerto represents the apotheosis of Romanian rhythmic- and motif-structure. Ex. 8.3 shows some of the bagpipe motifs transformed by Bartók for the composition of his masterpiece.

Ex. 8.3. *RFM*.i, Appendix I, motif nos. 173, 152, 236, and 323.

Note that the rhythmic-structure of motif 173 is identical with the opening motif (mm. 1–2) of the "Russian Dance" in Stravinsky's *Petrushka* (1911).

RFM VOLUME TWO: VOCAL MELODIES

The vocal material is grouped in ten classes, according to the purpose of the music or the singing serves:[18]

    A—F. Nonceremonial melodies (*doina,* in certain regions *hore*);
    G. Mourning-song melodies;
    H. Wedding song melodies;
    I. Harvest-song melodies;
    J. Rain-begging song melodies.

The melodies are composed of four, three, or two melody-sections. The text lines, including refrains, are almost exclusively of eight syllables and have a metrical structure completely different from that of the neighboring peoples. There is no stanza-structure, and rhyming verses are used.[19] The classification system is outlined as follows (Table 8.2).

TABLE 8.2
Classification of Romanian Vocal Folk Melodies

Class A. *Parlando* melodies (nos. 1–350)
    Subclass I. Isometric melodies
        Group 1. Two-section melodies
        Group 2. Three-section melodies, main caesura at the end of
            the first section
        Group 3. Three-section melodies, main caesura at the end of
            the second section
        Group 4. Four-section melodies
    Subclass II. Heterometric melodies
        Group 1–4. Same as in Subclass I.
Class B. *Tempo giusto* melodies (351–452)
    Subclass I. Isometric melodies
        Group 2–4. Same as in Class A. I.
    Subclass II. Heterometric melodies
        Group 1–4. Same as in Class A. II.

Class *C*. Dance melodies (453–529)
    Subclass I. Melodies with definite structure
        Group a) Isometric melodies with two-bar sections
            Subgroup 4. Four-section melodies
        Group b) Isometric melodies with four-bar sections
            Subgroup 3. Three-section melodies, main caesura at the end of the second section
            Subgroup 4. Four-section melodies
        Group c) Heterometric melodies
            Subgroup 3. Three-section melodies, main caesura at the end of the second section
            Subgroup 4. Four-section melodies
    Subclass II. Melodies with indefinite motif-structure
    Subclass III. Recited "dance-words"
Class *D*. *Tempo giusto* melodies in "dotted" rhythm (530–583)
    Subclass I. Isometric melodies
        Group 1. Two-section melodies
        Group 2. Three-section melodies, main caesura at the end of the second section
        Group 4. Four-section melodies
    Subclass II. Heterometric melodies
        Group 2. Three-section melodies, main caesura at the end of the first section
        Group 3. Three-section melodies, main caesura at the end of the second section
        Group 4. Four-section melodies
Class *E*. Melodies with indeterminate structure (584–612)
Class *F*. Variants of the *Cântec lung* (*Hora lungă*) "long-drawn" melody (613)
Class *G*. Mourning-song melodies (614–661)
    Subclass α) So-called *bocete* (proper melodies) with improvised texts
        Group 1. Two-section melodies
        Group 3. Three-section melodies, main caesura at the end of the second section
        Group 4. Four-section melodies
    Subclass β) *Zorilor* (at dawn)
        Group 1. Two-section melodies
        Group 3. Three-section melodies, main caesura at the end of the second section
        Group 4. Four-section melodies
    Subclass γ) *A bradului* (song of the fir)
        Group 4. Four-section melodies
    Subclass δ) *Hora mortului* (Dead Man's Song) or *La priveghiu* (At the Wake)
        Group 1. Two-section melodies
        Group 3. Three-section melodies, main caesura at the end of the second section

Group 4. Four-section melodies
Class *H*. Wedding-song melodies (662–666)
    Group 1. Two-section melodies
    Group 2. Three-section melodies, main caesura at end of first section
    Group 3. Three-section melodies, main caesura at end of second section
    Group 4. Four-section melodies
Class *I*. Harvest-song melodies (667–671)
    Group 1. Two-section melodies
    Group 3. Three-section melodies, main caesura at end of second section
Class *J*. Rain-begging song melodies (672–678)
    Subclass I. Melodies with definite structure
    Subclass II. Melodies with indefinite structure

Further partition of the Groups and Subgroups was made on the basis of the caesura relations of the melody sections. The divisions thus obtained were divided into Subdivisions according to the range of the melodies. The Z symbols used for the heterometric melodies in Subclass II of Class *A, B,* and *D* are the same as described in *HFS* (pp. 64–66).[20]

RFM VOLUME THREE: TEXTS

This volume contains 1,752 texts representing 1,335 text variants or single texts; altogether about 16,100 main text lines and 690 refrains lines, including the recited "dance words" from Vol. I. The texts are classified according to their content, since almost all of them have the same syllabic structure and there are no text stanzas. Although Bartók believed that the order of an ideal grouping system "should correspond to the order of events and sentiments in human life: beginning with birth and ending with death," his fieldwork in the villages of explored Romanian territory did not turn up texts connected with birth, christening or lullabies, or children's game texts connected with singing rather than recitation.[21] He therefore sorted the material according to the following classes, subclasses, and groups (Table 8.3).

TABLE 8.3
Classification of Romanian Folk Texts

Class *A*. Love Songs	5) Mistrust	12) Difficult to please
Subclass I. Subject:	6) Peaceful separation	14) Squeamishness
female; object: male	7) Forsaken	15) Imprecations on who
1) Description	8) Curses	divorced us
2) Longing	9) Repelling him	16) Impossible terms
3) Grief	10) Forsaking him	17) Charms
4) Jealousy	11) Recalling the past	18) Jeering at him

21) Diverse
II. Subject: male; object: female
  1) Description
  2) Longing
  3) Grief
  4) Jealousy
  5) Mistrust
  6) Peaceful separation
  7) Forsaken
  8) Curses
  9) Repelling him
  10) Forsaking him
  11) Recalling the past
  12) Difficult to please
  13) Having two or more sweethearts
  14) Squeamishness
  15) Imprecations on who divorced us
  17) Charms
  19) Ugly or bad wife
  20) Married woman
  21) Diverse
III. Subject and object: male and female
  1) Idyll
  3) Refusing to part
  4) No more love
  5) Separation
  6) Husband and wife
  7) Diverse
IV. Love (in general)
  1) Meditation
  2) Adversity
  3) Diverse
Class B. Songs of Sorrow
  I. Various subjects
    1) Meditation
    2) Too much distress
    3) I am a most distressed being
    4) Overcome by distress
    5) Simile
    6) Contrast
    7) Recalling the past

8) Reproaches to mother
9) Curses
10) Birds foretold my fate
11) Poverty
12) Old age
13) Diverse
II. Far from home
  1) Leaving home
  2) Leaving with sadness
  3) Saying goodbye
  4) Going to America
  5) Complaints from abroad
III. Bride or wife complaining about marital life
  1) General complaints
  2) Reproaches to parents
  3) Complaints about the mother-in-law
  4) Complaints about the mother-in-law and the husband
  5) Complaints about the husband
  6) Recalling girlhood
  7) Diverse
Class C. Soldiers' Songs
  1) Recruiting and leaving for the army
  2) Reproaches to mother
  3) Army life
  4) In the battlefield
  5) Returning home
  6) Diverse

Class D. Death
Class E. Worldly Wisdom
Class F. Nature
  1) Birds
  2) Plants
  3) Forests
  4) Stars
Class G. Jeering
  1) At girls
  2) At boys
  3) At women
  4) At men
  5) At women and men
  6) At Gypsies
Class H. Jesting Songs
Class I. Singing
Class J. Revelry (Drinking Songs)
Class K. At Dancing ("Dance-words")
Class L. Kryptadia[22]
  1) Man speaking
  2) About men
  3) Man about a woman or women
  4) Man to a woman
  5) Man and woman speaking
  6) Jesting at women
  7) About old men and women
  8) Girls
  9) Diverse
  10) Texts with indecent last lines
Class M. Enumerating Songs
Class N. About bad people
Class O. Against authority
Class P. About highwaymen
Class Q. Jail Songs
Class R. Miscellaneous subjects
Class S. Romany Texts
Class T. Epics

Class *U.* Wedding Songs
Class *V.* Rain-begging
    Songs
Class *W.* Harvest Songs
Class *X.* Songs of Mourn-
    ing
  I. *Bocete* (proper
    songs)
    1) For the father
    2) For the mother
    3) For a son

4) For a
    daughter
5) For a child
6) For a brother
7) For a sister
8) For the hus-
    band
9) For the wife
10) Birds foretold
    my fate
11) Fragments

12) Travesties
13) Diverse
II. *Zorilor* ([At]
    Dawn)
III. *A bradului* (song of
    the fir)
IV. *Hora mortului*
    (The Dead Man's
    [Mourning] Song) or
    La priveghiu (At the
    Wake)

Bartók chose the "Love Songs" as the first class (*A*), because they constitute more than one-third (5,599) of the 16,074 texts. Class *T* (2,093 Epics), *B* (2,016 Songs of Sorrow), and Class *C* (1,207 Soldier's Songs), make up another third of the collection. With regard to the subclasses and groups, Bartók states that he tried to "establish as logical a line as possible. The intention was, for instance, to give in entirety a quasi love story by means of the order of texts in *A* I and *A* II Subclasses."[23] In addition to the basic classification in Table 12, Bartók offers suggestions for further division of certain groups into subgroups by the use of arabic numerals (Table 13). In order to avoid complications, subgroups are not included in the Texts and Translations.[24]

The Introduction also includes remarks and tabulations concerning versification technique (rhyming lines), the use of refrains, including a list of those common to Bartók's Serbo Croatian material. An Addenda, added after Bartók had completed the Introduction, explores the relation of Italian lyrical folk texts—so-called *Stornelli* (Three-line ditties) and *Rispetti* (Love poems in eight- or six-line stanzas)—to the Romanian material, particularly in the use of the name of a flower as an introductory quinary line. As a case in point: *Fiore di canna* (It., Flower of cane reed) and *Floare rozmalin* (Rom., Bloom of rosemary). This common feature is "confined to the folk text material of Romance peoples, possibly only to the Rumanian and Italian folk texts. This fact may be considered as a sign of their great antiquity; indeed, they may date back to the epoch when the ancestors of the Rumanians left the soil of Italy."[25]

RFM VOLUME FOUR: CAROLS AND CHRISTMAS SONGS (*COLINDE*)

Part One

There are 484 melodies, including variants, in this collection of Romanian winter-solstice songs, which Bartók recorded from 1909 to 1917 in peasant villages situated in various counties of formerly Hungarian Transylvania. Exception: the 32 melodies, including variants, which he collected in Maramureş County during March 1913.[26]

The oldest genre is the *Colinde* (sg., *Colindă*), perhaps the only peasant-like melodies and texts of the Christmas ceremony in earlier times, and for the most part sung with one refrain. The newer genre is the *Cântece de stea* (Star or Bethlehem songs), probably introduced by priests and teachers, mostly sung by children, and strongly influenced by Western European music and poetry. The traditional Transylvanian Christmas practice is that:

> Caroling usually takes place according to the following custom: after several weeks of "study" (choral singing in unison) of the *Colinde*, on Christmas Eve a group of eight to ten boys and girls, under the leadership of a chief, set out on a caroling tour of the village (in Maramureș County, the groups are separated according to sex). They stop in front of each house and ask whether the hosts will receive them. Once inside the house, the group performs four or five carols. In Hundoara and Alba, the carolers divide themselves into two teams and sing alternately in antiphonal fashion; that is, the team of singers divides into two groups, each one singing in turn a verse of the song. At the end of the performance, the hosts present a gift to the carolers who go on to the neighbor's house.[27]

The antiphonal singing in the mentioned two counties is usually done as a "change" song, in which the new entry always occurs before the preceding stanza ends. Thus, the last one or two beats of the melody sung by one group sound together with the opening beats of the succeeding group.[28]

With regard to classification of the melodies, there are three major categories: melodies set to six-syllable proper lines (Class *A*), to eight-syllable proper lines (Class *B*), and the few melodies with indeterminate melodic structure, but mostly with text stanza structure (Class *C*).[29] In the following tabulation, the syllabic structure of proper text lines are designated by arabic numerals, separated one from the other by commas; italicized numerals represent the structure of refrain text lines (Table 8.4).

TABLE 8.4
Stanza Structure in the Colindă *Melodies*[30]

Class *A*. Six-syllable lines
    Subclass I. Two melody-lines
        Parlando (melody no. 1)
        Tempo giusto (2)
    II. Three melody-lines
        a) 6, *5,* 6, (3)
        b) 6, [= 6, 6, or 6, 6, *6,* or
            6, *6, 6,*] (4–8)
        c) 6 + 6, *6,* 6 + 6, (9–15)
        d) 6, 6, *7* (16)
        e) 6, 6, *8,* (17)
        f) 6, *9,* 6, (18–19)
        g) *8,* 6, 6 (20)

h) *8,* 6, *10* (21)
i) *9,* 6, 6 (22)
j) *9,* 6, *9* (23)
III. Four melody-lines
    a) 6, 6, *5,* 6 (24)
    b) 6, [6, 6, 6, 6,]
        α) isorhythmic (25–29)
        β) heterorhythmic (30–32)
    c) 6, *8,* 6, 6 (32)
    d) *8,* 6, 6, 6, (33–34)
Class *B*. Eight-syllable lines
    I. One melody-line (35–36)
    II. Two melody-lines

a) *6*, 8, (37)
b) *8*, 6, (38–40)
c) 8, [8, *8*,]
  α) isorhythmic (41–47)
  β) heterorhythmic (48)
d) 8, *12*, (50–51)
e) *12*, 8, (52–53)
f) *12*,
  α) isorhythmic (54)
  β) heterorhythmic (55–56)
III. Three melody-lines
  a) *5*, 8, 8, (57)
  b) 8, *5*, 8, (58–67)
  c) 8, *6*, *6*, (68)
  d) 8, *6*, 8, (69–70)
  e) 8, *6*, *11*, (71)
  f) 8, 8, *6*, (72–73)
  g) 8, [8, 8, *8*, or 8, *8*, 8,]

α) isorhythmic (74–96)
β) heterorhythmic
  (97–104)
h) 8, 8, *12*, (105)
i) *8*, *11*, 12, (106)
j) 8, *12*, 8, (107)
IV. Four melody-lines
  a) 8, *5*, 8, *5*, (108–110)
  b) 8, *6*, 8, *6*, (111–113)
  c) 8, [8, 8, 8, 8, or 8, *8*, 8, *8*,]
  α) isorhythmic (114–121)
  β) heterorhythmic (122–
    126)
  d) 8, *6* + *6*, 8, (127)
  e) 8, *14*, *14* ,8, (128)
  f) *10*, *8*, *13*, 8, (129)
Class *C*. Indeterminate forms (130–
  133)

The classifications thus established are further sorted according to the main and secondary caesuras (see Table 8.2 above). Bartók's other tabulations illustrate scale, range, and content-structure of the melodies.[31] Among the general characteristics of the *Colinde* are (a) three-line stanzas, (b) change of time (c) *Tempo giusto* rhythm, (d) change singing, and (e) use of refrain lines. It is noteworthy that twenty of the melodies in the collection are in so-called Bulgarian rhythm, where the smallest unit is a sixteenth note, and higher values are asymmetrically compounded from these short units, such as ♪. ♪ (or ♪ ♪.) .[32]

Part Two

The second part of the volume contains all the texts belonging to the melodies in Part One. Including variants and fragments, there are 467 texts whose tabulation represents Bartók's first attempt at the classification of folk texts."[33]

TABLE 8.5
Classification of the Colindă *Texts*

A. Secular texts
  I. Epic texts (secular subjects)
    a) Hunting (stags and lions) (text nos. 1–9)
    b) Pastorals (10–12)
    c) Ballads (13–24)
  II. Family life
    a) To young girls (25–40)
    b) To the man giving the bride away (41)
    c) To young men (or to the son of the family) (42–47)

  d) To the host of the house (48–50)
  e) To a married couple (51)

B. Secular Texts with Religious Allusions

  I. Texts about the Colinda custom in general
      a) Arrival of the Colinda singers (52–64)
      b) Congratulations (65–68)
      c) Allusions to expected gifts (69–72)
      d) Thanking and departing (52–64)
      e) Texts related to the *plugusor* (77–81)[34]

C. Religious Texts

  I. Religious legends
      a) About God (82–83)
      b) About the Holy Virgin (84–90)
      c) About the preeminence of God and John the Baptist (91)
      d) Pursuit of St. John (92)
      e) About Judas (93–94)
      f) The rebellion of the Jews against Christianity (95)
      g) Birth of Christ from a rock (96)
      h) About the Holy Mother and Christ (97)
      i) Origin of wine, wheat, and anointing oil (98)
      j) Preeminence of wine, wheat and anointing oil (99)
      k) About retribution in the future life (100)
      l) About the Last Judgment (101–102)
  II. Texts about events described in the Bible
      a) Creation of the World (103)
      b) The Fall of Man (104)
      c) The Birth of Christ (105–107)
      d) The three Magi (108)
      e) The Baptism of Christ (109–111)
      f) Judas' betrayal and Christ's crucifixion (112–114)
      g) Christ's ascension (115)

D. Religious Lyrics (116–133)

E. Humorous Texts (134–136)

F. Unclassifiable Fragments (137–138)

G. Romany Texts (139–141)

H. Appendix (nos. 142–164)

Bartók also grouped the 147 refrains into nine categories, according to key words. Group I, the largest category (Index nos. 1–39), contains syllabic variants of *Domn* (Lord!, Lord God!, etc.).[35] Among the refrains in Group II (nos. 40–61), the untranslatable word *Ler* occurs. Perhaps its origin and meaning stem from Romanian folk tales (Emperor Ler), or Celtic (the marine god *Ler*) sources.[36] Moreover, the usual *Colinde* performance gives the impression of a fiery warlike type of song rather than a pious and religious one.[37]

We must not think of the *Colinde*, however, in terms of the religious Christmas carols of the West. First of all, the most important part of these texts—perhaps one-third of them—have no connections with Christmas. Instead of the Bethlehem legend we hear about a wonderful battle between the victorious hero and the—until then—unvanquished lion (or stag), we are told the tale of the nine sons who—after hunting for so many years in the old forest—have been changed into stags, or we listen to a marvelous story about the sun who has asked in marriage the hand of his sister, the moon, and so on. Thus here are texts truly preserved from ancient, pagan times! One of the main festivals of pagan peoples was that observed at the time of the winter solstice. Afterwards, by chance or by design, the celebration of Christmas was established at the same time. It is not surprising that in the subconscious mind of Christianized pagan peoples the two holidays have become as one. What is really miraculous is the fact that after so many hundreds of years the pagan texts have been able to survive undisturbed.[38]

By way of comparing Bartók's English adaptation of Epic (hunting text) 4a for his *Cantata profana* (see p. 110 above) to the literal peasant text, the translation published in *RFM*.iv. is given below.

Behold, that old man,
He at one time
Had nine sons of his own;
Even taught them not
Cowherds how to be;
Only taught them how
In the hills to hunt.

They hunted so much,
Wherever they found
Spoor of a large stag,
Followed it so far,
Till they lost their way,
And until they changed
To nine mountain stags.

Their beloved father
Could hold out no more,
And he started out:
He fitted his bow,
Hunted in the hills,
Where he came upon

Nine fine mountain stags.
On one knee he went,
Arrow set to loose.

Of the stags the largest
Called aloud to say:
Father dear of ours,
Do not shoot at us,
For we'll pick you up
With these pointed antlers
And we'll toss you down,
From mountain to mountain,
From meadow to meadow,
And from stone to boulder,
You'll be torn to shreds.

Their dear father then
Loudly called to them:
Oh, dear sons of mine,
Come along back home
To your little mother!
Longing she awaits you

With the decked-out table,
With the candles burning,
With the glasses filled.

Of the stags the largest
Spoke and said to him:
Our beloved father,
Go back home without us
To our little mother,
Because our antlers
Can't go through the doorway,
Only through the mountains;
And these feet of ours
Do not step on ashes,
For they step through leafage;
And these lips of ours
Do not drink from glasses,
For they drink from well springs.

Example 8.4 shows the corresponding *Colindă* variant melody no. 12bb, collected by Bartók in 1914. Although the scalar degrees, E♮-F-G-A♭-B♭-C, form a nondiatonic (octatonic partition!) hexachord, F is the principal tone and G, the second degree, is the characteristic Romanian *tonus finalis*. Each section of the ternary (A B A) form has A♭-G as end tones (mm. 3, 6, 9), thus providing the melody with a basic Phrygian color. The same peculiarity occurs in the Phrygian source melody (no. 12a), whose secular ballad text intermixes a religious refrain ("To the Lord, to the Almighty"), a biblical figure ("Father Adam"), and the Romanian fairy princess ("Ana Sânziana"). Furthermore, the text itself is of pagan origin, narrating the journey of the mighty sun around the world, who, on his return, tells (his) sister, Sânziana, that she will be his wife when she has woven bolts of silken fabric.[39]

Ex. 8.4. *RFM*.iv, variant melody no. 14b. The key signature represents Bartók's innovative use of only those accidentals which apply to the principal tones of a folk melody.

Concurrent with Bartók's self-publication of *Melodien der rumänischen Colinde* (*Weihnachtslieder*) in 1935, he prepared a prospectus which the printer (Universal Edition, Vienna) mailed to a selected list of possible subscribers. In addition to his Preface and two pages of music examples in facsimile (melody nos. 81a–81n), he included the following comments:

> The [*Colinde*] material is treated according to rigorously scientific principle. It is for the first time that melodies if this type are published in such large number, in the most authentic manner, on the basis of the phonograph recordings.
> It seems that among all the Eastern European peoples the Rumanians have preserved best, till this day, these partly-ancient songs of the winter solstice. At all events, the extraordinary wealth (estimated to average 20 percent) of the Rumanian Christmas songs is outstanding. According to recent publications such songs are found only in comparatively small numbers among the neighboring peoples. For this reasons the Rumanian material is the richest source of this important folk custom of East European villages.
> The work should be of special interest to researchers in music folklore, to ethnologists, and to linguists.

RFM VOLUME FIVE: MARAMUREŞ COUNTY

Although the publication of this revised edition of *Volksmusik der Rumänen von Maramureş* brings to a close the posthumous series of volumes devoted to Bartók's monumental collection of Romanian musical folklore, the first edition, published in Munich in 1923, was intended to follow Bartók's other county-wide studies (Bihor in 1913, Hunedoara in 1914) of villages in Transylvania.[40]

Unlike the preceding four volumes, this one is all-inclusive: vocal melodies, including *Colinde*, instrumental melodies, and texts, collected by Bartók from 15–27 March 1913.

Bartók ordered the 365 melodies into five main classes, according to the occasions on which they would be sung or played, then further divided them into subclasses and groups (Table 8.6). The texts, many of them incomplete, were not classified, apparently because of wartime conditions and other obstacles which prevented Bartók from obtaining the written work of Ion Bîrlea, his Romanian collaborator.[41]

TABLE 8.6
Classification of Maramureş County Folk Melodies[42]

Class A (*Colinde*), melody nos. 1–19
    Group 1. Two-section melodies
    Group 2. Three-section melodies, main caesura at the end
    of the second section
    Group 3. Four-section melodies
Class B (Mourning-song melodies), 20–22
    Subclass I. Laments for the old (that is, married persons)
    Subclass II. Laments for the young (unmarried persons)
Class C (Non-ceremonial songs), 23–135
    Subclass I. The "long-drawn" melody (*Hora lungă*)
    Subclass II. The newer songs (*Hore*)
    Group 1. Two-section melodies
    Group 2. Three section melodies, main caesura at the end
    of the second section
    Group 3. Four-section melodies
Class D (Dance melodies), 136–92
    Subclass I. (Free form: varied repetitions of one or several two-
    measure motives)
    Subclass II.
    Group 1. Four-section melodies
    Group 2. Miscellaneous
Class E (Various instrumental melodies), 193–209
    Group 1. Alphorn (*bucium*)
    Group 2. Alphorn imitations: peasant flute (*fluer*), violin
    Group 3. Violin

It was in Maramureş that Bartók discovered the so-called long-drawn melody (*Hora lungă*), a genre which consists of variants of a single melody, always sung by only one person, and entirely improvisatory.

Nevertheless, in a general way three parts can be distinguished which alternately regularly or recur:
    1. A sustained c^2 or d^2 as a phrase opening;
    2. A richly ornamented middle section;

3. A declamatory cadence on g^1;

4. A variety of interjections are scattered before, after or between the text lines, such as *hei, și, că, măi,* and so forth.[43]

Example 8.5 illustrates *Hora lungă* melody no. 23a, the Class *C* source melody, which has seven variants.

Hey, you handsome youngster, you!
When I had a talk with you,
You were scared of witchery.

Ex. 8.5. *RFM*.v, melody no. 23a. The interjections are italicized.

The instrumental character of the entire *Hora lungă* melody indicates that its source may have been some kind of instrumental music. In older times, it undoubtedly was the only melody used in Maramureș for lyric and epic texts. And, Bartók states, the *Hora lungă* conforms closely to the melody of the Ukrainian *dumy.*[44]

The dance melodies (Class *D*) are played by professional musicians (mostly Gypsies) at weddings and social dances. The participants shout so-called dance-words (*strigături*) to the music, or sing these words along with the instrumental melody. The Gypsies use the ordinary European violin, and the accompaniment is played on the ordinary guitar, which, however, has only two strings and is tuned to D-A. The instrument is plucked (without plectrum) in the ostinato rhythm: 2/4 ♫♫, with the accented first and third eighths in one direction and the unaccented values in the other direction.

In the fifth movement (Finale) of Bartók's Concerto for Orchestra, the first section of the exposition begins with viola-cello fourth chords that emulate the performance of a Romanian guitar accompaniment in violin dance pieces.[45]

9

Arab Folk Music from the Biskra District

During May 1906, while Bartók was on tour in Portugal and Spain, he found the time for a short holiday in Tangier, north Morocco. One day he stumbled upon an Arab café and was struck by the unusual singing he heard, so much so that he resolved to return some day, when he had the time and funds.[1] It was not until the spring of 1913 that Bartók had the opportunity to return to North Africa, apparently sparked by his discovery of the Romanian *Hora lungă* in northern Transylvania during the last two weeks in March 1913.

It therefore seems evident that the *Hora lungă* recalled Bartók's musical experience in Tangier, inasmuch as he immediately began investigating the possibility of fieldwork in North Africa on his return to Budapest the next month: "This summer—in June and July, to be more exact—I want to go to Algeria; to be more precise, it is the region of Biskra to which I want to go first, then to the 'Grande Kabylie,' to collect Arab and Berber music (with a phonograph, of course)."[2]

Bartók's decision to visit Biskra was based on tour-book information that the summer temperature was cooler there than elsewhere. He encountered great difficulties when he began collecting instrumental and vocal music, because the first musicians he met played "coffeehouse music," and the only female singers permitted to perform before foreign men were Oueled-Nails (prostitutes). Nevertheless, he found a small number of suitable performers. Thereafter he visited Tolga, Sidi-Okba, and El-Kantara.[3] On 19 June, Bartók wrote that:

> The Arabs accompany almost all their songs with percussion instruments; sometimes in a very complicated rhythm (it is chiefly varying accentuations of equal bar lengths that produce the different rhythmic patterns). This is the most pronounced difference between their singing and ours. Apart from this, there are many primitive melodies (confined to three adjoining notes of the scale) and the compass of a fifth is hardly ever exceeded. None of their original string instruments have survived (they have the violin instead); their wind instruments have quite peculiar scales.[4]

Wind Instruments[5]

1. *Žăŭaq* (= fife) is the equivalent of the shepherd's pipe; 25 cm long, made of reed, has five keyholes.

189

2. *Gáṣba* (= reed-flute, *qâf* pronounced here as *g*): 62–63 cm. long, has neither "stopper" nor mouthpiece. With five or six keyholes. Very widely used. Its tone color approximately resembles the deepest register of the flute.

3. *Geiṭa* (= oboe): made of wood; length approximately 35 cm, diameter 2.5–3 cm. Diameter of the bell 7.5 cm. Has mostly seven (sometimes only six) keyholes and, near the bell, several smaller holes (probably for tuning). Its tone is much stronger than the deepest tones of the oboe and is almost equally penetrating and shrill in all ranges; it has a nearly ear-splitting effect when played indoors. The musicians have a particular technique to lengthen at will the duration of a tone without interruption; seemingly, while breathing through the nose, they press air out of their bloated cheeks into the instrument, in order to avoid "breathing pauses."

STRINGED INSTRUMENTS

In addition to the imported mandolin, Bartók found a kind of primitive "child's instrument," the *gombrí,* whose two strings are tuned to E♭ and A. The strings are strummed with the fingers: the melody is played on the E♭ string while the lower one (A) sounds a basso continuo–like pedal tone.

PERCUSSION INSTRUMENTS

1. *Darbuka (=* tamburin! [an earthenware drum]). A large-size clay jug whose diameter is approximately 20 cm, with a skin stretched over the space at its bottom (and therefore has only one percussion head). By holding the jug under the armpit, it can be played with both hands in alternation: the right hand systematically beats either the center or the border of the skin, the left one only the border. The difference in tone color resulting from the two methods of beating is strikingly apparent. This divergence, and the use of other accentuations, results in extremely interesting rhythmical motives when there is a planned division of right- and left-hand beats, even when the meter is unaltered.

2. *Băndír* (= drum). A snare drum of approximately 50 cm in diameter, with a skin stretched over one end (and therefore has only one percussion head). Two strings are extended over the inner surface of the skin, which provide the drum with a rattling tone. The instrument is held in the left hand, with the thumb and index finger (the thumb is inserted into a hole in the side of the drum), and it is beaten with the third, fourth, and fifth fingers of the left hand and the second, third, fourth, and fifth fingers of the right hand while the latter's thumb rests against the side of the drum. As in *darbuka* and *ṭábăl* performance, the right hand systematically beats the center or the border of the skin.

3. *Ṭábăl* (= drum) is the equivalent of the bass drum. It is played with two

sticks, one of them thin, long, and flexible; the other one thicker, shorter, rigid, and with a bent end that serves as a beating face.

4. In Sidi-Okba, Bartók found a small kettledrum (with a copper frame), 11 cm high and 19 cm in diameter, designated *naqarat* (possibly from the Arab word meaning "beat" [a drum]?). The instrument is played with two wooden sticks.

Vocal Melodies

With regard to the melodies, they can be divided into three categories according to the occasion at which they are sung.

1. *Knéja*, possibly *γneja* (?) from the Arab word meaning "song," is the song of the Arabs in the proper sense of the word. These songs have secular texts and are not performed at special occasions. They are subdivided into two major categories: (a) *rubato* (without accompaniment of percussion instruments), and (b) strict rhythm (accompanied by percussion instruments).

Both categories are again subdivided into the *Knéja*-songs sung by women and those sung by men. The unaccompanied *Knéja*-songs are performed by one singer or by two who alternate as in a dialogue. The men's *Knéja*-songs are performed by one singer or alternating with a *gásba* (or *zăŭaq*) player, never together. Those with strict rhythm may be performed by one singer, usually accompanying himself on the *darbuka*, or with a similar accompaniment in the case of the two singers who alternate couplets, or again, to a similar accompaniment where the singer and the *gásba* (see below) alternate the performance (in which case the singer beats the *darbuka*).

2. *Qṣeida* (Arab poem, 16–100 couplets) is a song with a religious subject (mostly in praise of a Marabout). It is performed only by men as a solo or change song, in strict rhythm with *darbuka* accompaniment;

3. Instrumental dance melodies, which are performed exclusively with drum accompaniment and are probably also partly sung with text. They are divided into two subcategories: (a) dance melodies in the proper sense of the term (tunes for dancing purposes), (b) dancelike melodies, performed at certain festive occasions but not for dancing.

In addition to the three principal categories are the funeral songs (dirges) called *Burda*.

Scale and Range

The *Knéja*-songs move without exception—the *Qṣeida* and dance melodies for the most part—only on two to three, possibly four, neighboring degrees, that is, their range is very narrow. Extension of these boundaries, however, does occur repeatedly, for instance: upward as an upper auxiliary tone; downward as a lower auxiliary tone (similar to a trill or other ornament); or the very frequent glissando at the end of a musical stanza, from the closing fundamental note to its (diminished?) lower fifth (in instrumental dance tunes, several times in the course of the stanzas too). However, these seeming extensions of range are disregarded: when the range is calculated, only the principal tones of the melody and not the ornamental accessory ones are considered.

The melodies of a more extended range occurring in the category of the *Qṣeida* and dance melodies are, in all probability, not an autochthonous product of the region Bartók visited but have been imported. How they have made their way into this area could not be established to date. A part of them, especially the dance melodies of a greater range, might possibly be attributed to the influence of urban Arab music.

Musical Form

In addition to the extremely narrow range, it is also a sign of primitivism that the melodies—especially the dance tunes—are for the most part not subdivided into stanzaic melody-lines but show continual repetition of short motives of one to two bars, possibly four to six bars. Often each pair of motives with two different reciprocally complementing cadences constitutes a period; that is their longest musical form. It should be noted that, in some instrumental dance melodies, a few bars with the character of an interlude are interpolated at certain intervals during the continuous repetition of the principal motive—they are always the same in the different pieces of music. In certain dances, some players reduced this interlude to a single tone sustained through several bars. On the other hand, in other melodies the leading motives sometimes alternate with a second or even a third motive.

In Sidi-Okba, a singularly undulating *rubato* introduction, without any drum accompaniment, preceded all the instrumental dance melodies. This introduction nearly makes the impression of a prelude for the purpose of tuning the instrument.

Rhythm

The high-level development of the rhythm is in contradistinction with the primitivism of the range and form. The syncopations met in melodies with strict rhythm are the chief characteristic differing from Eastern European folk music. These syncopations not only occur in the customary form but in an unfamiliar manner, where a short unaccented value is tied to a long accented one. Melodies in 6/8 (6/4) time are most frequent; there also are some 3/4 (3/2) and 2/4 (2/2) meters. Melodies with mixed time signatures do not occur (even if some bars accidentally differing from the main signature are occasionally met, they can not be considered as constituting a change of meter). The rhythm of the bars is either an ascending one (with an upbeat) or a descending one. The rhythm of the melody stanzas corresponds to the syllables of the metric verse stanzas or follows their changes in the same way as in German folk-song.

ACCOMPANIMENT

The intricacy of the melodic rhythm is further complicated by the accompanying rhythm of the percussion instruments. With very few exceptions, each melody has only one type of accompanying rhythm, undoubtedly interdependent with that melody, which rarely changes except when the rhythm takes on a variantlike form. There are fewer rhythmical motives than melodies, therefore several melodies have identical accompanying rhythm. Occasionally the accompaniment is independent to the extent that it nearly takes on a self-contained life alongside the melody. In this case—in point of fact met exceptionally—any connection of the melody and its accompaniment is lacking. The connection is stronger if at least a value of the melody corresponds with the smallest value of the accompaniment (for example, an eighth note on an eighth note), even if the motive of accompanying rhythm suffers a transformation resulting from a sudden interpolation of a bar or a beat (maybe only an eighth note) into the melody. Thus, for instance, if the singer interpolates half a bar into one of the melody stanzas of a song in 4/4 meter, the 4/4 motive of the accompaniment continues without change, as if the interpolation did not occur. And, finally, curious polyrhythms come into being when melodic and accompanying motives, although of identical length but fully divergent as far as rhythm, are united.

TEMPO

At the present time, a definite rule cannot be established concerning the tempo of the *Knéja-* and *Qṣeida*-songs; the tempo is very different among the given examples. However, we do find that the instrumental dance songs show some regularity. The tempo of certain kinds of dances (*Šaŭia, Făzzáj*) always is unaltered.

PECULIARITIES OF PERFORMANCE

It is just as difficult to describe with words as to indicate them with musical notation. As a matter of fact, only listening to the phonogram recordings can give us an exact idea. Namely, the *Knéja-* and partly the more primitive *Qṣeida*-songs are sung (especially by women) in a clucking kind of vibrato. Although one might notate them as a kind of trilled ornament, the tone color of these mournful clucking sounds cannot be represented by symbols. The songs are replete with ornaments, the most frequent being the shake with upper or lower auxiliary note. Sometimes, instead of the shake, there is a tremolo with upper or lower third. Melismata consisting of several notes are very frequent; in the more primitive songs, they have a strongly accented principal tone and several accessory tones sung with less accentuation. In the *Qṣeida*-song with larger range, the melismata consist of tones sung with identical accent.

CLASSIFICATION OF THE INSTRUMENTAL DANCE MELODIES[6]

Subdivision according to range seemed to be the most adequate system. The groups which were obtained were subdivided again into subclasses, according to structure, that is, the length of the motives. The primitive melodies are in the majority (with regard to the range as well as the length of the motive).

The group of dances with a three-tone range is especially peculiar: they have two alternating compulsory rhythmical motives as the accompaniment. The group consists of all the *Šaŭia*-dances, one *Făzzáj*, two wedding melodies of a marchlike type, and one melody supposedly with text. The principal accompanying rhythm (marked in the examples with 1.) is—with one exception—identical in all these melodies, likewise the accessory one (marked 2.). The latter rhythm shows up in certain intervals in a bar and yields its place to the principal rhythm after some bars have been played; or it shows up after the appearance of the above-mentioned interlude, or rather the sustained tone substituting for it, and returns to the principal rhythm at the same time as the principal motive of the melody. The second rhythm never occurs as an independent accompaniment, has a peculiarly solemn character, and gives the impression of intending to induce in the audience a certain tension which only disappears when the principal rhythm reappears. (A similar effect is induced, for instance, by the resolution of a dissonance in a chordal sequence). There undoubtedly is an interconnection of the choreography and the change of the two rhythms, but to my utmost regret I did not have the opportunity to research it.

The most primitive dances, the *Šaŭia*-, *Făzzáj*-, and wedding dances—with a range of three to four tones—are the genuine products of the regions Bartók visited, and the least primitive are the *Nuba* dances. In addition, the denominations of other dances give the impression that they were imports, inasmuch as the *Nuba* dances undoubtedly originate from Arab art music and were simplified in the Biskra region.

The earliest influence of Arab peasant music on Bartók's music is in the third movement of the Suite op. 14, for Piano (1916).[7] A more extensive influence is reflected in the Dance Suite for Orchestra (1923; see Ex. 4.36 above).[8] And no. 42 (Arabian Song) from Forty-Four Duos, for Two Violins (1931), is an arrangement of Biskra no. 15 ("*Knab bâl Äši . . .*").[9]

10

Ruthenian Folk Melody

Bartók's collection of Ruthenian folk music consists of eighty-one instrumental and vocal melodies, which he recorded in Ugocsa and Maramureş villages during 1911.[1] At that time, the Ruthenians (a tribe of the Ukrainian people) consisted of about 500,000 persons, who inhabited several counties to be found in the most eastern part of former Czechoslovakia proper.[2]

The most characteristic Ruthenian dance music, designated by the name *kolomyjka*, is based on the rhythm schema: 2/4 ♪♪♪♪ | ♪♪♪♪ | ♪♪♪♪ | ♪ ♪ ‖. Ex. 10.1 shows two of the collected Ruthenian folk songs in *kolomyjka* rhythm.

Ex. 10.1. (a) *BBSE*, 232, melody no. 63, and (b) 233, no. 64a.

The Hungarian melodies called *kanász-nóta* (swineherd's melody) show a striking resemblance to the Ruthenian *kolomyjka* melodies: the former probably constitute a more or less modified form of the latter.[3]

The importance of these swineherd melodies, probably created under Ruthenian influence, is due to two hypotheses that could be accepted, in my opinion, as a point of departure for further research:

(1) It is probably in the tunes of the swineherd songs that we will first look for the origin of the music of the *kuruc*- [soldier of the insurrectionist Rákóczi army] song (for example, the Tyukodi-song, similar to melody no. 304 in *The Hungarian Folk Song*), and after that the so-called *verbunkos* (dance music for recruiting). Principally the old Hungarian *verbunkos* melodies, but also those which have survived among the Romanians of Mezőség (Campie), show an obvious kinship with the old swineherd songs. Later on, of course, too many eighteenth-century Western European ornaments transformed the *verbunkos* music into one of such sophistication that its connection with the swineherd songs gradually blurred.

(2) It is possible that the new Hungarian folk melodies were created under the influence of the *verbunkos* music. But this influence had been crossed with many others (for instance, the pentatonic system and the dotted rhythm of the old Hungarian folk melodies; perhaps the recent urban folk songs), so that the connection between the new Hungarian style and the *verbunkos* style is even more difficult to demonstrate than that between the *verbunkos* music and the swineherd dance. According to my impressions—and I am guided here more by intuition than fact— the evolutionary process might have been this: the Ruthenian *kolomyjka* > Hungarian swineherd song > *verbunkos* music > new Hungarian folk melodies. This evolution—in the event it should be proven true—permits us to attach a far greater importance to indirect Ruthenian influence than that which results from the number of melodies created under direct borrowings.[4]

As part of the mentioned evolutionary process, Bartók included the Romanian *Ardeleana* dance genre as possibly stemming from *verbunkos* music. But he also considered the *Ardeleana* as a direct borrowing from the Ruthenian *kolomyjka* (Ex. 10.2).[5]

Ex. 10.2. *RFM*.i, melody no. 373. This *Ardeleana,* played on the violin, was collected by Bartók in Bihor County during July 1909.

Example 10.3 is a Slovak folk song (text omitted) in *kolomyjka* rhythm, which is closely related to several melodies in Bartók's Ruthenian, Hungarian, and Slovak folk music collections.[6] In this connection, he believed that there was "a certain predisposition, a certain spiritual kinship between the peoples of the Hungarian villages and those of the Slovak and Ruthenian ones. This circumstance evidently facilitated the borrowing of melodies."[7]

Tempo giusto

Ex. 10.3. *SV.*i, melody no. 420b. Collected by Bartók in Zvolenská County during April 1915.

We must take for granted a certain predisposition, a certain spiritual kinship between the peoples of the Hungarian villages and those of the Slovak and Ruthenian ones. Only one factor cannot have played a part in this propagation, and that is the aggressive Magyarization coming from above. And this for the very reason that the Hungarians had no such intention; indeed, leading Hungarians either had little regard for Hungarian village music or were hardly acquainted with it. At any rate, from the purely objective viewpoint, such artificial propagation is impossible. Village art cannot be other than a spontaneous manifestation; any attempt to interfere and direct it in an artificial manner would immediately result in its discontinuation. It is for this reason that it would be a vain effort to seek the development of music in this or that direction—as has been recently suggested from time to time—or the revival of the old village melodies, because the art of the village people dies the moment that its production ceases to be spontaneous and when they themselves no longer choose it.[8]

Bartók's first use of *kolomyjka* rhythm occurs in his remarkable childhood piano piece, *A Duna folyása* (The course of the Danube, op. 20).[9] In 1908, he composed "Bear Dance" (no. 10 from Ten Easy Piano Pieces), and the next year he arranged a swineherd song as no. 42 in *For Children,* for Piano. Among other arrangements, he incorporated two Ruthenian folk melodies in Forty-Four Duos for Two Violins (nos. 10 and 35). And the first dance in the Dance Suite for Orchestra combines Arab chromatic folk melody and Ruthenian *kolomyjka* rhythm.[10]

11

Yugoslav Folk Music

Bartók's first contact with Yugoslav folk music occurred in January 1910, while he was collecting Romanian folk music in Torontál County (now Torontal, Romania). Among the instrumental pieces he collected in Nagyszentmiklós (Sânnicolaul-Mare) was a Serbian dance melody played on a *fluer* (a recorder-like peasant flute) by a Romanian performer (Ex. 11.1).[1]

Fluer M.F. 833 b), Sânnicolaul-Mare (Torontal), a man, I. 1910.

Ex. 11.1. *RFM.*i, melody no. 252, mm. 1–8.

In addition, Bartók collected forty-eight vocal melodies, of which more than a third contained refrain lines of a type to be found outside of the Banat (that is, southwestern Hungary which contains Rumanian villages near Serbian and Slavonic territories).[2] One of the songs had a peculiar heterogeneous character, as if it were "a foreign body in the bulk of the Romanian material"(Ex. 11.2).[3]

8, M.F. 838 b), Sânnicolaul-Mare (Torontal), girls (15–18), I. 1910

Tra na na na na na na Tra na na na na na na

Ex. 11.2. *RFM.*ii, melody no. 360, mm. 1–8.

Apparently Bartók compared its melody with Fr. Kuhač's collection of Yugoslav folk songs and found three variants;[4] in fact, he was at first pleased with

Kuhač's transcriptions, commenting in 1912 that the melodies "are correctly notated as well as ordered according to the text. It is regrettable that the work has been expanded by the addition of wholly unnecessary piano accompaniments . . . we need to supplement Kuhač's collection which is of limited extent."[5] During March and November 1912, moreover, while collecting in the Banat counties of Temeş (now Timiş, Romania) and Torontal, Bartók sought, found, and recorded several Serbian folk musicians in the villages of Monostor (now Mănăştur) and Sárafalva (now Saravale, formerly Sarafola), respectively. He collected and transcribed twenty-one instrumental and vocal pieces. Probably on the basis of this small number of transcriptions, apparently the only Serbian folk music recorded by phonograph up to that time, Bartók revised his opinion of Kuhač's contribution. Thus, in 1919, Bartók complained in print that the folk music collections published by Yugoslavs were jotted down by amateurs and that systematic classification of the material, like that of Western Europe, was carried out almost exclusively according to the texts.[6] Two years later, he wrote that:

> Conditions are not such as would allow us to think of continuing our studies in musical folklore. They are a "luxury" we cannot afford on our own resources. Political conditions are another great impediment. The great hatred that has been worked up makes it almost impossible to carry out research in parts of countries that once belonged to Hungary.[7]

In particular, Bartók could no longer support his family on his Academy salary, and he devoted all his spare time to supplementing his income by writing articles for foreign periodicals and playing the piano at concerts. With regard to fieldwork abroad:

> No one is allowed to take phonographs across the frontier, neither one way or the other! They wouldn't even let me bring my own notebooks through! The most I could hope for would be to procure some special permits from heaven knows how many different authorities, and only after that I don't know how many weeks of running around for them! No, the curtain has been drawn over that work . . . [phonograph cylinders] would be confiscated at the border.[8]

The "drawn curtain" prevented Bartók from personal contact with South Slavic folk music, and he therefore turned to the collections made without the aid of the phonograph—published by Kuhač, Kuba, Bosiljevac, Kačerovski, Đorđević, and Žganec—since he needed source material in the 1920s for comparative purposes, during the preparation of his study of the Romanian *Colinde*.[9] Thus Bartók was able to state that Romanian Christmas carols ending with a half-cadence can be traced back to South Slavic influence, since the terminal half-cadence as well as certain scale patterns, diffused in Romanian areas, play a predominant role in Yugoslav peasant music.[10] In a letter dated 4 June 1926, in which Bartók refers to the main musical dialect of the Transylvanian Romanians in the counties of Alba, Hunedoara, Bihor, and in the Banat, he states that:

> As to the main musical dialect of the Rumanians, I think it must have come into existence under Yugoslav influence. Unfortunately I do not know Serbian folk music well enough to support my opinion, but I do know this much: in Serbian folk music the most characteristic structure is the F-major hexachord in which g^1 serves as final tone and half-cadence, and in which the first, third and fifth tones are the main degrees of the scale. Exactly the same scale is widespread among the Banat Rumanians. In Alba and Hunedoara, as the result of the tonal shift upward one step, the fourth and sixth degrees replace the third and fifth as the main ones. Out of the latter structure arose the Lydian hexachord in Bihor, with first, fourth (natural), and sixth main degrees.[11]

Bartók's reexamination of his Romanian material, coupled with a statistical survey he had made of aspects of Žganec's 1924 publication of Medumurje melodies,[12] may have prompted him to consider writing a documented comparative survey of all the East European musical folklore that he had investigated up to that time. Taking advantage of newly opened broadcasting opportunities, on 21 November 1933 Bartók gave a lecture on Budapest Radio, in which he discussed the influence of Hungarian folk song on that of its neighbors, illustrating the talk with piano and recorded examples. The lecture appeared in pamphlet form the next year, "appropriately enlarged," including 127 music examples in Bartók's autograph.[13] In the last chapter of the treatise, Bartók states that he had reviewed and classified about 2,500 melodies collected in Croatia, Slavonia, Dalmatia, Bosnia and other regions inhabited by the Serbs, for the most part from the collections of Kuhač and Kuba. He goes on to aver that there is hardly any connection between these melodies and the Hungarian material. But in Žganec's Medumurje collection of 636 melodies, Bartók found that a total of 66 percent were either Old Hungarian (190 melodies), New Hungarian (158), or other Hungarian "dotted" rhythm types (41). The most remarkable fact is that so many borrowings were made from the Old Hungarian tune types, and Bartók was astonished to find a greater proportion of Old Hungarian pentatonic melodies in Žganec's Yugoslav collection (33 percent) than in Bartók's Hungarian material (9 percent).

> There can be no doubt of the Hungarian origin of the pentatonic tunes of Muraköz [Medumurje]; on the one hand they are completely identical with the old Hungarian melodies propagated throughout Transdanubia, on the other hand no similarity between these tunes and the others of the Serbs and Croats can be found. It would truly be an exaggeration to concede that the melodies of this type had been propagated from the region of these two districts, throughout the Hungarian linguistic territory, and as far as the Székely-inhabited region of Transylvania.[14]

After Bartók took up his new duties at the Academy of Sciences in 1934, he set out to investigate the matter of Serbo-Croatian autochthonous material, by means of correspondence with Žganec and Kuba. In what appears to be the first letter between Bartók and Žganec, dated 27 October, Bartók mentions that he mailed his booklet containing Serbian and Bulgarian peasant music he collected in the Banat, and asks:

> How is the collecting activity proceeding in Yugoslavia at present? Could I study phonograph recordings somewhere? Is the phonograph used at all? Are there any-where any major (unpublished) collections, noted down and in a state suitable for study in Zagreb or Belgrade for instance? Is any major publication planned? I would be very interested to see such material, not from the Hungarian point of view, for, as one can see from Kuhač's and Kuba's great (Bosnian and Hercegovinian) collections (published in Sarajevo), with the exception of the items from Muraköz, there are hardly any points of contact. But it is with Rumanian folk music that I would like to compare it as thoroughly as possible; for I suspect, especially in the music of the Rumanians in the Banat, a strong Southern Slav influence; what is more, I even think that the music of the Rumanians in the Bihor region came into existence as the result of the crossing of pentatonic and Southern Slav melodies.

After discussing certain performance peculiarities he has noted in the Kuhač and Kuba materials, Bartók mentions that he would like to determine whether the so-called Bulgarian type of rhythm occurs in the Serbo-Croatian linguistic territory. The letter concludes with a postscript indicating that Bartók can "only understand the [Croatian] folk texts, but the literary language, hardly."[15]

On the same, day Bartók mailed the recently published "booklet containing my radio talks" to Žganec; a few weeks later it was "returned from the Yugoslav frontier, stamped 'ZABRANJENO, INTERDITE'! I don't suppose the frontier guard read the booklet; it rather seems he has imposed an intellectual blockade."[16] Another copy, with a dedication, probably sent out at the same time, was received in Prague by Ludvik Kuba. Bartók also sent a letter to Kuba, probably containing the same or similar lines as those in his letter to Žganec, since Kuba responded that "It will be a great pleasure to meet you in Prague and to cooperate with you in scholarly matters."[17] When the two met in Prague, during the last week in November—Bartók performed his Second Piano Concerto with the Czech Philharmonic Orchestra on November 28—it was decided that Kuba would correct his published material from Bosnia and Hercegovina, and send an edited copy, together with unpublished songs, for Bartók's use.[18] Not until May 1938, was Kuba able to complete the work: "It was no easy task to extricate these 160 vanished songs from my fifty-year-old notes, and I would not have undertaken this if you, dear Master, had not shown such keen interest in them. No wonder that it took such a long time."[19]

Other than information concerning source materials, Bartók's contact with Žganec was hardly fruitful. Their correspondence during 1934–1936, which included shipments of Bartók folk music publications, seems to focus on Bartók's candid references to the lack of folk music from Serbo-Croatia collected on phonograph records. In Bartók's letter, dated 3 July 1935, he states that:

> I am surprised to read in your letter that Kuhač still has 4,000 unpublished melodies. These are surely in some library where they can be studied, aren't they? In my opinion it would be better not to publish these, Kuhač's notations being very defective, but rather to use the money thus earmarked for new collecting activity, namely, collecting organized scientifically with all kinds of equipment (phonograph!).[20]

Toward the latter part of 1935, Bartók again attempted to mail his booklet of Serbian and Bulgarian peasant melodies to Žganec, this time successfully. The latter's response, perhaps their last communication, is dated 22 April 1936:

> The extremely interesting music material of the book that you collected with so much affection, gratified me exceedingly. I showed it to my friends, and all of them were amazed by the precision of your notation. Such accuracy as revealed by you is something new in the realm of folk music collecting.
>
> As soon as I shall have the leisure I intend to write a detailed and long review of this book and will mail it to you.[21]

Any lingering thoughts Bartók may have had about the possibility of still visiting Yugoslavia to collect folk music were diverted by negotiations leading to an official invitation, during the same month, to lecture in Turkey. Following his return to Hungary, he broadcast the results of his activities on Budapest Radio, including the fieldwork in South Anatolia, on 11 January 1937. Comparing Turkish and Serbo-Croatian materials, he found that:

> The "rain begging" songs are generally known by the Turks. These songs correspond in text and melody to the Yugoslav and Rumanian (*Dodola, Păpăruga*) songs used for the same purpose; their melodies are similar to the nursery rhymes and children's playsongs of the Hungarian, Slovak, or other Western European nations.[22]

It was not until the early 1940s that Bartók found another route toward achieving his goal of working with autochthonous Yugoslav folk music: the Parry Collection of recordings held by Harvard University.[23] After he transcribed and studied a number of the records, his conclusions and recommendations appear in the following letter, dated 18 April 1941:

> This unique collection of over 2,600 phonograph records—to my knowledge the only collection of Yugoslav folk music on acoustical recordings—contains a very large mass of epic song accompanied by the gusle, a primitive one-string instrument. The style and musical treatment of these heroic songs is probably as close to that of the Homeric poem as any folk music style found today may be. While from the historical, literary, and musicological point of view this material is invaluable, from the musical-esthetic point of view the lyric songs or "women's

songs" and the instrumental pieces in the collection are more rewarding. The epic songs are carried by a mode of chanting which, while on the whole simple, varies somewhat from region to region and singer to singer. The chant itself is undoubtedly part of old European folk heritage, but the gusle accompaniment occasionally shows parallels with Arabic melodic treatment—probably due to an influence during the long Turkish occupation.

There are two ends in view according to which the collection ought to be studied. One is the transcription into musical notation of the most important samples of the epic material, to be incorporated into its literary and textual study at Harvard University. The other is the transcription of the other materials in the collection, for an inclusive picture of Yugoslav folk music. This latter could well result, as you once suggested, in a book on Yugoslav folk music. I estimate that transcribing those parts of the collection which are the most important in these two respects would take a year's time, not including my work during the current semester.[24]

Although Bartók completed the first draft of his portion of *Serbo-Croatian Folk Songs* early in 1943, a combination of frustrating circumstances continuously delayed the attempt to arrive at the final form of the book. Wartime shortages; correspondence with Albert B. Lord concerning the texts and translations; multilingual text matter, including many special symbols devised by Bartók, which presented special problems for solution by the printer; and, above all, Bartók's struggle with the English language as well as the difficulties he had with the autographer of the exceedingly complex music examples— all contributed to one postponement after another. In 1951, six years after Bartók's death, Columbia University Press published *Serbo-Croatian Folk Songs*—the first full-length scholarly study of that subject in the English language. And in 1976, the book was incorporated in the expanded, four-volume edition published by the State University of New York Press, including facsimiles of the published and unpublished music examples comprising Bartók's collection of Yugoslav folk music.

YFM VOLUME ONE: SERBO-CROATIAN FOLK SONGS

Preceding the morphological study of the material is an extended essay in which Bartók presents his approach to problems concerning transcription, notation, pitch, variants, ornaments, objectivity, and variability in folk music.[25]

Method of transcription. Perceptible deviations in pitch are marked by arrow signs above notes or accidentals, pointing upward or downward to indicate raised or lowered pitch that almost reaches a quarter tone. Special signs are used to represent various types of *glissando.* The ordinary time-signature is used to indicate rigid dance rhythm [*tempo giusto*], but never in the transcription of *parlando-rubato* melodies.

Setting of bars and choice of values. The original meaning of the bar is an articulating accent on the value following the bar. In the case of vocal melodies with rigid dance rhythm, bars should be placed in accordance with the metrical structure of the text line. *Parlando-rubato* melodies which have lengthy and complicated measures can be transcribed with additional broken (i.e., dotted) bars to indicate subdivisions of the measure.

Melodic structure should be determined by the structure of the text lines, so that the single melody sections correspond with the respective lines of the text. The choice of values for the transcribed melodies should represent a compromise between unusually long or unusually short values: the former look too heavy and the latter make the transcription too difficult to read. With regard to *parlando-rubato* melodies, the choice of values presents more difficulties. To avoid using overly complicated dotted-values, M.M. figures can be changed to provide each melody section or stanza with its own metronome value.

Signs in the current notation which have a more or less vague meaning, such as the fermata, trill sign, mordent, comma, and so forth, should never be used. Four exceptions: a wavy line above a note to indicate *vibrato,* small semicircles to indicate slight shortening or lengthening, and the short grace-note.

Certain peculiarities appearing in the present publication. Beams are used instead of flags for a succession of notes sung to different syllables and to melismatic groups where different notes are sung to one syllable (each group is marked with a slur). With regard to key signatures, only those sharps and flats should be used which refer to the degrees actually occurring in the melody. In certain cases, both types of accidentals will be required, but this procedure will allow the reader to immediately perceive which scale is used in the melody.

Pitch of melodies. In order to facilitate the relationship of a melody to others, all melodies are transposed to a common *tonus finalis.* The original pitch is entered on the staff, with its own clef sign, preceding the melody. In certain cases, several pitches are required to indicate gradual changes of pitch during the performance of successive stanzas.

Methods in systematic grouping of folk melodies. Most editors have not used any musical principles in grouping their material. Thus the melodies are grouped according to texts, according to geographical units (villages, districts), or avoid grouping them in any way. The first large collections grouped according to systematic principles derived from the characteristics of the music were published by the Finns, others were later published by the Ukrainians.

The two predominant principles are the "lexicographical," and (what Bartók calls) the "grammatical." The former system makes it possible to locate each melody by comparatively simple means. The disadvantage consists in the fact that variants (sometimes even slightly differing variants) will have to be placed far from each other. Thus the reader will find it difficult to perceive the different styles, structures, or even the prevailing variant groups in the material.

The so-called grammatical system groups all melodies belonging to the same family, or being of similar structure and representing the same style, as near each other as possible. This complicated system uses the elements of the so-called lexicographical method intercrossed by various and numerous additional elements. While individual melodies can be located, in order to do so the reader must have some previous familiarity with the material and a thorough grasp of the grouping system. The following enumeration indicates the order of importance of melodic elements in creating a grammatical classification system:

(1) SECTION STRUCTURE. The portion of the melody corresponding to one line of text;

(2) METRIC STRUCTURE. Metric units such as feet or the number of text syllables in each section;

(3) RHYTHMICAL CHARACTER. For example, free rhythm, called *parlando-rubato* or, in short, *"parlando"*;[26]

(4) MELODIC STRUCTURE. Referring to the final notes of the sections or other significant melodic features;

(5) RANGE. The *ambitus* of the melody;

(6) SCALE SYSTEM; and

(7) VARIOUS SUBASPECTS.

The order of importance in the lexicographical system is approximately 1, 4, 2, and 5 (3, 6, and 7 are rarely considered in the Eastern European material). The order of importance in the grammatical system is 1, 2, 3, 4, and 5 (6 and 7 are rarely considered).

The Problem of Variants. What characterizes a melody as a variant of another? According to Bartók, variants are melodies in which the pitch relation of the various principal tones to each other shows a certain similarity; or, in other words, in which the contour line is entirely or partly similar.

Ornaments (Grace Notes). In vocal melodies, two or more notes sung to one syllable constitute ornaments. Usually one of the notes can be regarded as the principal one, since the ornamental notes are usually sung with a lighter tone emission. These ancillary notes should be transcribed with small note heads, in order to distinguish them from the heavier principal tone.

Objectivity and Subjectivity in Transcribing and Grouping Folk Music. Even if objective instruments are used for determining pitch and speed, subjective judgments remain in the determination of structure, range, and scale of folk music: (a) The last note of a section or even of the melody may not be the structural "final" note (*tonus finalis*); (b) if the metric system is based on syllable count, the number of syllables does not always correspond to the structurally essential syllables; (c) when certain sections or portions of the melody are repeated, determination must be made whether they are structurally essential or nothing but casual or playful ad hoc repetitions; (d) if a melody in rigid dance rhythm is sometimes performed in free *parlando-rubato* rhythm, it should be grouped as if it were in rigid rhythm; and sometimes it is difficult to determine the boundaries of a single section. While there are established rules and a tradition for deciding these issues, they are not always applicable.

Variability in Folk Music. One of the most conspicuous features of folk music is its continuous variability. Each individual of every living species of plant or animals is a unique phenomenon. The same is true of folk melodies—a given performance of a folk melody has never occurred before and will never occur again in exactly the same way.

The difference between the performance of folk music and art music is not one of contrast but of degree. Folk music shows an absolute variability, while art music varies in a far lesser, sometimes only in an infinitesimal degree. Even performance of the same work by the same performer will never occur in absolutely the same way. Even some of the notes of art music are subject to change, such as the particles of embellishments (trills and the like).

> This eternal changeableness gives life to music, be it folk or art music, whether the changes are considerable or scarcely perceptible. These intrinsic characteristics of music seem to be in contradistinction with the contemporary trend of producing music more and more by mechanical means, according to which the music would be compressed into a frozen and never changing form.[27]

MORPHOLOGY OF THE SERBO-CROATIAN VOCAL FOLK MELODIES

Bartók transcribed seventy-five women's songs in 54 variant groups, from the available recordings in the Parry Collection.[28] These were placed among the thousands of previously published and unpublished Yugoslav folk songs that he had studied and sorted prior to his arrival in New York in 1940. Then the complete, classified material was formatted in a unique "Tabulation of Material" during July 1942, which was intended to serve as a holographic appendix but not included in the posthumous publication of Bartók's work (Table 11.1).[29]

TABLE 11.1
Tabulation of Yugoslav Melodies
(Figures in Italics Indicate Syllabic Structure)

Class *A*. One-Section Melodies (nos. 1–35; Parry no. 1)
   7,–8, 8b, (3+2+3), 10, (Parry 1), *11,–13,*

Class *B*. Two-Section Melodies (36–619; Parry 2–17)

   Subclass I. Isometric Structure (36–460)
      5,–7, 8, (Parry 2–3), *8b,* (Parry 4–5), *9, 10,* (Parry 6–13),
      11, (Parry 14–15), *12,* (Parry 16a, 17), *13,*

   Subclass II. Heterometric Structure (461–619)

      Group 1) First section of higher syllabic number (461–581)
         6, –8, 10,–12, 14,–15,
      Group 2) Second section of higher syllabic number (582–619)
         5,–10, 12,

Class *C.* Three-Section Melodies (620–1023; Parry 18–21)

Subclass I. Isometric structure, main caesura at the end of
the first section (620–659)

5,–7, 8, (Parry 18), *8b, 10,* (Parry 19), *11,–12,*

Subclass II. Isometric structure, main caesura at the end
of the second section (660–727)

5,–7, 8, (Parry 20, 21a, b), *8b,–11, 13,*

Subclass III. Heterometric structure, main caesura at the
end of the first section (728–919; Parry 22–24)

Group 1) With two equal sections (728–832)
1. (Parry 22), 3.–4., 5. (Parry 23–24), 6.

Group 2) With double sections (833–861)
2.–6., 11.

Group 3) With unequal sections (862–919)
2.–6.

Subclass IV. Heterometric structure, main caesura at the
end of the second section (920–1023; Parry 25–30)

Group 1) With two equal sections, (920–993)
1., 2. (Parry 25), 3. (Parry 26–28), 4. (Parry 16b, 29)

Group 3) With unequal sections, (994–1023)
1. –2., 3. (Parry 30), 4.–6.

Subclass *V.* Melodics of Special Structure (1024–1053;
Parry 31–33)

Class *D.* Four-Section Melodies (1024–1830; Parry 34–53)

Subclass I. Isometric Structure (1054–1364)

5,–7, 8, (Parry 34–36), *8b,–11, 12,* (Parry 37), *13,–14,*

Subclass II. Heterometric Structure (1365 1830)
1.–4., 5. (Parry 38–52), 6.–17., 20.–24.

Class *E.* Melodies of Children's Play Type (1831–1855)

Class *F.* Melodies of Confused, Indeterminable Structure
(1856–1896; Parry 54)

The main characteristics of Bartók's Yugoslav folk song material are (a) heterometric, narrow-range melodies ending on the second degree as the final tone;
(b) without text-stanza structure, use of refrains, or so-called Bulgarian rhythm
formations; and (c) ten-syllable lines are preponderant.

There are examples of a "very peculiar" scale formation that is "intermediate
between the diatonic and the 'chromatic' scales."[30] and an "extremely peculiar
kind" of Dalmatian two-part singing in major seconds.[31]

Bartók offers two "tentative" hypotheses with regard to a possibly ancient
common Slavic musical style: (a) a common style of narrow-range melodies,
and (b) a common trait of performance, described as "syllable-interruption."[32]

In the second movement of the Concerto for Orchestra, Bartók emulates a

Dalmatian two-part folk song accompanied by a pair of *sopels* (a kind of folk oboe). The clarinets, substituting for the traditional *sopel* prelude, play their duet at the unusual but characteristic interval of a minor seventh. The muted trumpets are given the role of Dalmatian folk singers, that is, a duet in major seconds—the inverted form of the minor seconds—to follow the *sopel* prelude,

A Serbian instrumental dance melody appears as no. 39 in Forty-four Duos for Two Violins (see Example 5.9 above), and "In Yugoslav Mode" (no. 40) from *Mikrokosmos* for Piano, is in the "E-Mixolydian Mode. Ends on a half-cadence. Imitation of Yugoslav bagpipes: the piece is written for two pipes although the instrument has three."[33]

YFM VOLUME TWO: TABULATION OF MATERIAL

Table 11.2 is an extract from Bartók's remarkable classification of data assembled from his collection of Yugoslav folk music publications, for the most part the folk songs collected by Vladimir Đorđević, Fr. Kuhač, and Ludvik Kuba. The headings in the eight-column format are described as follows:[34]

No. The current number of entries: 3,449 melodies ordered in 1,896 variant groups; each group distinguished by small letters.

Original edition. The number of the melody or of the page in each collection.

Syllables. The number of syllables in each melody section, represented by an italicized arabic numeral with comma. Isometric melodies—those with melody sections of the same syllabic length—are represented by one number.

End notes. Main caesuras are indicated by bracketed degree-symbols and secondary caesuras by] or [brackets, where f^1 = VII, g^1 = 1, a^1 = 2, and so on.

Range. The same degree-symbols used for caesuras are applied to the designation of melodic ambitus, from lowest to highest principal tone.

Rhythm. Small letters and music notation indicate heterorhythmic melodies in which the sections are of unequal rhythm.

Content. Capital letters with subscript or superscript letters (v = variation, s = stepwise sequence) indicate melodic form.

Remarks. Indigenous and foreign variants, genres, performance peculiarities, and so forth.

TABLE 11.2

Selected Data from Bartók's "Tabulation of Material"

No.	Original ed.	Syl.	End notes	Range	Rhythm	Content	Remarks
1168a.	Kuba *B. H.*, 15	6,	1] [3] [2	V–5	a b b a	A B B$_s$ A	Slovak melody
1168b.	Kuba *B. H.*, 17	6,	1] [3] [2	V–6	a b b a	A B B$_s$ A	Slovak melody
1168c.	Đorđević *Nar. Pev.*, p. 107/1	6,	1] [3] [2	V–5	a b b a	A B B$_s$ A	Slovak melody
1168d.	Kuhać 381	6,	1] [3] [2	V–5	a b b a	A B B$_s$ A	Slovak melody
1168e.	Kuhać 113	6,	1] [3] [4	V–6	a b b a	A B B^{s}C	Slovak melody

12

Bulgarian Folk Music

While Bartók was meticulously revising his Romanian phonograph recordings during the mid-1930s, he observed that certain dance melodies previously notated as steady quarter-notes in 4/4 time were not only rhythmically incongruent but also in faster tempo. In fact, he had written on the old notations: "the ends of the bars drawn out in Gypsy fashion," and he prepared a revised transcription in additive rhythm (Ex. 12.1)[1]

Ex. 12.1. *RFM*.i, melody no. 382a for violin.

In addition, beginning in 1935, Bartók undertook the study of Vasil Stoin's Bulgarian folk music publications, including types of rhythm schemata and comparative analysis of the melodies. Thereafter, he examined smaller collections published by the Bulgarian Academy of Sciences.[2]

> In the two large volumes of Stoin's collections, he publishes more than 6,000 melodies, and lists the types of rhythm. It appears that the most frequent Bulgarian rhythms are as follows: 5/16 (subdivided into 3 + 2 or 2 + 3); 7/16 (2 + 2 + 3)— the rhythm of the well-known *Ruchenitza* dance); 8/16 (3 + 2 + 3); 9/16 (2 + 2 + 2 + 3); and about sixteen other less common rhythmic types, not counting the rhythmically-mixed formulas (that is, with different rhythmic patterns in alternation).[3]

Among the other folk music materials Bartók shipped to New York in 1940 are thirty-five large envelopes containing his Bulgarian folk music collection: approximately 9,500 published and unpublished melodies collected by A. Bukoreschliev, Đorđevic, Raina Katzarova, Kuba, and Stoin.[4] After he made his morphological entries in the material, he cut the published melodies apart for sorting purposes and extracted the data for comparison with his Hungarian, Romanian, Slovak, Turkish, and Yugoslav melodies. As Table 12.1 shows, the data were to a certain extent problematic: "The Bulgarians have so far worked without the phonograph, notating everything by ear."[5]

TABLE 12.1

Bartók's Classified Bulgarian Folk Music Collection

No. of Sections	Description	No. of Melodies
1	*5,–14,* syllables	500
2	Isometric	3,645
2	Heterometric	390
3	Isometric	560
3	Heterometric	200
4	Isometric	105
4	Heterometric	843
1–4	Isometric pentatonic: *5,–6,*	800
4	Isometric pentatonic: *8b = 3,+2,+3,*	310
4	Isometric pentatonic, *5—8, 8b, 10,* descending structure; heterometric; and melodies known in Hungary	278
4	Isometric *6,8,8b* (Set aside: perhaps to be placed among other groups?)	220
4	"Either ... or ..." melodies (indeterminate metric or syllabic structure, or section end notes)	310
–	Doubtful melodies	155
–	Instrumental dance melodies (not classified)	47
–	Game songs	18
–	German variants	7
–	Romanian variants	80
–	Slovak variants1	2
–	Fragments	20

According to Bartók's comparative studies, the so-called Bulgarian rhythm formations mentioned above are completely lacking in the Hungarian and Serbo-Croatian materials.[6] On the other hand, he states that:

> The existence of this kind of rhythm in Rumanian folk music is an extremely important fact, Except for the Bulgarian territory, they are rarely found elsewhere. The Turks of Asia Minor, and especially of Turkestan, have such rhythms in their music. . . .
>
> The various rhythm patterns called "Bulgarian," because of their frequency in Bulgarian folk music and because they have been discovered and described by Bulgarian musicologists, can be regarded as derivative of common, symmetrical 2/4 rhythm. The transformation is effected by addition or subtraction of a one-

sixteenth value to or from one or two value units of a symmetrical rhythm pattern in 2/4 time, the tempo of an eighth-note being M.M. 150 or more. In other words, these rhythmic patterns consist of unsymmetrical combinations of eighth-notes and dotted eighth-note values.[7]

Bartók's own use of Bulgarian rhythm in his compositions can be found for the most part in the *Mikrokosmos* for Piano: nos. 113 and 149: 2+2+3/8 (*ruchenitza* dance); no. 115: 3+2/8 and 2+3/8, and no. 150: 3+2/8 (*paidushko*); no. 148: 4+2+3; no. 151: 3+2+3/8; no. 152: 2+2+2+3/8; and no. 153: 3+3+2/8. In the Fifth String Quartet, the "Alla bulgarese" second movement shows 4+2+3/8 in the Scherzo and 3+2+2+3 in the Trio. And in the third movement ("Sebes") of *Contrasts* for Violin, Clarinet, and Piano, the unusual 8+5/8 schema can be interpreted as [3+2+3][2+3]/8. eighths, where the first group represents the *8b* designation used by Bartók to indicate the quintessential Bulgarian folk text structure of *3,+2,+3*. syllables (see Table 12.1), and the second group represents the 2+3/8 (*paidushko*) dance genre.

13

Turkish Folk Music from Asia Minor

The sequence of events which ultimately were to lead Bartók to the preparation of his Turkish folk music collection for publication—his last study in comparative music folklore—are narrated in Part One.[1] Moreover, other, important details of a scholarly nature, relating to Bartók's fieldwork, are worthy of further elaboration.

> The period available for the research work was unfortunately rather short; we had only nine or ten days at our disposal. In Ankara the plans for our journey were thoroughly discussed, especially the question concerning which area of the rather extended Turkish territory should be chosen for the work. . . . We finally decided on the winter quarters of the so-called Yürük tribes, a nomadic people living in the Taurus Mountains region during the summer and, during the winter, in the environs of Osmaniye, a place not far from the southern seashore, about fifty or sixty miles to the east of Adana (Seyhan). The presumption was that people exhibiting such ancient migratory customs may have better preserved their old musical material than a more settled people.[2]

Bartók recorded seventy-eight vocal melodies and nine instrumental pieces on Edison phonograph cylinders. He verified the tempo of each song with a metronome and the register of the voice by means of a pitch pipe. Unfortunately, the recording machine that Bartók brought with him could not clearly record both voice and accompanying instruments at the same time.[3] On the other hand, a momentous visit to a peasant cottage resulted in two unblemished cylinders of unique value.

> The owner of the place was an old man of seventy . . . We soon found out that he himself could play a four-stringed instrument, the so called "kemençe", which is like the "rebec", being played in the antique fashion, held like a violoncello though it is no larger than a violin. It is tuned almost in the same way as our violin. The old man began to sing a tune for us in the courtyard without any hesitation. It was an old narrative that he sang, about some war of the old days. I could hardly believe my ears, for it sounded just like a variant of an old Hungarian tune.[4]

After Bartók returned to Budapest at the end of November 1936, he set to work transcribing the sixty-four Turkish folk music cylinders. In January, he had researched his material to the extent that he was able to list the following conclusions: (1) the peasant music in the Adana region of Turkey has little in common with the music (possibly Arabic-influenced) in the Turkish cities; (2) rhymed prose hardly can be found in rural music; (3) Aeolian, Dorian, and, sporadically, Mixolydian modes occur; (4) deviations from the pure intonation of the diatonic scale do not exceed Hungarian ones in particular and those of east Europeans in general; and (5) augmented seconds are rarely encountered.[5]

During the correspondence with A. Adnan Saygun—who had been assigned as one of Bartók's research companions during the Adana fieldwork—the former sent his transcriptions of Turkish folk music material that he had collected in the northeastern (Black Sea area) part of the country.[6] On 20 June 1937, Bartók, noting that Saygun had not transcribed the melodies to a common *tonus finalis*, responded with the following comment:

> There were practical reasons that prompted us to select g^1 as the final tone. Because this tone is—up to the present time—applicable to melodies *of all peoples.* A lower tone (for example, f^1 or d^1) would be impossible for many Western European melodies, since they often descend as much as an octave below the final tone. A higher tone, on the other hand, would present inconveniences, since many Turkish and Hungarian melodies go higher than the final tone by as much as thirteen steps! With g^1 as the final tone we have at our disposal the compass of g through c^3 or d^3. . . .[7]

Table 13.1 shows the grouping of the collected melodies into twenty main classes. The "dotted" rhythm in classes 13–14 is defined by Bartók as a combination of ♪♩. and ♩.♪ patterns or—as their flattened form—of ♪♩ and ♩♪; ♩♩ will also occur in the first case, ♫. in the second case.[8]

TABLE 13.1
Classification of Turkish Folk Melodies

Class	Description of the Melodies	No. of Melodies
1.	*Parlando* isometric four-section, with 8-syllable sections	15
2.	*Parlando* isometric four-section, with 11-syllable sections	18
3.	*Parlando* isometric three-section, with 11-syllable sections	1
4.	*Parlando* isometric two-section, with 8-syllable sections	2
5.	*Parlando* isometric two-section, with 11-syllable sections	3
6.	*Parlando* isometric two-section, with 14-syllable sections	1
7.	*Parlando* isometric four-section, with 7-syllable sections	1

Class	Description of the Melodies	No. of Melodies
8.	*Parlando* isometric four-section, with 9-syllable sections	1
9.	*Parlando* isometric three-section, with 8- (= 3+2+3) syllable sections	1
10.	*Parlando* isometric three-section, with 10- (= 5+5) syllable sections	1
11.	*Parlando* heterometric four-section	1
12.	*Parlando* heterometric three-section	4
13.	*Tempo giusto* isometric four-section, with "dotted" rhythm and 7- or 7+7-syllable sections	7
14.	*Tempo giusto* isometric four-section, with "dotted" rhythm	1
15.	*Tempo giusto* isometric four-section	1
16.	*Tempo giusto* isometric three-section	1
17.	*Tempo giusto* heterometric four-section	2
18.	Rain-begging songs (with motif structure)	4
19.	Melodies with indeterminable structure or of suspicious origin	13
20.	Instrumental pieces	9

After thorough study of the Turkish material, Bartók determined that more than forty percent of the vocal melodies are either identical to or in near relation to the Old Hungarian material. In fact, he states that: "These kinships point to a common western-central Asiatic origin of both Turkish and Hungarian materials and determine their age to as being at least fifteen centuries.[9]

Following Bartók's completion of most of his Turkish transcriptions in May 1937, he made inquiries concerning the possibility of a joint Turkish-Hungarian publication. He interrupted these proceedings during July and August, however, in order to compose the Sonata for Two Pianos and Percussion. It is reasonable to conjecture that Bartók's timbral impression of his visit to the Turkish village of Çardak is vividly portrayed in the Sonata, particularly in the first movement, in approximation of the village drummer who "beat that drum [a bass drum called *davul*] with terrific energy with a wooden drumstick, and I really thought at times that either his big drum or my eardrum would break. Even the flames of the three flickering kerosene lamps jumped at every beat."[10]

Epilogue

When in the fall of 1899 Béla Bartók applied for admission to the Budapest Royal Academy of Music, it was his prodigious pianism and exceptional musicianship that enabled his acceptance as an advanced student of István Thomán—disciple of Liszt and caring teacher—whose nurturing molded his young charge into one of the great virtuosos of the twentieth century. But the creative juices that had inexorably driven Bartók to composing, beginning at the age of nine, were such that the felt need to create music, rather than pursue a career as concert artist, became his primary goal at the Academy and thereafter until his death in 1945.

At the turn of the century, Hungary was embroiled in a renewed thrust toward political separation from Austria. Bartók, caught up in the resurgent nationalism, was determined to work for "the good of Hungary and the Hungarian nation." Thus, inspired by the failed insurrection led by Lajos Kossuth in 1848, the fledgling composer set out on his lofty objective with the composition of the *Kossuth* symphonic poem in 1903. Because of its grotesque parody of the Austrian national anthem, *Kossuth* created a sensation in Hungarian musical circles and propelled Bartók into the national limelight as a composer. More important, Bartók's musical caricature of the anthem represents the innovation of new compositional devices: chromatic compression of a diatonic melody into a partition of the octatonic scale, or its extension in range to whole-tone construction.

In 1906, with the help of Zoltán Kodály, Bartók embarked on his first venture to collect autochthonous Hungarian folk music. He was convinced that the only viable source for composition would be found in the uncontaminated products of the peasant village, not the Gypsy-distorted melodies, composed by amateur musicians from the educated class, which pervaded urban Hungarian culture. The next year, during his visits to the Hungarian-Székely peasant enclaves of Transylvania, he was exhilarated by the discovery of an ancient, ornamented melodic style based on a specifically Hungarian form of the pentatonic scale and freely performed in *parlando-rubato* rhythm. In addition, he collected folk songs whose pitch collections were based on the Aeolian, Dorian, and Phrygian modes, and whose *giusto* tempos reflected a specifically Hungarian type of syncopation he called "dotted rhythm." All the mentioned characteristic features, together with other peculiarities he later found in Slovak, Transylvanian-Romanian, and other rural areas, were fused into a unique "musical mother

215

tongue" that, among other attributes, ultimately led to Bartók's posthumous designation as composer par excellence of the twentieth century.

His penchant for dissonances is illustrated in a 1903 letter to his mother, where he notates B-D-F♯-G in the bass staff as the chordal accompaniment to F♯ in the treble, followed by his query, "Beautiful??" This tendency was exacerbated in February 1908, immediately following the abrupt end of Bartók's unrequited love affair with the beautiful young violin virtuoso, Stefi Geyer. Her religious upbringing made it impossible to accept her suitor's vehement atheism, and he vented his anguish in the Janus-like Elegy no. 1 for Piano, op. 8b, which for the last time looks back to the Liszt style of virtuoso piano technique and for the first time points ahead to polymodal chromaticism, a new tonal language whose expressive dissonance is the outcome of juxtaposed pentatonic, modal, and nondiatonic configurations.

Following his appointment to the Academy as professor of piano and marriage to his pupil, Márta Ziegler, the inadequate performance of his orchestral works and their rejection by the public led to his self-imposed isolation from hostile musical circles in Budapest. As he wrote to Frederick Delius in 1910, "I am very much alone here apart from my one friend Kodály; I have nobody to talk to." These conversations were carried on from time to time until Bartók emigrated to the United States in 1940. Kodály's vivid recollections of Bartók were described in a Budapest lecture, "Béla Bartók the Man," on 22 February 1947.[1] In his effort to describe Bartók's character scientifically, he turned to the constitutional theory developed by the German psychiatrist Ernst Kretschmer (1888–1964). This theory of personality describes the relationships between morphological and physiological attributes with psychological and behavioral characteristics, and is a general term popularly referred to as characterology.[2] The following reminiscence of Bartók by H.W. Heinsheimer (b. 1900), who edited the composer's manuscripts for Universal Edition, Vienna (1924–1938), and Boosey & Hawkes, New York (from 1940), will be helpful in understanding Kodály's description that follows below.

> He was small and terribly frail. His very beautiful wise face was calm, stern, seldom ruffled by laughter. He was shy, very quiet spoken, constantly alert, very suspicious. Fragile in body and soul, he was hurt easily by the slightest deviation from what he believed to be right and true. His thin body, the penetrating, clear, serious eyes, the fine, sharply pointed nose, the noble forehead, the transparent, childlike hands—his was the appearance of an ascetic thinker. . . .
> When I saw him again here in Europe, I was amazed to see how little he had changed. He always seemed quite ageless. His hair had become white—but his face, his skin, his eyes seemed the same after all the years. Even through the years of his consuming sickness he changed little, outwardly.[3]

Kretschmer's three basic types are the *pyknic* (stocky), *asthenic* (slender), and *athletic* (muscular), and one mixed type, *dysplastic* (disproportioned).[4] The traits subsumed in the *cyclothyme* and *schizothyme* group divisions are, according to Kodály, only applicable to Bartók's personality and to a limited extent in the latter division:

> Grades from the uppermost extreme to the lowest: fragile, fine, sensitive, cool, severe, withdrawn (inapplicable: cold, dull, indolent). Categories of psychic tension, beginning from the bottom: fanatical, pedantic, unyielding, persevering, systematic (inapplicable: capricious, confused). The agility aspect, speed in reactions to stimuli: quicker than customary. The subtitles under this heading: restless, precipitate, hesitant, awkward, aristocratic, contrived, angular (inapplicable: rigid). With respect to social relations: self-contained, reserved. Grades: idealist, reformer, revolutionary, systematic, organizer, self-willed, crotchety, dissatisfied, mistrustful, lonely, unsociable (inapplicable: misanthropical, brutal, antisocial). He could have been a typical example of the *schizothyme* mental type.[5]

Kodály also cites Bartók's failure to win the Rubinstein Prize in piano performance (Paris, 1905) as a grave disappointment. "Bartók was a phenomenal pianist, but he was not attractive enough to become very popular. . . . And in Bartók's own words [regarding the collecting of folk songs]: he had spent the happiest days of his life among country people."[6]

The great success—at long last!—of Bartók's stage works in 1917, and the new contract with the Vienna publisher Universal Edition, were tempered by the difficult political and economic times following the end of the First World War. The dismemberment of Greater Hungary created new borders with Transylvania (now Romanian territory), Czechoslovakia, and Yugoslavia, ending his plans for future fieldwork. But his compensation was the time and energy to undertake contracts for the publication of folk music studies of the three major areas of his research: Hungary, Romania, and Slovakia. His pressing need to augment his income with new works for concert appearances, as well as satisfy the urging of his publisher, was intensified by the success of Stravinsky's tours, in which the latter was pianist and conductor, particularly as soloist in his Concerto for Piano and Wind Instruments (1923–1924). Bartok was in the audience when Stravinsky performed the work in Budapest, and its impact was such that Bartók was motivated to create his First Piano Concerto in 1926. Rather than follow Stravinsky's exploitation of Bach's contrapuntal style, Bartók turned to the keyboard works of Italian Baroque composers for inspiration. The added polyphonic dimension, his previous assimilation and extension of Beethoven's formal procedures and Debussy's innovative, nonfunctional chord progressions, together with the new "musical mother tongue" derived from his fusion of multinational folk music characteristics, are for the first time employed in the Concerto. And he subsequently referred to this new style of composition as "a synthesis of East and West."[7]

Kodály addressed "the secret dissonances" engendered by Bartók's music with the explanation that:

Since Bach, we have lost the habit of being able to pursue two voices of equal importance; coordination has been replaced by subordination. We concentrate our attention upon notes sounded below one another and are immediately searching for triads if groups of notes are sounded simultaneously. But music, melodious in its essence, is not to be listened to in this way. If we succeed in surveying a larger area with our glance, that is to say, if we hear horizontally, the grating dissonance comes to an end at once. . . . When two melodies meet, a stress is created that doubles the energy of movement and lends additional emphasis to one melody or to both. This renders Bartók's style particularly terse and implacably logical, creating a feeling of absolute inevitability.[8]

So far as Bartók's place in twentieth-century music is concerned, the pithy opinion of Mosco Carner is offered as a fitting conclusion to this book:

Of the three musicians who dominated the musical scene during the first half of the twentieth century—Stravinsky, Schoenberg, and Bartók—it is the Hungarian master who, despite his immense intellectual control, remained nearest to the instinctual, the irrational in music and thus to the Dionysian spirit in art. He is the supreme example of the artist who, in the dialectic between emotional "primitivism" and intellectual sophistication, never allowed the second ascendancy over the first.[9]

List of Compositions

This list is based on the comprehensive cataloging method designed by Elliott Antokoletz for his book, *Béla Bartók: A Guide to Research, Second Edition.* Among the differences is the replacement of his "Cat" headings by "PBA" and the prefixal abbreviations (as listed below) and alphanumeric designations that I had invented for encoding Bartók's manuscripts. During my tenure as curator of the New York Bartók Archive (*NYBA*), I stamped the encoded designation, including the Bartók Estate logo and the folio number, on each of the leaves comprising the New York Bartók Estate holdings of the composer's music manuscripts. As Dr. Victor Bator—then trustee of the Bartók Estate—states:

> The second person to join the staff was Dr. Benjamin Suchoff, who contributed to the building of the Archive by doing work that only a well-trained musician and musicologist can do. The separation of the sketches, the identification of much of the manuscript material which had been dispersed in scattered envelopes, the institution of systematic classification and of a special protective system of maintenance are to his credit (*The Béla Bartók Archives: History and Catalogue,* 1963, p. 15).

The holdings also include facsimiles of manuscripts in the possession of certain individuals and institutions, that were acquired after the mentioned designations had been in effect. In 1984, I transferred the archive to the composer's heir, Peter Bartók. It should be noted that the following *PBA* (Peter Bartók Archive) listings do not represent a precise chronology with regard to numerical order or specific drafts of a given work. In fact, in 1953 the trustee's primary objective was a procedure whereby the irreplaceable documents in his charge would be indelibly marked in the event of theft, misfiling, or other unforeseen incident, yet readily accessed for research purposes.

S: Sketch	VP: Violin and Piano
ID: Intermediary Draft	CP: Cello and Piano
FC: Final Copy	VoS: Vocal Score
T: Transcription	VoP: Voice and Piano
P: Piano	SA: Women's Chorus
PP: *Primo* Piano	TB: Men's Chorus
SP: *Secondo* Piano	SATB: Mixed Chorus
O: Orchestra	D: Percussion
V: Violin	I.: Volume I; II.: Volume II
VV: Violin Duo	A: Album

I. PIANO SOLO

Works of Youth

1. Three Piano Pieces (*Drei Klavierstücke*), op. 13
   1. Spring song (Tavaszi dal)
   2. Waltz (Valcer)
   3. In Wallachian style (Oláhos)
   Date—1896–1897
   Publication—No. 1, in Denijs Dille, *Der junge Bartók II*, Zeneműkiadó 1965

2. Scherzo or Fantasy for Piano (*Scherzo oder Fantasie für das Pianoforte*), op. 18
   Date—1897
   Dedication—Gabriella Lator
   Publication—in Denijs Dille, *Der junge Bartók II*, Zeneműkiadó 1965

3. Three Piano Pieces (*Drei Klavierstücke*), op. 13
   1. Adagio-Presto
   2. Intermezzo (The facsimile is untitled)
   3. Adagio, sehr düster
   Date—1898, Pozsony
   Dedication—Gabriella Lator
   Publication—Nos. 1-2, in Denijs Dille, *Der junge Bartók II*, Zeneműkiadó 1965

4. Twelve Variations on a Theme of F. F. (*Változatok F.F. egy témája fölött*)
   Date—1900-1901
   Publication—in Denijs Dille, *Der junge Bartók II*, Zeneműkiadó 1965

5. Oriental Dance *(Danse orientale)* [Six Dances for Piano, no. 1]
   Date—1900?
   Performance— 23 October 1954, Halsey Stevens, Bakersfield, California
   Publication—MS facsimile in *Pressburger Zeitung,* Christmas issue (1913)

Mature Works

6. Four Piano Pieces (*Négy zongoradarab*)
   1. Four Piano Pieces (*Tanulmány balkézre*)
   2. Fantasy I (*I. Ábránd*)
   3. Fantasy II (*II. Ábránd*)
   4. Scherzo
   Date—1903
   Publication—Ference Bárd 1904; Boosey & Hawkes 1950; Zeneműkiadó 1956, 1965; Archive Edition 1981
   PBA—6PS1

7. Funeral March (*Marche funèbre*), arrangement of *Kossuth*, tableau 10
   Date—1903

Publication—Kunossy Szilágy és Társa, Budapest 190?, *Magyar lant* 1905, Rozs-nyai 1910?, Zeneműkiadó 1950, Archive Edition 1981

8. Rhapsody (*Rapszódia*) op. 1 (also transcribed for piano and orchestra; and for two pianos)
   Date—November 1904
   Dedication—Emma Gruber
   Performance—solo version, 4 November 1906, composer, Pozsony
   Publication—Adagio mesto: Rózsavölgyi 1909. Complete: Rózsavölgyi 1923, Zeneműkiadó 1955, Archive Edition 1981
   PBA—8TFSS1, 8TSPS1, 8TPPFC1

9. Two Little Pieces for Piano (*Petits morceaux pour piano*), arrangement and transcription of the following songs:
   1. Kiss Me, for I Must Take My Leave (*Add reám csókodat, el kell már búcsúznom*)
   2. Autumn breeze (*Őszi szellő*), from Four Songs on poems of Lajos Pósa (1902)
   Date—1905–1907?
   Publication—in Denijs Dille, *Der junge Bartók II*, Zeneműkiadó 1965

10. Three Hungarian Folksongs from the Csík District (*Három csíkmegyei népdal*)
    1. Rubato
    2. L'istesso tempo
    3. Poco vivo
    Date—1907
    Publication—Rozsnyai 1910, Boosey & Hawkes 1950, Zeneműkiadó 1954, Archive Edition 1981

11. Fourteen Bagatelles (*Tizennégy zongoradarab*) op. 6
    1. Molto sostenuto
    2. Allegro giocoso
    3. Andante
    4. Grave (arr. of Hungarian folk song "Mikor gulyásbojtár voltam")
    5. Vivo (arr. of Slovak folk song "Ej' po pred naš, po pred naš")
    6. Lento
    7. Allegretto molto capriccioso
    8. Andante sostenuto
    9. Allegretto grazioso
    10. Allegro
    11. Allegretto molto rubato
    12. Rubato
    13. Elle est morte (Lento funebre)
    14. Valse: ma mie qui danse (Presto)
    Date—May 1908, Budapest
    Performance—29 June 1908, Vienna (Busoni's piano class)
    Publication—Rozsnyai 1908, Boosey & Hawkes 1950, Zeneműkiadó 1953, Archive Edition 1981
    PBA—18PFC1, 18PFC2

12. Ten Easy Pieces (*Tíz könnyű zongoradarab*)
Dedication (*Ajánlás*)
1. Peasant Song (*Paraszti nóta*)
2. Frustration (*Lassú vergődés*)
3. Slovakian Boys' Dance (*Tót legények tánca*)
4. Sostenuto
5. Evening in Transylvania (Evening with the Széklers) (*Este a székelyeknél*)
6. Hungarian Folk Song (*Gödöllei piactérre leesett a hó...*)
7. Dawn (*Hajnal*)
8. Slovakian Folk Song (*Azt mondják, nem adnak*)
9. Five-finger Exercise (*Ujjgyakorlat*)
10. Bear Dance (*Medvetánc*)
Date—June 1908, revised 1945
Performance—No. 10, 15 November 1909, Budapest; No. 5, 15 March 1910, Budapest
Publication—Rozsnyai 1909, Zeneműkiadó 1951, Archive Edition 1981
PBA—19PS1, 19PS2, 19PFC1

13. Two Elegies (*Két elégia*) op. 8b
1. Grave
2. Molto adagio, sempre rubato
Date—No. 1, February 1908; No. 2, December 1909
Performance—No. 1, 21 April 1919, composer, Budapest
Publication—Rozsnyai 1910, Boosey & Hawkes 1950, Zeneműkiadó 1955, Archive Edition 1981
PBA—21PS1

14. For Children (*Gyermekeknek; Pro dêti*)
Eighty-five pieces originally in four volumes. Volumes I and II (I: Nos. 1–21, II: Nos. 22–42) are based on Hungarian folk tunes, III and IV (III: Nos. I–22, IV: Nos. 23–42) are based on Slovakian folk tunes. The revised version (January 1945), which omitted Nos. II/25, II/29, IV/27, IV/33, and IV/34 of the original version, contains seventy-nine pieces in two volumes.

VOLUMES I AND II

1. Allegro. Let's Bake Something (*Süssünk, süssünk valamit*)
2. Andante. Dawn, O Day (*Süss fel nap*)
3. Andante. I Lost My Young Couple (*Elvesztettem páromat*)
4. Allegro. I Lost My Handkerchief (*Elvesztettem zsebkendőmet*)
5. Poco allegretto. Kitty, Kitty (*Cziczkom, Cziczkom*)
6. Allegro. Hey, Tulip, Tulip (*Hej tulipán, tulipán*)
7. Andante grazioso. Look for the Needle (*Keresd meg a tűt*)
8. Allegretto. Hey, Görbénye (*Ej görbénye, görbénye*)
9. Molto adagio. White Lily (*Fehér liliomszál*)
10. Allegro molto. The Wallachians Wear Wooden Shoes (*Az oláhok, az oláhok facipőbe járnak*)
11. Molto sostenuto. I Lost My Young Couple (*Elvesztettem páromat*)

12. Allegro. Chain, Chain, Floral Chain (*Láncz, láncz, este láncz*)
13. Andante. A Lad Was Killed (*Megöltek egy legényt*)
14. Allegretto. The Poor Lads of Csanád (*A csanádi legények*)
15. Allegro. Teeny-weeny is Stephen's Street (*Icike, picike az istvándi ucca*)
16. Andante rubato. I Never Stole in My Whole Life (*Nem loptam én életembe*)
17. Adagio. My Little Graceful Girl (*Kis kece lányom*)
18. Andante con molto. In the Harbor of Nagyvárad (*Nagyváradi kikötőbe*)
19. Allegretto. When I Go into the Inn at Doboz (*Ha bemegyek a dobozi csárdába*)
20. Poco Allegro. (Drinking Song)
21. Allegro robusto
22. Allegretto. One Ought to Go to Debrecen (*Debrecenbe kéne menni*)
23. Allegro grazioso. You Must Walk This Way, That Way (*Így kell járni, úgy kell járni*)
24. Andante sostenuto. Water, Water, Water (*Víz, víz, víz*)
25. Allegro. Three Apples Plus a Half (*Három alma meg egy fél*)
26. Andante. Go Round, Sweetheart, Go Round (*Kerülj rózsám kerülj*)
27. Allegramente.
28. Parlando. László Fehér Stole a Horse (*Fehér László lovat lopott*)
29. Allegro. Oh! Hey! What Do You Say (*Ej, haj, micsoda*)
30. Andante. They Brought Up the Rooster (*Felhozták a kakast*)
31. Allegro scherzando. Mother, Dear Mother (*Anyám édesanyám*)
32. Allegro ironico. The Sun Shines into the Church (*Besüt a nap a templomba*)
33. Andante sostenuto. Stars Brightly Shine (*Csillagok, szépen ragyogjatok*)
34. Andante. White Lady's Eardrop (*Fehér fuszujkavirág*)
35. Allegro non troppo. I picked Flowers in the Garden (*Kertbe virágot szedtem*)
36. Allegretto. Margitta Isn't Far Away (*Nem messzi van ide Margitta*)
37. Poco vivace. When I Go Up Buda's Big Mountain (*Ha felmegyek a budai*)
38. (no tempo indication) Ten Liters Are Inside (*Tíz litero bennem van*)
39. Allegro. The Cricket's Wedding (*Házasodik a trücsök*)
40. Molto vivace. May the Lord Give (*Adjon az úr isten*)
41. Allegro moderato. Do You Go, Darling? (*Elmész ruzsám?*)
42. Allegro vivace.The Cricket's Wedding (*Házasodik a trücsök*)

VOLUMES III AND IV

1. Allegro. If There Were Cherries, Morellos (*Keby boly čerešne, višne*)
2. Andante. Kite Settled On the Branch (*Kalina, malina*)
3. Allegretto. Above the Tree, Under the Tree Two Roses Bloom (*Pod lipko, na lipko edná mala dve*)
4. Andante. Wedding song (*Lakodalmas*). Hey, Lado, Lado (*Ej, Lado, Lado*)
5. Molto andante.Variations (*Változatok*). The Peacock Flew (*Lecela pava*)
6. Allegro. Rondo I. There Is an old witch (*Stará baba zlá*)
7. Allegro. Highwayman's Tune (*Betyárnóta*)
8. Allegro. Dance Song (*Táncdal*). Hey, Two Pigeons Sit On Prešov Tower (*Hej, na prešovskej tudni dva holubky šedza*)
9. Andante. Rondo II. Children's Song (*Gyermekdal*). Unfold Yourself, Blossom. (*Zabelej sa, zabelej*)
10. Largo. Mourning Song. In Mikulás Barracks (*V mikulásskej kompanii*)
11. Lento. On Bystrov's Field (*V tej bystrickej bráne*)

12. Poco andante. Mother of My Lover (*Suhajova mati*)
13. Allegro. Anička Mlynárova
14. Moderato. Plowing Are Six Oxen (*Ore šest volov*)
15. Molto tranquillo. Bagpipe Tune (*Dudanóta*). Dance, Maiden (*Tancuj, dievča*)
16. Lento. Lament (*Panasz*).
17. Andante. The Girl Was the Priest's Maidservant (*Sluzilo dievča na fare*)
18. Sostenuto. Satirical Song (*Gúnydal*). Once I Was Your Lover (*Mau som ta dievča*)
19. Assai lento. Romance (*Románc*). Bird On the Branch (*Daťel na dube, žalostne dube*
20. Prestissimo. Game of Tag (*Kergetőző*). Don't Go at Dawn, Hanulienka (*Nechocže ty, Hanulienka*)
21. Allegro moderato. Pleasantry (*Tréfa*). She Flew Down and Was in Tears (*Sadla dola, plakala*)
22. Molto allegro. Revelry (*Duhajkodó*). The Lads Caught a Goat (*Hnali švarní šuhj c kozy do dúbravy*)
23. Molto rubato, non troppo lento. I Am Already an Old Shepherd (*Ja som bača velmi starí*)
24. Poco andante. I Passed Through the Forest (*Koj som išol cez horu*)
25. Andante. Bird on the Branch (*Daťel na dube, žalostne dube*)
26. Scherzando Allegretto.
27. Allegro. Teasing Song (*Csúfolódás*)
28. Andante molto rubato. Peasant's Flute (*Furulyaszó*)
29. Allegro. Another Pleasantry (*Még egy tréfa*)
30. Andante molto rubato. I Have Wandered a Lot (*Dosti som sa nachodil*)
31. Poco vivace. Canon (*Kánon*)
32. Vivace. Bagpipe II. Little Garden (*Zahradka*)
33. Poco andante. The Orphan (*Rvagyerek*). Hey, Forest, Green Forest (*Ej, hory, zelené hory*)
34. Poco allegretto. Romance (*Románc*). I Know a Little Forest (*Viem ja jeden hájiček*)
35. Allegro. The Highway Robber. Jánošik Is a Big Bully (*Bol by ten Jánošik*)
36. Largo. If I Knew Where My Darling (*Kebych ja vedela*)
37. Molto tranquillo. The Danube's Bank is Green at Bratislava (*Pri Prešporku, pri čichom Dunajku*)
38. Adagio. Farewell (*Búcsú*). I Look Back Upon You Once More (*Ešťe sa raz obzrieť mám*)
39. Poco largo. Ballad (*Ballada*). Janko Drives Out Two Oxen (*Pásol Janko dva voly*)
40–41. Parlando molto rubato–Allegro moderato. Rhapsody (*Rapszódia*). Hey!Blow, You Summer Wind; Hey! What a Beautiful House (*Hej! pofukuj povievaj; Hej! ten stoličny dom*)
42. Lento. Mourning Song (*Sirató ének*)
43. Lento. Funeral Song (*Halotti ének*). There In the Deep Valley (*Dolu dolinami*)

Date—1908-9; revised January 1945
Performance—1 February 1913, Kecskemét?
Publication—Rozsnyai 1910-1912, Zeneműkiadó 1950; revised Boosey & Hawkes 1947, Archive Edition 1981
PBA—22PS1, 22PI./II.ID1, 22PFC1, 22TVPS1, 22TVPFC1/2, 22 TVFC1

15. Two Romanian Dances (*Két román tánc*) op. 8a
   1. Allegro vivace
   2. Poco Allegro
   Date—No. 1, 1909; No. 2, March 1910
   Performance—No. 1, 12 March 1910, composer, Paris
   Publication—Rózsavölgyi 1910, Boosey & Hawkes 1950, Zeneműkiadó 1951,
      Editio Musica (facsimile) 1974, Archive Edition 1981
   PBA—25PID1, 25PFC1, 25TFSS1

16. Seven Sketches (*Vázlatok*) op. 9b
   1. Andante (con moto). Portrait of a Young Girl (*Leányi arckép*)
   2. Comodo. See-Saw, Dickory Daw (*Hinta palinta*)
   3. Lento
   4. Non troppo lento
   5. Andante. Romanian Folk Song (*Román népdal*)
   6. Allegretto. In Wallachian Style (*Oláhos*)
   7. Poco lento
   Date—1908-August 1910; revised January 19, 1945
   Dedication—No. 1, Márta Ziegler [Bartók]; No. 3, Emma and Zoltán [Kodály]
   Publication—Rozsnyai 1912, Boosey & Hawkes 1950, Zeneműkiadó 1954, Archive
      Edition 1981
   PBA—23PID1, 23PFC1

17. Four Dirges (*Négy siratóének*) (*Quatre nénies*) op. 9a
   1. Adagio
   2. Andante
   3. Poco lento
   4. Assai andante
   Date—1909-1910; No. 2 transcribed for orchestra 1931
   Performance—in part, 17 October 1917, Ernő Dohnányi, Budapest
   Publication—Rózsavölgyi 1912, Boosey & Hawkes 1950, Zeneműkiadó 1955,
      Archive Edition 1981
   PBA—26PID1

18. Three Burlesques (*Három burleszk*) op. 8c
   1. Quarrel (*Perpatvar*)
   2. A Bit Drunk (*Kicsit ázottan*)
   3. Molto vivo capriccioso
   Date—No. 1, November 1908; No. 2, May 1911; No. 3, 1910; No. 2 transcribed for
      orchestra as No. 4 of Hungarian Sketches, 1931
   Dedication—Márta [Ziegler-Bartók]
   Performance—one piece, 12 April 1912, composer, Tîrgu Mureş, Romania; two
      pieces, 1 February 1913, composer, Kecskemét; nos 1 and 2, 17 October 1917,
      Ernő Dohnányi, Budapest; complete November 12, 1921, Budapest
   Publication—Rózsavölgyi 1912, Boosey & Hawkes 1950, Zeneműkiadó 1954,
      Archive Edition 1981
   PBA—24PS1, 24PID1, 24PFC1

19. *Allegro barbaro*
    Date—1911
    Performance—27 February 1921, composer, Budapest
    Publication—Universal Edition 1918, K.M.P., Kiev 1927, Boosey & Hawkes 1939,
        Béla Bartók 1945, Universal Edition (UE 5904, Revision: Péter Bartók) 1992
    PBA—29PS1, 29PFC1

20. The First Term at the Piano (*Kezdők zongoramuzsikája*)
    Eighteen pieces from the Béla Bartók-Sándor Reschofsky piano method
    1. Moderato
    2. Moderato
    3. Moderato. Dialogue (*Párbeszéd*)
    4. Moderato. Dialogue (*Párbeszéd*)
    5. Moderato
    6. Moderato
    7. Moderato. Folk Song (*Népdal*)
    8. Andante
    9. Andante
    10. Allegro. Folk Song (*Népdal*)
    11. Andante. Minuet (*Menüett*)
    12. Allegro. Swineherd's Dance (*Kanásztánc*)
    13. Andante. Folk Song (*Népdal*). Where Have You Been Little Lamb? (*Hol voltál
        báránykám?*)
    14. Andante
    15. Moderato. Wedding Dance (*Lakodalmas*)
    16. Allegro moderato. Peasant's Dance (*Paraszttánc*)
    17. Allegro deciso.
    18. Tempo di Valse. Waltz (*Keringő*)
    Date—1913
    Publication—Rózsavölgyi 1929, Boosey & Hawkes 1950, Zeneműkiadó 1952, 1955,
        Archive Edition 1981
    PBA—32TPFC1

21. Sonatina (*Szonatina*)
    Three movements based on Romanian folk tunes
    I. Bagpipers (*Dudások*)
    II. Bear Dance (*Medvetánc*)
    III. Finale
    Date—1915; transcribed for orchestra as Transylvanian Dances (*Erdélyi táncok*),
        1931
    Performance—March 8, 1920, Berlin?
    Publication—Rózsavölgyi 1919, Muzghis (Moscow) 1933, Boosey & Hawkes 1950,
        Zeneműkiadó 1952, Archive Edition 1981
    PBA—36PS1, 361VPS1, 36TFSS1

22. Romanian Folk Dances (*Román népi táncok*)
    1. Stick Dance (*Jocul cu bâtă*)
    2. Sash Dance (*Brâul*)

3. In One Spot (*Pe loc*)
4. Horn Dance (*Buciumeana*)
5. Romanian Polka (*Poarg· româneasca*)
6. Fast Dance (*Mărunţelul*)
   Date—1915; transcribed for small orchestra 1917
   Dedication—Professor Ion Buşiţia
   Publication—Universal Edition 1918, Boosey & Hawkes 1945, Universal Edition (UE 5802, Revision: Peter Bartók) 1993
   PBA—37PS1, 37PFC1, 37TVPFC1

23. Romanian Christmas Carols (*Román kolinda-dallamok*).

SERIES I

1. Allegro. *Pă cel plai de munte*
2. Allegro. *Intreabă şi intreaba*
3. Allegro. *D-oi roagă sa roagă*
4. Andante. *Ciucur verde de mătasă*
5. Allegro moderato. *Coborât-o coborât-o*
6. Andante. *In patru cornuţi de lume*
7. Andante. *La lină fântână*
8. Allegretto. *Noi umblăm d-a corindare*
9. Allegro. *Noi acum ortacilor*
10. Più allegro. *Tri crai dela răsăritu*

SERIES II

1. Molto moderato. *Colo'n jos la munte'n josu*
2. Moderato. *Deasupra pa răsăritu*
3. Andante. *Creşte-mi Doamne creştiu*
4. Andante. *Sculaţl, sculaţi boieri mari*
5. Moderato. *Ai, Colo'n josu mai din josu*
6. Andante. *Si-o luat, luată*
7. Variante della precedente. *Colo sus, mai susu*
8. Allegro. *Colo sus pă după lună*
9. Allegretto. *De ce-i domnul bunu*
10. Allegro. *Hai cu toţii să suimu*
    Date—1915
    Publication—Universal Edition 1918
    PBA—38PS1, 38PFC1, 38PFC2

24. Suite (*Szvit*) op. 14
    1. Allegretto
    2. Scherzo
    3. Allegro molto
    4. Sostenuto
    Date—February 1916, Rákoskeresztúr
    Performance—21 April 1919, composer, Budapest
    Publication—Universal Edition 1918, the abandoned Andante between the first two

movements published in *Új zenei szemle* 5 (1955), Béla Bartók 1945, Universal
Edition (UE5891, Revision: Peter Bartók) 1992
PBA—43PS1, 43PF1, 43PFC2

25. **Three Hungarian Folk Tunes** (*Három magyar népdal*)
   1. The Peacock (*Leszállott a páva*)
   2. At the Jánoshida Fairground (*Jánoshidi vásártéren*)
   3. White Lily (*Fehér liliomszál*)
   Date—1914–1918
   Publication—No. 1, in an earlier version, published in *Periszkôp* (Arad, Romania,
   June-July 1925); complete in collection "Homage to Paderewski," revised 1942,
   Boosey & Hawkes 1942
   PBA—35PFC1, 35PFC2

26. **Fifteen Hungarian Peasant Songs** (*Tizenöt magyar parasztdal*)
   1-4. Four Old Tunes (*Négy régi keserves ének*)
   5. Scherzo
   6. Ballade (Tema con variazioni)
   7–15. Old Dance Tunes (*Régi táncdalok*)
   Date—1914–1918; Nos. 6–12, 14–15 transcribed for orchestra as Hungarian Peasant Songs, 1933
   Publication—Universal Edition 1920, Boosey & Hawkes 1948, Universal Edition
   (UE 6370, Revision: Peter Bartók) 1994
   PBA—34PFC1, 34PFC2, 34TFSFC1, 34TFSFC2, 34TFSFC3

27. **Three Studies** (*Etüdök*) op. 18
   1. Allegro molto
   2. Andante sostenuto
   3. Rubato; Tempo giusto, capriccioso
   Date—1918, Rákoskeresztúr
   Performance—21 April 1919, composer, Budapest
   Publication—Universal Edition 1920, Boosey & Hawkes 1939, Muzghis (Moscow) 1957
   PBA—48PS1, 48PFC1

28. **Eight Improvisations on Hungarian Peasant Songs** (*Improvizációk magyar
   parasztdalokra*) op. 20
   I. Molto moderato (*Sütött ángyom rétest*)
   II. Molto capriccioso
   III. Lento rubato (*Imhol kerekedik*)
   IV. Allegretto scherzando (*Kályha vállán az ice*)
   V. Allegro molto
   VI. Allegro moderato, molto capriccioso (*Jai istenem, ezt a vént*)
   VII. Sostenuto, rubato (*Beli fiam, beli*)
   VIII. Allegro (*Télen nem jó szántani*)
   Date—1920
   Dedication—No. VII dedicated to the memory of Claude Debussy

Performance—27 February 1921, composer, Budapest
Publication—Universal Edition 1922; no. VII in the *Tombeau de Claude Debussy,*
  Boosey & Hawkes 1939
PBA—50PS1

29. Dance Suite (*Táncszvit*), reduction of Dance Suite for Orchestra (1923)
  I. Moderato
  II. Allegro molto
  III. Allegro vivace
  IV. Molto tranquillo
  V. Comodo
  [VI]. Finale
  Date—arranged 1925
  Publication—Universal Edition 1925, Boosey & Hawkes 1952, Universal Edition
    (UE 8397, Revision: Peter Bartók) 1991
  PBA—53PS1, 53FSS1, 53FSFC1

30. Sonata (*Szonáta*)
  I. Allegro moderato
  II. Sostenuto e pesante
  III. Allegro molto
  Date—June 1926, Budapest
  Dedication—Ditta [Pásztory-Bartók]
  Performance—8 December 1926, composer, Budapest
  Publication—Universal Edition 1927, Boosey & Hawkes 1939, 1955, Editio Musica
    1980, Universal Edition (UE 8772, Revision: Peter Bartók) 1992
  PBA—55PS1, 55PID1, 55PFC1

31. Out of Doors (*Szabadban*)
  1. With Drums and Pipes (*Síppal, dobbal*)
  2. Barcarolla
  3. Musettes
  4.The Night's Music (*Az éjszaka zenéje*)
  5. The Chase (*Hajsza*)
  Date—1926
  Dedication—No. 4 dedicated to Ditta [Bartók]
  Performance—Nos 1 and 4, 8 December 1926, composer, Budapest
  Publication—Universal Edition 1927, Boosey and Hawkes 1954, Universal Edi-
    tion (UE 8892a, Revision: Peter Bartók) 1990
  PBA—56PS1, 56PFC1

32. Nine Little Piano Pieces (*Kilenc kis zongoradarab*)

BOOK I

  (1–4): Four Dialogues (*Négy párbeszéd*)
  1. Moderato
  2. Andante

3. Lento
4. Allegro vivace

BOOK II

5. Menuetto
6. Air (*Dal*)
7. Marcia delle bestie
8. Tambourine (*Csörgő-tánc*)

BOOK III:

9. Preludio, All' ungherese
Date—31 October 1926
Performance—8 December 1926, composer, Budapest (one dialogue omitted)
Publication—Universal Edition 1927
PBA—57PS1, 57PID1, 57PFC1

33. Three Rondos on (Slovak) Folk Tunes (*Három rondó népi dallamokkal*)
1. Andante
2. Vivacissimo
3. Allegro molto
Date—No. 1, 1916; nos. 2 and 3, 1927
Publication—Universal Edition 1930, Boosey & Hawkes 1957, Universal Edition
(UE 9508, Revision: Peter Bartók) 1995
PBA—45PS1, 45PFC1

34. Petite Suite (*Kis szvit*), transcriptions of nos. 28, 38, 43, 16, 36, of Forty-
Four Duos for two violins
1. Slow Tune (*Lassú*)
2. Whirling Dance (*Forgatós*)
3. Quasi pizzicato (*Pengetős*)
4. Ruthenian Dance (*Oroszos*)
5. Bagpipes (*Dudás*)
Date—1936
Publication—Universal Edition 1938; no. 36 unpublished; original version for two
violins, 1931
PBA—69TPS, 69TPFC1, 69TPFC2, 69TPFC3

35. *Mikrokosmos,* 153 Progressive Pieces for Piano

VOLUME I

1–6. Six Unison Melodies
7. Dotted Notes
8. Repetition
9. Syncopation
10. With Alternate Hands
11. Parallel Motion
12. Reflection

148–153. Six Dances in Bulgarian Rhythm
Date—1926, 1932-1939
Dedication—Vols. I–II to Peter Bartók; Nos. 148–153 to Harriet Cohen
Publication—Boosey & Hawkes 1940, (New Definitive Edition: Peter Bartók) 1987
PBA—59PS1, 59PID1, 59PID2, 59PFC1, 59PFC2

36. *Seven Pieces from Mikrokosmos* (nos. 113, 69, 135, 123, 127, 145, 146) for two pianos, four hands
Date—1940
Publication—Boosey & Hawkes 1947
PBA—59TPPS1, 59TPPID1, 59TPPFC1

37. *Suite for Two Pianos* (arrangement of Suite no. 2 for Orchestra. op. 4, 1905)
Date—1941
Publication—Boosey & Hawkes 1960
PBA—12TPPS1, 12TPPID1, 12TPPFC1, 12TSPFC1

II. CHAMBER MUSIC

38a. Andante for Violin and Piano (*hegedűre és zongorára*)
Date—November 1902
Publication—Editio Musica 1980, Editio Musica (MS facsimile) 1980
Performance—5 July 1955, Adila Fachiri, London

38b. Sonata for Piano and Violin (*Szonáta zongorára és hegedűre*)
1. Allegro moderato
2. Andante
3. Vivace
Date—February–August 1903
Publication—Editio Music 1968, B. Schott's Söhne (Mainz) 1969

38c. Piano quintet (*Zongoraötös*)
Date—1903-1904, revised 1920?
Publication—Editio Musica 1970
PBA—7FSFC1

39. Three folk songs from the Csík District (*Három csík megyei népdal*), for long peasant-flute (*tilinkó*) and piano)
1. Rubato
2. L'istesso tempo
3. Poco vivo
Date—1907
Publication—Zeneműkiadó 1961

40. String Quartet no. 1 (*I. Vonósnégyes*) op. 7
I. Lento
II. Allegretto

(Introduzione)
III. Allegro vivace
Date—1908–27 January 1909
Performance—19 March 1910, Waldbauer-Kerpely Quartet, Budapest
Publication—Rózsavölgyi 1910, Boosey & Hawkes 1939, Zeneműkiadó 1956 and 1964
PBA—20FSS1

41. String Quartet no. 2 (*II. Vonósnégyes*) op. 17
I. Moderato
II. Allegro molto capriccioso
III. Lento
Date—1915–October 1917, Rákoskeresztúr
Dedication—Waldbauer-Kerpely Quartet
Performance—3 March 1918, Waldbauer-Kerpely Quartet, Budapest
Publication—Universal Edition 1920, Boosey & Hawkes 1939
PBA—42FSS1, 42FSFC1

42. Sonata No. 1 for Violin and Piano (*I. Szonáta*; MS only: op. 21)
I. Allegro appassionato
II. Adagio
III. Allegro
Date—October–12 December 1921, Budapest
Dedication—Jelly d'Arányi
Performance—8 February 1922, Mary Dickenson-Auner and Edward Steuermann, Vienna; 24 March 1922, Jelly d'Arányi and composer, London
Publication—Universal Edition 1923, Boosey & Hawkes 1950, Universal Edition (UE 7247, Revision: Peter Bartók) 1991
PBA—51VPS1, 51VFC1, 51VFC2, 51VPFC1, 51VPFC2

43. Sonata No. 2 for Violin and Piano (*II. Szonáta*)
I. Molto moderato
II. Allegretto
Date—July–November 1922, Budapest
Dedication—Jelly d'Arányi
Performance—7 February 1923, Imre Waldbauer and composer, Berlin; 7 May 1923, Jelly d'Arányi and composer, London
Publication—Universal Edition 1923
PBA—52VS1, 52VFC1, 52VPFC1, 52VPFC2

44. String Quartet No. 3 (*III. Vonósnégyes*)
Prima parte. Moderato
Seconda parte. Allegro
Ricapitulazione della prima parte. Moderato
Coda. Allegro molto
Date—September 1927, Budapest
Dedication—Musical Fund Society of Philadelphia

Performance—30 December 1928, Philadelphia, Mischa Mischakoff, David Dubinsky, Samuel Lifschey, and William Van der Berg; 12 February 1929, Vienna (Kolisch) Quartet, London; 19 February 1929, Waldbauer-Kerpely Quartet, London
Publication—Universal Edition 1929, Boosey & Hawkes 1939
PBA—60FSS1, 60 FSFC1

45. Rhapsody No. 1 for Violin and Piano (*I. Rapszódia*) (also versions for violoncello and piano, and for violin and orchestra)
I. Moderato. *Lassú*
II. Allegretto moderato. *Friss*
Date—1928
Dedication—Joseph Szigeti
Performance—4 March 1929, Zoltán Székely and composer, London; 22 November 1929, Joseph Szigeti and composer, Budapest; orchestral version, 1 November 1929, Joseph Szigeti with unspecified orchestra, cond. Hermann Scherchen, Königsberg (Kaliningrad); violoncello and piano version, 30 March, 1929, Jenő Kerpely and composer, Budapest
Publication—Universal Edition 1929
PBA—61VS1, 61VPS1, 61VPFC1, 61VPFC2, 61VPFC3, 61TFSS1

46. Rhapsody No. 1 for Violoncello and Piano (*I. Rapszódia*) (transcription of Rhapsody No. 1 for Violin and Piano
I. Moderato. *Lassú*
II. Allegretto moderato. *Friss*
Date—1928
Performance—30 March 1929, Jenő Kerpely and composer, Budapest
Publication—Universal Edition 1929
PBA—61TCPFC1

47. Rhapsody No. 2 for Violin and Piano (*II. Rapszódia*) (also for violin and orchestra)
I. Moderato. *Lassú*
II. Allegretto moderato. *Friss*
Date—1928; revised 1945
Dedication—Zoltán Székely
Performance—19 November 1928, Zoltán Székely and Géza Frid, Amsterdam; for violin and orchestra, 26 November 1929, Zoltán Székely and Philharmonic Society Orchestra (Ernő Dohnányi, conducting), Budapest
Publication—Universal Edition 1929, Boosey & Hawkes (1945 revision) 1947
PBA—63VPFS1, 63VPID1, 63VPFC1, 63TFSS1, 63TFSFC1

48. String Quartet No. 4 (*IV. Vonósnégyes*)
I. Allegro
II. Prestissimo, con sordino
III. Non troppo lento
IV. Allegretto pizzicato

V. Allegro molto
Date—July-September 1928, Budapest
Dedication—Pro Arte Quartet
Performance—22 February 1929, Hungarian (Waldbauer) Quartet, London
Publication—Universal Edition 1929, Boosey & Hawkes 1939
PBA—62FSS1, 62FSFC1, 62FSFC2, 62FSFC3

49. Forty-Four Duos (*Negyvennégy duó*) (for two violins)

VOLUME I

1. Teasing Song (*Párosító*)
2. Dance (*Kalamajkó*)
3. Menuetto.
4. Midsummer Night Song (*Szentivánéji*)
5. Slovak Song (*Tót nóta*)
6. Hungarian Melody (*Magyar nóta*)
7. Wallachian Song (*Oláh nóta*)
8. Slovak Song (*Tót nóta*)
9. Play (*Játék*)
10. Ruthenian Song (*Rutén nóta*)
11. Lullaby (*Gyermekrengetéskor*)
12. Hay-Harvesting Song (*Szénagyűjtéskor*)
13. Wedding Song (*Lakodalmas*)
14. Cushion Dance (*Párnás-tánc*)

VOLUME II

15. Soldier's Song (*Katonanóta*)
16. Burlesque (*Burleszk*)
17. Marching Song (*Menetelő nóta*)
18. Marching Song (*Menetelő nóta*)
19. Fairy Tale (*Mese*)
20. Song (*Dal*)
21. New Year's Greeting (*Újévköszöntő*)
22. Mosquito Dance (*Szúnyogtánc*)
23. Wedding Song (*Menyasszony-búcsúztató*)
24. Gay Song (*Tréfás nóta*)
25. Hungarian Melody (*Magyar nóta*)

VOLUME III

26. Teasing Song (*Ugyan édes komámasszony*)
27. Limping Dance (*Sántatánc*)
28. Sorrow (*Bánkódás*)
29. New Year's Greeting (*Újévköszönto*)
30. New Year's Greeting (*Újévköszönto*)
31. New Year's Greeting (*Újévköszönto*)
32. Dance from Máramaros (*Máramarosi tánc*)
33. Harvest Song (*Aratáskor*)

34. Counting Song (*Számláló nóta*)
35. Ruthenian Round Dance (*Rutén kolomyjka*)
36. Bagpipes (*Szól a duda*)

VOLUME V

37. Prelude and Canon (*Preludium és kánon*)
38. Romanian Whirling Dance (*Forgatós: Invărtita bâtrănilor*)
39. Serbian Dance (*Szerb tánc: Zaplet*)
40. Wallachian Dance (*Oláh tánc*)
41. Scherzo
42. Arab Song (*Arab dal*)
43. Pizzicato
44. Transylvanian Dance (*Erdélyi tánc: Ardeleana*)
    Nos. 28, 32, 38, 43, 16, and 36 were transcribed for piano (1936) as *Petite Suite*
    Date—1931
    Performance—in part, 20 January 1932, Imre Waldbauer and György Hannover, Budapest
    Publication—seven pieces, Schott 1932; complete, Universal Edition 1933
    PBA—69VVS1, 69VVID1, 69VVID2, 69VVFC1, 69VVFC2, 69VVFC3

50. String Quartet No. 5 (V. Vonósnégyes)
    I. Allegro
    II. Adagio molto
    III. Scherzo
    IV. Andante
    V. Finale
    Date—6 August–6 September 1934, Budapest
    Dedication—Mrs. Elizabeth Sprague Coolidge
    Performance—8 April 1935, Kolisch Quartet, Washington
    Publication—Universal Edition 1936, Boosey & Hawkes 1939
    PBA—71FSS1, 71FSFC1, 71FSFC2, 71 (Parts) FC1,

51. Sonata for Two Pianos and Percussion
    I. Assai lento—Allegro molto
    II. Lento ma non troppo
    III. Allegro non troppo
    Date—July–August 1937, Budapest; transcribed as Concerto for Two Pianos, Percussion, and Orchestra, December 1940
    Performance—16 January 1938, Béla and Ditta Bartók, Fritz Schiesser, and Philipp Rühlig, Basel; Concerto, 21 January 1943, Béla and Ditta Bartók, New York Philharmonic Symphony (Fritz Reiner conducting), New York
    Publication—Boosey & Hawkes 1942
    PBA—75FSS1, 75FSID1, 75FSID2, 75FSID3, 75DID1, 75DID2, 75DID3

52. Contrasts (*Kontrasztok*) (for violin, clarinet, and piano)
    I. Recruiting dance (*Verbunkos*)
    II. Relaxation (*Pihenő*)
    III. Fast Dance (*Sebes*)

Date—24 September 1938, Budapest
Dedication—Benny Goodman and Joseph Szigeti
Performance—9 January 1939, Joseph Szigeti, Benny Goodman, Endre Petri, New York
Publication—Boosey & Hawkes 1942
PBA—77FSS1, 77FSFC1

53. String Quartet No. 6 (*VI. Vonósnégyes*)
   I. Mesto—Più mosso, pesante—Vivace
   II. Mesto—Marcia
   III. Mesto—Burletta
   IV. Mesto
   Date—August–November 1939, Saanen-Budapest
   Dedication—Kolisch Quartet
   Performance—20 January 1941, Kolisch Quartet, New York
   Publication—Boosey & Hawkes 1941
   PBA—79FSS1, 79FSFC1

54. Sonata for Solo Violin
   I. Tempo di ciaccona
   II. Fuga
   III. Melodia
   IV. Presto
   Date—14 March 1944, Asheville, NC
   Dedication—Yehudi Menuhin
   Performance—26 November 1944, Yehudi Menuhin, New York
   Publication—Boosey & Hawkes 1947, Urtext Edition (Preface by Peter Bartók): Boosey & Hawkes 1994
   PBA—81VS1, 81VFC1, 81VFC2

3. SOLO INSTRUMENTS AND ORCHESTRA

55. Rhapsody (*Rapszódia*) op. 1, for Piano and Orchestra (first version for piano)
   Date—November 1904; piano and orchestra version 1905
   Dedication—Emma Gruber
   Performance—15 November 1909, Jenő Hubay, violin, and the Academy of Music Orchestra, Budapest
   Publication—Rózsavölgyi 1910, Zeneműkiadó 1954
   PBA—8TFSS1, 8TPPS1, 8TPPFC1

56. Scherzo (originally known as Burlesque) op. 2, for Piano and Orchestra
   Date—1904
   Performance—28 September 1961, E. Tusa, Hungarian Radio Orchestra (György Lehel conducting), Budapest
   Publication—Zeneműkiadó 1961

57. Violin Concerto no. 1 for Violin and Orchestra (*Hegedűverseny*) (first

movement revised as no. 1 of Two Portraits)
I. Andante sostenuto
II. Allegro giocoso
Date—1 July 1, 1907, Jászberényi–5 February 1908, Budapest
Dedication—Stefi Geyer
Performance—30 May 1958, Hans-Heinz Schneeberger and the Basel Chamber Orchestra (Paul Sacher conducting), Basel
Publication—Boosey & Hawkes 1959
PBA—15VFC1, 15FSFC1

58. Concerto no. 1 for Piano and Orchestra (*I. Zongoraverseny*)
I. Allegro
II. Andante
III. Allegro
Date—August–12 November 1926, Budapest
Performance—1 July 1927, composer (Wilhelm Furtwängler conducting), Frankfurt am Main
Publication—Universal Edition 1927, 1928; two-piano version, Universal Edition 1927
PBA—56PPS1, 58FSS1, 58TPPFC1

59. Rhapsody no. 1 for Violin and Orchestra (*Rapszódia*) (transcription of Rhapsody No. 1 for Violin and Piano)
I. Moderato. *Lassú*
II. Allegretto moderato. *Friss*
Date—1928
Dedication—Joseph Szigeti
Performance—1 November 1929, Joseph Szigeti (Hermann Scherchen conducting), Königsberg
Publication—Universal Edition 1929
PBA—61TFSS1

60. Rhapsody No. 2 for Violin and Orchestra (*II. Rapszódia*) (transcription of Rhapsody No. 2 for Violin and Piano)
I. Moderato. *Lassú*
II. Allegretto moderato. *Friss*
Date—1928; revised 1944
Dedication—Zoltán Székely
Performance—26 November 1929, Zoltán Székely (Ernő Dohnányi conducting), Budapest
Publication—Universal Edition 1929, Boosey & Hawkes (1944 revision) 1949
PBA—61TFSS1, 63TFSFC1

61. Concerto no. 2 for Piano and Orchestra (*II. Zongoraverseny*)
I. Allegro
II. Adagio-Presto-Adagio
III. Allegro molto

Date—October 1930 to September–October 1931
Performance—23 January 1933, composer (Hans Rosbaud conducting), Frankfurt am Main
Publication—Universal Edition 1932, 1941, 1955
PBA—68FSS1, 68FSFC1, 68FSFC2, 68TPSPFC1

62. Concerto no. 2 for Violin and Orchestra
   I. Allegro non troppo
   II. Andante tranquillo
   III. Allegro molto
   Date—August 1937–31 December 1938, Budapest
   Dedication—Zoltán Székely
   Performance—23 March 1939, Zoltán Székely and the Concertgebouw Orchestra (Willem Mengelberg conducting), Amsterdam
   Publication—Boosey & Hawkes 1946, Muzghis (Moscow) 1964
   PBA—76VPS1, 76FSID1, 76FSFC1, 76TVPFC1, 76TVPFC2

63. Concerto for Two Pianos, Percussion, and Orchestra (original version: Sonata for Two Pianos and Percussion)
   I. Assai lento—Allegro molto
   II. Lento ma non troppo
   III. Allegro non troppo
   Date—transcribed, December 1940
   Performance—21 January 1943, Béla and Ditta Bartók and the New York Philharmonic Symphony (Fritz Reiner conducting), New York
   Publication—Boosey & Hawkes 1970
   PBA—75 TFSID1, 75TFSFC1, 75TPPPFC1, 75TPSPFC1, 75TDFC1, 75TDFC2

64. Concerto No. 3 for Piano and Orchestra
   I. Allegretto
   II. Adagio religioso—poco più mosso—tempo I
   III. Allegro vivace
   Date—1945, last 17 measures completed by Tibor Serly
   Performance—8 February 1946, György Sándor and the Philadelphia Orchestra (Eugene Ormandy conducting), Philadelphia
   Publication—Boosey & Hawkes 1946 and 1947
   PBA—84FSS1, 84FSFC1

65. Viola Concerto for Violin and Orchestra
   I. Moderato (attacca)
   II. Adagio religioso—allegretto (attacca)
   III. Allegro vivace
   Date—1945, unfinished; reconstructed and orchestrated by Tibor Serly
   Dedication—written for William Primrose
   Performance—2 December 1949, William Primrose and the Minneapolis Symphony Orchestra (Antal Dórati conducting)
   Publication—Boosey & Hawkes 1950, Bartók Records 1995 (facsimile of the au-

tograph manuscript)
PBA—85FSS1

4. FULL OR SMALL ORCHESTRA

66. Scherzo from Symphony in E-Flat Major
Date—Symphony in piano reduction only, 1902; Scherzo orchestrated 1903
Performance—29 February 1904, Budapest Opera Orchestra (István Kerner conducting), Budapest; two movements of the Symphony orchestrated by Denijs Dille and performed 28 September 1961, Hungarian Radio Orchestra (György Lehel conducting), Budapest
Publication—Symphony unpublished except for recording of the Scherzo, *Bartók Béla, Posztumusz művek* (Béla Bartók, Posthumous Works), edited by Ferenc Bónis, LPX11517

67. *Kossuth* symphonic poem (*Kossuth szimfoniai költemény*)
Date—2 April–18 August 1903
Performance—13 January 1904, Philharmonic Society (István Kerner conducting), Budapest
Publication—Zeneműkiadó 1963
PBA—3FSFC1

68. Suite No. 1 (*I. Szvit*) op. 3 (for full orchestra)
I. Allegro vivace
II. Poco adagio
III. Presto
IV. Moderato
V. Molto vivace
Date—1905, Vienna; revised 1920
Performance—three movements only (I, III, V), 29 November 1905, Gesellschaftkonzerte (Ferdinand Loewe); complete, 1 March 1909 (Jenő Hubay conducting), Budapest
Publication—Rózsavölgyi 1912, revised Zeneműkiadó 1956, 1961
PBA—10FSS1

69. Suite No. 2 (*II. Szvit*) op. 4 (for small orchestra; also arranged for two pianos)
I. Comodo
II. Allegro scherzando
III. Andante
IV. Comodo
Date—Movements I–III, November 1905, Vienna; Movement IV, 1 September 1907, Rákospalota; rev. 1920 and 1943; version for two pianos, 1943
Performance—Movement II only, 2 January 2, 1909, composer conducting, Berlin; complete, 22 November 1909, Philharmonic Society (István Kerner conducting), Budapest
Publication—Bartók 1907, Universal Edition 1921, Boosey & Hawkes 1939, 1948

PBA—12FSS1, 12FSID1, 12FSFC1, 12FSFC2

70. Two Portraits (*Két portré*) op. 5
    1. One Ideal (*Egy ideális*)
    2. One Grotesque (*Egy torz*)
    Date—1907–1908
    Performance—1909, Imre Waldbauer (violin) and Budapest Symphony (László Kun), Budapest
    Publication—Rozsnyai 1914, Boosey & Hawkes 1950, Zeneműkiadó 1953; no. 1 from Movement I of the First Violin Concerto, no. 2 also appears as no. 14 ("Ma Mie qui danse") of the Fourteen Bagatelles, op. 6
    PBA— 15FSS1, 15VFC1

71. Two Pictures (*Két kép*) (*Deux Images*) op. 10 (also arranged for piano)
    1. In Full Flower (*Virágzás*)
    2. Village Dance (*A falu tánca*)
    Date—August 1910, Budapest; piano version, ca. 1911
    Performance—25 February 1913, Philharmonic Society (István Kerner), Budapest
    Publication—Rózsavölgyi 1912, Boosey & Hawkes 1950, Zeneműkiadó 1953; same for piano version
    PBA—27FSS1, 27TPS1

72. Four Pieces for Orchestra (*Négy zenekari darab*) op. 12
    1. Preludio
    2. Scherzo
    3. Intermezzo
    4. Marcia funebre
    Date—1912, orchestrated 1921
    Performance—9 January 1922, Philharmonic Society (Ernő Dohnányi conducting), Budapest
    Publication—Universal Edition 1923
    PBA—31FSFC1, 31TPPS1

73. Romanian Folk Dances (*Román népi táncok*) (originally for piano)
    Date—transcribed 1917; original piano version, 1915
    Performance—11 February 1918, E. Lichtenberg conducting, Budapest
    Publication—Universal Edition 1922; Boosey & Hawkes 1945
    PBA—37FSFC1

74. The Miraculous Mandarin, Suite (*A csodálatos mandarin*) op. 19
    Date—1919, 1927
    Performance—15 October 1928, Philharmonic Society (Ernő Dohnányi conducting), Budapest; 1, 2, 4 October 1948, Philadelphia Orchestra (Eugene Ormandy conducting
    I. Introduction, street noises. The orders of the ruffians to the girl
    II. The first siren call of the girl; Entrance of the shabby gentleman
    III. Second siren call of the girl, summoning the shy youth

IV. Third call of the girl. The Mandarin appears
V. The girl dances before the Mandarin
VI. The Mandarin catches the girl after a wild chase
Publication—Universal Edition 1927
PBA—Philadelphia Orchestra program note, prepared by György Kroó

75. Dance Suite for Orchestra (*Táncszvit*)
    I. Moderato
    II. Allegro molto
    III. Allegro vivace
    IV. Molto tranquillo
    V. Comodo
    (VI). Finale
    Date—August 1923, Radvány, North Hungary, composed to celebrate the fiftieth
        anniversary of the merging of Pest, Buda, and Obuda into the city of Budapest
    Performance—19 November 1923, Budapest Philharmonic Society (Ernő Dohnán-
        yi conducting), Budapest
    Publication—Universal Edition 1924; piano reduction, Universal Edition 1925
    PBA—53PS1, 53FSS1, 53FSFC1

76. The Wooden Prince, Suite (*A fából faragott királyfi*) op. 13
    I. Preludium (Nature awakening)
    II. The Princess
    III. The Forest
    IV. The Prince's "Work Song"
    V. The Dance of the Wooden Puppet
    VI. Postludium (Nature in Repose)
    Date—three dances from the ballet, 1921–1924?
    Performance—23 November 1931, Philharmonic Society (Ernő Dohnányi con-
        ducting), Budapest
    Publication—Universal Edition
    PBA—TFSFC2. See György Kroó, "Ballet: The Wooden Prince," in *BC,* 370

77. Transylvanian Dances (*Erdélyi táncok*) (transcription of Sonatina,
    for piano
    I. Bagpipers (*Dudások*)
    II. Bear Dance (*Medvetánc*)
    III. Finale
    Date—1931
    Performance—24 January 1932, M. Freccia conducting, Budapest
    Publication—Rózsavölgyi 1932, Zeneműkiadó 1955
    PBA—36TFSS1

78. Hungarian Sketches (*Magyar képek*)
    1. An Evening at the Village (*Este a székelyeknél*)
    2. Bear Dance (*Medvetánc*)
    3. Air (*Melódia*)
    4. A Bit Tipsy (*Kicsit ázottan*)

5. Dance of the Ürög Swineherds (*Ürögi kanásztánc*)
   Date—transcribed from piano works, 1931, Mondsee
   Performance—Nos. 1–3, 5, 24 January 1932, Budapest; complete, 26 November
   1934, Philharmonic Society (Heinrich Laber conducting), Budapest
   Publication—Rozsnyai-Rózsavölgyi 1932, Zeneműkiadó 1954
   PBA—A1TFSS1. See the listings in Nos. 12, 14, 17, and 18

79. Hungarian Peasant Songs (*Magyar parasztdalok*)
    I. Ballade (Tema con variazioni)
    II.Old Dance Tunes (*Régi táncdalok*)
    Date—transcription of Nos. 6–12, 14–15 from 15 Hungarian Peasant Songs for Pi-
    ano (1914–1917) 1933
    Performance—18 March 1934, Gyula Baranyai conducting, Szombathely
    Publication—Universal Edition 1933
    PBA—34TFSFC1, 34TFSFC2, 34TFSFC3

80. Music for Strings, Percussion, and Celesta (*Zene húros hangszerekre, ütőkre
    és celestára*)
    I. Andante tranquillo
    II. Allegro
    III. Adagio
    IV. Allegro molto
    Date—7 September 1936, Budapest
    Dedication   commissioned for the tenth anniversary of the Basel Chamber Orches-
    tra
    Performance—21 January 1937, Basel Chamber Orchestra (Paul Sacher conduct-
    ing), Basel
    Publication—Universal Edition 1937, Boosey & Hawkes 1939, Muzghis (Leningrad)
    1961
    PBA—74FSS1, 74FSFC1, 74FSFC2

81. Divertimento (for string orchestra)
    I. Allegro non troppo
    II. Molto adagio
    III. Allegro assai
    Date—2–17 August 1939, Saanen
    Dedication—Basel Chamber Orchestra
    Performance—11 June 1940, Basel Chamber Orchestra (Paul Sacher conducting),
    Basel
    Publication—Boosey & Hawkes 1940
    PBA—78FSS1, 78FSID1, 78FSFC1

82. Concerto for Orchestra
    I. Introduzione
    II. Giuoco delle coppie
    III. Elegia
    IV. Intermezzo interrotto

V. Finale
Date—15 August–8 October 1943, Saranac Lake; revised February 1945
Dedication—for the Koussevitzky Music Foundation in memory of Mrs. Natalie
Koussevitzky
Performance—1 December 1944, Boston Symphony Orchestra (Serge Koussevitz-
ky conducting), Boston
Publication—Boosey & Hawkes 1946
PBA—80FSS1, 80FSID1, 80FSFC1, 80FSFC2, 80TPFC1

5. SOLO VOICE AND PIANO

83. Love Songs (*Liebeslieder*)
    2 I Pluck This Rose (*Diese Rose pflück ich hier*) (Lenau)
    4. I Feel Your Breath (*Ich fühle deinen Odem*) (Lenau)
    Date—1900, Budapest
    Publication—Nos. 2 and 4, in Denijs Dille, *Der junge Bartók I,* Zeneműkiadó 1963

84. Four Songs (*Négy dal*) (texts by Lajos Pósa)
    1. Autumn Breeze (*Őszi szellő*)
    2. They Are Accusing Me (*Még azt vetik a szememre*)
    3. There Is No Greater Sorrow (*Nincs olyan bú*)
    4. Alas, Alas! (*Ejnye! Ejnye!*)
    Date—1902
    Publication—Bárd 1904

85. Evening (*Est*) (text by Kálmán Harsányi)
    Date—April 1903?
    Publication—in Denijs Dille, *Der junge Bartók I,* Zeneműkiadó 1963

86. Székely Folk Song (*Székely népdal*): "Piros alma leesett a sárba" (The Red
Apple Has Fallen in the Mud)
    Date—1904
    Publication—in the supplement to *Magyar lant* 1905

87. Hungarian Folk Songs (*Magyar népdalok*)
    First Series, four songs, no. 4 incomplete, only one published
    1. They Have Mowed the Pasture Already (*Lekaszálták már a rétet*)
    Second Series, ten songs, only four published
    4. Down at the Tavern (*Ha bemegyek a csárdába*)
    6. My Glass Is Empty (*Megittam a piros bort*)
    7. This Maiden Threading (*Ez a kislány gyöngyöt fűz*)
    8. The Young Soldier (*Sej, mikor engem katonának visznek*)
    Date—First Series 1904–1905; Second Series 1906
    Publication—First Series, no. 1, in Denijs Dille, *Der junge Bartók I,* Zeneműkiadó
    1963; Second Series, nos. 4, 6, 7, 8, Zeneműkiadó 1963

88. Hungarian Folk Songs (*Magyar népdalok*)

(The first ten set by Bartók, the remaining ten by Zoltán Kodály)
1. I Left My Fair Homeland (*Elindultam szép hazámbul*)
2. I Would Cross the Tisza in a Boat (*Által mennék én a Tiszán ladikon*)
3. László Fehér Stole a Horse (*Fehér László lovat lopott*)
4. Behind the Garden of Gyula (*A gyulai kert alatt*)
5. Behind the Garden of Kertmeg (*A kertmegi kert alatt*) [in the original edition: The Street Is on Fire (*Ucca, ucca, ég az ucca*)]
6. In My Window Shone the Moonlight (*Ablakomba, ablakomba*)
7. From the Withered Branch Far Rose Blooms (*Száraz ágtól messze virít a rózsa*)
8. I Walked to the End (Végigmentem a tárkányi)
9. Not Far from Here Is Little Margitta (*Nem messze van ide kis Margitta*)
10. My Sweetheart Is Plowing (*Szánt a babám csireg*)
Date—1906; revised 1938
Publication—Rózsavölgyi 1938, Zeneműkiadó 1953
PBA—13VoPS1

89. Two Hungarian Folk Songs (*Két magyar népdal*)
1. My Sweetheart, You Are Beyond the Málnás Woods (*Túl vagy rózsám, túl vagy a málnás erdejin*)
2. My Mother's Rosebush (*Édesanyám rózsafája*)
Date—1907
Publication—Béla Bartók Estate, 1958 (MS facsimile), no. 1, Zeneműkiadó 1963; no. 2 in *Documenta bartókiana* 4, 1970
PBA—66ID1

90. Four Slovak Folk Songs (*Négy szlovák népdal*)
1. Near the Borders of Bistritz (*V tej bystrickej bráne*)
2. Dirge (*Pohřební písen*)
3. The Message (*Prilelel pták*)
4. Tony Turns His Spindle Round (*Kruti tono vretana*)
Date—No. 1, 1907; Nos. 2–3, ?); No. 4, 1916
Publication—Denijs Dille, *Der junge Bartók I*, Zeneműkiadó 1963

91. Five Songs (*Öt dal*) op. 15
1. Spring: My Love (*Tavasz: Az én szerelmem*) (text by Klára Gombossy)
2. Summer (Nyár) (Gombossy)
3. Night of Desire (*A vágyak éjjele*) (text by Wanda Gleiman)
4. Winter: in Vivid Dreams (*Tél*) (Gombossy?)
5. Autumn (*Ősz*) (Gombossy)
Date—1915–1916
Publication—*NYBA*/Pallas Gallery (London) *1958,* Universal Edition 1961, 1966
PBA—41VoPS1, 41VoPID1, 41VoPFC1

92. Five Songs (*Öt dal*) op. 16 (texts by Endre Ady)
1. Three Autumn Tears (*Három őszi könnycsepp*)
2. Sounds of Autumn (*Az őszi lárma*)
3. Lost Content (*Az ágyam hívogat*)
4. Alone with the Sea (*Egyedül a tengerrel*)

5. I Cannot Come to You (*Nem mehetek hozzád*)
Date—1916
Dedication—Béla Reinitz 1920
Publication—Universal Edition 1923
PBA—44VoPS1, 44VoPID1, 44VoPFC1, 44VoPFC2

93. Eight Hungarian Folk Songs (*Nyolc magyar népdal*)
   1. Black Is the Earth (*Fekete főd, fehér az én zsebkendöm*)
   2. My God, My God, Make the River Swell (*Istenem, istenem, áraszd meg a vizet*)
   3. Wives, Let Me Be One of Your Company (*Asszonyok, asszonyok*)
   4. So Much Sorrow Lies in My Heart (*Annyi bánat az szívemen*)
   5. If I Climb Yonder Hill *Ha kimegyek arr' a magos tetőre*)
   6. They Are Mending the Great Forest Highway (*Töltik a nagyerdő útját*)
   7. Till Now My Work Was Plowing (*Eddig való dolgom*)
   8. The Snow Is Melting (*Olvad a hó, csárdás kis angyalom*)
   Date—Nos. 1–5, 1907; nos. 6–8, 1917
   Performance—Nos. 6–8, 12 January 1918, Vienna, Ferencz von Székelyhidy and composer
   Publication—Universal Edition 1922, Boosey & Hawkes 1939, 1955
   PBA—17VoPS1, 17VoPID1, 17VoPFC1, 17VoPFC2

94. Village Scenes (*Falun*; *Dedinské scény*)
   Slovak Folksongs (nos. 3–5 arranged for female voices and chamber orchestra)
   1. Haymaking (*Ej! hrabajže len*)
   2. At the Bride's (*Letia pávy, letia*)
   3. Wedding (*A ty Anča krásna*)
   4. Lullaby (*Beli žemi, beli*)
   5. Lad's Dance (*Poza búčky, poza peň*)
   Date—December 1924
   Dedication—Ditta [Pásztory-Bartók]
   Performance—8 December 1926 (?), Mária Basilides and composer
   Publication—Universal Edition 1927, Boosey & Hawkes 1954
   PBA—54VoPS1, 54VoPFC1

95. Twenty Hungarian Folk Songs (*Húsz magyar népdal*)

VOLUME I: SAD SONGS (*Szomorú nóták*)

   1. In Prison (*A tomlöcbën*)
   2. Old Lament (*Régi keserves*)
   3. The Fugitive (*Bujdosó ének*)
   4. Herdsman's Song (*Pásztornóta*)

VOLUME II: DANCING SONGS (*Táncdalok*)

   5. Slow Dance (*Székely "lassú"*)
   6. Fast Dance (*Székely "friss"*)
   7. Swineherd's Dance (*Kanásztánc*)

8. Six-Florin Dance (*"Hatforintos" nóta*)

VOLUME III: DIVERSE SONGS (*Vegyes dalok*)

9. The Shepherd (*Juhászcsúfoló*)
10. Joking Song (*Tréfás nóta*)
11. Nuptial Serenade (*Párosító I*)
12. Humorous Song (*Párosító II*)
13. Dialogue Song (*Pár-ének*)
14. Complaint (*Panasz*)
15. Drinking Song (*Bordal*)

VOLUME IV: NEW STYLE SONGS (*Új dalok*)

I. Oh, My Dear Mother (*Hej, édesanyám*)
II. Ripening Cherries (*Érik a ropogós cseresznye*)
III. Long Ago at Doboz Fell the Snow (*Már Dobozon régen leesett a hó*)
IV. Yellow Cornstalk (*Sárga kukorícaszár*)
V. Wheat, Wheat (*Búza, búza*)
Date—1929; Nos. 1, 2, 11, 14, 12 orchestrated in 1933 as Hungarian Folk Songs
Performance—30 January 1930, Mária Basilides and the composer, Budapest; for
Voice and orchestra, 23 October 1933, Mária Basilides and the Philharmonic So-
ciety (Ernő Dohnányi conducting), Budapest
Publication—Universal Edition 1932, 1933 (transcription, not issued?), Boosey
& Hawkes 1939
PBA—64VoPS1, 64PFC1, 64PFC2, 64TFSS1

96. Hungarian Folk Song (*Debrecennek van egy vize*) (arrangement of *For Children* I, no. 16)
Date—1937?
Publication—in Béla Paulini, *Gyöngyösbokréta* [Crown of Pearls], Budapest: Vajna
és Bokor, 1937, p. 10

97. Ukrainian Folk Song: "It was not I alone . . ."
Date—1945, New York
PBA—82VoPS1

98. Goat Song: The Husband's Grief (*A férj keserve*)
Date—February 1945, New York
Dedication—Pál Kecskeméti
Publication—in János Demény, ed., *Bartók Béla levelei*, Budapest: Művelt Nép,
1951, p. xiv (sketch facsimile)
PBA—83VoPS1, 83VoPFC1

6. CHORUS, A CAPPELLA AND WITH PIANO

99. Evening (*Est*) (for four-part male chorus, a capella) (K. Harsányi)
Date—April 1903
Publication—Denijs Dille: *Documenta bartókiana* I, 1964

100. Four Old Hungarian Folk Songs (*Négy régi magyar népdal*) (for four-part male chorus, a cappella)
1. Long Ago I Told You (*Rég megmondtam bús gerlice*)
2. Oh God, Why Am I Waiting? (*Jaj Istenem, kire várok*)
3. In My Sister-in-Law's Garden (*Ángyomasszony kertje*)
4. Farmboy, Load the Cart Well (*Béreslegény, jól megrakd a szekeret*)
Date—1910, revised 1912
Performance—13 May 1911, Szeged (Hungary) Chorus, Peter König conducting
Publication—Universal Edition 1928
PBA—30TBS1

101. Slovak Folk Songs (*Tót népdalok; Slovácké l'udové piesne*) (for four-part male chorus, a capella)
1. Hey, Listen Now My Comrades (*Ej, posluchajte málo*)
2. If I Must Go to the War (*Ked'ja smutny pojdem*)
3. Let Us Go, Comrades (*Kamarádi mojí*)
4. Hey, If Soon I Fall in Battle (*Ej, a ked'mna zabiju*)
5. To Battle I Went Forth (*Ked'som šiou na vojnu*)
Date—1917
Performance—15 December 1917, Vienna
Publication—Universal Edition 1918, Boosey & Hawkes 1939
PBA—46TBS1

102. Four Slovak Folk Songs (*Négy tót népdal; Štyri slovenské piesne*) (for four-part mixed chorus and piano)
1. Wedding Song (*Zadala mamka*)
2. Song of the Hay-Harvesters (*Naholi, naholi*)
3. Song from Medzibrod (*Rada pila, rada jedla*)
4. Dancing Song (*Gajdujte, gajdence*)
Date—1917
Performance—5 January 1917, Emil Lichtenberg conducting, Budapest
Publication—Universal Edition 1927, Boosey & Hawkes 1939, Zeneműkiadó 1950
PBA—47SATBPS1

103. Hungarian Folk Songs (*Magyar népdalok*) (for mixed chorus, a cappella)
1. The Prisoner (*Elhervadt cidrusfa*)
2. The Wanderer (*Ideje bujdosásimnak*)
3. Finding a Husband (*Adj el, anyám*)
4. My Ox Is Grazing (*Sarjut eszik az ökröm*)
5. Love Song (*Az én lovam szajkó*)
Date—May 1930, Budapest
Performance—11 May 1936, Kecskemét (Hungary) Municipal Choir, Zoltán Vásárhelyi conducting
Publication—Universal Edition 1932, Boosey & Hawkes 1939
PBA—65SATBS1, 65SATBFC1, 65SATBFC2, 65SATBFC3

104. Székely Songs (*Székely dalok*) (for male chorus, a cappella)

1. How Often I've Grieved for You (*Hej de sokszor megbántottál*)
2. My God, My Life (*Istenem, életem nem igen gyönyörü*)
3. Slender Thread, Hard Seed (*Vékony cérna, kemény mag*)
4. Girls Are Gathering in Kilyénfalva (*Kilyénfalvi közeptizbe*)
5. Do a Dance, Priest (*Járjad pap a táncot*)
6. Slender Thread, Hard Seed (*Vékony cérna, kemény mag*)
Date—November 1932, Budapest
Publication—Nos. 1–2, Magyar Kórus 1938; complete Zenemu...kiadó 1955
PBA—70TTBBFC1, 70TTBBFC2

104. Twenty-Seven Choruses (*27 két- és háromszólamú kórus*) (for two- or three-part children's or women's chorus). Vols. I-VI, children's voices; Vols. VII-VIII, women's voices

VOLUME I

1. Spring (*Tavasz*)
2. Only Tell Me (*Ne hagyj itt!*)
3. Enchanting Song (*Jószág-igéző*)

VOLUME II

4. Letter to Those at Home (*Levél az otthoniakhoz*)
5. Candle Song (*Játék*)
6. Choosing of a Girl (*Leánynéző*)
7. Thieving Bird (*Héjja, héjja, karahéjja*)

VOLUME III

8. Don't Leave Me (*Ne menj el*)
9. The Fickle Girl (*Van egy gyűrűm*)
10. Song of Loneliness (*Senkim a világon*)
11. Breadbaking (*Cipósütés*)

VOLUME IV

12. Hussar (*Huszárnóta*)
13. Loafer (*Resteknek nótája*)
14. Lonely Wanderer (Bolyongás)
15. Mocking of Girls (*Lánycsúfoló*)

VOLUME V

16. Mocking of Youth (*Legénycsúfoló*)
17. Michaelmas Greeting (*Mihálynapi köszöntő*)
18. The Wooing of a Girl (*Leánykérő*)

VOLUME VI

19. Lament (*Keserves*)
20. Song of the Bird (*Madárdal*)
21. Stamping Feet (*Csujogató*)

21. Stamping Feet (*Csujogató*)

VOLUME VII

22. The Sorrow of Love (*Bánat*)
23. Had I Never Seen You (*Ne láttalak volna!*)
24. The Song-Bird's Promise (*Elment a madárka*)

VOLUME VIII:

25. Pillow Dance (*Párnás táncdal*)
26. Canon (*Kánon*)
27. Lover's Farewell (*Isten veled!*)
Date—1935
Performance—Nos. 1, 17, 25, 7 May 1937, conducted by Paula Radnai, László Preisinger (Perényi), Mme. Ferenc Barth, Benjamin Rajecky, and Adrienne Stojanovics, Budapest
Publication—Magyar Kórus 1937, 1938, Zeneműkiadó 1953; 9 pieces, Boosey & Hawkes 1955, remaining 18 pieces, Zeneműkiadó 1972; nos. IV/1, III/1, IV/2, IV/3, III/4 arranged with school orchestra, Magyar Kórus 1937, Zeneműkiadó 1962, 1963; Nos. I/2, V/1 arranged with small orchestra, Boosey & Hawkes 1942
PBA—72SAS1, 72SAFC1, 72SAFC2, 72SA-OS1, 72SA-OFC1

105. From Olden Times (*Elmúlt időkből*) (after old Hungarian folk song and art art song texts, for three-part male chorus, a cappella)
1. No One's More Unhappy Than the Peasant (*Nincs boldogtalanabb*)
2. One, Two, Three, Four (*Egy, kettő, három, négy*)
3. No One Is Happier Than the Peasant (*Nincsen szerencsésebb*)
Date—1935
Performance—7 May 1937, Béla Endre Chamber Chorus (Béla Endre conducting), Budapest
Publication—Magyar Kórus 1937
PBA—73TBBS1, 73TBBID1, 73TBBFC2

7. VOICE AND ORCHESTRA

107. Hungarian Folk Songs (*Magyar népdalok*) (arrangement of nos. 1, 2, 11, 14, 12 from Twenty Hungarian Folk Songs for Voice and Piano)
1. In Prison (*Tömlöcben*)
2. Old Lament (*Régi kerserves*)
3. Nuptial Serenade (*Párosító I*)
4. Complaint (*Panasz*)
5. Humorous Song (*Párosító II*)
Date—1933; original voice and piano version, 1929
Perf—23 October 1933, Ernő Dohnányi conducting, Budapest
Publication—Original voice and piano version, Universal Edition 1932
PBA—64TFSS1

8. CHORUS AND ORCHESTRA

108. Three Village Scenes (*Falun; Tri dedinské scény*) (for four or eight women's voices and chamber orchestra; transcription of nos. 3, 4, and 5 from Five Village Scenes for voice and piano)
1. Wedding (*Lakodalom*)
2. Lullaby (*Bölcsődal*)
3. Lad's Dance (*Legénytánc*)
   Date—May 1926, Budapest
   Performance—1 February 1927, Serge Koussevitzky conducting, New York
   Publication—Full score, Universal Edition 1927; vocal score, Universal Edition 1927
   PBA—54TVoSFC1, 54TFSS1, 54TFSFC1

109. Cantata Profana (The Nine Enchanted Stags) (*Cantata profana. A kilenc csodaszarvas*) (text based on Romanian *colinde* collected and translated by the composer), for double mixed chorus, tenor and baritone solos, and orchestra)
   I. Molto moderato (attacca)
   II. Andante (attacca)
   III. Moderato
   Date—8 September 1930, Budapest
   Performance—25 May 1934, Trefor Jones (tenor), Frank Phillips (baritone), BBC Symphony and Wireless Chorus (Aylmer Buesst conducting the English libretto), London; 9 November 1936, Endre Rösler (tenor) and Imre Palló (baritone), Philharmonic Orchestra and Palestrina Chorus (Ernő Dohnanyi conducting the composer's Hungarian libretto), Budapest; 14 June 1984, Cristian Caraman (tenor), Choir "George Enescu" (Remus Tzincoca conducting the composer's Romanian libretto), Bucharest
   Publication—Full score, Universal 1934, 1957; vocal score, Universal 1934, 1951, Boosey & Hawkes 1939, 1955 (English translation copyright)
   PBA—67VoSS1 (Romanian text), 67FSS1, 67FSFC1, 67FSFC2, 67PFC1, 67 Texts

9. STAGE WORKS

110. Duke Bluebeard's Castle (*A kékszakállú herceg vára*) op. 11; opera in one act, libretto by Béla Balázs
   Date—September 1911, Rákoskeresztúr; revised 1912, 1918
   Dedication—Márta [Bartók]
   Performance—24 May 1918, Hungarian State Opera House, Olga Haselbeck as Judith, Oszkar Kálmán as Bluebeard (Egisto Tango conducting), Budapest
   Publication—Vocal score, Universal Edition 1922; full score, Universal Edition 1925, 1963
   PBA—S28FSS1, 28FSFC1, 28VoSFC1, 28VoSFC2

111. The Wooden Prince (*A fából faragott királyfi*) op. 13; ballet in one act, libretto by Béla Balázs

Date—1914–1916, orchestrated 1916–1917; suite, 1932
Dedication—Egisto Tango
Performance—12 May 1917, Hungarian State Opera House (Egisto Tango con ducting), Budapest; 23 November 1931, Hungarian State Opera House (Ernő Dohnanyi conducting the small orchestral suite), Budapest
Publication—Piano score, Universal Edition 1921; full score, Universal Edition 1924
PBA—33PS1, 33PFC1, 33FSFC1, 33FSFC2,33TFSFC1, 33TFSFC2

112. The Miraculous Mandarin (*A csodálatos mandarin*) op. 19; pantomime in one act, libretto by Menyhért Lengyel
Date—October 1918–May 1919, Rákoskeresztúr; also suite
Performance—27 November 1926, Jenő Szenkár conducting, Cologne Opera; 8 April 1926 and 1 April 1927, selections for two pianos (the composer and György Kósa), Budapest Radio
Publication—Piano four-hands score, Universal Edition 1925; full score, Universal Edition 1955
PBA—49PS1, 49FS1, 40FSFC1, 49FSFC2, 49TPPS1, 49TPPFC1

10. ADDENDA

113. Two Romanian Folk Songs, for four-part women's chorus
Date—1915
Publication—Unpublished
PBA—39SAS1

114. Nine Romanian Folk Songs, for voice and piano
Date—1915
Publication—Unpublished
PBA—40VoPS1

11. BARTÓK'S EDITIONS AND TRANSCRIPTIONS OF STANDARD KEYBOARD WORKS

For earlier listings, see: Halsey Stevens. *The Life and Music of Béla Bartók.* New York: Oxford University Press ((1953, 1964), 333–34; Victor Bator. *The Béla Bartók Archives: History and Catalogue.* New York: Bartók Archives publication (1963), 37–38; David Yeomans. *Bartók for Piano: A Survey of His Solo Literature.* Bloomington (Indianapolis): Indiana University Press (1988), Appendix C; László Somfai/Vera Lampert. "Béla Bartók." *The New Grove Dictionary of Music and Musicians,* II., 6th ed. Stanley Sadie. London: Macmillan Publishers Ltd. (1980), 223; László Somfai's essay in *19th Century Music* 11, no. 1 (Summer. 1987), 78, 84; and Elliott Antokoletz, *Béla Bartók: A Guide to Research,* 2nd ed. New York and London: Garland Publishers (1997).

The period of transcription or edition is indicated by *Date*; publisher and date of publication, by *Publication*; publisher's plate number, indicated by *Plate no.*; and source of original composition, by *Source*.

115. Bach, Johann Sebastian. *Wohltemperirtes Klavier* (Well-tempered Clavier)

Publication—Rozsnyai Károly, Budapest, vols. I–IV; Rózsavölgyi, Budapest, vol.
I; Editio Music, Budapest, vols. I–II
Plate no.—R.K. 246 (vol. I); R.K. 247 (vol. II); R.K. 248 (vol. III); R.K. 249 (vol.
IV)

116. Bach, Johann Sebastian. *Tizenhárom könnyű kis zongoradarab* (Dreizehn
Leichte kleine Klavierstücke aus dem "Notenbuchlein für Anna Magdalena
Bach") (Thirteen easy little piano pieces from the "Notebook for Anna
Magdalena Bach"
Publication—Rozsnyai Károlyi, Budapest; Rózsavölgyi és Társa, Budapest, 1917;
Zeneműkiadó Vallalat, Budapest, 1950
Plate no.—Z. 30

117. Bach, Johann Sebastian. *Sonata VI,* BWV. 530
Date—arr. c1930
Publication—Rózsavölgyi és Társa, Budapest, 1930
Plate no.—R. & Co. 5172

118. Beethoven, Ludwig van. *Sonatas for Piano* (complete; issued separately;
nos. 15–32 edited by Ernő Dohnányi)
Publication—Rózsavölgyi és Társa, Budapest
Plate no.—R. és Tsa: 3281 (1), 3515 (2), 3318 (3), 3516 (4), 3282 (5), 3319 (6),
3517 (7), 3283 (8), 3320 (9), 3321 (10), 3518 (11), 3377 (12), 3519 (13), 3284
(14), 3520 (15), 3521 (16), 3522 (17), 3523 (18), 3322 (20), 3382 (21), 3378
(23), 3379 (24), 3381 (27)

119. Beethoven, Ludwig van. *Sonata in C-sharp Minor,* op. 27, no. 2
Publication—Zeneműkiadó Vallalat, Budapest, 1955
Plate no.—Z. 2042

120. Beethoven, Ludwig van. *7 Bagatelles,* op. 33
Publication—Rozsnyai Károly, Budapest

121. Beethoven, Ludwig van. *11 New Bagatelles,* op. 119
Publication—Rozsnyai Károly, Budapest
Plate no.—R.K. 477

122. Beethoven, Ludwig van. *Polonaise in C,* op. 89
Publication—Rozsnyai Károly, Budapest
Plate no.—R.K. 493

123. Beethoven, Ludwig van. *6 Variations in F,* op. 34
Publication—Rozsnyai Károly, Budapest

124. Beethoven, Ludwig van. *Ecossaises*

Publication—Rozsnyai Károly, Budapest; Zeneműkiadó Vallalat, Budapest, 1951
Plate no.—Z. 116

125. Beethoven, Ludwig van. *15 Variations and Fugue,* op. 35
Publication—Rozsnyai Károly, Budapest
Plate no.—R.K. 476

126. Chopin, Frédéric. *Valses*
Publication—Rozsnyai Károly, Budapest

127. Ciaia, Azzolino Bernardino della. *Sonata (in G Major)*
I. Toccata
II. Canzone
III. Primo tempo
IV. Secondo tempo
Date—arr. c1926–1928
Publication—in Béla Bartók, *XVII and XVIII Century Italian Cembalo and Organ Music Transcribed for Piano,* Carl Fischer, New York, 1930, reprinted 1990 with introduction by László Somfai
Plate no.—25272-7 P1816 (Toccata), 25272-10 P1817 (Canzone), 25274-4 P1818 (P. Tempo), 25275-4 P1819 (S. Tempo)
Source—Buonamici, ed., *3 Sonate per Cembalo (op. 4) del Cavaliere Azzolino Bernardino Della Ciaja di Siena* (C. Bratti et Co., 1912)

128. Couperin, François. *Selected Keyboard Works*
Publication—Editio Musica, Budapest, 1950

129. Couperin, François. *18 Pieces*
Publication—Rozsnyai Károly, Budapest, October 1924; Zeneműkiadó, Budapest, 1955
Plate no.—R.K. 1641 (vol. II), R.K. 1642 (vol. III); Z. 1769 (1–10) (vol. II), (see D. Scarlatti for vol. I)

130. Cramer. *Etudes* (nos. 29–56 Inc.)
Publication—Rózsavölgyi és Társa, Budapest
Plate no.—5387

131. Duvernoy, V.A. *L'école du Mécanisme,* op. 120
Publication—Bárd Ferenc és Fia, Budapest, 1920
Plate no.—B.F.F. 2255

132. Frescobaldi, Girolamo. *Fuga (G Minor).* This piece composed by Gottlieb Muffat (1690–1770); see Frederick Hammond, *Girolamo Frescobaldi* (Cambridge, MA and London: Harvard University Press,1983): 96.
Date—arr. c1926–1928
Publication—See entry under No. 127

Plate no.—25277-6 P1821
Source—Torchi, ed., *L'arte musicale in Italia,* vol. 3 (Ricordi, n.d.)

133. Frescobaldi, Girolamo. *Toccata (G Major)*
Date—arr. c1926–1928
Publication—See entry under No. 127
Plate no.—25276-7 P1820
Source—Torchi, ed., *L'arte musicale in Italia,* vol. 3 (Ricordi (n.d.)

134. Händel, George Frederic. *Sonatas*
Publication—Rozsnyai Károly, Budapest

135. Haydn, Franz Joseph. *Deux Sonates*
Publication—Rózsavölgyi és Társa, Budapest
Plate no.—4346

136. Haydn, Franz Joseph. *Sonatas,* vols. I–II (nos. 1–10; nos. 11–19)
Publication—Rozsnyai Károly, Budapest
Plate nos.—R.K. 879-888 (nos. 1–10), R.K. 889-895 (nos. 11–17), R.K. 1550-1551
(nos. 18–19)

137. Haydn, Franz Joseph. *Sonata No. 53 in E Minor,* Hob. XVI/34
Publication—Editio Musica, Budapest

138. Heller, Stephen. *25 Etudes,* Op. 45, vols. I–III
Publication—Rózsavölgyi és Társa, Budapest
Plate no.—R. és Tsa: 3913 (vol. I), 3914 (vol. II), 3915 (vol. III)

139. Heller, Stephen. *30 Etudes,* Op. 46, vols. I–III
Publication—Rózsavölgyi és Társa, Budapest
Plate no.—R. és Tsa: 3926 (vol. I), 3927 (vol. II), 3928 (vol. III)

140. Heller, Stephen. *25 Etudes,* Op. 47, vols. I–II
Publication—Rózsavölgyi és Társa, Budapest

141. Heller, Stephen. *Tarantella,* Op. 85, No. 2
Publication—Rózsavölgyi és Társa, Budapest

142. Heller, Stephen. *24 Etudes,* Op. 125, vols. I–II
Publication—Rózsavölgyi és Társa, Budapest

143. Heller, Stephen. *Album,* vols. I–III
Publication—Rózsavölgyi és Társa, Budapest

144. Marcello, Benedetto. *Sonata in B-flat Major*
Date—arr. c1926–1928

Plate no.—25268-14 P1812
Source—Pauer, ed., *Alte Meister,* Band V (Breitkopf & Härtel, n.d.)

145. Mendelssohn, Felix. *Scherzo in B Minor*
Publication—Rozsnyai Károly, Budapest

146. Mendelssohn, Felix. *Prelude and Fugue in E Major*
Publication—Rozsnyai Károly, Budapest

147. Mozart, Wolfgang Amadeus. "Marcia alla Turka" (published separately from *Sonata in A Major,* K. 331)
Publication—Zeneműkiadó, Budapest, 1952
Plate no.—Z. 1102

148. Mozart, Wolfgang Amadeus. *Fantasie in C Minor*
Publication—Rozsnyai Károly, Budapest

149. Mozart, Wolfgang Amadeus. *Sonatas for Piano* (complete), vols. I (nos. 1–10) and II (nos. 11–20)
Publication—Rozsnyai Károly, Budapest; Editio Musica, Budapest
Plate no.—R.K.: 640 (1), 632 (2), 727 (3), 731 (4), 732 (5), 733 (6), 686 (7), 734 (8), 550 (9), 735 (10), 736 (11), 737 (12), 738 (13), 739 (14), 740 (15), 551 (16), 741 (17), 435 (18), 872 (19), 873 (20)

150. Mozart, Wolfgang Amadeus. *Twenty Sonatas*
Publication—Rozsnyai Károly, Budapest, 1911; Kalmus-Belwin Mills

151. Mozart, Wolfgang Amadeus. *Sonata in G Major,* K. 545
Publication—Editio Musica, Budapest

152. Purcell, Henry. *Two Preludes* (in G, C)
Publication—Delkas, Los Angeles

153. Rossi, Michelangelo. *Toccata No. 1 in C Major*
Date—arr. c1926–1928
Publication—See entry under No. 127
Plate no.—25269-7 P1813
Source—Torchi, ed., *L'arte musicale in Italia,* vol. 3 (Ricordi, n.d.), no. 1 of "Dieci Toccate"

154. Rossi, Michelangelo. *Toccata No. 2 in A Minor*
Date—arr. c1926–1928
Publication—See entry under No. 127
Plate no.—25270-7 P1814
Source—Torchi, ed., *L'arte musicale in Italia,* vol. 3 (Ricordi, n.d.), no. 9 of "Dieci Toccate"

155. Rossi, Michelangelo. *Tre correnti*
Date—arr. c1926–1928
Publication—See entry under No. 127
Plate no.—25271-5 P1815
Source—Torchi, ed., *L'arte musicale in Italia,* vol. 3 (Ricordi, n.d.), nos. 5, 1, and 2
of "Dieci Correnti"

156. Scarlatti, Domenico. *Sonatas,* vols. I and IV
Publication—Rozsnyai Károly, Budapest, May 1921
Plate no.—R.K.: 1552 (vol. I, Nos. 1-5), 1651 (vol. IV, Nos. 6-10), (see F. Couperin
for vols. II, III

157. Scarlatti, Domenico. *Selected Sonatas,* vols. I and II
Publication—Editio Musica, Budapest

158. Scarlatti, Domenico. *Five Pieces*
Publication—Kalmus-Belwin Mills

159. Scarlatti, Domenico. *Essercizi*
Publication—Rozsnyai Károlyi, Budapest

160. Schubert, Franz. *Sonata in G Major*
Publication—Rozsnyai Károlyi, Budapest

161. Schubert, Franz. *Sonata in A Minor,* op. 143
Publication—Rozsnyai Károlyi, Budapest

162. Schubert, Franz. *Fantaisie oder Sonate*
Publication—Rozsnyai Károlyi, Budapest

163. Schubert, Franz. *2 Scherzi*
Publication—Rozsnyai Károlyi, Budapest
Plate no.—R.K. 685

164.–165. Schumann, Robert. *Jugend-Album,* op. 68; *Phantasiestücke*
Publication—resp. : Rozsnyai Károlyi, Budapest; Universal Edition, New York

166. Zipoli, Domenico. *Pastorale in C Major*
Date—arr. c1926–1928
Publication—See entry under No. 127
Plate no.—25278-5 P1822
Source—Torchi, ed., *L'arte musicale in Italia,* vol. 3 (Ricordi, n.d.)

Personalia

ADY, ENDRE (1877–1919), Hungarian poet who rejuvenated ancient Hungarian versification. He was one of the founders of *Nyugat* (West), a progressive journal which influenced Hungarian artists of all kinds.

ARÁNYI, JELLY (1893–1966), Hungarian violinist, younger sister of violinist Adila (nee Arányi) Fachiri, pupil of Hubay and great-niece of the noted Hungarian violinist József Joachim (1831–1907).

BACKHAUS, WILHELM (1884–1969), noted piano virtuoso and, beginning in 1905, professor of piano at the Royal Manchester College of Music.

BALÁZS, BÉLA (1884–1949), well-known Hungarian poet. Author of the libretto of Bartók's opera, *Duke Bluebeard's Castle* and of the ballet *The Wooden Prince*. Also friendly with Zoltán Kodály, who set some of his poems to music.

BARTÓK, BÉLA (1855–1888), father of the composer. He was an agricultural school principal, technical writer, and amateur musician. He proclaimed himself a member of the Hungarian lesser nobility (thus far unsubstantiated), and his son carried on the pretension by signing his youthful compositions as Béla von Bartók.

BARTÓK, BÉLA, JR. (1910–1994), elder son of the composer, was brought up by his mother, Márta, following her divorce in 1923. After his retirement as a civil engineer for the Hungarian State Railways, he was the author of important chronologies, reminiscences, and a compendium of his father's family correspondences.

BARTÓK, DITTA (EDITA), nee Pásztory (1903–1982), the composer's second wife. She was Bartók's pupil at the Budapest Academy of Music, married him in 1923, and returned to Hungary after his death in 1945. She was the dedicatee of a number of Bartók compositions and performed with him as duo-pianist in concerts.

BARTÓK, ELZA (ERSZÉBET) (1895–1955), sister of the composer and wife of Emil Oláh-Tóth.

BARTÓK, MÁRTA, nee Ziegler (1893–1967), the composer's first wife. She was Bartók's pupil at the Budapest Academy of Music, married him in 1909 and was divorced in 1923. She was a tireless helpmate in Bartók's preparation of drafts of his folk music transcriptions and German translations.

BARTÓK, PAULA, nee Voit (1857–1939), the composer's mother. She was thirty-one years old when her husband died and left her virtually penniless. In order to support her son and daughter, she worked as an itinerant schoolteacher until she found permanent employment in Pozsony (Bratislava) in 1894.

BARTÓK, PÉTER (b. 1924), the composer's younger son and dedicatee of the first two volumes of *Mikrokosmos* for Piano. He arrived in the United States in 1942, enlisted in the U.S. Navy, and subsequently trained as a specialist in sound recording. He then founded Bartók Records in New York and set out to record his father's works. Following his mother's death in 1982 and in accordance with Bartók's will, he inherited the copyrights and other holdings as remainderman of his father's New York estate. Thereafter he devoted his career to the preparation of revised performing editions of Bartók works.

BOBÁL, SÁMUEL, Slovak village pastor. He accompanied Bartók during the latter's fieldtrips in the Slovak areas of then Greater Hungary. He was of great help in grasping the dialectal pronunciation of the peasant singers.

BRĂILOIU, CONSTANTIN (1893–1958), preeminent scholar of Romanian musical folklore. He served as a consultant and associate during Bartók's preparation of his collection of Romanian carols and Christmas songs for publication in Britain and Romania. When these projects could not be achieved, in 1935 Bartók brought out an abridged German edition of the melodies, published at his own expense by Universal Edition.

BUŞIŢIA, ION (1876–1953), Romanian schoolteacher. He accompanied Bartók during the latter's fieldtrips in Transylvanian-Romanian villages. Their correspondence provides an invaluable source for information regarding Bartók's fieldwork in musical folklore.

DOHNÁNYI, ERNŐ VON (1877–1960), Hungarian composer, pianist, and conductor. A former Bartók schoolmate in Pozsony (Bratislava), he was helpful in guiding his younger colleague toward acceptance as a piano student at the Budapest Academy of Music. He also served as conductor of premieres of Bartók works.

FÁBIÁN, FELICIE (1884–1908), composer-pianist classmate of Bartók at the Budapest Academy of Music, who idolized the youthful genius.

GEYER, STEFI (1888–1956), Hungarian violinist. She was a pupil of Hubay and a successful concert artist. Because she was unable to cope with Bartók's atheism, she ended their budding love affair in 1908. She was the inspiration and dedicatee of his First Violin Concerto.

HORTHY, MIKLÓS (1868–1957), Hungarian naval officer. Chief architect of the reign of white terror, he acted as Hungary's Regent from March 1920 to October 1922.

HUBAY, JENŐ (1858–1938), Hungarian violinist and conductor. A pupil of Joachim, who became the outstanding violin teacher at the Budapest Academy of Music and, later on, its director.

JURKOVICS, IRMY (1882–1945), childhood friend of Bartók. She and her sister, Emsy, idolized the composer following his first public recital at his birthplace, Nagyszentmiklós (now Sinnicolau Mare, Romania).

KODÁLY, ZOLTÁN (1882–1967), distinguished Hungarian composer, folklorist, educator, and professor of composition at the Budapest Academy of Music. He introduced Bartók to methods of gramophone recording of folk music in 1905, and became his friend, confidant, and coauthor.

KODÁLY, EMMA, nee Sándor (18?–1958), accomplished Hungarian pianist and composer, who married Kodály in 1910. She was also noted for the musical soirées in her Budapest home, where Bartók and Kodály met for the first time.

KOESSLER, HANS (1853–1926), composer and friend of Johannes Brahms. Professor of composition at the Budapest Academy of Music. Among his pupils were Bartók, Dohnányi, and Kodály.

KOSSUTH, LAJOS (1802–1894, Hungarian minister of finance in 1848–1849 and later governing president. He was the figure of greatest historical importance in the nineteenth-century struggle for national independence. He went into exile after the defeat of the War of Independence in 1849.

LENGYEL, MENYHÉRT (1880–1974), Hungarian writer and dramatist. He was the author of *The Miraculous Mandarin*, on which Bartók based his music.

MIHALOVICH, ÖDÖN (1842–1929), composer, teacher, and director of the Academy of Music from 1887 to 1919.

MÜLLER-WIDMANN, ANNIE (d. 1965), Basel admirer and friend of Bartók, who helped save his manuscripts following his emigration to the United States in October 1940.

RÁKÓCZI, FERENC II (1676–1735), Prince of Transylvania. In 1686 he was taken from his mother and reared in Bohemia under supervision of the Vienna court. When he returned to Hungary, he was influence by the aristocrats and gentry who chafed under Habsburg rule. Following an unsuccessful insurrection with French assistance and capture in 1701, he escaped from prison to Poland, where he launched the liberation struggle which bears his name. In 1704, he was elected Prince of Transylvania.

RICHTER, HANS (1843–1916), Hungarian-born conductor. In 1904, he conducted the English premiere of Bartók's *Kossuth* symphonic poem in Manchester. It was this work that caused a sensation during its first performance in Budapest and brought Bartók instant fame as a composer.

SACHER, PAUL (b. 1906–1999), Swiss conductor. He commissioned Bartók's Music for Strings, Percussion, and Celesta, Sonata for Two Pianos and Percussion, and the Divertimento for String Orchestra.

SZÉKELY, ZOLTÁN (b. 1903), Hungarian violinist and composer, pupil of Hubay and Kodály. He commissioned Bartók's Second Violin Concerto.

SZABOLCSI, BENCE (1899–1973), Hungarian scholar and student of Zoltán Kodály. Bartók considered Szabolcsi to be one of Hungary's foremost musicologists and entrusted him with the translation into German of Bartók's *Cantata Profana* Hungarian text. Szabolcsi's major field was investigation of the origin of the oldest strata in Hungarian folk music. His findings corroborated in a conclusive way the assertions previously made by others, and proved that the earliest strata of Hungarian folk music is more than 1,500 years old.

SZIGETI, JÓZSEF (1892–1983), Hungarian-born violinist and pupil of Hubay, whose concerts were mainly given in Switzerland and the United States. He was the dedicatee of Bartók's First Rhapsody for Violin and Piano and *Contrasts* for Violin, Clarinet, and Piano. It was at Szigeti's suggestion that Benny Goodman commissioned Bartók to compose *Contrasts*.

TANGO, EGISTO (1873–1951), Italian conductor, was musical director of the Budapest Opera and conducted the premiere of Bartók's *The Wooden Prince* in 1917 and *Duke Bluebeard's Castle* in 1918.

THOMÁN, ISTVÁN (1862–1941), Hungarian pianist, favored pupil of Liszt, and professor of piano at the Budapest Academy of Music. Among his pupils were Bartók—who succeeded him as professor in 1907—and Dohnányi.

VECSEY, FERENC VON (1893–1935), prodigious Hungarian violinist and pupil of Joachim and Hubay. In 1906, Bartók travelled with him on an Iberian tour as accompanist and soloist. Bartók's excursion to Tangier was marked by an impromptu visit to an inn, where the performance of Arab music made a lasting impression.

VIKÁR, BÉLA (1859–1945), Hungarian folklorist. He was the first collector to use the Edison phonograph for recording folk music in the rural areas of then Greater Hungary. These invaluable documents were transcribed by Bartók and published in his folk-music studies.

WALDBAUER, IMRE (1892–1952), Hungarian violinist, pupil of Hubay, and professor of violin at the Budapest Academy of Music. He founded the Waldbauer-Kerpely string quartet, which gave the premieres of Bartók's String Quartet nos. 1 and 2, and joined with Bartók in chamber music concerts.

Abbreviations

BBA   Budapest Bartók Archívum
BBCL   Béla Bartók Jr.: *Bartók Béla családi levelei*, ed. Adrienne Konkoly Gombozné. Budapest: Zeneműkiadó, 1981
BBCO   Benjamin Suchoff: *Béla Bartók: Concerto for Orchestra: Understanding Bartók's World*. New York: Schirmer, 1995
BBE   Béla Bartók: *Béla Bartók Essays*, selected and edited by Benjamin Suchoff. Reprint. Lincoln and London: University of Nebraska Press, 1992
BBGR   Elliott Antokoletz: *Béla Bartók: A Guide to Research*. 2d ed., rev. and enl. New York: Garland, 1997
BBL   *Béla Bartók Letters,* ed. János Demény. Trans. Péter Balabán and István Farkas, rev. trans. Elisabeth West and Colin Mason. New York: St. Martin's Press, 1971
BBMW   Tibor Tallián: *Béla Bartók: The Man and His Work*. Trans. Gyula Gulgás, rev. trans. Paul Merrick. Budapest: Corvina, 1981
BBRP   *Denijs Dille: Béla Bartók. Regard sur le passé*, ed. Yves Lenoir. Louvain-la-neuve: Institut supérieure, 1990
BBSE   *Béla Bartók: Béla Bartók Studies in Ethnomusicology,* selected and ed. Benjamin Suchoff. Lincoln and London: University of Nebraska Press, 1997
BC   *The Bartók Companion*, ed. Malcolm Gillies. Portland, OR: Amadeus Press, 1994
BR   Malcolm Gillies: *Bartók Remembered*. London: Faber, 1990
CEBB   *Complete Edition Béla Bartók*. Budapest: Hungaroton Records
HFS   Béla Bartók: *The Hungarian Folk Song*, ed. Benjamin Suchoff. Trans. M.D. Calvocoressi, with annotations by Zoltán Kodály. Albany: State University of New York Press, 1981
LMBB   Halsey Stevens: *The Life and Music of Béla Bartók*. 3d edition. Prepared by Malcolm Gillies. Oxford: Clarendon Press. 1993
MBB   Elliott Antokoletz, *The Music of Béla Bartók: A Study of Tonality and Progression in Twentieth-Century Music*. Berkeley and Los Angeles: University of California Press, 1984
NYBA   New York Bartók Archive (now in *PBA*)

PBA	Peter Bartók Archive, Homosassa, Florida
RFM.i–v	Béla Bartók: *Rumanian Folk Music*, ed. Benjamin Suchoff, trans. E.C. Teodorescu. The Hague: Martinus Nijhoff, 1967, 1975
SV.i–iii	Béla Bartók: *Slowakische Volkslieder*, ed. Alica Elscheková, Oskár Elschek, and Jozef Kresánek. Bratislava: Academia Scientiarum Slovaca, 1959, 1970 (vol. iii is unpublished)
TFM	Béla Bartók: *Turkish Folk Music from Asia Minor*, ed. Benjamin Suchoff. With an Afterword by Kurt Reinhard. Princeton: Princeton University Press, 1976
TVJB	Denijs Dille: *Thematisches Verseichnis der Jugenwerke Béla Bartóks: 1890–1904*. Budapest: Akadémiai Kiadó, 1974
YFM.i–iv	Béla Bartók: *Yugoslav Folk Music*, ed. Benjamin Suchoff (Albany: State University of New York Press, 1978

Notes

PART ONE

Life

Chapter 1: Historic Events and Musical Developments in Hungary to the Close of the Nineteenth Century

1. This chapter is an enlarged revision of my editorial preface to *HFS*, ix–xvi.

2. The singing style of one Ugar woman was "just like that of we Hungarians." See John Pomfret, "Foreign Journal; Hungry for Their Roots," *Washington Post* Foreign Service.

3. Bence Szabolcsi, *A Concise History of Hungarian Music,* 109. The parallels between the skeleton form of the two melodies (that is, ornamental notes are excluded) include the symmetrical pentatonic scale (D-F-G-A-C), four melody sections, and the second half of the melody is a fifth lower than the first half. Note, too, that the metrical structure (six syllables) and the end notes of the first two sections (D and A, respectively) are identical. The Hungarian-Csángó melody appears as no. 106 in Zoltán Kodály, *A magyar népzene,* 146. Such ancient melodic style "has been preserved quite intact by the Székely emigrants, called Csángó-s, who settled in Bukovina in the eighteenth century." See *BBSE,* 77.

4. Ervin Pamlényi, ed. *A History of Hungary,* 15–22. See also László Pusztaszeri, "On the Highway of the Steppes" (an interview with István Fodor, Director of the Hungarian National Museum), 31.

5. The unabridged melodies appear in Szabolcsi, *A Concise History,* 110. Latin texts were soon followed by Hungarian translations, and the most popular melodies eventually were transformed into a musical base for rural folk song, such as Ex. 1.2b. This folk song, originally published in Béla Bartók and Zoltán Kodály, *Transylvanian Hungarians: Folk Songs* (melody no. 83), is reprinted in *BBSE,* 111. *HFS* melody no. 2 is another example of the ancient style that has been preserved by the Hungarian-speaking Székely people in Transylvania as well as in Bukovina (see also note 3).

6. Szabolcsi, *A Concise History,* 33. Jacob Paix (b 1550) was a German organist and composer. The folk song was collected by Béla Vikár in Lengyelfalva (Udvárhely) in 1903 and transcribed by Bartók. See *BBSE,* 130 (melody no. 139).

7. A facsimile of the complete Tinódi example with text appears in Szabolcsi, *A Con-*

cise History, 30. The variant folk song was collected by Kodály in Székelydobó (Udvarhely) in 1910.

8. C.A. Macartney, *Hungary,* 75–86.

9. László Dobszay, *A History of Hungarian Music,* 92.

10. Pamlényi, ed. *A History of Hungary,* 172–6.

11. Jörg K. Hoensch, *A Modern History of Hungary,* 3.

12. Szabolcsi, *A Concise History,* 43–5, 48.

13. According to Kerényi's note to the melody, the text of Ex. 1.6a, written by Gyula Pap, appears as no. 37 in a collection of popular poems printed in 1865. The melody is published in *Magyar Dalok és Népdalok* (Hungarian Songs and Folk Songs), series 37, no. 6 (1902).

14. See Donald Jay Grout, *A History of Western Music,* 413–4, 433–4, and Paul Henry Lang, *Music in Western Civilization,* 581–2.

15. The Bihari piece is transcribed for piano solo in *A magyar zongoramuzsika 100 éve* (100 years of Hungarian keyboard music: From *verbunkos* to Bartók's *"Kossuth"*), ed. Ervin Major and István Szelényi. Budapest: Zeneműkiadó Vállalat (1954): 10–2.

16. See also Zoltán Kodály, *Hungarian Folk Music,* 62–5.

17. Hoensch, *A History of Modern Hungary,* 4–5.

18. Pamlényi, ed. *A History of Hungary,* 255–84.

19. Ervin Major and István Szelényi, *A magyar zongoramuzsika 100 éve,* 28.

20. Szabolcsi, *A Concise History,* 69–71.

21. Ibid., 188–9, 250.

22. Ibid., 80–1.

23. Hoensch, *A Modern History of Hungary,* 16–9.

24. Ibid., 31–3.

25. Emil Lengyel, *1,000 Years of Hungary,* 164–9.

Chapter 2: Childhood and Youth: 1881–1899

1. Ferenc Bónis, *Béla Bartók. His Life in Pictures and Documents,* 33. The town of about 10,000 inhabitants—located near the junction of present-day Hungary, Romania, and Yugoslavia—included Serbian, Swabian (South German), and Romanian minorities. No. 229 Rácznagyszentmiklós is presumed to be the house in which Bartók was born—the Rác prefix indicating the Serbian quarter of the town—and its photograph appears in a Romanian commemorative leaflet *Sînnicolaul Mare oraşul natal a lui Béla Bartók* (n.p., n.d.).

2. Denijs Dille, *Généalogie sommaire de la famille Bartók,* 53. It is interesting to note (p. 51) that the composer used the title as late as 1923, the year of his second marriage.

3. *BBMW,* 9–10.

4. *BBE,* 408.

5. Jenő Glück and Éva Wetzler, "Bánsági adatok a Bartók-kutatáshoz" (Contribution to Bartók-research from the Banat), 83–4.

6. *BBRP,* 281.

7. János Demény, "Adatok Bartók szülővárosának művelődéstörténetéhez" (Data on the cultural history of Bartók's birthplace), 218–22.

8. János Demény, ed. *Bartók Béla levelei* (Béla Bartók's letters, 1951), 203–4.

9. Ibid., 205.

10. Demény, "Adatok Bartók . . . ," 219–20.

11. Demény, ed. *Bartók Béla levelei* (1951), 205.

12. Ibid., 206.

13. Ibid. See also *TVJB,* 53.

14. *TVJB,* 53, 282. According to a 1941 interview reprinted in *BBRP,* 284, Bartók recalled the piece as "in the style of Lanner." Josef Lanner (1801–1843), Austrian orchestra leader, violinist, and composer of waltzes, was noted for his lyric melodies.

15. Demény, ed. *Bartók Béla levelei* (1951), 206.

16. Bartók added a violin part in 1894. See *TVJB,* 63–9 and *BBCO,* 14–5.

17. Demény, ed. *Bartók Béla levelei* (1951), 207.

18. According to the Hungarian-born musicologist Otto Gombosi (1902–55), Bartók played "the opening movement of Beethoven's C Major Sonata op. 2, no. 3, not of the 'Waldstein' Sonata (This was confirmed to me in a conversation by Bartók, in 1943)." See Gombosi's unfinished biography of Bartók in the *PBA.*

19. Erkel was the third son of Hungary's outstanding opera composer, Ferenc Erkel (1810–1893).

20. *BBE,* 408.

21. Demény, ed. *Bartók Béla levelei* (1951), 208.

22. Bartók designated this piece as op. 1, to underscore its stylistic difference from the preceding dance pieces and programmatic compositions. The themes and approximate durations are given in *TVJB,* 76–7.

23. Lajos Lesznai, *Bartók,* 12–3. See *TVJB,* 82–3, for a discussion, including thematic excerpts, of Bartók's three-movement violin sonata.

24. Pongrácz Kacsóh, "Bartók Béla," 212–3. Bartók was also tutored by János Batka (1846–1917), a librarian and writer on music.

25. *BBE,* 408. See also Tadeusz A. Zieliński, *Bartók,* 27–8.

26. *BBL,* 76–7, letter of 6 September 1907.

27. See *TVJB,* 92, for the thematic excerpts of the first two movements (I. Allegro, II.

Scherzo and Trio: Allegro molto). The estimated time of performance is ca. 25'.

28. It is interesting to note that the composer signed his manuscript with the titular "von Bartók" family name. My condensed score is based on the composer's full score facsimile (see *TVJB*, 289). The work apparently represents Bartók's first orchestral score.

29. *BBL*, 369.

Chapter 3: Summary of Hungarian Musical Dialect: 1899–1905

1. Klára Hamburger, *Liszt*, 172.

2. Demény, ed. *Bartók Béla levelei* (1951), 210.

3. Ibid., 210–1.

4. *BBE*, 489–90.

5. Otto Gombosi, unfinished biography of Bartók in the *PBA*.

6. *BBCL*, 17.

7. This work was inspired by a talented young girl, Felicie Fábián, classmate and friend of Bartók in Koessler's composition class, who composed the second theme in the reprise of the fourth song. See the thematic excerpts and commentaries in *TVJB*, 112–6.

8. See *TVJB*, 212.

9. On 10 January, Bartók completed a piano piece titled *Változatok* (Variations), twelve variations based on an original theme. See *TVJB*, 119–20.

10. Zoltán Kodály, "Bartók the Folklorist," in *The Selected Writings of Zoltán Kodály*, 103.

11. Demény, ed. *Bartók Béla levelei* (1951), 213.

12. *BBE*, 453.

13. Lesznai, *Bartók*, 27–8.

14. *BBE*, 409.

15. Text translation: "Come, Come! that's an angry little girl." In his unpublished biography, Gombosi writes: "good old Lajos Pósa, known to three generations of Hungarian children as a bore of a magazine 'uncle,' spared no efforts to exclude any novel idea from their folkish jingling." Analysis of the first song appears in *BBCO*, 21–2. This was Bartók's first published work, printed in 1904 by Ferencz Bárd, Budapest.

16. *BBE*, 409.

17. *BBCL*, 56. English translation appears in *BBMW*, 30.

18. Other structural analyses will be found in *BBCO*, 23–4, and John Williamson, *Strauss: Also Sprach Zarathustra*, 79–81.

19. Another emphatic rendition of the octatonic scale occurs in the seventh section, "das Tanzlied" (The dance song). See also the illustrated discussion in *BBCO*, 23–4.

This nondiatonic scale is an eight-note, symmetrical configuration based on alternating half- and whole-steps or whole- and half-steps.

20. Béla Bartók, Jr., *Apám eletének krónikája* (Chronicles of my father's life), 41. Stefi Geyer (1888–1956) began her studies with violin virtuoso and Academy professor Jenő Hubay (1858–1937) in 1898. After the concert she left Budapest for an international concert tour.

21. *BBCL*, 60. Adila Arányi Fachiri (1886–1966), then age sixteen and another violin prodigy of Hubay, entered the Academy in 1897.

22. Bartók, Jr., *Apám eletének krónikája*, 43.

23. In his unpublished biography, Gombosi recalls a conversation he had with Koessler during the summer of 1924, in which the latter still questioned Bartók's real talent as a composer and rejected him as "oversophisticated and as one that replaces originality with a *tour de force*."

24. Bartók, Jr., *Apám eletének krónikája*, 45.

25. *BBCL*, 75. See also the remainder of this fragmentary English translation in *A Memorial Review*, 12. The excerpt shown in Ex. 3.5 appears in *TVJB*, 126.

26. The Scherzo was also performed in 1961 and later recorded by the Budapest Symphony Orchestra, György Lehel, conducting (Hungaroton LPX 11517, with program notes by Ferenc Bónis). See also the analytic commentary in Gunter Weiss-Aigner, "Youthful Orchestral Works," in *BC*, 441–5.

27. *BBCL*, 74–5.

28. *BBCL*, 76.

29. József Ujfalussy, *Béla Bartók*, 37. A vignetted biography of Emma Gruber appears in Lajos Lesznai, *Bartók*, 25.

30. A facsimile of the complete autograph appears in Joseph Mcleod, *The Sisters d'Aranyi*, 29. See also the illustrated discussion in *TVJBB*, 130–1.

31. *BBL*, 18–9. Bartók's letter is curious. While Joachim (1831–1907) and his sister Johanna were Jews, her second marriage was to Lajos Arányi—a typically anti-Semitic member of the lesser nobility, ardent nationalist, and head of Pest University—who persuaded her sons by a former marriage to convert to Catholicism and be ordained as priests. Arányi's own child, Taksony, married Adrienne de Ligenza (she spoke only Polish and French). See Joseph Mcleod, *The Sisters d'Aranyi*, 15-7.

32. The manuscript and various postcards are listed and annotated in the 16 May 1967 Sotheby (London) catalogue as "The Property of a Lady," 111–6. See Gillies, *Bartók in Britain*, 134, n. 19. See also the illustrated discussion in *TVJBB*, 131–2, and the publication of the *Andante* by Editio Musica Budapest, 1981. The Mcleod biography (see n. 58) is based on many interviews with Jelly d'Arányi as well as Adila's typescript of her talk on Bartók given at the International Cello Centre (London) on 23 June 1955.

33. József Ujfalussy, *Béla Bartók*, 38.

34. Originally titled "Sonata" *(BBL*, 27). See also *PBA* 6PS1.

35. János Demény, brochure notes to Hungaroton LPX 1300, 6.

36. *BBMW,* 36–7. The Hungarian publication will be found in *BBCL,* 91.

37. *BBMW,* 38 and Lesznai, *Bartók,* 17–8.

38. *BBL,* 23.

39. See *BBE,* 399–403 and my essay, "The Genesis of Bartók's Musical Language," in *Bartók Perspectives,* 115–6. For multilingual versions of the program notes and *Kossuth* reviews, see János Demény, "Bartók Béla tanulóévei és romantikus korszaka" (Béla Bartók's student years and romantic period), 411–34.

40. *BBL,* 29.

41. See Roswitha Schlötterer-Traimer, "Béla Bartók und die Tondichtungen von Richard Strauss" (Béla Bartók and the tone poems of Richard Strauss), 312-3.

42. The notated song, for voice and piano, appears in Judit Frigyesi, *Béla Bartók and Hungarian Nationalism,* 146–7.

43. *LMBB,* 20–1.

44. Lesznai, *Bartók,* 36–7.

45. *BBL,* 39–40.

46. See Demény, "Bartók Béla tanulóévei," 412.

47. *Manchester Guardian,* 19 February 1904. See also Gillies, *Bartók in Britain,* 5–8.

48. Günter Weiss-Aigner, "Youthful Chamber Works, 223. The score of the first two movements are published in Denijs Dille, ed., *Documenta Bartókiana* 1 (1964): "Musikbeilagen" appendix, without page nos.

49. *BBCO,* 26–7. The third movement is published in Dille, ed., *Documenta Bartókiana* 2 (1965): 175–200.

50. *TVJB,* 156.

51. *BBE,* 409.

52. The Hungarian peasant adaptation was collected in 1909 by Zoltán Kodály in northern Hungary (now Slovakia).

53. *HFS,* melody no. 313. The music has been transposed to B as final tone, in order to facilitate comparison with the source melodies in Ex. 3.17.

54. Cseke, Péter. "Aki Bartóknak énekelt" (Who sang to Bartók), 90. See also Ferenc László, "Bartók's First Encounter with Folk Music," 67–8.

55. A Slovak folk song variant of the popular art song appears in *HFS,* 77 and the unpublished *SV.*iii, melody no. 1084b. The original art song is reprinted in György Kerényi, *Népies Dalok* (p. 141), with the remark (p. 221) that it was first published in 1883.

56. *HFS,* 77. Rhythm contraction is a structural peculiarity of Slovak peasant music (see *BBSE* 263n. 15).

57. Bartók transcribed another of her songs, *HFS,* 234a, which is an isometric (same number of text syllables in each verse) variant of a heterometric art song. See the Remark in *HFS,* 63, and the related melody no. 234b.

58. The song was published in the musical supplement of the *Magyar Lant* (Hungarian Lyre) issue of 15 February 1905. A reprint appears in Dille, ed., *Documenta Bartókiana* 4 (1970): 25–6.

59. Bach's ostinato—a repeated chromatic hexachord—serves as the instrumental bass in his Easter church cantata (1714).

60. Bartók, Jr., *Apám eletének krónikája,* 68.

61. *BBL,* 44.

62. László Eősze, *Zoltán Kodály: His Life in Pictures,* 41.

63. *HFS,* 5. Vikár (1859–1945) recorded 1,492 melodies in Hungarian villages, beginning in 1898, which he deposited in the ethnographical section of the Hungarian National Museum. Kodály expected to undertake fieldwork in Hungarian villages during the summer, in order to record additional data for his Ph.D. dissertation, "The Stanzaic Structure of Hungarian Folk Song," at Eötvös College, Budapest.

64. *BBE,* 452–4.

65. Béla Bartók, Jr., *Bartók Béla műhelyében* (In Béla Bartók's workshop), 271.

66. *BBL,* 45-6. Bartók later heard that there was not enough money to award cash prizes, only diplomas.

67. Ibid., 50.

68. Ibid., 53.

69. Gillies, *Bartók in Britain,* 13–4.

70. See *PBA* 10FSS1.

71. *BBL,* 54.

72. Ibid., 132, 396. Only three movements were played on 9 November, and a repetition of this incomplete performance was played in Budapest on 6 December.

73. Ferenc Bónis, ed. *The Selected Writings of Zoltán Kodály,* 104. The collection, published in the periodical without explanatory annotations, appears in vol. 16 (1905): 300–5.

74. *BBE,* 409.

Chapter 4: Fusion of National Styles: 1906–1925

1. See Kodály, "A magyar népdal strófa-szrkezete (Stanza-structure in Hungarian folk song)," in *Kodály Zoltán. Visszatekintés* (Zoltán Kodály. Retrospection), 14–22. See also Stephen Erdely, *Methods and Principles of Hungarian Ethnomusicology,* 2–8.

2. Béla Bartók and Zoltán Kodály, *Hungarian Folksongs for song with piano*, 50.

3. *BBSE*, xii.

4. József Ujfalussy, *Béla Bartók*, 65.

5. *BBSE*, x.

6. *BBL*, 67.

7. The preface, titled Foreword, appears in *The Selected Writings of Zoltán Kodály*, 9-10, and the reprint of the original 1906 publication (Budapest: Editio Musica, 1970, 5), where Kodály is listed as the only author. However, the facsimile edition, *Hungarian Folksongs for song with piano* (Kodály's holographic preface, p. 26), ends with "Bartók Béla [and] Kodály Zoltán dr."

8. Bartók and Kodály, *Hungarian Folksongs for song with piano*, 51.

9. Lesznai, *Bartók*, 59–60.

10. The melody, reprinted in *BBSE*, 272, was transcribed by Bartók as no. 3 in *For Children* for Piano, vol. 2.

11. Denijs Dille, "Angaben zum Violinkonzert 1907," 91. According to *HFS* (pp. 84, 94), Bartók collected twenty-nine folk songs, of which three (dated VII, 1907) appear in Bartók, *Hungarian Folk Songs. Complete Collection*, nos. 248h (1, 2) and 273a.

12. Bartók, *Briefe an Stefi Geyer, 1907–1908*, 17–8.

13. *BBSE*, 77. See also the variant melody *HFS*, no. 2. Another indicator of antiquity is twelve syllables in each of the four verses.

14. *BBE*, 262–3.

15. Inasmuch as Stefi's letters to Bartók have not been completely published up to the present time, the only reference to them appears in Bartók's letters to her.

16. *BBL*, 70–4. See also Bartók, *Briefe*, 27–30. In addition to the folk songs Bartók collected in the Székely villages of Csík County during the summer of 1907, he found instrumental versions of vocal material in the village of Gyergyótekerőpatak. Three melodies, played on the *tilinkó* (long peasant-flute) by a sixty-year-old man, were transcribed for piano solo as "Három csíkmegyei népdal" (Trois chansons hongroises populaires), and published in 1910 by Rozsnyai Károly, Budapest. A description of the instrument appears in *BBE*, 269–70.

17. Bartók, *Briefe an Stefi Geyer*, 31. He later placed an extended variant of the melody as mm. 14–25 in the second movement of his First String Quartet, op. 7 (1909).

18. Ibid., 33.

19. *BBL*, 82.

20. Ibid., 83–7. The "Leitmotiv" is an arpeggiated major-seventh chord, a horizontal projection of the vertical sonority that appears in *Tristan und Isolde*.

21. Ibid., 88. Printed in 1908, the essay represents Bartók's first publication of Hungarian folk music (see the discussion and music example in *BBSE*, viii–ix).

22. In October 1906. See melody no. 31b in *SV.*i.

23. Bartók, *Briefe an Stefi Geyer*, 47.

24. Paul Sacher, "Begegnungen mit Béla Bartók," 19–20.

25. Dille, "Angaben zum Violinkonzert 1907," 94–5.

26. Bartók, *Briefe an Stefi Geyer*, 70–1. See also *PBA* 15FSS1.

27. "Les Préludes," no. 15 from Méditations Poétiques (1820), by the French poet, A. M. Louis de Lamartine (1790–1869). It is noteworthy that Bartók studied the symphonic poem during his second year as a student at the Budapest Academy of Music.

28. Dille, "Angaben zum Violinkonzert 1907," 92. Bartók completed the quartet on 27 January 1909.

29. Eősze, *Zoltán Kodály: His Life in Pictures*, 17. Kodály was on a visit to Berlin and Paris for study purposes, particularly the score of Debussy's opera, *Pelléas et Mélisande*.

30. *BBE*, 518.

31. Ibid., 410.

32. Ibid., 432.

33. Such sequences of parallel fifths and octaves are justified, in accordance with Bartók's assertion that: "Melodies in such an archaic style can very well be provided also with the most daring harmonies. It is an amazing phenomenon that just the archaic features will admit of a much wider range of possibilities in harmonizing and treating melodies of a pentatonic kind, than would be the case with the common major or minor scale melodies" (*BBE*, 374).

34. Dille, "Angaben zum Violinkonzert 1907," 101–2.

35. According to the original edition published in 1908 by Rozsnyai Károly, Budapest. The English subtitle translations are, respectively, "She is dead" and "My dancing sweetheart."

36. Günter Weiss, "Zwei unbekannte Briefe von Béla Bartók," 384–5.

37. *BBL*, 92.

38. *BBE*, 426–7. The lecture-recital, "Contemporary Music in Piano Teaching," was presented at various American colleges and universities from December 1940 to March 1941.

39. Letter from Rozsnyai Károly, dated 9 December 1909, quoted in Bartók, *The Piano Music of Béla Bartók*. The Archive Edition, Series II, vii. It is interesting to note that the last two (Slovak) volumes of *For Children* deviate even more radically from the "rules of classical harmony" than those of the first two (Hungarian) volumes.

40. *BBL*, 93–4.

41. *BBCL*, 187–9. The folk song is published in *SV.*i as melody no. 113b.

42. *BBSE,* xi.

43. *BBE,* 119–20.

44. *RFM.*ii, 37–8.

45. Bartók, *Chansons populaires du département Bihar (Hongrie),* melody nos. 5 and 65. The revised notation is published in *RFM.*ii as melody nos. 62b and 395, respectively.

46. *BBSE,* 3, 20.

47. *RFM.*i, 13.

48. *RFM.*i, melody no. 648. The original transcription appears in Bartók, *Chansons populaires . . . ,* melody no. 362.

49. *BBMW,* 76.

50. *BBL,* 96. See also Bartók's letter to his mother, dated 12 January, in *BBCL,* 193–4.

51. His Paris performance consisted of thirteen Bagatelles (1908), the First Romanian Dance (1908), and "Fantaisie" (probably no. 2 from Four Piano Pieces, 1903). During 1910, therefore, he composed the second Romanian Dance and completed the Seven Sketches (begun in 1908) and Four Dirges (1909–1910).

52. Julia Szegő, *Bartók Béla a népdalkutató* (Béla Bartók the folk song researcher), 92.

53. See note 41. The English translation appears in *BBMW,* 76–7.

54. *RFM.*1, 3. Bartók's fieldwork ended in July 1915.

55. *BBSE,* 4–5.

56. Between 1908 and 1909, the Academia Română published the first six volumes of popular music, poetry, and literature that had been collected not only in Romania proper but in northern Transylvania (Máramaros, now Maramureş, Romania) as well. The publications are cited in *RFM.*iv, 34–5, and v, 34.

57. *BBL,* 102. It was apparently at this time that Bartók prepared the first draft of his Four Old Hungarian Folk Songs (for unaccompanied four-part male chorus), perhaps with the intention of sending a copy to his Romanian colleague.

58. C. A. Macartney, *Hungary and Her Successors,* 264–5.

59. The correspondence between Bartók and members of the Romanian Academy appears in Dille's editorial preface to *Béla Bartók: Ethnomusikalische Schriften Faksimile-Nachdrucke* 3, 8*–14*.

60. *BBE,* 396.

61. Ibid., 254. Two of the pipers were Slovaks.

62. Ibid., 108.

63. See note 59.

64. György Kroó, Brochure notes to *Duke Bluebeard's Castle*, op. 11 (Hungaroton LPX 11486), 7.

65. Cf. *BBE*, 280–2 and *SV*.ii, melody no. 831.

66. *HFS*, melody no. 180. The melody is reprinted together with its bagpipe variant in *BBE*, 251–2. There are many Slovak folk songs with similar structural characteristics (see *Sv*.i, 409–17).

67. *BBL*, 111.

68. *BBE*, 410.

69. Bartók was so exacerbated by UMZE administrative and other problems that on 24 November his postcard to Etelka Freund states: "Well, this UMZE has been such a nuisance that I would like to consign it to the depths of hell" (Ujfalussy, *Béla Bartók*, 117).

70. Demény, "Bartók Béla művészi kibontakozásának (1906–14)" (Béla Bartók's years of artistic development), 411–34.

71. *BBL*, 123–4.

72. *RFM*.ii, 24–5.

73. Reschofsky, a recognized pianist, composer, and teacher, attended the Academy of Music beginning in 1901. The details concerning his work with Bartók are given in his letters to me during 1954.

74. Hoensch, *A Modern History of Hungary*, 77.

75. *BBL*, 118.

76. Ibid., 119–20.

77. *BBSE*, xiii.

78. Benjamin Suchoff, "Bartók's Odyssey in Slovak Folk Music," in *Bartók Perspectives*, 18–9.

79. *BBL*, 128. Bartók is referring to previously published collections (see the list in *SV*.i, 61).

80. The letter, published in *Ethnographia* 24, no. 5 (1913), 313–6, is reprinted in *BBSE*, 24–8. It is noteworthy that the society failed to respond to their request.

81. *TVJB*, 107–10. The original composition, the first piece in a set of six dances for piano, was also transcribed for orchestra as *Valcer* (Waltz). The facsimile is reproduced in the Budapest music journal, *Zenei Szemle* 5, nos. 7–8 (1954): 34.

82. *RFM*.i, xxvi. During 1914, he added to his Hungarian folk music collection while he was traveling in Maros-Torda County (now Mureş). See, for example, the *HFS* Class C melody nos. 181, 194, 283, and 299c.

83. According to Oskár Elschek's editorial estimate in *SV*.1, 23.

84. The essay is reprinted in *BBE*, 195–200. It is noteworthy that no Hungarian re-

view of the Bihor book appeared.

85. The essay, "The Folk Music Dialect of the Hunedoara Romanians," including music examples, is reprinted in *BBE,* 103–14. Although Bartók had completed his monograph on the folk music of the Maramureş Romanians, under an agreement with the Academia Română, the lecture discloses for the first time that Bartók's research on Romanian music dialects proves that they transcend certain Transylvanian county borders. This finding thus prompted his determination to incorporate the Hunedoara material as well as the eventually retranscribed Bihor collection in a much larger compilation of Transylvanian-Romanian folk music (cf. *RFM.*i–ii).

86. *BBL,* 132. Bartók began composing *The Wooden Prince* in 1914 but "put it aside for a long time" (see *BBE,* 406).

87. *RFM.*i, ix.

88. János Demény, ed. *Bartók Béla levelei* (1955), 90.

89. *BBL,* 131.

90. *RFM.*i, 16, 364–6.

91. *BBL,* 132.

92. Cf. *BBRP,* 257–77, and Jenő Platthy, *Bartók. A Critical Biography,* 34–6.

93. The first posthumous edition appeared in 1958, as a publication of the Béla Bartók Archives, New York. The second edition, published by Universal Edition in 1961, has introductory remarks by Ivan Waldbauer and Denijs Dille.

94. János Liebner, "Unpublished Bartók Documents," *The New Hungarian Quarterly* 2, no. 6 (April–June 1962): 222.

95. *BBE,* 432.

96. Ibid., 338.

97. János Demény, ed. *Bartók Béla levelei* (1955), 374, n.1. Cf. *PBA* 43PS1, 43PFC1, and 43PFC2.

98. János Demény, "Bartók Béla pályaja delelőjén" (Béla Bartók at the height of his career), 209, 228, 370.

99. Bartók Jr., *Apám életének krónikája,* 148–9.

100. *BC,* 362–3.

101. Universal-Edition no. 6635, © 1921.

102. *BBL,* 133.

103. *BR,* 38.

104. Bartók Jr., *Apám életének krónikája,* 157.

105. Carl Leafstedt, "Pelléas Revealed: The Original Ending of Bartók's Opera, *Duke Bluebeard's Castle,*" in *Bartók Perspectives,* 238.

106. *BBE*, 411.

107. Hoensch, *A Modern History of Hungary*, 79–86.

108. *BBE*, 377–9.

109. BBSE, 32–3, 60. See also melody nos. 12–15.

110. *BC*, 117–22. See also Elliott Antokoletz, "The Musical Language of Bartók's 14 Bagatelles for Piano," 12–5.

111. *PBA*, Universal Edition correspondence files. The extant sources do not indicate whether the projected additional etudes were composed for op. 18.

112. *BBE*, 376. See also 338–9.

113. Demény, "Bartók Béla pályaja . . . ," 114.

114. *BBE*, 168.

115. Ibid., 226–7.

116. Ibid., 140–1. The letter is dated 14 September 1918.

117. Vera Lampert, "*The Miraculous Mandarin*: Melchior [Menyhért] Lengyel, His Pantomime, and His Connections to Béla Bartók," 159–62.

118. Ibid., 163.

119. See Menyhért Lengyel, "The Miraculous Mandarin," trans. István Farkas, *The New Hungarian Quarterly* 4, no. 11 (1963): 30–5.

120. Zsuzsa L. Nagy, "Revolution in Hungary (1918–9)," 421–5.

121. *BBL*, 142–3.

122. Under the title, "Hungary in the Throes of Reaction." See *BBE*, 460–3.

123. *BBL*, 146.

124. Ibid., 144. In this letter to his mother in Pozsony, dated 23 October 1919, Bartók lists "Transylvania, Vienna, and Germany" as the "three other countries."

125. Ibid., 151. Dohnányi and Kodály were the most prominent musicians among those who had not been included as council members.

126. Demény, ed. *Bartók Béla levelei* (1976), 241, 246. See also *SV.*1.,

127. Ibid., 259–60.

128. Lesznai, *Bartók*, 109. In this case, "Walachian" is a Hungarian pejorative substitution for "Romanian."

129. Ibid., 109–10.

130. *BBE*, 201–3.

131. Ibid., 375.

132. Ibid., 318.

133. *HFS* melody no. 46. The translation of the folk text reads: To plough in winter is hard work: / One can hardly hold the plough, / 'Tis better to remain abed, / Disporting with a young woman.

134. *BBE,* 118. See the discussion of octatonicism in *Pribaoutki* no. 4 in Pieter C. van ten Toorn, *The Music of Stravinsky,* 40–1. See also *MBB,* 213–7, for a study of octatonicism in the Eighth Improvisation.

135. Ibid., 375.

136. Gillies, *Bartók in Britain,* 22.

137. Ibid., 23.

138. *BBL,* 153–4. From the spring of 1920 to the spring of 1922, the Bartóks accepted banker József Lukács's offer of lodging as house guests in his Budapest villa.

139. Published in 1923 and reprinted in *BBSE,* 77–134 (150 melodies).

140. Suchoff, "Bartók's Odyssey in Slovak Folk Music," in *Bartók Perspectives,* 19.

141. Editions were published in Hungarian (1924), German (1925), and English (1932, as *Hungarian Folk Music*), and a reprint of the latter, edited by the present writer, as *HFS* (1981).

142. Joseph Mcleod, *The Sisters d'Arányi,* 139–40.

143. Included in the program were Bartók's performance of ten pieces from Fourteen Bagatelles op. 6 (see Plate 4 in Claude Kenneson, *Székely and Bartók*). It is conceivable that the omission of nos. 13 and 14—which reflects Bartók's failed relationship with Stefi Geyer—was subconsciously prompted by his attraction toward Jelly d'Arányi.

144. *BBCL,* 325 (trans. Gillies, *Bartók in Britain,* 137). It is noteworthy that the dedicatee of the 1923 publication is Jelly d'Arányi and not Márta Bartók.

145. See Alistair Wightman, "Szymanowski, Bartók and the Violin," 159–63.

146. Gillies, *Bartók in Britain,* 41.

147. Ibid. 138–9. It is interesting (see n. 143) that the concert began with Bartók's performance of the First Elegy, op. 8b (1908), which he composed immediately after his breakup with Stefi Geyer.

148. *BBE,* 475–6. See *Musikblätter des Anbruch* 3, no. 5 (March): 87–90.

149. Ibid., 410. See *Il Pianoforte* 2, no. 7 (July): 193–7.

150. See *PBA* 52VPFC2, p. 45, and Universal Edition correspondence files. During his published interview with Henry Cassin Becker, Bartók stated that his two violin sonatas are among his most complicated works, with distinct evidences of tonality: no. 1 in C-sharp Minor and no. 2 in C Major.

151. See the comparative analysis in *BBCO,* 75–80.

152. Suchoff, "Notes on the Music," in *Béla Bartók: A Celebration,* 10–1. See also *RFM.*i, 55.

153. Demény, ed. *Bartók Béla levelei* (1976), 286.

154. PBA, Universal Edition correspondence files.

155. Reprinted in 1975 as *RFM*.v.

156. Vladimír Čižík, *Bartóks Briefe in die Slowakei*, 45.

157. Demény, ed. *Bartók Béla levelei* (1976), 301–2.

158. Ibid., 300 (trans. Halsey Stevens, *The Life and Music of Béla Bartók*, 66).

159. Gillies, *Bartók in Britain*, 60–5. See also the study of Bartók's approach to piano touch in Suchoff, *Béla Bartók and a Guide to the Mikrokosmos* (1957), 117–62 .

160. Letter to Halsey Stevens, dated 10 October 1950, in *LMBB*, 67.

161. Letter to Otto Gombosi, in *PBA* correspondence files.

162. *BBL*, 167, letter to János Bușiția, dated 15 May 1925.

163. László Somfai, Introduction to *Béla Bartók. XVII and XVIII Century Italian Cembalo and Organ Music Transcribed for Piano*. Reprint. New York: Carl Fischer (1990), v–vi.

164. See Suchoff, "The Impact of Italian Baroque Music on Bartók's Music," in *Bartók and Kodály Revisited*, ed. György Ránki, 189–93.

165. József Ujfalussy, *Béla Bartók*, 221.

Chapter 5: Synthesis of East and West: 1926–1945

1. It should be noted that the Philharmonic had never offered the Budapest public a concert devoted to Bartók's works.

2. *BBE*, 360. According to Roman Vlad, "In the majority of cases Stravinsky employs the "pre-existing" material (chord, harmonic groups, and melodic phrases) in such an entirely novel and original manner that it is hardly fair to speak of his neo-classical compositions as so many 'throwbacks' to Bach . . ." (*Stravinsky*, 78). See also Paul Griffiths, *Stravinsky*, 81–3.

3. Winthrop P. Tryon, "How Bartók Composes," 15. Bartók prefaces his remark with: "Schönberg and his 12-tone music is foreign to me. . . . I take as the basis of composing, folk music. That gets me away from the nineteenth century and romanticism, from which escape for many is so difficult."

4. Letter (n.d.) to Edwin von der Null, quoted in the latter's monograph, *Béla Bartók. Ein Beitrag zur Morphologie der neuen Musik* (Béla Bartók. A contribution to the morphology of the new music), 108–9.

5. Serge Moreux, *Béla Bartók*, 92.

6. *BBCL*, 376–7. The delay in communication apparently resulted from the publisher's problem with translation of the original Hungarian publication. D. C. Ráz—London cor-

respondent for the Hungarian Telegraph Correspondence Bureau in Budapest—had been given the assignment but was unable to cope with its difficulties. The job was then turned over to M. D. Calvocoressi for translation of the German edition.

7. Vladimír Čižik, *Bartóks Briefe in die Slowakei*, 48–9.

8. Béla Bartók, Jr., "Remembering my father, Béla Bartók," 203.

9. *BR,* 111.

10. Ibid., 112.

11. Comparison of the *Lyric Suite* and Bartók's Third String Quartet only shows certain similarities that reflect parallel historical developments. See Elliott Antokoletz, "Middle Period String Quartets," in *BC,* 258.

12. Demény, "Bartók Béla pályája delelőjén" (Béla Bartók at the height of his career), 229. See also Ex. 4.32.

13. Harry Cassin Becker, "Béla Bartók and His Credo." *Musical America* (17 December 1927): 7, 35.

14. See "The Folk Songs of Hungary" in *BBE,* 331–9.

15. Demény, "Bartók Béla pályája delelőjén," 246–64.

16. *BBL,* 188–9.

17. *RFM.*i., 33. See also Stevens, Halsey. "The Sources of Bartók's Rhapsody for Violoncello and Piano," 65–6; and Suchoff, "Notes on the Music," in *Béla Bartók: A Celebration,* 13–5.

18. *BBE,* 412. See also Elliott Antokoletz, *Twentieth-Century Music,* 124–5.

19. A fair copy of the Ruthenian melody appears in Bartók's Ruthenian folk music collection at the *PBA.* A facsimile of the preliminary draft is published in László Somfai, *18 Bartók-tanulmány* (Eighteen Bartók studies), 309.

20. *BBL,* 189–90.

21. Ibid., 191. This letter marks the first of many communications between Bartók and book publishers concerning the inordinate delays in the printing of his various folk music collections.

22. *BBE,* 492–6 ("About Béla Bartók's Russian Tour"). See also Werner Fuchss, *Béla Bartók en Suisse,* 39, 44, and 46. In 1920, Stefi Geyer married Walter Schulthess, Swiss conductor and composer. Bartók also met Frau Müller-Widmann in Basel, who later helped him export his manuscripts prior to the Second World War. And Paul Sacher was another admirer, who founded the Basel Chamber Orchestra in 1926 and commissioned Bartók to compose works for it during the mid-1930s.

23. Gillies, *Bartók in Britain,* 75. It may have been this unfortunate event that prompted Bartók to concertize with the score later on.

24. *BBL,* 194.

25. *BBMW,* 158–9. Bartók's opinion of his critic, written in a letter dated 10 January

1931, states that: "I must inform you that Haraszti is a stupid and, in addition, a malicious man *who, moreover, understands as much of music as a hen does of the ABC!* (*BBL*, 202). Haraszti's pretentious 1938 monograph on Bartók's life and works, however, represents a recantation of his previously held opinions.

26. Demény, ed. *Bartók Béla levelei* (1955), 249. Bartók's letter addresses the first in a series of what would prove to be insuperable problems with his publisher.

27. The *colindǎ* melody appears as a "támlap" (proof-sheet) facsimile in Ferenc Bónis, *Bartók Béla élete képekben és dokumentumokben* (p. 183)—a revised edition of *Béla Bartók. His Life in Pictures and Documents*—which was published by Zeneműkiadó, Budapest, in 1980. Bartók commingled text nos. 4a and (its variant) 4b for the creation of the Cantata.

28. *BBE,* 120.

29. *BBL,* 51, 76–87.

30. Elliott Antokoletz, "Modal Transformation and Musical Symbolism in Bartók's *Cantata Profana,* in *Bartók Perspectives,* 74–5ß.

31. He also asked the Hungarian musicologist Bence Szabolcsi (1899–1973) to provide a better German version.

32. *BBL,* 440.

33. Ibid., 349–50.

34. *PBA,* Universal Edition correspondence files.

35. *BBL,* 201.

36. Ujfalussy, *Béla Bartók,* 290. With regard to the French award, on 20 December Bartók commented that he would have been more pleased if, instead of the decoration, "they would play my works more often in Paris" (*BBL,* 220).

37. Ibid., 292–3. The original publication of Aladár Tóth's article in *Pesti Napló* is reprinted in Demény, "Bartók Béla pályája delelőjén," 397.

38. See nos. 68–74 in *BBE* and no. 7 in *BBSE.*

39. Ujfalussy, *Béla Bartók,* 294. See also *BBE,* 498.

40. *BBE,* 499–500.

41. *BBL,* 221.

42. Kárpáti, Brochure notes to *Bartók Béla. Complete Edition* III. Chamber Music (44 Duos for Two Violins), 7.

43. "The *tambura* is a stringed instrument with frets, about the size of a viola, played with a plectrum. It has four pairs of strings, both strings of a pair are tuned to the same pitch, the pairs themselves are tuned differently" (*YTM.*i., 239).

44. *BBL,* 217.

45. *BBE,* 419.

46. Demény, ed. *Bartók Béla levelei* (1955), 250–2. The correspondent was Ján Valašťan-Dolinský the third in the succession of editors appointed by *Matica* to work with Bartók.

47. Ibid., 256–7.

48. Ibid., 258.

49. *BBE,* 38.

50. Suchoff, "Synthesis of East and West: *Mikrokosmos,*" 190.

51. In the 1940s, Bartók stated that the work is "a series of pieces in (all) of different styles to represent a small world," and that "it appears as a *synthesis* of all the musical and technical problems which were treated and only partially solved in the previous piano pieces" (ibid., 191).

52. Demény, ed. *Bartók Béla levelei* (1976), 378. It was Brăiloiu who received the manuscript in 1926, checked it for errors, and served as Bartók's intermediary for arranging parallel English and Romanian editions of the book (*BBL,* 168–70).

53. Ibid., 414.

54. At this time Oxford University Press was also involved with translation and production problems with the forthcoming publication of Bartók's *Hungarian Folk Music.*

55. *PBA,* Universal Edition correspondence files. The printing method, also used in producing blueprints, requires special music paper called transparencies or tissue masters.

56. Demény, ed. *Bartók Béla levelei* (1955), 263. It is interesting that Bartók uses the prewar Hungarian Pozsony designation instead of the current Bratislava.

57. Ibid., 265.

58. Bartók had offered to group the complete folk texts according to their content.

59. Suchoff, "Bartók's Odyssey in Slovak Folk Music," in *Bartók Perspectives,* 59.

60. *BBL,* 224–5.

61. Pamlényi, ed. *A History of Hungary,* 487–9.

62. Demény, "Bartók Béla pályája delelőjén," 437–49.

63. Particularly in English. See the listings in *BBE* and *BBSE.*

64. In the January–February and September–October (1933) issues, respectively. See *BBE,* 71–9, 119–27.

65. Bartók, Jr., *Apám eletének krónikája,* 326. The first English edition appears in *BBSE,* 174–240.

66. *BBL,* 227, 415.

67. *RFM.*i., 1–2.

68. *BR,* 156.

69. See the listings in *RFM*.i, 44; ii, 40–1; and iv, 32, 35–6.

70. *RFM*.i, 43.

71. Bartók, Jr., *Apám életének krónikája,* 343. The commission of $1,000 was sponsored by the Elizabeth Sprague Coolidge Foundation of Washington, D.C.

72. *PBA* 71FSFC1, p. 50 (copy of MS in the Library of Congress).

73. Bartók designated such asymmetrical schemata as Bulgarian rhythm "because of their frequency in Bulgarian folk music and because they have been discovered and described by Bulgarian musicologists." See *RFM*.i, 43.

74. *RFM*.i, xiv. This truncated German edition was distributed in 1935 by Universal Edition, Vienna.

75. Zoltán Kodály, "Bartók the Man," in *The Selected Writings of Zoltán Kodály,* 100.

76. *BBL,* 357.

77. Ibid., 283.

78. The C-Major scale with raised fourth degree (F♯).

79. *TFM,* 3. Halkevi is the designation of the social institutes established throughout Turkey. Paul Hindemith (1895–1963) was then in residence to organize a High School for Music in Ankara.

80. *TFM,* 4.

81. *BBL,* 245, 419–20.

82. Ibid., 245–7, *BBE,* 501–10.

83. *TFM,* 4.

84. The English translation appears in *BBE,* 9–24.

85. *TFM,* 5.

86. Sacher, "Begegnungen mit Béla Bartók," 16.

87. *BBE,* 381.

88. *TFM,* 5–6.

89. Ibid., 6.

90. A. Adnan Saygun, "Bartók in Turkey," 8–9. See also *TFM,* 6.

91. *TFM,* 7.

92. Ujfalussy, *Bartók,* 327.

93. *BBE,* 289.

94. Ibid., 298.

95. Suchoff, *Béla Bartók and a Guide to the Mikrokosmos* (1957), 94–5.

96. Gillies, *Bartók in Britain*, 108.

97. Kenneson, *Székely and Bartók*, 158–9.

98. Sacher, "Begegnungen mit Béla Bartók," 17. The Basel musicians had scheduled their Jubilee Concert for 16 January 1936 (see *BBE*, 417).

99. Demény, "Bartók Béla pályája delelőjén," 592–604.

100. Kenneson, *Székely and Bartók*, 178–80, 183–4, 387–94.

101. *TFM*, 8.

102. Sacher, "Begegnungen mit Béla Bartók," 17. Sacher thereafter informed Bartók (ibid.) that "a quartet for 2 Pianos and Percussion would be of special interest."

103. *BBL*, 259–61.

104. Kenneson, *Székely and Bartók*, 185–6.

105. Sacher, "Begegnungen mit Béla Bartók," 17. In fact, Bartók and his wife played the piano parts during Székely's visit (see n. 104).

106. *BBL*, 262.

107. Ujfalussy, *Bartók*, 338. The author adds that: "But all his attempts to show that the ban had no political implications were in vain. The excuse might well have had some validity, but everyone was perfectly aware of the greater truth that lay behind the decision [his feelings about the fascist countries, especially Hitler's Germany]."

108. Pamlényi, ed. *A History of Hungary*, 493–4.

109. Kenneson, *Székely and Bartók*, 178.

110. *BBL*, 264, 425.

111. Kenneson, *Székely and Bartók*, 187.

112. Ralph Hawkes, "Béla Bartók: A Recollection by His Publisher," 14, 16..

113. *BBL*, 267–9.

114. The related correspondence is published in Demény, ed. *Bartók Béla levelei* (1976), 587–91.

115. Suchoff, Béla *Bartók and a Guide to the Mikrokosmos* (1957), 75.

116. Gillies, *Bartók in Britain*, 110.

117. Čížik, ed. *Bartóks Breife in die Slowakei*, 225.

118. Demény, ed. *Bartók Béla levelei* (1955), 320–1.

119. Todd Crow, ed. *Bartók Studies*, 130.

120. Kenneson, *Székely and Bartók*, 191.

121. See Pamlényi, ed. *A History of Hungary*, 497, and Hoensch, *A Modern History of Hungary*, 141–2.

122. *BBL,* 273.

123. Ibid., 275.

124. Suchoff, "Bartók's Odyssey in Slovak Folk Music," in *Bartók Perspectives,* 26.

125. Demény, "Bartók Béla pályája delelőjén," 689–709.

126. Kenneson, *Székely and Bartók,* 208–9.

127. Ibid., 211.

128. Sacher, "Begegnungen mit Béla Bartók," 18.

129. *BBE,* 278.

130. Suchoff, "Structure and Concept in Bartók's Sixth String Quartet," 5–9.

131. Ibid., 10.

132. Suchoff, "A History of Béla Bartók's *Mikrokosmos,*" 190.

133. Suchoff, "Structure and Concept in Bartók's Sixth String Quartet," 10.

134. Bartók, Jr., *Apám életének krónikája,* 416–8.

135. *BBL,* 281.

136. Ibid., 280.

137. Ibid., 282.

138. *New York Sun,* 13 April 1940.

139. *Chicago Daily News,* 20 April 1940.

140. *BBE,* 186.

141. Suchoff, "Bartók and Serbo-Croatian Folk Music," 568.

142. Letter from CBS Records to the author, dated 12 March 1968.

143. Letter dated 1 April 1940.

144. Letter dated 3 May 1940.

145. Suchoff, "Bartók and Serbo-Croatian Folk Music," 569.

146. *BBL,* 282–3.

147. *RFM.*i, xviii. The trust was later terminated at Bartók's request.

148. Letter to the university president, Nicholas Murray Butler. On 11 June, his staff indicated it was unlikely that any income from the Ditson Fund would be available during 1940-1941 academic year.

149. *BBL,* 283–4.

150. *RFM.*i, 2. See the listed collections in Victor Bator, *The Béla Bartók Archives History and Catalogue,* 32–3. The remaining materials were stored in the home of his

elder son.

151. Letter to Ralph Hawkes, dated 5 September 1940.

152. Demény, ed. *Bartók Béla levelei* (1976), 651. The funds were provided by Sacher, and Stefi Geyer stayed with the Bartóks in Geneva until their departure. Bartók's elder son, an engineer, remained in Hungary. Péter, at that time still a student, subsequently followed his parents to the United States.

153. See *BBL,* Bartók, Jr., *Apám életének krónikája,* 426.

154, Lesznai, *Bartók,* 159.

155. Péter Ruffy, "The Dispute over Bartók's Will." Reprinted from the *New Hungarian Quarterly* 7, no. 22 (Summer 1988: 204–9) in Crow, *Bartók Studies,* 144, 146. In 1943, Bartók signed a second will in New York and set aside the Hungarian will he had made in Hungary.

156. *BBL,* 284. Letter to Mrs. Annie Müller Widmann, mailed in Geneva on 14 October 1940.

157. *BBL,* 290. The Bartóks were temporarily registered at the Buckingham Hotel in Manhattan.

158. Letter from Boosey & Hawkes to Bartók, dated 26 November 1940. See the list in Tibor Tallián, *Bartók fogadtatása Amerikában 1940–1945* (Bartók's reception in America 1940–1945), 57–9. One lacuna is the CBS Radio broadcast of the Sonata for Two Pianos and Percussion on 10 November.

159. Suchoff, "Bartók in America," 123.

160. *BBL,* 293.

161. *BBE,* 426.

162 *BBL,* 292.

163. Douglas Moore, "Bartók at Columbia University," 16.

164. *BBE,* 348–51. About fifty Barnard College and Columbia students attended.

165. *LMBB,* 94.

166. *BBE,* 151.

167. *BBL,* 302.

168. Ibid., 303–4.

169. The circumstances concerning the change of residence are narrated in Agnes Fassett [nee Agota Illés], *The Naked Face of Genius: Bartók's American Years,* chap. 5.

170. *BBL,* 306.

171. Milman Parry, coll. *Serbocroatian Heroic Songs,* 437. The *gusle* is a one-stringed instrument played with a bow, and the place name Temišvar refers to Temesvár, the former Hungarian region in western Transylvania, now Romanian Timişoara. Other than

musical values, the references to Hungarian events may have influenced Bartók's decision to transcribe both epics. A facsimile of the unpublished transcription appears in Stephen Erdely, "Bartók on Southslavic Epic Song," in *Bartók Perspectives*, 33–9.

172. Hawkes, "Bela Bartók," 17.

173. *BBL,* 306–7.

174. *RFM*.i, 2; *RFM*.ii, ix–x, xxx. This material had been autographed in Budapest and subsequently sent to London for transshipment to New York. See also Fassett, *The Naked Face of Genius,* 120–1.

175. *BBL,* 318.

176. Erdely, "Bartók on Southslavic Epic Song," in *Bartók Perspectives.*

177. *BBL,* 320.

178. Ibid., 321.

179. Ibid., 324. The letter is dated 31 December 1942. Bartók was not informed that the official medical finding was "atypical mycloid leukaemia." See Bartók, Jr., "Béla Bartók's Diseases," 438.

180. *BBE,* 29–31. The essay has appeared in a substantial number of international publications, beginning in 1944.

181. *YFM*.i., xxv.

182. Ibid.

183. *BBL,* 324–5.

184. Fassett, *The Naked Face of Genius;* 261–2.

185. *BBCO,* 114.

186. *BBE,* 392.

187. Ibid., 185–6. This supposition is supported by the fact that additional music examples were on hand in his classified collection of melodies from Bulgarian folk music publications, whose shipment arrived in New York in 1941.

188. Joseph Szigeti, *With Strings Attached,* 271.

189. Balogh, "Bartók in America," 21–2.

190. Ibid. Balogh, a noted pianist and former pupil of Bartók, became an intimate friend of the Bartóks after their arrival in New York. ASCAP is the acronym for the American Society of Composers, Authors and Publishers.

191. Victor Bator (1891–1967), a Hungarian-born banker and graduate of the University of Budapest law school, was an acquaintance of Bartók since 1919 and a voluntary exile in the United States beginning in 1939. After Bartók sought his assistance with regard to immigration and other matters, which Bator provided without fee, the latter was treated as a friend of the family and entrusted with the safekeeping of Bartók's manuscripts. In fact, on 28 March Bartók signed a new will which set up his estate as a

trust and designated Bator and Dr. Gyula Baron as joint executors and trustees. See also the Bator obituary in the *New York Times*, 13 December 1967.

192. Suchoff, "Bartók in America," 123.

193. *BBL,* 326. Letter to Szigeti, dated 23 May 1943.

194. *RFM*.i, xviii. Bartók was quite agitated about Schirmer's refusal to use the unfolded sheets of music—he had paid $1,200 for their production— which in his opinion were indeed suitable.

195. *BBL,* 326–7.

196. *LMBB,* 98.

197. *TFM,* 13.

198. Suchoff, "Notes on the Music," 6.

199. Ibid. It is also noteworthy that Bartók describes the *Elegia* as "the lugubrious death song."

200. *RFM*.iii, 1x. The letter cites wartime paper shortages and the current lack of a qualified editor.

201. *TFM,* 14.

202. Yehudi Menuhin, *Unfinished Journey,* 164–5.

203. *BBL,* 328. He was scheduled to resume his lectures at Harvard University during that month.

204. *TFM,* 14.

205. *LMBB,* 101.

206. Demény, ed. *Bartók Béla levelei* (1976), 699. This statement represents a peculiar lapse. Bartók had undergone a traumatic experience with Oxford University Press in the 1930s, resulting from the unsatisfactory translations of the classified *colinde* texts (see p. 123).

207. Bartók, Jr., *Apám életének krónikája,* 456. Apparently he made jottings of the birdsongs which were later transformed as "Night's music" elements in the second movement of the Third Piano Concerto.

208. *BBE,* 394–5.

209. *BBL,* 334.

210. *New York Times,* 27 November 1944.

211. *BBL,* 342.

212. *Boston Herald,* 2 December 1944.

213. *BBL,* 344. Letter dated Christmas day 1944.

214. *New York Times,* 11 January 1945.

215. *New York Times,* 28 April 1945.

216. *BBCO,* 116–7.

217. *BBL,* 346–7, 439.

218. *YFM.*i, xxvi. Bartók was dissatisfied with the quality of his collaborator's contributions.

219. Bartók, Jr., *Apám eletének krónikája,* 463.

220. *LMBB,* 105.

221. Ditta Bartók, "26. SEPTEMBER 1945. Zum 20. Todestag von Béla Bartók," 449.

PART TWO

Folk Music Research

Chapter 6: Hungarian Folk Music

1. *BBE,* 156.

2. Paavö Helistö, "Zoltán Kodály und Ilmari Krohn," 47–8. Krohn's collection was published in 1904 by the Finnish Literary Society.

3. Ilmari Krohn, "Welche ist die beste Methode, um Volks- und volksmässige Lieder nach ihrer melodischen Beschaffenheit lexikalisch zu ordnen?" (Which is the best method to put in order folk- and folk-related songs by their melodic nature from a lexicographic standpoint?), 1 ff. See also *BBE,* 156–7 and *HFS,* 6.

4. *HFS,* xxxiv.

5. *BBSE,* 27.

6. *Erdélyi magyar népdalok,* completed in 1921 and published in Budapest by the Popular Literary Society. The work is reprinted without the indices in *BBSE* (chap. 4).

7. See the editorially constructed Appendix Three (Tabulation of Material) in *HFS,* 339–60.

8. Suchoff, "The Bartók-Kodály Connection," 155–6.

9. Cf. *HFS,* 16–9.

10. Ibid., 38.

11. *BBE,* 95.

12. *HFS,* 52

13. *BBE,* 93.

14. *HFS*, xli. During 1938 or 1939, Bartók revised the classification as shown in pp. xlii–xliii and Figure 6 (liii). See also the editorial presentation in Bartók, *Hungarian Folk Songs. Complete Collection*. ed. Sándor Kovács and Ferenc Sebő (Budapest: Akadémiai Kiadó, 1993), 26–31.

15. *HFS*, 212.

16. *BBE*, 409.

17. Ibid., 410.

18. *BBCO*, 129.

19. *BBE*, 384.

Chapter 7: Slovak Folk Music

1. See p. 52.

2. This enumeration results from my preparation of a facsimile edition of Bartók's Slovak material in 1981–1982. See my essay, "Bartók's Odyssey in Slovak Folk Music," in *Bartók Perspectives*, 27n. 26.

3. *BBSE*, 243.

4. Group a) isometric melodies are published in *SV.*i. The types are further sorted as described and illustrated in *BBSE*, 241–2.

5. Group b) heterometric melodies are published in *SV.*ii.

6. That is, in terms of the letters "z" and "Z" to indicate the proportion of lesser (z) and greater (Z) number of syllables in the stanza. Thus, $z\,z\,Z\,Z$ may represent $6,6,8,8$, or $6,6,9,9$, or $7,7,11,11$, syllabic structure, and so forth. Double-line stanzas, such as $Z\,Z\,z+z$ Z, may represent quaternaries with $6,6,4+4,4$, syllabic structure, and so forth. See *BBSE*, 245–7.

7. The treatment of Subclass *A*. II conforms to that of Subclass *A*. I., with the exception that Type α) *parlando-rubato* rhythm does not occur. It should be noted that the melodies of Subclass II, II, and of Class *B, C, D*, and *E*, intended by Bartók as *SV.*iii, have not been published as of the present writing, and that the first two volumes were posthumous publications that appeared in 1959 and 1970, respectively. For further details, see the current index entries for *Matica Slovenská* and my essay, "Bartók's Odyssey in Slovak Folk Music," in *Bartók Perspectives*, 15–6.

8. This subclass is further ordered as described in *BBSE*, 247.

9. Class *A* and Class *B* are further ordered as described in *BBSE*, 247.

10. Class *D* melodies are generally ordered according to ambitus only.

11. Class *E* melodies are arranged according to type of instrument, type of dance, and collectors. See *BBSE*, 250–3.

12. See *SV.*i, nos. 16a–z, and *BBSE*, 178, 256–8.

13. *BBE,* 130.

14. Ibid., 132.

15. Suchoff, "The Ethnomusicological Roots of Bartók's Musical Language," 51. See also *BBSE,* 263.

16. Slovak variants of Hungarian Class *B* (New Style) melodies are listed in *HFS,* 324–5 (Appendix II, nos. 75–151b).

Chapter 8: Romanian Folk Music

1. Current English literary practice uses "Romanian" rather than Bartók's "Rumanian" as the appellative. The Hungarian orthography, "román," is denominated in English as "R(o)umanian" (n.b.: Fr., "roumain"; Ger., "rumänische").

2. *RFM.*i, xxv–xxvi.

3. The excluded melodies and the translated preface and notes appear in *BBSE,* 1–23.

4. The treatise appears in English translation in *BBE,* 103–14.

5. *RFM.*v, xv.

6. *RFM.*iv, vii. This paragraph, probably written during the first half of 1942, appears in a discarded draft of Bartók's preface to *RFM.*i.

7. *RFM.*iv, 7.

8. This subclass corresponds to Class *A* in *RFM.*ii.

9. This subclass corresponds to Class *B* in *RFM.*ii.

10. This subclass corresponds to Class *G* in *RFM.*ii.

11. This group corresponds to Class *F* in *RFM.*ii.

12. *RFM.*i, 41–2.

13. Ibid., 42–3.

14. Ibid., note 88.

15. The tempo is M.M. $\eighthnote$ = 552.

16. *RFM.*i, 49–50.

17. *BBCO,* 76–80.

18. The tenth class, consisting of the *Colinde* (that is, Winter-solstice songs), is classified in *RFM.*iv.

19. *RFM.*ii, 37.

20. In Table 6 of *RFM.*ii, however, three sizes of Z are used in *B* II 4, *Z Z z + z Z,* to represent the heterometric structure of *12, 12, 6 + 6, 11,* syllables in melody no. 438a.

21. *RFM*.iii, xxix, xxlii.

22. That is, Indecent Texts, for the most part belonging to the category of so-called dance-words. See *RFM*.iii, xciv.

23. *RFM*.iii, xlviii.

24. Ibid., xlix–liv.

25. Ibid., cii–ciii, cvi.

26. See *RFM*.v, Class *A* melodies (nos. 1–19).

27. Tiberiu Alexandru, *Béla Bartók despre folclorul rominesc* (Béla Bartók about Romanian folklore), 44.

28. *RFM*.iv, 25, 28–9.

29. Class *A* and Class *B* melodies are without text stanza structure.

30. For practical reasons, the notated rhythm patterns in *RFM*.iv, Table 1, are not included here. The patterns are ordered from simpler to more complex, are marked with punctulated arabic numbers (1. to 5.), and serve as a further means of classifying the melodies.

31. *RFM*.iv, Table 2 and Table 3.

32. *RFM*.iv, 24–32.

33. *RFM*.iv, 199–200.

34. Ritual ploughing songs.

35. See *RFM*.iv, 202, and Index of Refrains.

36. *RFM*.iv, 217 (Translator's Note).

37. *BBE*, 121.

38. Ibid., 120.

39. See *RFM*.iv, 253–7.

40. The Torontal material, consisting of 229 vocal and 156 instrumental melodies, was classified but not prepared for publication purposes. See *RFM*.v, xv.

41. *RFM*.v, 195.

42. Bartók excluded variant melodies from this tabulation.

43. *RFM*.v, 9–10.

44. Ibid., 11. The *dumy* is a kind of improvisational epic song of irregular rhythm, sung by women (see *Grove 5* [1954], 3: 345).

45. *BBCO*, 171, and exx. 9.1, 9.8.

Chapter 9: Arab Folk Music from the Biskra District

1. Béla Balázs, "Az oszthatatlan ember" (The indivisible man: A reminiscence of Bartók), 957–8.

2. *BBL*, 119–20.

3. Márta Ziegler, "Bartóks Reise nach Biskra," in Dille, ed., *Documenta Bartókiana* 2 (1965): 9–11.

4. *BBL*, 122–3.

5. *BBSE*, 29–31.

6. The tabulated classification of the dance melodies will be found in *BBSE*, 35–7.

7. *BBE*, 338, 350.

8. Ibid., 396.

9. Cf. the source melody in *BBSE*, 52.

Chapter 10: Ruthenian Folk Melody

1. Victor Bator, *The Béla Bartók Archives: History and Catalogue*, 33. The unpublished collection is in *PBA*, Envelope no. 105b.

2. *BBSE*, 187.

3. See *HFS*, melody nos. 301–4.

4. *BBSE*, 187–8.

5. *RFM*.i, 49–50.

6. Cf. Ex. 10.3 and *HFS*, melody no. 303a.

7. *BBSE*, 189.

8. Ibid.

9. *BBCO*, 14–5.

10. Ibid., 80.

Chapter 11: Yugoslav Folk Music

1. The Hungarian town—Bartók's birthplace—had Romanian, Serbian, and Swabian ethnic groups.

2. Unlike the Romanian double refrains which alternate in melody stanza pairs, the Serbo-Croatian type occurs always in the same melody stanza. In addition, the Serbo-Croatian refrains may contain Turkish words (invariably unintelligible to the singer); the Romanian refrains do not. See *RFM*.iii, lxxix–lxxx.

3. Melody no. 94c in *RFM*.ii. See also p. 22 for Bartók's discussion of Class *B* (*tempo*

giusto) melodies.

4. Nos. 601–3 in Kuhač, *Južno-slovenske narodne popievke* (Yugoslav folk songs).

5. *BBE,* 155, 158.

6. Ibid., 159.

7. Ibid., 411.

8. *BBL,* 154.

9. See Bartók's description of published and unpublished source materials in *YFM*.i, 22–7.

10. *RFM*.iv, 30.

11. János Demény, ed. *Bartók Béla levelei* (1955), 164. The description of the scales appears in music notation.

12. Vinko Žganec, *Hrvatske pucke popijevke is Medumurje* (Croatian folk songs from the Mur island). This triangle of land (Muraköz in Hungary), about 795 sq. km. in area, is situated between the Mur River, the Drave River, and the old Austrian frontier.

13. See *BBE,* 545–6 for bibliographic details and *BBSE,* 174–240, for the English translation.

14. *BBSE,* 199.

15. *BBL,* 229–33.

16. Ibid., 236.

17. Dille, ed., *Documenta Bartókiana* 3 (1968): 171.

18. Ibid., 178–9.

19. Ibid., 222. Kuba was then more than seventy-five years old. Bartók's regard for this material is evident by the fact that he brought it with him when he emigrated to the United States in 1940.

20. *BBL,* 239. It seems reasonable to conjecture that Bartók was subtly attempting to suggest that Žganec—a lawyer in the city of Zombor (formerly Hungarian territory)—might be able to arrange for a subsidy or at least official permission for Bartók to undertake fieldwork in Yugoslavia.

21. Dille, ed., *Documenta Bartókiana* 3 (1968): 191–2.

22. *BBE,* 146.

23. See chapter 5 for the discussion of this crucial period in Bartók's life. See also Stephen Erdely, "Bartók on Southslavic Epic Song," in *Bartók Perspectives,* 28–31; and *BBE,* 148–51.

24. See *YFM*.i, xxii–iii, letter to Professor Douglas Moore, Columbia University. See also *PBA* correspondence files.

25. The following discussion represents abridgments of the subject matter in *YFM*.i, 3–20.

26. Another example is strict rhythm, called *tempo giusto.*

27. *YFM*.i, 20.

28. Parry collected approximately 205 women's songs. Of these, about sixty had been made by Samuel Bayard of Pennsylvania State University but were not available to Bartók for comparative purposes. The remainder were sung by an unreliable performer, chanted, or otherwise unsuitable for transcription purposes. See *YFM*.i, xxvi–ii, 255.

29. The tabulation appears in *YFM*.ii.

30. *YFM*.i, 61–2. The quoted F-G-A♭-B♭-C♭ pitch collection is a pentachord of the octatonic scale.

31. Ibid., 72.

32. Ibid., 87.

33. Suchoff, *Guide to Bartók's Mikrokosmos*, 38.

34. See further details in *YFM*.ii, xv–xviii.

Chapter 12: Bulgarian Folk Music

1. *BBE,* 44–5.

2. *BBL,* 237. The 1927, 1938, and 1931 Stoin editions are listed in the bibliography. Other collections are mentioned in *RFM*.ii, 52–3.

3. *BBE,* 44.

4. Bator, *The Béla Bartók Archives: History and Catalogue*, 32.

5. *BBE,* 46.

6. *YFM*.i, 86.

7. Ibid., 43–4. See also *RFM*.iv, 31–2.

Chapter 13: Turkish Folk Music from Asia Minor

1. See chap. 5, 125–9, 151–5.

2. *TFM,* 30.

3. A. Adnan Saygun, "Bartók in Turkey," 7.

4. *BBE,* 139–40. Bartók's essay includes his transcription of the melody and the notation of the corresponding Hungarian variant.

5. János Demény, ed. *Bartók Béla levelei* (1976), 542.

6. Saygun served as interpreter, and he also notated the folk texts on the spot.

7. Demény, ed. *Bartók Béla levelei* (1976), 553–5.

8. *TFM,* 36–7.

9. Ibid., 211–2.

10. Suchoff, "Ethnomusicological Roots of Béla Bartók's Musical Language," 60–1. The quotation can be found in *BBE,* 141.

Epilogue

1. Zoltán Kodály, "Béla Bartók the Man." In Ferenc Bónis, ed. *The Selected Writings of Zoltán Kodály,* 97–101.

2. Arthur S. Reber. *The Penguin Dictionary of Psychology,* 2d ed. London: Penguin Books (1995): 121, 156–7.

3. H. W. Heinsheimer, "Béla Bartók: A Personal Memoir," 30.

4. Reber, *The Penguin Dictionary of Psychology,* 156. He states that there is little or no evidence to support Kretschmer's claims.

5. Kodály, "Béla Bartók the Man," 97–8. See also the essays by the Hungarian psychologist Bertalan Pethő, "Béla Bartók's Personality," *Studia Musicologica* 23 (1981): 443–58, and "The Meaning of Bartók's Secret Path," *Studia Musicologica* 24 (1982): 465–73.

6. Ibid., 100.

7. Serge Moreux, *Béla Bartók,* 92.

8. Zoltán Kodály, "Béla Bartók," In Ferenc Bónis, ed. *The Selected Writings of Zoltán Kodály,* 90.

9. *Mosco Carner,* "Béla Bartók," 299.

Select Bibliography

Alexandru, Tiberiu. *Béla Bartók despre folclorul romînesc* (Béla Bartók about Romanian folklore). Bucharest: Editura Muzicală, 1958.

Antokoletz, Elliott. *The Music of Béla Bartók: A Study of Tonality and Progression in Twentieth-Century Music.* Berkeley and Los Angeles: University of California Press, 1984.

————. "Bartók's *Bluebeard*: The Sources of Its 'Modernism.'" *College Music Symposium* 30, no.1 (Spring 1998): 75–95.

————. *Twentieth-Century Music.* Englewood Cliffs, N.J.: Prentice Hall, Inc. 1992.

————. "'At last something truly new': Bagatelles," "Concerto for Orchestra," and "Middle-period String Quartets." In *The Bartók Companion*, ed. Malcolm Gillies. London: Faber & Faber, 1993, 110–23, 257–77, 526–37.

————. *Béla Bartók: A Guide to Research, Second Edition.* New York: Garland Publishing, 1997.

————. "Perspectives in Bartók Research," "Modal Transformation and Musical Symbolism in Bartók's *Cantata Profana,*" and "Organic Expansion and Classical Structure in Bartók's Sonata for Two Pianos and Percussion." In *Bartók Perspectives,* ed. Elliott Antokoletz, Victoria Fischer, and Benjamin Suchoff. New York: Oxford University Press, 2000, 1–11, 61–76, 77–94.

Antokoletz, Elliott, Victoria Fischer, and Benjamin Suchoff, eds. *Bartók Perspectives.* New York: Oxford University Press, 2000.

Austin, William. "Bartók's Concerto for Orchestra." *The Music Review* 18, no.1 (February 1957): 21–47.

Balázs, Béla. "Az oszthathatlan ember" (The indivisible man). *Forum* (December 1948): 956–65.

Balogh, Ernő. "Bartók in America." *The Long Player* 2, no. 10 (October 1953): 18–23.

Bartók, Béla. "Székely balladák" (Székely Ballads). *Ethnographia* 19, nos. 1–2 (January–March 1908): 43–52, 105–15.

————. *Chansons populaires roumaines du département Bihar (Hongrie).* Bucharest: Academia Română,1913. See the reprint in *Bartók Béla: Ethnomusikologische Schriften, Faksimile-Nachdrucke* 3, ed. Denijs Dille. Budapest: Editio Musica, 1967. See also *Béla Bartók Studies in Ethnomusicology,* 1–23.

————."Dunántuli balladák" (Transdanubian Ballads). *Ethnographia* 20, no. 5 (October 1909): 301–5.

————. "Der Musikdialekt der Rumänen von Hunyad." *Zeitschrift für Musikwissenschaft* 2, no. 6 (March 1920): 352–60. See also *Béla Bartók Essays*, 103–14.

————. "Ungarische Bauernmusik." *Musikblätter des Anbruch* 2, nos. 1–2 (June 1920). See also *Béla Bartók Essays*, no. 304–15.

————. "Die Volksmusik der Araber von Biskra und Umgebung." *Zeitschrift für Musikwissenschaft* 9 (November 1920): 489–522. See also *Béla Bartók Studies in Ethnomusicology*, 29–76.

————. "La musique populaire hongroise." *La Revue Musicale* 11, no. 1 (November 1921). See also *Béla Bartók Essays*, 58–70.

————. "Musique paysanne serbe (No. 1–21) et bulgare (No. 22–8) du Banat: Budapest, 1935." In *Documenta Bartókiana* 4, ed. Denijs Dille. Budapest: Akadémiai Kiadó, 1970: 221–44. Nos. 1–21 are reprinted in *YFM*.i, 453–71.

————. "La musique populaires des hongrois et des peuples voisins." Ed. Béla Bartók. Offprint (1937) published by *Archivum Europae Centro Orientalis* 2, nos. 3–4 (Budapest, 1936): 197–232. See also *Béla Bartók Studies in Ethnomusicology*, 174–240.

————. "Réponse à une attaque roumaine." Ed. Béla Bartók. Offprint (1937) from *Archivum Europae Centro Orientalis* 2, nos. 3–4 (Budapest, 1936): 233–44. See also *Béla Bartók Essays*, 227–36.

————. "Debussyről" (About Debussy). In *Bartók Béla válagatott irásai* (Béla Bartók selected writings). Collected and arranged by András Szőllősy. Budapest: Művelt Nép Tudományos, 1956, 342–3.

————. *Slowakische Volkslieder*. Ed. Alica Elscheková, Oskár Elschek, and Jozef Kresánek. Bratislava: Academia Scientiarum Slovaca, vol. I, 1959; vol. II, 1971; vol. III, unpublished. See also *Bartók Perspectives*. Ed. Elliott Antokoletz, Victoria Fischer, and Benjamin Suchoff. New York: Oxford University Press, 2000, 15–27.

————. *Rumanian Folk Music*. Ed. Benjamin Suchoff, trans. E. C. Teodorescu et al. Foreword by Victor Bator. The Hague: Martinus Nijhoff, 1975. 5 vols. The five volumes appear as vols. 2–6 of the New York Bartók Archive Studies in Musicology series, ed. Benjamin Suchoff: 2) I. Instrumental Music (1967); 3) II. Vocal Melodies (1967); 4) Texts (1967); 5) Carols and Christmas Songs (*Colinde*) (1975); 6) Maramureş County (1975).

————. *Turkish Folk Music from Asia Minor*. Ed. Benjamin Suchoff. Princeton and London: The Princeton University Press, 1976. Appears as vol. 7 of the New York Bartók Archive Studies in Musicology series, ed. Benjamin Suchoff.

————. *Béla Bartók Essays*. Selected and edited by Benjamin Suchoff. London: Faber & Faber Ltd.; New York: St. Martin's Press, 1976. Reprint. Lincoln and London: University of Nebraska Press, 1992. Appears as vol. 8 of the New York Bartók Archive Studies in Musicology series, ed. Benjamin Suchoff.

————. *Yugoslav Folk Music*. Ed. Benjamin Suchoff. Albany: State University of New York Press, 1978. 4 vols. The four volumes appear as vols. 9–12 of the New York Bartók Archive Studies in Musicology series, ed. Benjamin Suchoff: 9) I. Serbo-Croatian Folk Songs (with Albert B. Lord); 10) II. Tabulation of Material; 11) III. Source Melodies: Part One; 12) IV. Source Melodies: Part Two.

———. *Briefe an Stefi Geyer, 1907–1908.* Ed. Lajos Nyikos. With a foreword by Paul Sacher. Basel: Paul Sacher Stiftung, 1979.

———. *The Hungarian Folk Song.* Ed. Benjamin Suchoff, trans. M. D. Calvocoressi, with annotations by Zoltán Kodály. Albany: State University of New York Press, 1981. Appears as vol. 13 of the New York Bartók Archive Studies in Musicology series, ed. Benjamin Suchoff.

———. *Piano Music of Béla Bartók.* The Archive Edition, ed. Benjamin Suchoff. New York: Dover Publications, Inc., 1981. Series I appears as vol. 14, Series II as vol. 15 of the New York Bartók Archive Studies in Musicology series, ed. Benjamin Suchoff.

———. *XVII and XVIII Century Italian Cembalo and Organ Music Transcribed for Piano.* Ed. László Somfai. New York: Carl Fischer, Inc., 1990.

———. *Hungarian Folk Songs. Complete Collection.* Ed. Sándor Kovács and Ferenc Sebő. Budapest: Akadémiai Kiadó, 1993.

———. *Studies in Ethnomusicology.* Ed. Benjamin Suchoff. Lincoln and London: University of Nebraska Press, 1997.

Bartók, Béla and Zoltán Kodály. *Magyar népdalok* (Hungarian folk songs for voice and piano). With an introduction prepared by Kodály for joint signature. Budapest: Rozsnyai Károly, 1906. See also *The Selected Writings of Zoltán Kodály*, ed. Ferenc Bónis, 9–10.

———. *Transylvanian Hungarians: Folk Songs* (English edition). Budapest: The Popular Literary Society, 1923.

———. *Hungarian Folksongs for Voice and Piano.* Facsimile of the original 1906 manuscript. With commentaries by Denijs Dille. Trans. Nancy Bush and Ilona L. Lukács. Budapest: Editio Musica, 1970.

Bartók, Béla, Jr. "Remembering My Father, Béla Bartók." *The New Hungarian Quarterly* 7, no. 22 (Summer 1966): 201–3.

———. *Apám eletének krónikája* (Chronicles of my father's life). Ed. Adrienne Konkoly Gomboczné. Budapest: Zeneműkiadó, 1981.

———. *Bartók Béla családi levelei,* (Béla Bartók's family letters. Ed. Adrienne Konkoly Gombocz. Budapest: Zeneműkiadó, 1981.

———. "Béla Bartók's Diseases." *Studia Musicologica* 23 (1981): 427–41.

———. *Bartók Béla műhelyében* (In Béla Bartók's workshop). Budapest: Szépirodalmi Könyvkiadó, 1982.

Bartók, Ditta. "26 September 1945 zum 20 Todestag von Béla Bartók." *Österreichische Musikzeitschrift* 20, no. 9 (September 1965): 445–9.

Bartók, Peter. "Correcting Printed Editions of Béla Bartók's Viola Concerto and Other Compositions." In *Bartók Perspectives.* Ed. Elliott Antokoletz, Victoria Fischer, and Benjamin Suchoff. New York: Oxford University Press, 2000, 243–59.

Bator, Victor. *The Béla Bartók Archives: History and Catalogue.* New York: Bartók Archives Publication, 1963. Cataloging preparation (pp. 22–39) by Benjamin Suchoff.

Béla Bartók: A Memorial Review. New York: Boosey & Hawkes, 1950.

Becker, Harry Cassin. "Béla Bartók and His Credo." *Musical America* (17 December 1927): 7, 35.

Berger, Arthur. "Problems of Pitch Organization in Stravinsky." *Perspectives of New Music* 2 (Fall–Winter 1963): 11–42.

Bónis, Ferenc. "Quotations in Bartók's Music: A Contribution to Bartók's Psychology of Composition." *Studia Musicologica* 5 (1963): 355–82.

———. *Béla Bartók. His Life in Pictures and Documents.* Trans. Lili Halápy, trans. rev. Kenneth McRobbie. Budapest: Corvina Press, 1972.

———, ed. *The Selected Writings of Zoltán Kodály.* Trans. Lili Halápy and Fred Macnicol. London: Boosey & Hawkes Music Publishers Ltd., 1974.

Botstein, Leon. "Out of Hungary: Bartók, Modernism, and the Cultural Politics of Twentieth-Century Music." In *Bartók and His World,* ed. Peter Laki. Princeton: Princeton University Press, 1995, 3–63.

Bukoreschliev, A., Vasil Stoin, and Raina Katzarova. *Rodopski pesni* (Rhodope [mountains] songs). Sofia, 1934.

Carner, Mosco. "Béla Bartók." In *The Modern Age 1890–1960,* ed. Martin Cooper. Vol. 10 of the *New Oxford History of Music.* London: Oxford University Press, 1974.

Čížik, Vladimír, ed. *Bartóks Breife in die Slowakei.* Bratislava: Slowakischen Nationalmuseum, 1971.

Crawford, Dorothy L. "Love and Anguish: Bartók's Expressionism." In *Bartók Perspectives,* ed. Elliott Antokoletz, Victoria Fischer, and Benjamin Suchoff. (New York: Oxford University Press, 2000, 129–39.

Crawford, John C., and Dorothy L. *Expressionism in Twentieth-Century Music.* Bloomington: Indiana University Press, 1993.

Crow, Todd, comp. and ed. *Bartók Studies.* Detroit: Information Coordinators, 1976.

Cseke, Péter. "Aki Bartóknak énekelt" (Who sang to Bartók). In *Bartók-könyv* (Bartók-book), ed. Ferenc László, Bucharest: Kriterion, 1971, 89–92.

Csobádi, Peter. "Béla Bartók und das Ungarn seiner Zeit." In *Béla Bartók Zu Leben und Werk.* Bonn: Boosey & Hawkes, 1982, 9–23.

Dellamaggiore, Nelson. "Deciphering Béla Bartók's Viola Concerto Sketch." In *Bartók Perspectives,* ed. Elliott Antokoletz, Victoria Fischer, and Benjamin Suchoff. New York: Oxford University Press, 2000, 260–70.

Demény, János, ed. *Bartók Béla levelei* (Béla Bartók's letters). Budapest: Művelt Nép Könyvkiadó, 1951.

———. "Bartók Béla tanulóévei és romantikus korszaka" (Béla Bartók's student years and romantic period). In *Erkel Ferenc és Bartók Béla emlékére* [*Zenetudományi tanulmányok,* 2], ed. Bence Szabolcsi and Dénes Bartha. Budapest: Akadémiai Kiadó, 1954: 323–487.

————."Bartók Béla művészi kibontakozásának évei (1906–14) (Béla Bartók's years of artistic development). In *Liszt Ferenc és Bartók Béla emlékére* [*Zenetudományi tanulmányok,* 3], ed. Bence Szabolcsi and Dénes Bartha. Budapest: Akadémiai Kiadó, 1955: 286–447.

————, ed. *Bartók Béla levelei* (Béla Bartók's [Czechoslovak, Hungarian, and Romanian] letters). Budapest: Zeneműkiadó Vállalat, 1955.

————. "Bartók Béla művészi kibontakozásának évei. II. rész (1914–1926)" (Béla Bartók's years of artistic development, Part 2). In *Bartók Béla (1914–1926)/Liszt Ferenc hagyatéka* [*Zenetudományi tanulmányok,* 7], ed. Bence Szabolcsi and Dénes Bartha. Budapest: Akadémiai Kiadó, 1959: 7–425.

————. "Bartók Béla pályája delelőjén" (Béla Bartók at the height of his career: 1927–40). In *Bartók Béla emlékére* [*Zenetudományi tanulmányok,* 10], ed. Bence Szabolcsi and Dénes Bartha. Budapest: Akadémiai Kiadó, 1962: 189–727.

————, ed. *Béla Bartók Letters.* Trans. Péter Balabán, et al. New York: St. Martin's Press, 1971.

————. "Adatok Bartók szülővárosának művelődéstörténetéhez" (Data on the cultural history of Bartók's birthplace). In *Magyar zenetörténeti tanulmányok: Mosonyi Mihály és Bartók Béla emlékére,* ed. Ferenc Bónis. Budapest: Zeneműkiadó Vállalat, 1973: 213–24. See also the plate facing p. 209.

————. *Bartók Béla a zongoraművész* (Béla Bartók the pianist). Budapest: Zeneműkiadó Vállalat, 1973.

————, ed. *Bartók Béla levelei* (Béla Bartók's letters). Budapest: Zeneműkiadó, 1976.

————. Brochure notes to *Bartók Béla. Complete Edition* II. Piano Music (Four Piano Pieces, Rhapsody for Piano op. 1). Trans. Rosemarie Trockl. Budapest: Hungaroton LPX 1300.

Densmore, Frances. *Chippewa Music II.* Bulletin 53 of the Bureau of American Ethnology. Washington, D.C., 1913.

Dille, Denijs. [*Kossuth* program notes] *Documenta Bartókiana* 1. Mainz: B. Schott, 1964: 70–103, facsimiles 16–18.

————."Angaben zum Violinkonzert 1907, den Deux portraits, dem Quartett Op. 7 und den Zwei rumänishen Tänzen." *Documenta Bartókiana* 2, ed. Denijs Dille. Budapest: Akadémiai Kiadó, 1965: 91–102.

————. *Béla Bartók: Ethnomusikologische Schriften, Faksimile-Nachdrucke,* ed. Denijs Dille. 4 vols. Budapest: Editio Musica, 1965–1968.

————."Gerlice puszta: Mai bis November 1904." *Documenta Bartókiana* 4, ed. Denijs Dille. Budapest: Akadémiai Kiadó, 1970: 15–49.

————. *Thematische Verzeichnis der Jugendwerke Béla Bartóks 1890–1904.* Budapest: Akadémiai Kiadó, 1974.

————. *Genealogie sommaire de la famille Bartók.* Antwerp: Metropolis, 1977.

————. *Béla Bartók: Regard sur le passé.* Études bartókiennes 1, ed. Yves Lenoir. Louvain-la-neuve, Belgium: Institut supérieure d'archéologie et d'histoire de l'art, Collège Érasme, 1990.

Dobszay, László. *A History of Hungarian Music.* Trans. Mária Steiner, trans. rev. Paul Merrick. Budapest: Corvina, 1993.

Dorati, Antál. "Bartókiana (Some Recollections)." *Tempo* 136 (March 1981): 6–13.

Downey, John W. *La musique populaire dans l'oeuvre de Béla Bartók.* Preface by Jacques Chailley. Paris: L'institut de Musicologie de l'Université de Paris no. 5, 1966.

Drăgoi, Sabin V. *303 Colinde* (Christmas songs). Craiova, 1925.

Eősze, László. *Zoltán Kodály: His Life and Work.* Trans. István Farkas and Gyula Gulyás. London: Collett's Holdings, 1962.

———, ed. *Zoltán Kodály: His Life in Pictures.* Budapest and New York: Corvina Press and Belwin Mills, 1971.

Erdely, Stephen. *Methods and Principles of Hungarian Ethnomusicology.* Bloomington: Indiana University Press, 1965.

———. "Bartók on Southslavic Epic Song." In *Bartók Perspectives,* ed. Elliott Antokoletz, Victoria Fischer, and Benjamin Suchoff. New York: Oxford University Press, 2000, 28–40.

Erdélyi, János. *Magyar Népdalok és Mondák* (Hungarian folk songs and folk tales). Pest, 1846.

Fassett, Agatha. *The Naked Face of Genius; Béla Bartók's American Years.* Boston and New York; Houghton Mifflin Company; Cambridge: Riverside Press, 1958. Reprinted as *Béla Bartók–the American Years.* New York· Dover Publications, Inc., 1970.

Fischer, Victoria. "Bartók's Fourteen Bagatelles op 6, for Piano: Toward Performance Authenticity." In *Bartók Perspectives,* ed. Elliott Antokoletz, Victoria Fischer, and Benjamin Suchoff. New York: Oxford University Press, 2000, 273–86.

Frigyesi, Judit. *Béla Bartók and Hungarian Nationalism.* Ann Arbor, Mich.: UMI, 1989.

———. *Béla Bartók and Turn-of-the-Century Budapest.* Berkeley and Los Angeles: University of California Press, 1998.

———. 'The Verbunkos and Bartók's Modern Style." In *Bartók Perspectives,* ed. Elliott Antokoletz, Victoria Fischer, and Benjamin Suchoff. New York: Oxford University Press, 2000, 140–52.

Fuchss, Werner. *Béla Bartók en Suisse.* Trans. Laurent Jospin. Lausanne: Éditions Payot, 1975.

Gillies, Malcolm. *Bartók in Britain.* New York: Oxford University Press, 1989.

———. "Stylistic Integrity and Influence in Bartók's Works: The Case of Szymanowski." *International Journal of Musicology* 1 (1992): 139–60.

———, ed. *The Bartók Companion.* Ed. Malcolm Gillies. London: Faber & Faber Ltd. 1993; Portland, Oreg: Amadeus Press, 1994.

———. "Analyzing Bartók's Works of 1918–1922: Motives, Tone Patches, and Tonal Mosaics," and "The Canonization of Béla Bartók." In *Bartók Perspectives,* ed. Elliott Antokoletz, Victoria Fischer, and Benjamin Suchoff. New

York: Oxford University Press, 2000, 43–60, 289–302.

Glück, Jenő, and Éva Wetzler, "Bánsagi adatok a Bartók kutatáshoz" (Contribution to Bartók-research from the Banat). In *Bartók-könyv 1970–1971*, ed. Ference László. Bucharest: Kriterion, 1971, 81–5.

Griffiths, Paul. *Stravinsky*. New York: Schirmer Books, 1992.

Grout, Donald Jay. *A Short History of Opera*. New York: Columbia University Press, 1947.

———. *A History of Western Music*. New York: W.W. Norton, 1960.

Hamburger, Klára. *Liszt*. Budapest: Corvina, 1987.

Hawkes, Ralph. "Béla Bartók: A Recollection by His Publisher." In *Béla Bartók: A Memorial Review*. New York: Boosey & Hawkes, 1950, 14–6.

Haraszti, Emil. *Béla Bartók; His Life and Works*. Trans. Dorothy Swainson. Paris: The Lyrebird Press, 1938.

Hawthorne, Robin. "The Fugal Technique of Béla Bartók." *The Music Review* 10 (November 1949): 277–85.

Heinsheimer, Hans W. "Béla Bartók: A Personal Memoir," *Tomorrow* (October 1949), 30–4.

Helistö, Paavö. "Zoltán Kodály und Ilmari Krohn," in *International Kodály Conference: Budapest 1982*, ed. Ferenc Bónis, L. Vikar, and E. Szőnyi. Budapest: Editio Musica, 1986, 47–50.

Hoensch. Jörg K. *A History of Modern Hungary*. 2d ed. Trans. Kim Traynor. London and New York: Longman, 1996.

Hornbostel, Erich von. "Phonografierte tunesiche Melodien." *Sammelbände für Vergleichende Musikwissenschaft* 8 (1907).

———. *Musik des Orients* recording series 19, Odéon 0-5168.

Kacsóh, Pongrácz. "Bartók Béla." *Zenevilág* 4, no. 25 (3 July 1903): 211–4.

Kárpáti, János. "Béla Bartók et la musique arabe." *Musique Hongroise* 74–75 (Paris, 1962): 92–105.

———. "Béla Bartók and the East." *Studia Musicologica* (Budapest, 1964): 179–94.

———. *Bartók's String Quartets*. Trans. Fred Macnicol. Budapest: Corvina Press, 1975.

———. "Bartók in North Africa: A Unique Fieldwork and Its Impact on His Music." In *Bartók Perspectives*, ed. Elliott Antokoletz, Victoria Fischer, and Benjamin Suchoff. New York: Oxford University Press, 2000, 171–84.

———. Brochure notes to *Bartók Béla. Complete Edition* III. Chamber Music (44 Duos for Two Violins). Trans. Rosemarie Trockl. Budapest: Hungaroton LPX 11320.

Kenneson, Claude. *Székely and Bartók: The Story of a Friendship*. Portland Oreg.: Amadeus Press, 1994.

Kerényi, György. *Népies dalok* (Popular songs). Budapest: Akadémiai Kiadó, 1961.

Kiss, Áron. *Magyar Gyermekjáték gyűjtemény* (Hungarian children's play songs collection), 1891.

Kodály, Zoltán. "Mátyusföldi gyűjtés" (Mátyusföld collection). *Ethnographia* 16 (Budapest, 1905): 300–5.

———. "Nagyszalontai gyűjtés" (Nagyszalonta collection). *Magyar népköltési gyűjtemény* 14 (Budapest, 1924): 257–302, 361–70.

———. *Kodály Zoltán. Visszatekintés* (Zoltán Kodaly. Retrospection). Ed. Ferenc Bónis. Budapest: Zeneműkiadó, 1964. 2 vols.

———. *Folk Music of Hungary*, trans. Ronald Tempest, et al. New York: Praeger Publishers, Inc., 1971.

———. *A magyar népzene* (The Hungarian folk music). Ed. Lajos Vargyas. Budapest: Zeneműkiadó, 1973.

———. *The Selected Writings of Zoltán Kodály*. Ed. Ferenc Bónis, trans. Lili Halápy and Fred Macnicol. London: Boosey & Hawkes Music Publishers, Ltd., 1974.

Kolessa, Philaret. *Melodien der ukrainischen rezitierenden Gesange (Dumy)*, 13–14. Lemberg: Beiträge der ukrainschen Ethnologie, 1910–1913.

Kovács, János. Brochure notes to *Béla Bartók Complete Edition*. Budapest: Hungaroton SLPX 1142.

Kresánek, Jozef. "Bartók's Collection of Slovak Folk Songs." In *Studia Memoriae Bélae Bartók Sacra*, ed. Benjamin Rajeczky and Lajos Vargyas. London: Boosey & Hawkes Ltd., 1959, 55–71.

Krohn, Ilmari. "Welche ist die beste Methode, um Volks- und volksmässige Lieder nach ihrer melodischen Beschaffenheit lexikalisch zu ordnen?" *Sammelbände der Internationalen Musikgesellschaft* 4 (1902–1903): 1 ff.

Kroó, György. "Bartók Concert in New York on July 2, 1944." *Studia Musicologica* 11 (1969): 253–7.

———. "Unrealized Plans and Ideas for Projects by Bartók." *Studia Musicologica* 12 (1970): 11–27.

———. *A Guide to Bartók*. Trans. Ruth Pataki, et al. Budapest: Corvina Press, 1974.

———. Brochure notes to *Bartók Béla. Complete Edition* I. Orchestral Music (*Bluebeard's Castle*. Opera in One Act, op. 11). Trans. Rosemarie Trockl. Budapest: Hungaroton LPX 11486.

———. "Opera: *Duke Bluebeard's Castle*," "Ballet: *The Wooden Prince*," and "Pantomime: *The Miraculous Mandarin*." In *The Bartók Companion*, ed. Malcolm Gillies. London: Faber and Faber, 1993, 349–59, 360-71, 372–84.

Kuba, Ludvik. *Pjesme i napjevi iz Bosne i Hercegovine* (Songs and melodies from Bosne and Hercegovina). Sarajevo, 1906–1910. Also 160 unpublished melodies copied by Kuba and sent to Bartók in the summer of 1938.

Kuhač, Fr. *Južno-Slovjenske Narodne Popijevke* (Yugoslav folk songs). Zagreb, 1879–81.

Kunst, Jaap. *Ethnomusicology*. The Hague: Martinus Nijhoff, 1959.

Laade, Wolfgang. "The Diaphonic Music of the Island of Krk, Yugoslavia," Recorded 1961 by Wolfgang and Dagmar Laade. In *Music from the Island of Krk, Yugoslavia*. New York: Ethnic Folkways Records FE 4060, 1975, 1–4.

Laki, Peter, ed. *Bartók and His World.* Princeton N.J.: Princeton University Press, 1995.

Lampert, Vera. "Quellenkatalog der Volksliedbearbeitungen von Bartók. Ungarische, slowakische, rumänische, ruthenische, serbische und arabische Volkslieder un Tänze." In *Documenta Bartókiana* 6, ed. László Somfai. Budapest: Akadémiai Kiadó, 1981, 15–149.

————. "*The Miraculous Mandarin*: Melchior Lengyel, His Pantomime, and His Connections to Béla Bartók." In *Bartók and His World,* ed. Peter Laki Princeton N.J.: Princeton University Press, 1995, 149–71.

Lampert, Vera, and László Somfai. "Béla Bartók." In *The New Grove Modern Masters: Bartók, Stravinsky, Hindemith,* 1–101, ed. Stanley Sadie. New York and London: W.W. Norton, 1984.

Lang, Paul Henry. *Music in Western Civilization.* New York: W.W. Norton, 1941.

László, Ferenc, ed. *Bartók-könyv* (Bartók-book). Bucharest: Kriterion, 1971.

————. "Bartók's First Encounter with Folk Music." *The New Hungarian Quarterly* 19, no. 72 (Winter, 1978): 68–74.

Leafstedt, Carl S. "Pélleas Revealed: The Original Ending of Bartók's Opera, *Duke Bluebeard's Castle.*" In *Bartók Perspectives,* ed. Elliott Antokoletz, Victoria Fischer, and Benjamin Suchoff. New York: Oxford University Press, 2000, 226–44.

Lendvai, Ernő. *Béla Bartók, An Analysis of His Music.* London: Kahn & Averill, 1971.

Lengyel, Emil. *1,000 Years of Hungarian History.* New York: John Day, 1958.

Lenoir, Yves. *Folklore et transcendance dans l'oeuvre américaine de Béla Bartók* (1940–1945). Preface by Denijs Dille. Louvain-la-Neuve, Belgium: Institut Supérieur de Archéologie et d'Histoire de l'Art, 1986.

————. "Contributions à l'étude de la Sonate pour Violon Solo de Béla Bartók (1944)." *Studia musicologica* 23 (1981): 209–60.

Lesznai, Lajos. *Bartók.* Trans. Percy M. Young. London: Dent, 1973.

Liebner, János. "Unpublished Bartók Documents," *The New Hungarian Quarterly* 3, no. 6 (April–June 1962): 221–4.

Lyudkevitch, St. *Halitschsko-ruski Narodni Melyodii.* Lemberg: Chevtchenko Society, 1906.

Macartney, C. A. *Hungary.* Foreword by H. A. L. Fisher. London: Benn, 1934.

————. *Hungary and Her Successors.* London: Oxford University Press, 1937.

Mcleod, Joseph. *The Sisters d'Aranyi.* London: George Allen & Unwin, 1969.

Menuhin, Yehudi. *Unfinished Journey.* London: Macdonald & Jane's Publishers, 1977.

Moore, Douglas. "Bartók at Columbia University," *The Long Player* 2, no. 10 (October 1953): 16.

Moravcsik, Géza. *Országos M. Kir. Zeneakadémia története 1875–1907* (Records of the National Hungarian Royal Music Academy 1875–1907. Budapest: Athenaeum, 1907.

Moreux, Serge. *Béla Bartók.* Preface by Arthur Honegger. Trans. G. S. Fraser and Erik de Mauny. London: The Harvill Press, 1953.

Nagy, Zsuzsa l. "Revolution in Hungary (1918–1919)." In Pamlényi, ed., 419–49.

Newmarch, Rosa. "Folk Music: Russian." In *Grove* 5, ed. Erich Blom. New York: St. Martin's Press, 1954, 345.

Novak, John K. "The Benefits of 'Relaxation': The Role of the 'Pihenő' Movement in Béla Bartók's *Contrasts.*" In *Bartók Perspectives,* ed. Elliott Antokoletz, Victoria Fischer, and Benjamin Suchoff. New York: Oxford University Press, 2000, 95–109.

Nüll, Edwin von der. *Béla Bartók. Ein Beitrag zur Morphologie der neuen Musik.* Halle: Mitteldeutsche Verlags A.G., 1930.

Pamlényi, Ervin, ed. *A History of Hungary.* Budapest: Corvina Press, 1973; London: Collet's, 1975.

Parry, Milman, coll. *Serbocroatian Heroic Songs.* Ed. and trans. Albert B. Lord. With musical transcriptions by Béla Bartók and prefaces by John H. Finley, Jr. and Roman Jakobson. Vol. 1. Novi Pazar: English Translations. Cambridge: Harvard University Press; Belgrade: Serbian Academy of Sciences, 1954.

Platthy. Jenő *Bartók. A Critical Biography.* Santa Claus, Ind.: Federation of International Poetry Associations of UNESCO, 1988.

Pomfret, John. "Foreign Journal; Hungry for Their Roots." *Washington Post* Foreign Service. Budapest, 6 February 1995.

Porter, James, "Bartók's Concerto for Orchestra (1943) and Janáček's Sinfonietta (1926): Conceptual and Motivic Parallels." In *Bartók Perspectives,* ed. Elliott Antokoletz, Victoria Fischer, and Benjamin Suchoff. New York: Oxford University Press, 2000, 152–68.

Pusztaszeri, László, "On the Highway of the Steppes." *Magyar Hirek* 41, no. 2 (22 January 1988): 31.

Ránki, György, ed. *Bartók and Kodály Revisited.* Budapest: Akadémiai Kiadó, 1987.

Rice, Timothy. "Bartók and Bulgarian Rhythm." In *Bartók Perspectives,* ed. Elliott Antokoletz, Victoria Fischer, and Benjamin Suchoff. New York: Oxford University Press, 2000, 196–210.

Sacher, Paul. "Begegnungen mit Béla Bartók." *Das Orchester* 1 (1982): 16–20.

Sárosi, Balint. *Gypsy Music.* Trans. Fred Macnicol. Budapest: Corvina Press, 1978.

Saygun A. Adnan. "Bartók in Turkey." *Musical Quarterly* 37 (1951): 5–9.

———. *Béla Bartók's Folk Music Research in Turkey.* Ed. László Vikár. Budapest: Akadémiai Kiadó, 1976.

Schauffler, Robert H. *Beethoven: The Man who Freed Music.* New York: Tudor Publishing Co., 1946.

Schlötterer-Traimer, Roswitha. "Béla Bartók und die Tondichtungen von Richard Strauss." *Österreichische Musik Zeitschrift* 38, nos. 5–6 (May–June 1981): 311–8.

Sebestyén, Gyula. *Regös-énekek* (Christmas songs). *Magyar népköltési gyűjtemény* 4 (Budapest, 1902).

Serly, Tibor. "Story of a Concerto." *New York Times*, 11 December 1949.

———. "Béla Bartók's Last Works." *The Long Player* 2, no. 10 (October 1953): 26–7.

———. "The Reconstruction of a Musical Masterpiece." *College Music Symposium* 15 (Spring 1975): 7–25.

Slovenské Spevy. Turčiansky Svätý Martin, 1880, 1890, 1899–1926.

Somfai, László. *18 Bartók-tanulmány* (Eighteen Bartók studies). Budapest: Editio Musica, 1981.

———. "Bartók's Notations in Composition and Transcription." In *Bartók Perspectives*, ed. Elliott Antokoletz, Victoria Fischer, and Benjamin Suchoff. New York: Oxford University Press, 2000, 213–25.

Stevens, Halsey. "The Sources of Bartók's Rhapsody for Violoncello and Piano." In *International Musicological Conference in Commemoration of Béla Bartók 1971*, ed. József Ujfalussy and János Breuer. Budapest: Editio Musica; Melville, New York: Belwin Mills, 1972: 65–76.

———. *The Life and Music of Béla Bartók*. 3d ed. prepared by Malcolm Gillies. New York: Oxford University Press, 1993.

Stoin, Vasil. *Grundriss der Musik unter Rhythmik der bulgarischen Volksmusik.* Sofia, 1927.

———. *Chants populaires bulgares de Timok à l Vita*. Sofia: Ministère Bulgare de l'instruction publique, 1928.

———. *Chants populaires bulgares de la partie centrale de la Bulgare du Nord.* Sofia: Ministère Bulgare de l'instruction publique, 1931.

Suchoff, Benjamin. "Errata in the *Mikrokosmos* Publication." *Piano Quarterly Newsletter* 16 (Summer 1956): 11, 24.

———. *Béla Bartók and a Guide to the Mikrokosmos*. Ann Arbor, Mich.: UMI, 1957.

———. "History of Béla Bartók's *Mikrokosmos*." *Journal of Research in Music Education* 7, no. 2 (Fall 1959): 186-96.

———. "Bartók's *Rumanian Folk Music* Publication." *Ethnomusicology* 15, no. 2 (May 1971): 220–30.

———. "Bartók and Serbo-Croatian Folk Music." *The Musical Quarterly* 58, no. 4 (October 1972): 557–71.

———. "Bartók in America." *Musical Times* 117, no. 1596 (February 1976): 123–4.

———. "Some Observations on Bartók's Third Piano Concerto." *Tempo* 65 (Summer 1963): 8–10.

———. "Structure and Concept in Bartók's Sixth String Quartet." *Tempo* 83 (Winter 1967–1968): 2–11.

———. *Guide to Bartók's Mikrokosmos*. London: Boosey & Hawkes Ltd., 1971. Reprint, with foreword by György Sandor. New York: Da Capo Press, 1983.

———. "Notes on the Music." *Béla Bartók: A Celebration*. With an introduction by Harold C. Schonberg. Camp Hill, Pennsylvania: Book-of-the-Month Club, 1981: The Classics Record Library 81-6407, 41-6444.

———. "Introduction to *Piano Music of Béla Bartók.*" The Archive Edition, ed. Benjamin Suchoff. New York: Dover Publications, Inc., 1981. Series 1: vii–xii, 2: vii–xxv.

———. "Folk Music Sources in Bartók Works." In *Weine meine laute... Gedenkschrift Kurt Reinhard*, ed. Christian Ahrens, et al. Laaber: Laaber-Verlag, 1984: 197–218.

———. "Ethnomusicological Roots of Béla Bartók's Musical Language." *The World Of Music* 29, no. 1 (1987): 43–65.

———. "The Bartók-Kodály Connection." *The New Hungarian Quarterly* 34, no. 118 (Summer 1990): 154–7.

———. "Fusion of National Styles: Piano Literature 1908–1911," and "Synthesis of East and West: *Mikrokosmos.*" In *The Bartók Companion*, ed. Malcolm Gillies. London: Faber & Faber, 1993, 124–45, 189–211.

———. "The Genesis of Bartók's Musical Language," and "Bartók's Odyssey in Slovak Folk Music." In *Bartók Perspectives*, ed. Elliott Antokoletz, Victoria Fischer, and Benjamin Suchoff. New York: Oxford University Press, 2000, 15–27, 113–28.

Szabolcsi, Bence. *A Concise History of Hungarian Music*. Afterword ("Hungarian History since 1945") by György Kroó. 2d, enlarged ed. Trans. Sára Karig and Fred Macnicol, trans. rev. Florence Knepler. Budapest: Corvina Press, 1964.

Szabolcsi, Bence, and Aladár Tóth. *Zenei Lexikon*, 2 vols. Budapest, 1931.

Szegő, Julia. *Bartók Béla népdalkutató* (Béla Bartók the folk song researcher). Bucharest: Állami Iroldalmi és Művészeti Kiadó, 1956.

Szigeti, Joseph. *With Strings Attached*. New York: Alfred A. Knopf, 1947.

Szőllősy, András, ed. *Bartók Béla Összegyűjtött írásai* (Béla Bartók collected writings), vol. 1. Budapest: Zeneműkiadó Vállalat, 1967.

Tallián, Tibor. *Béla Bartók: The Man and His Work*. Trans. Gyula Gulás, trans. rev. Paul Merrick. Budapest: Corvina, 1981.

Tryon, Winthrop P. "How Bartók Composes." *Christian Science Monitor* (31 December 1927): 14–5.

Ujfalussy, Jószef. *Béla Bartók*. Trans. Ruth Pataki, trans. rev. Elisabeth West. Budapest: Corvina Press; Boston: Crescendo, 1971.

van den Toorn, Pieter C. *The Music of Stravinsky*. New Haven, Conn.: Yale University Press, 1983.

Vargyas, Lajos. *Researches into the Mediaeval History of the Folk Ballad*. Budapest: Akadémiai Kiadó, 1967.

Veress, Sandor. "Bluebeard's Castle." In *Béla Bartók: A Memorial Review*. New York: Boosey & Hawkes, Inc., 1950, 36–53.

———. "Béla Bartóks 44 Duos für zwei Violinen." In *Erich Doflein: Festschrift zum 70. Geburstag* (7 August 1970). Mainz: Schott, 1972, 31–57.

Vinton, John. "Toward a Chronology of the *Mikrokosmos*." *Studia Musicologica* 8, nos. 1–4 (1966): 41–69.

Vlad, Roman. *Stravinsky.* 2d ed. Trans. Frederick Fuller and Ann Fuller. London: Oxford University Press, 1967.

Waldbauer, Ivan. "Bartók's 'Four Pieces' for Two Pianos." *Tempo* 53–4 (1960): 17–22.

Walacínski, Adam. Preface to *Karol Szymanowski Complete Edition* 9. Vienna: Universal Edition (1978): ix–xii.

Webster, J. H. Douglas. "Golden-Mean Form in Music." *Music and Letters* 31 (1950): 237–8.

Weiss, Günther. "Zwei unbekannte Briefe von Béla Bartók zu einem Violinkonzert (op. posth.) 1907–1908 und seinem ersten Streichquartett (op. 7)." *Studia Musicologica* 27 (1985): 379–92.

———."Youthful Orchestral Works." In *The Bartók Companion*, ed. Malcolm Gillies. London: Faber & Faber, 1993, 441–53.

Wightman, Alistair. "Szymanowski, Bartók and the Violin." *The Musical Times* 122 (March 1981): 159–63.

Williamson, John. *Strauss: Also sprach Zarathustra.* Cambridge: Cambridge University Press, 1993.

Yeomans, David. "Background and Analysis of Bartók's Romanian Christmas Carols for Piano (1915)." In *Bartók Perspectives,* ed. Elliott Antokoletz, Victoria Fischer, and Benjamin Suchoff. New York: Oxford University Press, 2000, 185–95.

Yafil, E. and J. Rouanet. *Répertoire de musique arabe et maure*, Algiers, 1904.

Ziegler, Márta. "Bartóks reise nach Biskra." In *Documenta Bartókiana* 2, ed. Denijs Dille. Mainz: B. Schotts Söhne, 1965, 9–12.

Zieliński, Tadeusz A. *Bartók.* Trans. Bruno Heinrich. Zurich: Atlantis, 1973.

Index

322

"*Passamezzo Ongaro*" 6
Pásztory, Ditta. *See* Bartók, Ditta
Pest 10, 12, 100
Pest University 270n.31
Petchenegs 4
Petrograd 87
Philadelphia
  Curtis Institute of Music 140
  Music Fund Society 110
  Orchestra 108
piano
  percussive character of 83, 101, 130,
    280n.159
Pittsburgh 140, 144
Poland 138, 262
Polikeit, Károly 20
polymodal chromaticism. *See* Bartók, Béla:
  musical language
Portland (Oreg.) 109, 149
Portugal 50, 189
  Bartók's concert tour of 116
Pósa, Lajos 28, 269n.15
Pozsony (Pressburg; Bratislava, Slovakia) 14,
    18, 21, 24, 26–7, 30, 34–5, 44–5,
    283n.56
  Catholic Grammar School 21
  Catholic Gymnasium 19
  municipal theater 20
  Pressburger Zeitung 78
  Teachers' Training College 19
Prague 201
  Czech Philharmonic Orchestra 102, 201
Prill-Jeral Quartet 44
Primrose, William 158–60
Pro-Musica Society 107
  French section 111
Protestantism 6

Rácznagyszentmiklós 267n.1
Rákóczi, Ferenc II 8, 262
Rákospalota 55
Rameau, Jean-Phillipe 75
Rásonyi, László 127–8
Ravel, Maurice 75
Ráz, D. C. 281n. 6
Reed College (Portland, Oreg.) 149
Reger, Max 75
Reiner, Fritz 102, 108–110, 144, 150, 152
Reschofsky, Sándor 76, 276n.73
rhythm
  Arab syncopated 192
  Bulgarian 81, 124–5, 138, 153, 175,

182, 201, 209–10, 284n.73
  hemiola 168
  Hungarian "dotted" 112, 168, 215
  parlando-rubato 205, 215, 291n.19
  Romanian "shifted" 176
  Ruthenian *kolomyjka* 18, 100, 195
  Slovak contraction of 42, 74, 171, 271n.5
  Slovak schemata 168
  tempo giusto 215, 296n.26
  verbunkos 49
Richter, Hans (János) 39–40, 262
Riverdale (Bronx, NY) 147
Riverton (VT) 148
Rodzinski, Artur 155
Romania 7, 77, 96, 117
Romanian
  fieldwork by Bartók 66, 79, 88, 172, 179
  Ministry of Culture 102
  people 4, 6–8, 15
Rome 102
  Café Greco 111
  Santa Cecilia Society 111
Rosbaud, Hans 123
Rossi, Michelangelo 102
Roth Quartet 111
Rothchild, Mr. 121
Rózsavölgyi és Társa 76, 117, 120
Rozsnyai, Károly 53, 63, 274, 273n.16,
    274n.35
Rubinstein Competition 45–7, 217
Rückert, Friedrich 26
Ruppeldt, Miloš 93, 111, 262
Russia 35, 77, 135, 138
  Bartók's tour of 110
  Bolshevik October Revolution 87
Ruthenia (Carpatho-Ukraine) 135
Ruthenian (Ukrainian) people 4, 7

Saanen 137–8
Sacher, Paul 129, 131–2, 137, 142
Sackbut 96
San Francisco 109
Sárafalva (Saravale, formerly Sarafola) 199
Sarajevo 77
Sarasate, Pablo de 11
Saxons 6
Saygun, A. Adnan 213, 296n.296
Scales
  chromatic 46
  diatonic
    chromatic compression of 215
    Hungarian-Gypsy 39, 60
    nondiatonic 216

About the Author

Benjamin Suchoff is adjunct professor in the Department of Ethnomusicology at the University of California, Los Angeles, and a member of the American Society of Composers, Authors, and Publishers (ASCAP, 1960–). Dr. Suchoff was curator of the New York Bartók Archive (1953–1967), successor-trustee of the New York Bartók estate (1968–1984), and editor of the thirteen volumes comprising the Bartók Archive Studies in Musicology series and the two volumes of piano works in the Bartók Archive Edition. His most recent books are *Bartók: Concerto for Orchestra: Understanding Bartók's World* (1995), *Béla Bartók Studies in Ethnomusicology* (1997), and, as coeditor, *Bartók Perspectives* (2000). He was awarded the Béla Bartók Diploma and Memorial Plaque from the Hungarian Republic in 1981 for his "great contributions to the understanding of Bartók's oeuvre" and is generally recognized as the dean of Bartók scholars.